Drug Control and International Law

This book provides for an extensive legal analysis of the international drug control system in light of the growing challenges and criticism that this system faces. In the current debate on global drug policy, the central pillars of the international drug control system – the UN Drug Conventions as well as its institutions – are portrayed as outdated, suppressive and seen as an obstacle to necessary changes. This book's objective is to provide an in-depth and positivist insight into drug control's present legal framework and thus provide for a better understanding of the normative assumptions upon which drug control is currently based. This is attained by clarifying the objectives of the international drug control system and the premises by which these objectives are to be achieved.

The objective of the current global framework of international drug control is the limitation of drugs to medical and scientific purposes. The meaning of this objective and its concrete implications for States' parties as well as its problems from the perspective of other regimes of international law, most notably international human rights law, are extensively analysed. Additionally, the book focuses on how the international drug control system attempts to reach the objective of confining drugs to medical and scientific purposes, i.e. by setting up a universal system that exercises a rigid control on drug supply. The consequences of this heavy focus on the reduction of drug supply are outlined, and the book concludes by making suggestions on how the international drug control system could be reformed in the near future in order to better meet the existing challenges.

The analysis occurs from a general international law perspective. It aims to map the international drug control system within a wider context of international law and to understand whether the problems that the international drug control system faces are exemplary for the difficulties that institutionalized systems of global scope face in the twenty-first century.

Daniel Wisehart is an associate at Wach + Meckes LLP, Munich. He has previously worked as a researcher at the Universität Potsdam and the Universität Freiburg and clerked for the European Court of Human Rights.

Routledge Research in International Law

Available:

International Criminal Law and Sexual Violence against Women
The Interpretation of Gender in the Contemporary International Criminal Trial
Daniela Nadj

Unilateral Acts
A History of a Legal Doctrine
Betina Kuzmarov

Regional Developmentalism through Law
Establishing an African Economic Community
Jonathan Bashi Rudahindwa

China's One Belt One Road Initiative and Private International Law
Edited by Poomintr Sooksripaisarnkit and Sai Ramani Garimella

Transnational Terrorist Groups and International Criminal Law
Anna Marie Brennan

Confronting Cyberespionage under International Law
Oğuz Kaan Pehlivan

Russian Discourses on International Law
Sociological and Philosophical Phenomenon
Edited by P. Sean Morris

For a full list of titles in this series, visit www.routledge.com/Routledge-Research-in-International-Law/book-series/INTNLLAW

Drug Control and International Law

Daniel Wisehart

Routledge
Taylor & Francis Group
NEW YORK AND LONDON

First published 2019
by Routledge
52 Vanderbilt Avenue, New York, NY 10017

and by Routledge
2 Park Square, Milton Park, Abingdon, Oxon OX14 4RN

First issued in paperback 2020

Routledge is an imprint of the Taylor & Francis Group, an informa business

Library of Congress Cataloging-in-Publication Data
Names: Wisehart, Daniel, author.
Title: Drug control and international law / Daniel Wisehart.
Description: Abingdon, Oxon ; New York, NY : Routledge, 2018. |
Series: Routledge research in international law
Identifiers: LCCN 2018021609 | ISBN 9781138486041 (hardback)
Subjects: LCSH: Drugs of abuse—Law and legislation. | Drug control—International cooperation. | Public health laws, International.
Classification: LCC K5282 .W57 2018 | DDC 344.05/45—dc23
LC record available at https://lccn.loc.gov/2018021609

ISBN 13: 978-0-367-58499-3 (pbk)
ISBN 13: 978-1-138-48604-1 (hbk)

Typeset in Galliard
by codeMantra

Für Cléa und Liv

Contents

Acknowledgments

This book would not have seen the light of the day without the help of various people, who inspired, guided and accompanied me, during my long journey into the international drug control system.

First of all, I am deeply grateful to my PhD supervisor, Professor Robin Geiß, for introducing me to the intriguing subject of drug control. He has always supported me in developing my own ideas, guided me throughout this long process and taught me a great deal about legal writing and structuring a sound legal analysis. I would also like to thank Professor Andreas Zimmermann, who was so kind as to examine this work as a co-supervisor. I started working for him as a law student almost eight years ago, and the invaluable insights into legal scholarship which I have gained at his chair have marked me ever since. Many thanks also to Routledge/Taylor and Francis for helping me to transform my PhD thesis into a book, as well as thanks to the two anonymous peer reviewers for their helpful comments on an earlier version of the manuscript.

The bulk of this work was written while I was a research associate at the University of Potsdam and the University of Freiburg, Germany. It was a true pleasure working with fabulous colleagues who have become dear friends during the last years. Many of them were so kind to proofread earlier drafts of this book: Jakob Jürgensen, Lena Hammel, Simon Schädler, Constantin Teetzmann, Anne-Katrin Wolf and Julie-Enni Zastrow. Sincere thanks for your friendship and your dedicated help!

I also want to *dire merci beaucoup à Olga Bodnarchuk*. I feel incredibly blessed meeting her in the final stages of writing this book. Moreover, I am forever indebted to my parents, who have always given me everything they could and whose support to me has been enormous in these last years. Finally, I want to express my deepest gratitude to my wonderful daughters Cléa and Liv. *Ihr seid mein Glück und mein ganzer Stolz. Ihr habt mir mehr über mich selbst und das Leben gelehrt, als ein Buch es jemals vermag!*

Munich, March 2018

Abbreviations

ACHR	American Convention on Human Rights
AFDI	*Annuaire français de droit international*
AJICL	*Arizona Journal of International & Comparative Law*
AJIL	*American Journal of International Law*
AmULR	*American University Law Review*
BFSP	British and Foreign State Papers
BYBIL	*The British Yearbook of International Law*
Can. Y. B. Int'l	*Canadian Yearbook of International Law*
Cardozo J. Int'l & Comp. L	*Cardozo Journal of International and Comparative Law*
CAT	Convention against Torture and Other Cruel, Inhuman or Degrading Treatment or Punishment
CESCR	Committee on Economic, Social and Cultural Rights
CLR	*Columbia Law Review*
CND	Commission on Narcotic Drugs of the Economic and Social Council
Colum. J. Transnat'l L.	*Columbia Journal of Transnational Law*
CRC	United Nations Convention on the Rights of the Child
CTS	Consolidated Treaty Series
DJILP	*Denver Journal of International Law and Policy*
ECDD	WHO Expert Committee on Drug Dependence
ECDDA	European Monitoring Centre for Drugs and Drug Addiction
ECHR	Convention for the Protection of Human Rights and Fundamental Freedoms
ECOSOC	Economic and Social Council of the United Nations
ECtHR	European Court of Human Rights
EJIL	*European Journal of International Law*

EMCDDA	European Monitoring Centre of Drugs and Drug Addiction
EU	European Union
Eur. J.L. Reform	*European Journal of Law Reform*
FIILJ	*Fordham International Law Journal*
GAOR	General Assembly Official Records
GATT	General Agreement on Tariffs and Trade
GoJIL	*Goettingen Journal of International Law*
HRC	Human Rights Committee
HRLR	Human Rights Law Review
HRQ	*Human Rights Quarterly*
IACHR	Inter-American Courts of Human Rights
ICCPR	International Covenant on Civil and Political Rights
ICESCR	International Covenant on Economic, Social and Cultural Rights
ICJ	International Court of Justice
ICLQ	*International & Comparative Law Quarterly*
IDPC	International Drug Policy Consortium
IJDP	*International Journal of Drug Policy*
IJHRL	*International Journal of Human Rights Law*
ILA	International Law Association
ILC	International Law Commission
ILM	International Legal Materials
ILO	International Labour Organization
INCB	International Narcotics Control Board
Int'l L.	*International Lawyer*
Iowa L. Rev.	*Iowa Law Review*
Isr.Y.B. Hum.Rts	*Israel Yearbook on Human Rights*
JCHLP	Journal of Contemporary Health Law and Policy
JDI	*Journal of Drug Issues*
JICJ	*Journal of International Criminal Justice*
J. Int'l L. & Econ.	*The Journal of International Law and Economics*
JLAS	*Journal of Latin American Studies*
J. L. Med. & Ethics	*Journal of Law Medicine and Ethics*
JPPCP	*Journal of Pain & Palliative Care Pharmacotherapy*
LN Doc.	League of Nations Document
LNTS	League of Nations Treaty Service
Md. J. Int'l L.	*Maryland Journal of International Law*
Mich. J. Int'l L.	*Michigan Journal of International Law*
Minn. J. Int'l L.	*Minnesota Journal of International Law*
MN	Marginal Number

MPEPIL	*Max Planck Encyclopaedia of Public International Law*
MPYbUNL	*Max Planck Yearbook of United Nations Law*
NILR	*Netherlands International Law Review*
NJW	*Neue Juristische Wochenschrift*
NUJHR	*Northwestern Journal of Human Rights*
NYU JILP	*NYU Journal of International Law and Politics*
OAC	Advisory Committee on Traffic in Opium and Other Dangerous Drugs (Opium Advisory Committee)
OAS	Organization of American States
PCB	Permanent Central Board
PCIJ	Permanent Court of International Justice
QHR	*Netherland Quarterly of Human Rights.*
RdC	*Recueil des Cours Collected Courses of the Hague Academy of International Law*
RGDIP	*Revue général de droit international public*
Rutgers L. Rev.	*Rutgers Law Review*
SB	Supervisory Body
TCLR	*Trinity College Law Review*
TJICL	*Tulane Journal of International and Comparative Law*
Trends Organ. Crim.	*Trends in Organized Crime*
UN	United Nations
UN Doc.	United Nations Document
UNDCP	United Nations Drug Control Programme
UNDRIP	United Nations Declaration on the Rights of Indigenous Peoples
UNGA	United Nations General Assembly
UNGASS	United Nations General Assembly Special Session
UNODC	United Nations Office on Drugs and Crime
UNSC	United Nations Security Council
UNTS	United Nations Treaty Service
UNYB	*Yearbook of the United Nations*
VCLT	Vienna Convention on the Law of Treaties
Vand. J. Trant'l L.	*Vanderbilt Journal of Transnational Law*
WHA	World Health Assembly
WHO	World Health Organization
WTO	World Trade Organization
YIL	*Netherland Yearbook of International Law*
YJIL	*Yale Journal of International Law*

1 Introduction

1.1 International drug control after UNGASS 2016: more of the same or towards a fundamental turning point?

Ja; mach nur einen Plan
sei nur ein großes Licht!
Und mach dann noch´ nen zweiten Plan
gehn tun sie beide nicht.[1]

For more than a century the international community has tried to resolve the 'world drug problem'. Thirteen multilateral treaties and protocols on drug control were adopted between 1912 and 1988.[2] An infamous 'war on drugs' has been declared[3] and drug abuse has been labelled as 'public enemy number one'.[4] Billions of dollars have been spent. Countless resolutions in various international fora have been adopted. Three special sessions of the United Nations General Assembly (UNGA) on the world drug problem have been carried out.

The international community has made specific pledges in order to underline the determination to reduce illicit demand for, and supply of, drugs: In 1990 – at the closure of its first special session on drugs – the UNGA 'resolve[d] to protect mankind from the scourge of drug abuse and illicit trafficking in narcotic drugs and psychotropic substances'.[5] Accordingly, a plan of action was adopted, foreseeing prevention and reduction of drug abuse as well as an eradication of

1 Bertold Brecht, Das Lied von der Unzulänglichkeit des Menschlichen Strebens.

2 https://treaties.un.org/pages/Treaties.aspx?id=6&subid=A&lang=en (all websites were last accessed in April 2018).

3 The 'war on drugs' terminology goes back to Richard Nixon: 'This Administration has declared all-out, global war on the drug menace.' Message to the Congress Transmitting Reorganization Plan 2 of 1973 Establishing the Drug Enforcement Administration, 28 March 1973 (available online at: www.presidency.ucsb.edu/ws/index.php?pid=4159#axzz1PCJydjl5). No direct references of such a war can be found within the UN Drug Conventions, although they are frequently associated with the war on drugs; cf. for the 1988 Convention, Neil Boister, book review: *Commentary on the United Nations Convention Against Illicit Traffic in Narcotic Drugs and Psychotropic Substances*, UN Doc. E/CN.7/590', *ICLQ* Vol. 55 2001, 466.

4 US President Richard Nixon, Remarks About an Intensified Program for Drug Abuse Prevention and Control, 17 June 1971 (available online at: www.presidency.ucsb.edu/ws/?pid=3047).

5 UNGA, Political Declaration and Global Programme of Action, 1990, UN Doc. A/Res-17/2, para. 1.

illicit drug production and a suppression of the illicit traffic in drugs;[6] the 1990s were envisioned as the 'United Nations Decade against Drug Abuse'.[7]

In 1998, the second UNGA special session on drugs assembled. The 'unwavering determination and commitment to overcoming the world drug problem through domestic and international strategies to reduce both the illicit supply of and the demand for drugs' was reaffirmed.[8] The year 2008 was set as a target date 'with a view to eliminating or reducing significantly the illicit manufacture, marketing and trafficking of psychotropic substances'.[9] Furthermore, it was decided that in same year 'measurable results in the field of demand reduction' should be achieved[10] and that the illicit cultivation of the coca bush, the cannabis plant and the opium poppy should be eliminated or significantly reduced.[11]

In 2009, the Commission on Narcotic Drugs of the Economic and Social Council (CND) – the primary organ of the United Nations on drug control – carried out an extensive review of the progress made since 1998 on the occasion of a High Level Segment. This time it was

> [d]ecide[d] to establish 2019 as a target date for States to eliminate or reduce significantly and measurably: (a) The illicit cultivation of opium poppy, coca bush and cannabis plant; (b) The illicit demand for narcotic drugs and psychotropic substances; and drug related health and social risks; (c) The illicit production, manufacture, marketing and distribution of, and trafficking in, psychotropic substances, including synthetic drugs.[12]

In 2016, the UNGA convened for the third special session on drugs. It included a review of the progress made with the implementation of the 2009 Action Plan.[13] Albeit the UNGA now refrains from adopting clear target dates, the 'determination to tackle the world drug problem' is reaffirmed and a 'society free of drug abuse' is promoted.[14] *Plus ça change, plus ça reste la même chose?*

Not forcibly, looking exclusively at consensus-driven resolutions does not capture the dynamics that have surrounded the international drug control system in the last 20 years, and it seems possible that in the near future different outcomes will be achieved.[15] For the last 20 years, a seemingly growing number of NGOs and elder statesmen have been criticizing the current

6 *Ibid.*
7 *Ibid.*, para. 29.
8 UNGA, Political Declaration Annex, 1998, UN Doc. A/Res/S-20/2, para. 1.
9 *Ibid.*, para. 14.
10 *Ibid.*, para. 17.
11 *Ibid.*, para. 19.
12 CND, Plan of Action on International Cooperation towards an Integrated and Balanced Strategy to Counter the World Drug Problem, 2009, UN Doc. E/2009/28, para. 36.
13 UNGA Resolution 69/200, 2014, UN Doc. A/Res/69/200.
14 UNGA, Our Joint Commitment to Effectively Addressing and Countering the World Drug Problem, A/RES/S-30/1, 2016, preambular para. 2.
15 But cf. for a more pessimistic account, Francisco E. Thoumi, 'The International Drug Control Regime's Straight Jacket: Are there any Policy Options?', *Trends Organ. Crim.* Vol. 13 2010, 75 (86), cf. also in this regard before UNGASS 2016, Martin Jelsma, 'UNGASS 2016: Prospects for Treaty Reform and UN System-Wide Coherence on Drug Policy', 2016.

approaches of the international community with regard to drugs.[16] These critiques do not act as a monolithic bloc, their critique of the international drug control system is not coherent and accordingly they have so far not developed a precise alternative of an international drug control system that they would adhere to.[17]

The critique of the international drug control system is often based upon a purported failure of the system to universally reduce drug demand and supply.[18] It is argued that despite all efforts, illicit production and use of drugs remain unabated.[19] Conversely, the United Nations Office on Drugs and Crime (UNODC) claims that the international drug control system is a success story, since only a marginal portion of the world population are problematic drug users.[20] These arguments may give the impression that the debate over the international drug control system is a debate of mere effectiveness: is the international drug control system attaining the goals that were set? This impression needs to be rebutted. The fact that the international drug control system fails to reach its goals, in itself is ill-suited in order to explain growing discontent.

International law contains many utopian goals, such as the 'ideal of free human beings enjoying civil and political freedom and freedom from fear and want' announced in the preamble of the International Covenant on Civil and Political Rights (ICCPR).[21] Although frustration is caused by the fact that these goals are very often not attained and the law is neglected, the lack of success in reaching these goals does not lead to an open rejection of the system that has been erected for their protection. Nobody would deny, for instance, that human rights are

16 For instance, the former UN Secretary General Kofi Annan or the former US Secretary of State George Shultz are also active within the opposition to the drug control system and have gathered within a Global Commission on Drugs (see www.globalcommissionondrugs.org/). Their regional predecessor has been the Latin American Commission on Drugs and Democracy, which had been founded by the former Brazilian President Fernando Henrique Cardoso; cf. Latin American Commission on Drugs and Democracy, 'Drugs and Democracy: Toward a Paradigm Shift', 2009. This initiative has also inspired the West African Commission on Drugs, chaired by the former President of Nigeria, Olusegun Obasanjo, cf. for further details, West African Commission on Drugs, 'Not Just in Transit: Drugs, the State and Society in West Africa', 2014, p. 2.

17 Cf. as to the persisting lack of agreement within the 'reform camp', David Courtwright, 'Drug Use and Prohibition: Three Reform Traditions', in: Beatriz Caiuby Labate and Clancy Cavnar (eds), *Prohibition, Religious Freedom, and Human Rights: Regulating Traditional Drug Use*, v (vii).

18 Cf. e.g. Latin American Commission on Drugs and Democracy, 'Drugs and Democracy: Toward a Paradigm Shift', 2009, p. 5; cf. also Global Commission on Drug Policy, 'War On Drugs', 2011, p. 2. This critique is of course far from new, cf. already in this regard, Robin Room and Angela Pagila, 'The International Drug Control System in the Post-Cold War Era. Managing Markets or Fighting a War', *Drug and Alcohol Review* Vol. 18 1999, 305 (311 et seq.).

19 Cf. e.g, Latin American Commission on Drugs and Democracy, 'Drugs and Democracy: Toward a Paradigm Shift', 2009, p. 3.

20 UNODC, 'World Drug Report 2008', UN Publication, Sales No. E.08.XI.1, p. 213; Daniel Heilmann, 'The International Control of Illegal Drugs and the UN Treaty Regime: Preventing or Causing Human Rights Violations?', *Cardozo J. Int'l & Comp. L* Vol. 19 2011, 237 (285).

21 International Covenant on Civil and Political Rights of 19 December 1966, entered into force 23 March 1976, UNTS Vol. 999, p. 171.

violated very often. Furthermore, one can very well call into doubt whether international human rights protection effectively prevents international human rights violations from occurring. However, nobody would claim that because human rights are violated, international human rights protection is senseless. To the contrary, many would ask for an even more elaborated and effective system of international human rights protection in order to curb human rights violations.

This example shows that in reality the debate surrounding the international drug control system is not – at least not exclusively – about effectiveness. It is – at least partly – a normative discussion. It is the viability of *the goals* of the international drug control system themselves that are questioned. Additionally, States are divided by *the premises* by which these goals are to be attained. This explains why review processes of a more substantial kind are carried out within universal and regional fora. The run-up to the 2016 UNGASS was determinatively influenced by a joint declaration of Uruguay, Guatemala and Colombia, demanding a review of the current approach of the international community towards drugs, where 'all available options' – including regulatory market options should be considered.[22] By the same token, the Organization of American States (OAS) is currently involved in a process of 'analysing the results of the current policy on drugs in the Americas and to explore new approaches to strengthen this struggle and to become more effective'.[23]

Thus the criticism of the international drug control system has spurred processes, whose outcome can hardly be predicted today.[24] The system is under pressure; States have already shown their willingness to unilaterally experiment with new approaches and are starting to consider legalization of certain drugs. In 2012, voters in Colorado and Washington approved the creation of a regulatory market for cannabis on a state level.[25] In 2013, Uruguay followed suit on a national level and likewise established a regulated market for cannabis.[26]

Whether this wind of change will advance the consensus that is necessary to make substantial decisions is far from certain. To the contrary, it seems that

22 Joint Declaration of Colombia, Guatemala and Mexico to the United Nations, 2012, UN Doc. A/67/493; cf. also for the need to evaluate contemporary drug policies by Colombian President Juan Manuel Santos, 'Re-examining the Drug Problem through a Fresh Lens', in: John Collins (ed.), *Governing the Global Drug Wars*, Special Report, p. 2.

23 Closing Statement of the President of the Republic of Colombia Juan Manuel Santos, Sixth Summit of the Americas, Cartagena de Indias, Colombia', 2012, p. 2 (available online at: www.summit-americas.org/SIRG/2012/041412/statement_santos_closing_en.pdf). The Secretariat of the OAS has issued the 'Report on the Drug Problem in the Americas' (2013) of which the member States have taken note; OAS, 'Report on the Drug Problem in the Americas in 2013', 2013, p. 5; OAS, 'Declaration for a Comprehensive Policy against the World Drug Problem in the Americas', 2013, AG/DEC. 73 (XLIII-O/13) corr. 1.

24 Cf. also for a similar assessment, Neil Boister, *An Introduction to Transnational Criminal Law*, p. 61: 'There is growing pressure to reform the Conventions.'

25 David Bewley-Taylor, Tom Blickman and Martin Jelsma, 'The Rise and Decline of Cannabis Prohibition: The History of Cannabis in the UN Drug Control System and Options for Reform', TNI, 2014, pp. 52 et seq.

26 *Ibid.*, pp. 56 et seq.

States find it increasingly difficult to agree on questions of fundamental importance. As Bewley-Taylor has it, the consensus that once existed between States parties to the UN Drug Conventions, today is 'fractured'.[27]

This might be exemplified with regard to two very different issues. First, States parties are unable to reach an agreement on health-oriented approaches for treatment of drug users (harm reduction). It has been impossible until now to adopt a resolution within the United Nations supporting such interventions.[28] Second, the events surrounding the Bolivian strive for the traditional use of the coca leaf stand as proof that States will opt for unilateral solutions if they do not achieve the desired results multilaterally.[29] In 2008, Bolivia called for an amendment of the Single Convention on Narcotic Drugs, aiming for the removal of traditional coca leaf consumption from the international drug control regime.[30] The rejection of the amendment proposal led to a 'creative step' by Bolivia. In order to attain the desired result of allowing traditional use of the coca leaf on its territory,[31] Bolivia denounced the Single Convention on 30 June 2011[32] with the intention to re-accede to the instrument subject to the acceptation of a permanent reservation, providing 'the right [of Bolivia] to allow on its territory: coca leaf chewing; the consumption and use of the coca leaf in its natural state'.[33] The re-accession, including the said reservation, became effective on 11 January 2013.[34] Therefore, the international drug control system is currently in a situation of uncertainty.[35] Old objectives and approaches are increasingly openly challenged without a consensus on a new direction and goals. This requires a careful analysis of the current status quo, which is the object of this book.

27 David Bewley-Taylor, *International Drug Control: Consensus Fractured*, 2012.

28 Cf. in this regard the 2008 session of the CND; CND, Report on the Fifty-Second Session, UN Doc. E/2009/28 E/CN.7/2009/12 2009, paras 155 et seq.

29 Cf. as to the link between Bolivia's re-accession and legalization of cannabis within the US New York City Bar, 'The International Drug Control Treaties: How Important are They to US Drug Reform', August 2012, pp. 5 et seq.

30 Proposal of Amendment, 'Depositary Notification of the Secretary General of 6 April 2008' C.N.194.2009.TREATIES-2.

31 Bulgaria, Canada, Denmark, Estonia, France, Germany, Italy, Japan, Latvia, Malaysia, Mexico, Russian Federation, Singapore, Slovakia, Sweden, United Kingdom and United States; INCB Annual Report 2011, para. 276, fn. 18; cf. e.g. note verbale of Sweden of 20 January 2011, 'Depositary Notification of the Secretary General', C.N.24.2011.TREATIES-4; note verbale of Bulgaria of 28 January 2011, 'Depositary Notification of the Secretary General' C.N.34.2011. TREATIES-7.

32 According to Art. 46 (2) of the Single Convention, the denunciation of Bolivia entered into force 1 January 2012; Depositary Notification of the Secretary General of 30 June 2011, C.N.421.2011.TREATIES-26.

33 Depositary Notification of the Secretary General of 10 January 2012, C.N.829.2011. TREATIES-28.

34 Depositary Notification of the Secretary General of 22 January 2013, C.N.94.2013. TREATIES-VI.18. According to Art. 40 (2) of the Single Convention, the accession entered into force on 10 February 2013.

35 See for the same view Bernard Levroy, 'Drug Trafficking', in: Neil Boister and Robert J. Currie (eds), *Routledge Companion of Transnational Criminal Law*, 229 (246).

1.2 Objectives and methodology of this book

This book provides an extensive legal analysis of the international drug control system in light of the growing challenges and criticism that the system faces.

First, it lays bare the sources of the international drug control system as well as the role of its central actors (Chapter 2).

Next it outlines the emergence of the international drug control system. Chapter 3 shows how throughout the decades, the limitation of drugs to medical and scientific purposes eventually became the fundamental bedrock of international drug control. Nineteenth-century bilateralism was eventually replaced by today's objective of confining all psychoactive substances covered to medical and scientific purposes. Additionally, the material scope of the limitation of drugs to medicine and science expanded throughout this period. Drug control has constantly struggled with changing patterns of recreational use of psychoactive substances. Historically, it expanded from opium to opiates and other narcotic drugs – i.e. plant-based drugs – and finally to psychotropic substances.

Chapter 4 lays bare the entire international drug control system's objective to reduce all drug-related activities – production, trade and use alike – to medical and scientific purposes. The task of the obligation to restrict drugs to medical and scientific purposes can hardly be overestimated. Despite the central function of the limitation of drugs to medical and scientific purposes for the entire drug control system, it will be examined whether exceptions to this rule can be identified. On the one hand, it will be explored whether the international drug control system contains 'intrinsic exceptions' to this rule, by allowing States parties to opt out of the requirement to limit substances to medical and scientific purposes. On the other hand, it will be established whether there exist 'extrinsic exceptions' to the reduction of drugs to medical and scientific purposes, emanating from international human rights law, i.e. whether human rights law contains norms allowing individuals to use drugs for other than medical or scientific purposes.

Chapter 5, on the scope *ratione materiae* of the international drug control system, identifies the substances covered. The international drug control system embodies enough flexibility to modify its scope of control, in order to extend to substances previously left unaffected. However, the drug market nowadays is evolving with unprecedented speed and the time-costly mechanisms to enlarge drug control's scope of application appear to be too slow to react to the plethora of 'new psychoactive substances' that flood the drug market each year. This causes major actors to blur the line between substances inside and outside of the international drug control system. Furthermore, the current scope of application of the international drug control system is controversial with regard to certain substances, such as cannabis. If and how these substances could be removed from drug control's scope of application will be examined.

Finally, Chapter 6 analyses the means by which the international drug control system collaborates to reach the objective of confining drugs to medical and scientific purposes: i.e. by setting up a universal system that exercises a rigid control on drug supply. The system is based upon the unspoken premise that a surplus of drugs is available which must be reduced to the amount required for medical and scientific purposes only. To this end, it has established a controlled economy for the licit production, trade and distribution of drugs. Illicit production and traffic of drugs is suppressed by a requirement for States to adopt enforceable penal sanctions. This heavy focus on the control of drugs via a reduction of supply is deficient in two ways. First, it does not contain enough safeguards to ensure the availability of drugs for medical and scientific purposes. While the system involves obligations to reduce the supply of drugs to the amount required for medical and scientific purposes, it does not contain operative obligations that require States to take effective steps in order to increase the availability of drugs for these ends. Second, it only contains very vague obligations on how to reduce illicit demand and provide for treatment measures for drug users. Although soft law instruments have strengthened both aspects – i.e. the guarantee of availability of drugs for medical and scientific purposes as well as the reduction of demand – they have so far not corrected the impreciseness and vagueness of the hard law with regard to these issues. The book concludes by making suggestions on how the international drug control system could be reformed in the near future in order to better meet the existing challenges.

Before proceeding *in medias res*, one preliminary remark about what this book is *not* about seems necessary. This book is not a piece of advocacy. This approach may seem self-evident for most fields of international law. Albeit the international drug control system has been analysed by many, international lawyers in general have ignored it in the last years and decades.[36] Hence, many analysing the international drug control system either aim to change it or defend it against the growing critique. Conversely, this book neither aims to change the current international drug control system nor can it be read as defending the current status quo. Instead of taking a definite position with regard to the viability of international drug control, this book takes one step back and analyses the premises and means of the current legal framework. It focuses on what this legal framework actually allows or inhibits and how the contemporary problems of the international drug control system can be evaluated from a legal perspective. Such a study of the international drug control system so far has been lacking.

36 See in that regard Harry Levine, 'Global Drug Prohibition: Its Uses and Crises', *IJDP* Vol. 14 2003, 145: 'The invisible system'. Even a well-known and influential legal scholar as Paul Reuter, who has published widely on many different fields of international law, did not see drug control fit for a substantive and elaborated treatise. Although being a member of the INCB for decades, he only wrote one short note on the Single Convention; Paul Reuter, 'The Obligations of the States under the Single Convention on Narcotic Drugs, 1961' *Bulletin on Narcotics* Vol. 20 No. 4 1968.

2 The sources and actors of the international drug control system

This chapter introduces the international drug control system by presenting its source (2.1) and its institutions (2.2). Understanding the sources and actors of the international drug control system is of vital importance for this book, which captures the contemporary status quo of the international drug control system.

The international drug control system is evolving constantly due to the myriad of legal instruments adopted by the various actors. Thus, for example drug control's institutions are vested by the UN Drug Conventions with the power to decide on which substances will be effectively covered by these treaties. The CND can modify the substances covered by the international drug control system upon the recommendation of the World Health Organization (WHO).[1] Second, even outside of the particular constellation of binding decisions of such actors, their interpretation of the UN Drug Conventions shapes the way in which these treaties are understood and perceived in general. Thus, the fact that the International Narcotics Control Board (INCB) has constantly argued against health-oriented measures in the treatment of drug users, in particular the operation of drug consumption rooms, has led to the image of the international drug control system as not paying adequate attention to the needs of vulnerable drug users.[2]

These rather cursory examples may explain why this book cannot be limited to an isolated assessment of the 'hard law' of the international drug control system that can be found in the UN Charter and the UN Drug Conventions, but also encompasses an analysis of 'soft law' and other secondary instruments of the principle institutions of the international drug control system. Their mandate and role in drug control matters need to be addressed and the normative value of their secondary instruments has to be understood.

Capturing the legal relevance of the soft law instruments of the international drug control system is far from self-evident. The normative uncertainties

1 Cf. *infra* Chapter 5 for further details.

2 Cf. *infra* 6.3 for further details.

surrounding such instruments are, of course, not an exclusive attribute of the international drug control system, but form part of a wider and more profound confusion over an exact delimitation of the sources of international law, in the light of ever-multiplying actors and instruments at an international level since World War II.[3]

Nevertheless, it is particularly difficult to connect subsequent instruments of the international drug control system with the UN Drug Conventions. These difficulties are related to the fractured structure of the international drug control system. States have not set up an international organization vested with exclusive competence in drug control matters. Furthermore, and different from many other so-called 'autonomous arrangements' in other fields of international law,[4] the UN Drug Conventions lack a formal Assembly of States parties.[5] These assemblies play an important role within the normative life of treaty systems; they shape and modify the way in which a treaty is understood. Such a body is lacking within the international drug control system, making its normative setting more fuzzy and fragmentized. The international drug control system (the exception of the INCB notwithstanding) relies on organs and institutions of the United Nations. Hence, the institutions of the international drug control system are given functions under the UN Drug Conventions, as well as the UN Charter, and act under an interwoven set of obligations in drug control matters. This interwoven set of obligations needs to be briefly outlined.

2.1 The primary sources of the international drug control system

2.1.1 The UN Drug Conventions: The 'cornerstones' of the international drug control system[6]

There are currently three UN Drug Conventions in force. The first is the Single Convention on Narcotic Drugs of 1961.[7] This treaty applies to certain plant-based drugs – i.e. cannabis, opiates and cocaine/coca leaf – as well as substances with similar properties. The Single Convention was soon updated in 1972 by the

3 Cf. as to this issue, Prosper Weil, 'Towards Relative Normativity in International Law?', *AJIL* Vol. 77 1983, 413.

4 Robin Churchill and Geir Ulfstein, 'Autonomous Institutional Arrangements in Multilateral Environmental Agreements: A Little Noticed Phenomenon in International Law', *AJIL* Vol. 94 2000, 623.

5 *Ibid.* A 'conference of parties' may be defined as a permanent association of the parties which institutionalizes intergovernmental cooperation in a permanent form that is distinct from the parties; cf. Volker Röben, 'Conference (Meeting) of States Parties', in: Rüdiger Wolfrum (ed.), *MPEPIL*, 2012, MN 1.

6 Cf. in this regard UNGA Resolution 64/182, UN Doc. A/Res/64/182, para. 3.

7 Single Convention on Narcotic Drugs, 1961, of 30 March 1961, entered into force 13 December 1963, UNTS Vol. 520, p. 151.

Protocol amending the Single Convention on Narcotic Drugs, 1961.[8] The Single Convention has been ratified by 186 States, of which 185 are also bound by its Protocol.[9] The Single Convention terminated all earlier drug control treaties (Art. 47), which had been drafted between 1912 and 1953, and therefore marks the beginning of the contemporary drug control system.[10] The treaty limits the production, trade and use of narcotic drugs to medical and scientific purposes (Art. 4 (c) Single Convention).

The rise of hitherto uncontrolled synthetic psychoactive substances during the 1960s, which were not *narcotic* drugs required the adoption of a new instrument: The Convention on Psychotropic Substances of 1971.[11] This treaty was ratified by 183 States parties.[12] It limits the manufacture, traffic and use of psychotropic substances to medical and scientific purposes (Arts 5 (2) and 7 (1) 1971 Convention).

The third UN Drug Convention is the United Nations Convention against the Illicit Traffic in Narcotic Drugs and Psychotropic Substances. This treaty was drafted in order to counter international drug trafficking cartels by enhancing international cooperation against the illicit traffic in drugs; it is ratified by 187 States.[13] The treaty does not fundamentally alter the approach chosen by the Single Convention and the 1971 Convention, it was rather crafted from the 'need to reinforce and supplement' these treaties.[14] Thus, sanctions penalizing illicit activities regarding drugs were strengthened and their effective implementation was to be ensured by a system of international cooperation.

2.1.2 The UN Charter and international drug control[15]

International drug control is not only 'treaty based', but also partly 'charter based'. Article 55 (b) – contained in Chapter IX of the UN Charter on 'International Economic Cooperation' – reads:

> With a view to the creation of conditions of stability and well-being which are necessary for peaceful and friendly relations among nations based on respect for the principle of equal rights and self-determination of peoples, the United Nations shall promote [...] b. solutions of international economic, social, health, and related problems [...].

8 Protocol amending the Single Convention on Narcotic Drugs, 1961, of 25 March 1972 entered into force 8 August 1975, UNTS Vol. 976, p. 3 [hereinafter referred to as 1972 Protocol]. A consolidated version of the Single Convention on Narcotic Drugs, 1961, as amended by the 1972 Protocol can be found at UNTS Vol. 976, p. 3. This book uses 'Single Convention' in order to quote the Single Convention as amended by its 1972 Protocol, unless otherwise stipulated.

9 Cf. INCB Annual Report 2016, para. 64

10 Cf. *infra* Chapter 3 for further details.

11 Convention on Psychotropic Substances of 21 February 1971, entered into force 16 August 1976, UNTS Vol. 1019, 175 [hereinafter referred to as 1971 Convention].

12 INCB Annual Report 2016, para. 64,

13 *Ibid.*, para. 65.

14 Preambular para. 13, 1988 Convention.

15 The Charter of the United Nations of 26 June 1945, entered into force 24 October 1945, UNCIO Vol. 15, p. 335.

Drug control is not mentioned *expressis verbis* in this provision. This had been different under the Charter's predecessor, i.e. the Covenant on the League of Nations, where the League had been expressively entrusted with regard to the agreements concerning the 'traffic in opium and other dangerous drugs' (Art. 23 (c) Covenant of the League of Nations).[16] Albeit no concrete reference to drugs is contained within the UN Charter, it was understood among the delegates that the United Nations disposed of the competence to deal with this issue.[17]

Article 55 (b) thus vests the United Nations with the competence in drug control matters. The *telos* of Art. 55 is to lay out the areas of international cooperation that the United Nations should be preoccupied with[18] and thus provides the United Nations with the competence to adopt measures on drug control and develop a regulatory framework in that regard.[19] The Charter fails, however, to lay out a concrete *démarche* that the United Nations would be required to adopt with regard to drugs. As will be seen, several organs of the United Nations have made use of this competence and effectively laid out an extensive framework on drug control in the last decades. Article 56 of the Charter complements Art. 55 (b) by clarifying that not only the United Nations but all member States are to cooperate in order to achieve "the purposes set forth in Article 55".[20]

2.2 The institutions of the international drug control system and a typology of their secondary instruments

The central actors within the international drug control system are the UNGA, the Economic and Social Council of the United Nations (ECOSOC), the CND and the WHO. Furthermore, these treaties are monitored by the INCB which is assisted by the UNODC.

2.2.1 The United Nations General Assembly: A (potentially) central actor for the international drug control system

The UNGA from 1967 onwards has adopted annual resolutions on drug control and dedicated three special sessions to the World Drug Problem. International drug control is discussed within the UNGA's third committee, which is

16 Covenant of the League of Nations of 10 January 1920, entered into force 10 January 1920, CTS Vol. 225, p. 188. Before the adoption of the Charter it had been expected that the final document would contain a similar provision to Art. 19 (c); cf. Adolf Lande, 'The Adjustments of the International Opium Administration to an Eventual Dissolution of the League of Nations', *CLR* Vol. 45 1945, 392 (397).

17 Cf. in this regard UNICO Vol. X, pp. 196 et seq. It does not clearly derive from the *travaux préparatoires*, whether drug control was considered an economic, social, health or related problem; cf. UNICO Vol. VIII, p. 252; UNICO Vol. X, p. 390.

18 Alain Pellet, 'Art. 55 alinéas a et b', in: Alain Pellet, Jean Pierre Cot and Mathias Forteau (eds), *La Charte des Nations Unies*, MN 11 et seq.

19 Cf. as to this framework Peter-Tobias Stoll, 'Art. 55 (a)-(b)', in: Bruno Simma et al. (eds), *The Charter of the United Nations*, MN 99.

20 Alain Pellet, 'Art. 55 alinéas a et b', in: Alain Pellet, Jean Pierre Cot and Mathias Forteau (eds), *La Charte des Nations Unies*, MN 8.

concerned with social and humanitarian issues.[21] The UNGA consists out of all 193 UN member States (Art. 9 (1) UN Charter) and is the sole UN institution where each member is represented. Additionally, the UNGA is the only forum where all the States parties to the UN Drug Conventions assemble regularly to discuss drug control.

2.2.1.1 Mandate with regard to drug control

The UNGA (the 'universal conference within the organizational structure of the UN'[22]) is vested with a mandate as broad as the scope of the UN Charter (Art. 10 UN Charter). It 'may initiate studies and make recommendations' for the purpose of *inter alia* 'promoting international cooperation in the economic, social, cultural, educational, and health fields [...] (Art. 13 (1) (b) UN Charter)'. This also comprises international drug control – as drug control is classified among the economic, social and health fields mentioned in Art. 55 (b) of the Charter

Additionally, the Single Convention and the 1971 Convention provide the UNGA with treaty-based functions. In accordance with Art. 6 Single Convention and Art. 24 1971 Convention, the UNGA decides on the expenses of the INCB and the CND and on the remuneration of the members of the INCB (Art. 10 (6) Single Convention). Furthermore, Art. 7 Single Convention vests the UNGA with the authority to review all recommendations and decisions of the CND together with the ECOSOC. The only exception to this are those decisions of the ECOSOC that concern the 'scheduling', i.e. the modification of the substances controlled by the UN Drug Conventions, where the UNGA cannot intervene (Art. 3 Single Convention).[23]

2.2.1.2 Normative value of drug-related instruments of the UNGA

The normative value of UNGA resolutions under the UN Charter has been the subject of long and vivid debates among legal scholars, as well as States. Such debate will not be recaptured here.[24] It is held today by most scholars that the UN Charter does not provide the UNGA with the authority to take

21 www.un.org/en/ga/third/index.shtml; cf. also Daniel-Erasmus Khan, 'Art. 20', in: Bruno Simma et al. (eds), *The Charter of the United Nations*, MN 12.

22 Christian Tomuschat, 'United Nations General Assembly', in: Rüdiger Wolfrum (ed.), *MPEPIL*, 2012, MN 1; 37.

23 It is possible to modify the substances controlled by the UN Drug Conventions. It is also possible to modify the scope of control exercised on individual substances. This procedure (scheduling) is foreseen within Art. 3 Single Convention; Art. 2 1971 Convention and Art. 12 1988 Convention; cf. also as to further details *infra* 5.2.

24 For a comprehensive account with regard to this issue cf. e.g. Blaine Sloan, 'General Assembly Resolutions Revisited (Forty Years Later)', *BYIL* Vol. 58 1987, 39 with further references.

any binding measures on UN member States.[25] The UNGA, in general, merely adopts recommendations with the exception of so-called internal matters, where the UNGA may take binding decisions in order to ensure its continuous functioning.[26] One example for an internal matter that the UNGA may address in a binding manner is the call for an UNGA special session (Art. 20 UN Charter).[27] This call has been made three times for the world drug problem, the last time in 2014 by UNGGA Resolution 69/200 for UNGASS 2016.[28] Furthermore, the UNGA has a superior role to other UN organs and institutions, and it therefore reviews decisions of the CND and the ECOSOC.

Apart from the exceptions mentioned above, UNGA resolutions do not generate rights and obligations for UN member States or other international organisations per se.[29] This reading is confirmed by the wording of the Charter, referring to UNGA instruments as 'recommendations' (cf. in that regard, e.g. Arts 11 (1) (2) and 12 (1).[30] This absence of mandatory effect, however, as has been explained authoritatively by Pellet and others, does not mean that such instruments are deprived of any normative value.[31] The content of UNGA resolutions may in certain situations have an evolving effect on the law. The fact that 193 States agree on certain issues at a universal level has an impact within the legal sphere. The UNGA has effectively shaped and changed international law by the adoption of mere non-binding resolutions.[32]

Most importantly for the present inquiry of the international drug control system – where the normative development of the hard law of the UN Drug Conventions will have to be assessed in the light of UNGA resolutions on the same matter – UNGA resolutions possibly influence the interpretation of treaty provisions. It has to be borne in mind that all the parties to the UN Drug Conventions are members of the United Nations and meet during the UNGA. It is thus not the form of an UNGA resolution which is important here, but the fact that all States parties to the UN Drug Conventions agree on a certain modality of their interpretation in occurrence of the adoption of such a resolution

25 Cf. in this regard Eckart Klein and Stefanie Schmahl, 'Art. 11', in: Bruno Simma et al. (eds), *The Charter of the United Nations*, 48 et seq.

26 Patrick Daillier, Mathias Forteau and Alain Pellet (Nguyen Quoc Dinh †), *Droit International Public*, 2009, MN 243; as an example, one may mention the election of the president of the UNGA, the acceptance of credentials of a Member State and so forth; *ibid.*, MN 247.

27 Cf. as to this issue in detail Christophe Eick, 'Art. 20', in: Bruno Simma et al. (eds), *The Charter of the United Nations*, MN 25 et seq. with further details.

28 UNGA Resolution 69/200, 2014, UN Doc. A/Res/69/200.

29 Christian Tomuschat, 'United Nations General Assembly', in: Rüdiger Wolfrum (ed.), *MPEPIL*, 2012, MN 22.

30 *Ibid.*, MN 17 et seq., 22; Eckart Klein and Stefanie Schmahl, Art. 11, in: Bruno Simma et al. (eds), *The Charter of the United Nations*, MN 47 et seq.

31 Patrick Daillier, Mathias Forteau and Alain Pellet (Nguyen Quoc Dinh †), *Droit International Public*, 2009, MN 248.

32 Cf. e.g. in that regard UNGA Resolution 2625, 1970, UN Doc. A/Res/2625 (XXV) on the peaceful relations among States; cf. also UNGA Resolution 3314 (XXIX), 1974, UN Doc. A/Res/3315 (XXIX) on the definition of aggression.

Hence, UNGA resolutions can be used as a source for treaty interpretation of the UN Drug Conventions in the sense of subsequent practice according to Art. 31 (3) (b) Vienna Convention on the Law of Treaties (VCLT).[33] Article 31 (3) (b) provides that '[a]ny subsequent practice in the application of the treaty which establishes the agreement of the parties regarding its interpretation' has to be taken into account when a treaty is interpreted. Indeed, the International Law Commission (ILC) as well as legal scholarship agree that voting for UNGA resolutions can amount to subsequent practice in accordance with Art. 31 (3) (b) VCLT.[34] Furthermore, in order to amount to a practice in the sense of Art. 31 (3) (b) VCLT, the practice has to be concordant, i.e. the parties have to consistently interpret a certain stipulation of the UN Drug Conventions in a given matter.[35]

Additionally, it has to be established that a given interpretation of the UN Drug Conventions contained in an UNGA resolution has been taken 'in application' of the UN Drug Conventions. The ILC has interpreted this criterion restrictively as it required '[c]areful consideration, in particular of whether the parties, by an agreement or a practice, assume a position regarding the interpretation of a treaty'.[36] Certainly not all the resolutions of the UNGA on the World Drug Problem can be considered as having been adopted in application of the UN Drug Conventions. The annual resolutions comprise several pages and more than 54 paragraphs.[37] They cover a variety of topics, examples of which range

33 Of 23 May 1969, entered into force 27 January 1980, UNTS Vol. 1155, p. 331. This study relies heavily on the rules of treaty interpretation, as expressed by the VCLT, regardless of the fact that two of the UN Drug Conventions entered into force before the VCLT and Art. 4 VCLT prohibits its retroactive application. The rules of treaty interpretation contained within Art. 31 et seq. VCLT may be applied, since these rules merely codify preexisting customary international law; cf. Jean-Marc Sorel and Valérie Boré Eveno, 'Art. 31', in: Olvier Corten and Pierre Klein (eds), *The Vienna Convention on the Law of Treaties: A Commentary*, 2011, MN 15 with further references; cf. also more generally Fréderic Dopagne 'Art.4', in: *ibid.*, MN 18; for a different view on the applicability of the rules expressed in the Single Convention, cf., however, Mark A. Leinwand, 'The International Law of Treaties and United States Legalization of Marijuana,' *Colum. J. Transnat'l L.* Vol. 10 1971, 413 (426).

34 Cf. in that regard Oliver Dörr, 'Art. 31', in: Oliver Dörr and Kirsten Schmalenbach (eds), *Vienna Convention on the Law of Treaties: A Commentary*, 2012, MN 78; Draft Conclusion 5th Report of the ILC to the UNGA 65th Session, 2013, UN Doc. A/68/10, GAOR Supplement No. 10 (A/68/10), 2013; cf. also Georg Nolte, Second Report on Subsequent Agreements and Subsequent Practice in relation to the Interpretation of Treaties, 2014, UN Doc. A/CN.4/671, paras 42 et seq.

35 Cf. in that regard International Court of Justice (ICJ), Kaskili/Sedudu Island (*Botswana v. Namibia*); Judgment of 13 December 1999, ICJ Rep 1999 1045, para. 74; cf. also Gerhard Hafner, 'Subsequent Agreements and Practice: Between Interpretation, Informal Modification and Formal Agreement', in: Georg Nolte (ed.), *Treaties and Subsequent Practice*, 105 (113); Richard Gardiner, *Treaty Interpretation*, pp. 226 et seq.

36 Georg Nolte, Special Rapporteur, Second Report on Subsequent Agreements and Subsequent Practice in relation to the Interpretation of Treaties, 2014, UN Doc. A/CN.4/671, para. 19, Draft Conclusion 6.

37 Cf. in this regard UNGA Resolution 69/201, 2014, UN Doc. A/Res/69/201.

from availability of drugs for medical and scientific purposes[38] to concerns over drug-affected driving.[39] However, a resolution of the UNGA on the world drug problem is made in application of the UN Drug Conventions when it contains a direct reference to those treaties. The same is true when it is clear from its adoption that a certain statement contained therein relates directly to the UN Drug Conventions' provisions.[40]

Furthermore, in order to fulfil the criteria of Art. 31 (3) (b) VCLT, the resolutions in question have to amount to agreement of the parties to the UN Drug Conventions. In order to constitute an agreement, the practice has to be universally consented to by all the States parties. This is especially important for multilateral treaties such as the UN Drug Conventions. While it is true that an agreement does not require that all the parties 'must have individually engaged in practice', it is equally certain that agreement means consensus of all the parties.[41] This also derives from of the International Court of Justice's (ICJ) jurisprudence. In the *Whaling in Antarctica* case, the latter refrained from interpreting the International Convention for the Regulation of Whaling against the background of resolutions adopted by the States parties to this treaty, since many of them had not met the parties' universal consensus.[42]

Accordingly, an UNGA resolution on the world drug problem might be considered when interpreting the UN Drug Conventions if:

1 There exists a concrete nexus between the resolution and a provision of the UN Drug Conventions;
2 The practice amounts to a certain degree of coherence, i.e. is repeated in a certain number of situations and thus appears in a certain number of resolutions;
3 All the States parties agree to the given interpretation.

In conclusion, it may be said, that the UNGA enjoys a central function within the international drug control system. Although the UN Drug Conventions do not vest the UNGA with an extensive mandate, it plays an influential role in how

38 UNGA Resolution 69/201, 2014, UN Doc. A/Res/69/201, para. 14.

39 *Ibid.*, para. 13.

40 Cf. in that regard UNGA Resolution 68/196, 2013, UN Doc. A/Res/68/196. The resolution was has adopted while 'bearing in mind the content of Article 14 of the 1988 Convention (preambular para. 2)'.

41 Oliver Dörr, 'Art. 31', in: Oliver Dörr and Kirsten Schmalenbach (eds), *Vienna Convention on the Law of Treaties: A Commentary*, MN 83; cf. also Richard Gardiner, *Treaty Interpretation*, pp. 235 et seq.

42 ICJ, Whaling in Antarctica (*Australia v. Japan*: New Zealand intervening), Judgment of 31 March 2014, para. 83. Cf. however Separate Opinion Whaling in Antarctica (*Australia v. Japan*: New Zealand intervening) of Judge ad hoc Charlesworth, para. 4: 'I note that resolutions adopted by a vote [and thereby without consensus] of the IWC have some consequence although they do not come within the terms of art. 31.3 of the Vienna Convention'; this assessment, however, leaves open the crucial question what legal consequences might be attributed to these instruments.

the terms of these treaties are to be understood. Its singularity lies in the fact that it is only within the UNGA that all States parties to the UN Drug Conventions discuss and decide on international drug control. This turns the UNGA into a central actor for drug control, whose importance may not be grasped by its mandate under the UN Drug Conventions alone. The UNGA has played this vital role in the past; it has set the central benchmarks with regard to drugs for the international community in the last decades.[43] However, it has so far failed in many cases to use its potential fully and to substantially advance the interpretation of the UN Drug Conventions. This can be seen, for instance, with regard to more health-oriented approaches to drug demand, which have so far not been laid out precisely enough by the UNGA.[44]

2.2.2 The Economic and Social Council of the United Nations: Drug control as an economic and social problem

The Economic and Social Council of the United Nations (ECOSOC) consists out of 54 member States of the United Nations, elected by the UNGA for a three-year term (Art. 61 (1) and (2) of the UN Charter).

2.2.2.1 Mandate with regard to drug control

The mandate of the ECOSOC under the UN Charter is laid out by Art. 62 (1). Thereby the ECOSOC is assigned with the responsibility to carry out the functions of the United Nations as far as 'international economic and social cooperation' are concerned; as has been shown this also includes international drug control.[45] It may 'initiate studies and reports' in this field and make recommendations in that regard; these recommendations may be addressed to the UNGA, the member States and to the specialized agencies concerned (Art. 62 UN Charter). Additionally, Art. 62 (4) of the Charter allows the ECOSOC to 'call [...] international conferences on matters falling within its competence'. The conferences drafting all three UN Drug Conventions, as well as the 1972 Protocol, were all called by the ECOSOC according to this provision.[46]

The ECOSOC together with the UNGA carries out a general review of all decisions taken by the CND under Art. 7 Single Convention. Additionally, by all three UN Drug Conventions the ECOSOC is provided with the ultimate authority to reverse any decision of the CND as far as the scheduling of a substance

43 Cf. only the goals set by 1990 and 1998 UNGASS; UNGA, Political Declaration Annex, 1998, UN Doc. A/Res/S-20/2, paras 14, 17 and 19; UNGA, Political Declaration and Global Programme of Action, 1990, UN Doc. A/Res-17/2, para. 1.

44 Cf. *infra* 6.3 for further details.

45 Volker Röben, 'Art. 60', in: Bruno Simma et al. (eds), *The Charter of the United Nations*, MN 1; cf. as to Art. 55 (b) of the Charter *supra* 2.1.2.

46 For the Single Convention, cf. ECOSOC Resolution 689 (XXVI) J, 1958, UN Doc. E/Res/ 1958/ 689 (XXVI) J, para. 4; for the 1971 Convention, cf. Resolution 1474 (XLV1H), 1970, UN Doc. E/RES/1970/1474(XLVIII), para. 2; for the 1972 Protocol, cf. ECOSOC Resolution 1577 (L), 1971, UN Doc. E/Res/1971/1577 (L), para. 1; for the 1988 Convention, cf. ECOSOC Resolution 1988/8, 1988, UN Doc. E/Res/1988/8, para. 7.

is concerned, upon the demand of a party (Art. 3 (7) Single Convention; Art. 2 (8) 1971 Convention; Art. 12 (7) (c) 1988 Convention).[47] The ECOSOC elects the members of the INCB (Art. 9 (1) Single Convention) and may, on the request of nine of 15 INCB members, dismiss members of the board (Art. 10 (4) Single Convention). Lastly, all UN Drug Conventions provide the ECOSOC with the competence to decide on treaty amendments; the ECOSOC may either decide to submit such amendments to the States parties individually or call for a conference of the parties to the issue (Art. 47 Single Convention; Art. 30 1971 Convention; Art. 31 (2) 1988 Convention).

2.2.2.2 Normative value of drug-related instruments of the ECOSOC

The UN Charter only gives the ECOSOC the authority to adopt 'recommendations';[48] thus its resolutions are of non-binding character.[49] Given that ECOSOC resolutions are only adopted by 54 States, these instruments cannot be considered as subsequent practice of all the States parties to the UN Drug Conventions in accordance with Art. 31 (3) (b) VCLT. However, a resolution of the ECOSOC initiates a certain interpretation of this treaty, on which consensus of all the States parties to the UN Drug Conventions may emerge. Additionally, the UN Drug Conventions have not provided the ECOSOC with the task of authoritatively developing their obligations. Its decisions are only legally binding when carrying out the above-mentioned treaty-based functions. In practice, the ECOSOC has not been very active with regard to drug control in the last years, and for the most part has left this issue to its functional commission, the Commission on Narcotic Drugs of the Economic and Social Council of the United Nations (CND).[50]

2.2.3 The Commission on Narcotic Drugs of the Economic and Social Council: The UN organ with 'prime responsibility for drug control'[51]

The CND was founded in 1946 and meets annually in March in Vienna; it takes decisions without vote by consensus.[52]

47 As to this issue cf. *supra* note 59. This decision does not fall under Art. 7 Single Convention and therefore may not be subsequently reversed by the UNGA.

48 Cf. in this regard Arts 62, 63, 64 and 66.

49 Georg Schwarzenberger, *Economic World Order: A Basic Problem of International Economic Cooperation*, p. 40.

50 Cf. in this regard the resolutions and decisions adopted by the CND and the ECOSOC in the last years (www.unodc.org/unodc/en/commissions/CND/Resolutions_Decisions/Resolutions-Decisions_2010-2019.html).

51 CND Resolution 57/5, UN Doc. E/2014/28, 2014, preambular para. 4. Although being formally merely a subsidiary organ of the ECOSOC, the UNGA today recognizes that the CND plays the 'principal role' and is vested with the 'prime responsibility' for drug control matters; cf. e.g. UNGA Resolution 68/197, 2013, UN Doc. A/Res/68/197, preambular para. 23.

52 This practice, although far from infrequent on an international level, referred to by some as 'Vienna consensus' is criticized, since it would forestall changes within the international drug control system; David Bewley-Taylor, *International Drug Control: Consensus Fractured*, p. 23; *passim*.

When drafting the UN Drug Conventions, the States parties entrusted the central governance of these treaties to a functional commission of the ECOSOC that had already been in existence before the entry into force of the Single Convention.[53] The States parties were aware that they were assigning treaty-based functions to a charter-based entity but assumed that this would not create any specific practical problems.[54] However, the problems arising out of the duality of the CND manifested themselves during the drafting process of the Single Convention. Thus, the initial idea to modify the name of the CND to the International Narcotics Commission[55] was soon dropped since 'it was considered inappropriate' to change the name of a charter-based institution by virtue of a multilateral treaty.[56]

The membership of the CND has constantly been extended and today comprises 53 States.[57] The members of the CND are elected by the ECOSOC. In order to be eligible, States either have to be members of the United Nations or its specialized agencies, or to be a State party to the Single Convention.[58]

2.2.3.1 Mandate and relationship with the UNGA and the ECOSOC

The CND has been established as a subcommission by the ECOSOC.[59] The ECOSOC has been granted the power to establish such subcommissions in 'economic and social fields' by the virtue of Art. 7 (2) and Art. 68 of the UN Charter, 'as may be required for the performance of its functions'.[60] Being an

53 The CND was the ECOSOC's first functional committee; Robert W. Gregg, 'The United Nations and the Opium Problem', *ICLQ* Vol. 14 1964, 96.

54 Cf. in this regard statement by the President of the United Nations Conference for the Adoption of a Single Convention on Narcotic Drugs New York, 24 January, 25 March 1961 Official Records Volume I: Summary Records of Plenary Meetings, 1964, UN Doc. E/CONF.34.24 [hereinafter referred to as OR I Single Convention], p. 1.

55 Cf. Art. 10 (2) Third Draft Single Convention on Narcotic Drugs of 11 September 1958, UN Doc E/CN.7/AC.3/9 [hereinafter referred to as Third Draft Single Convention].

56 OR I Single Convention, pp. 87 et seq.

57 Initially, the CND was composed of 15 UN members; ECOSOC Resolution 9 (1) 1946, 1946, UN Doc. E/Res/1946/9, para. 4. In 1966, the ECOSOC decided to enlarge the membership to 24 members, ECOSOC Resolution 1147 (XLI), 1966, UN Doc. E/RES/1147 (XLI), para. 4. The membership was raised again in 1972 to 30 members; ECOSOC Resolution 1663 (LII), 1972, UN Doc. E/Res/1663 (LII). In 1983, the CND was enlarged to 40 members; ECOSOC Resolution 1983/5,1983, UN Doc. E/Res/1983/5. Finally, in 1991, the CND membership expanded to its contemporary size of 53 member States; ECOSOC Resolution 1991/49, 1991, UN Doc. E/Res/1991/49; cf. also to the expansion of the CND, Daniel Heilmann, 'Narcotic Drugs and Psychotropic Substances', in: Rüdiger Wolfrum (ed.), *MPEPIL*, 2012, MN 36

58 ECOSOC Resolution 845 (XXXII), 1977, UN Doc. E/Res/845 (XXXII), para. II 1. This is not of practical relevance today as the membership to the United Nations is quasi-universal. However, it shows the hybridity of the CND as both assuming treaty and charter-based functions.

59 ECOSOC Res. 9 (1) 1946, 1946, UN Doc. E/Res/1946/9.

60 Gilles Giacca and Eibe Riedel, 'Art. 68', in: Bruno Simma et al. (eds), *The Charter of the United Nations*, MN 14.

'auxiliary organ' of the ECOSOC, the charter-based powers of the CND cannot be more extensive than the powers of the ECOSOC itself.[61]

The mandate of the CND is set out by ECOSOC Resolution 9/1946 and very broadly comprises the right to 'advise the Council on all matters pertaining to the control of narcotic drugs'.[62] The term 'narcotic drugs' should not be perceived too narrowly in that regard and comprises all psychoactive substances under international control, regardless of whether psychotropic substances – i.e. substances covered by the 1971 Convention – or narcotic drugs – i.e. substances covered by the Single Convention.[63]

The UN Drug Conventions provide the CND with three types of functions. First, the CND takes decisions on the scheduling of drugs (Art. 3 Single Convention; Art. 2 1971 Convention; Art. 12 1988 Convention). Second, the CND is vested with the authority to 'call attention' of the INCB to any matter considered relevant (Art. 8 (c) Single Convention; Art. 21 (c) 1988 Convention). Third, and more generally, States parties to all three UN Drug Conventions provide the CND with a general mandate 'to consider all matters pertaining to the aims of this Convention' (Art. 8 Single Convention; Art. 17 (1) 1971 Convention; Art: 21 Convention). According to the Commentary to the Single Convention, this means that under the Single Convention, the CND 'has under this article to deal with all aspects of the fight against drug abuse, whether political, legal, administrative, economic, social medical or scientific'.[64]

As the CND is a subsidiary organ of the ECOSOC, it assumes its functions under the authority of the latter.[65] In practice, the ECOSOC approves the decisions of the CND indirectly by taking note of the report of the CND to the ECOSOC which also contains the relevant resolutions.[66] Furthermore, the ECOSOC also approves the agenda of the CND.[67] In the words of the Commentary to the Single Convention, the ECOSOC 'has complete authority' over the CND's instruments and 'may modify them in any way it may see fit'.[68] In practice, however, the assessment that most of the recommendations of the

61 *Ibid.*, MN 94.

62 ECOSOC Res. 9 (1) 1946, 1946, UN Doc. E/Res/1946/9.

63 United Nations, Commentary on the Single Convention on Narcotic Drugs 1961, UN Publication, Sales No. E.73.XI.1 1973, Art. 8, MN 3 [hereinafter referred to as Commentary Single Convention]. The Commentary was prepared by the Secretary General in accordance with ECOSCO Resolution 914 (XXXIV) (D), 1961, UN Doc. E/Res/914 (XXXIV) (D); where the ECOSOC had 'requested' the Secretary General 'to prepare a legal commentary, giving an interpretation of the provisions of the Convention in the light of the relevant conference proceedings and other material'; *ibid.*, para. 1.

64 Commentary Single Convention, Art. 8, MN 3.

65 See also Art. 7 Single Convention.

66 Cf. in that regard e.g. ECOSOC Decision 2014/233, 2014; Decision 2013/249, 2013; Decision 2012/240, 2012; Decision 2011/260, 2011; Decision 2010/244, 2010.

67 *Ibid.*

68 Commentary Single Convention, Art. 7, MN 4. The decisions of the CND regarding the scheduling of certain substances are binding and may only be reviewed by the ECOSOC if a party appeals; cf. Art. 3 (8) Single Convention and *infra* Chapter 5.

ECOSOC are 'initiated by the Commission despite the fact that the Council has complete authority over the recommendations and decisions of the Commission regarding its functions' remains valid.[69]

2.2.3.2 Normative value of drug-related instruments of the CND

The UN Charter does not recognize any right for subsidiary organs of the ECOSOC – including the CND – to make any binding decisions. Additionally, a resolution of 53 States cannot amount to subsequent practice establishing an agreement of all the parties in accordance with Art. 31 (3) (b) VCLT. When exercising functions under the UN Drug Conventions, however, two situations have to be distinguished.

On the one hand, the CND takes binding decisions as far as the scheduling is concerned. These decisions are binding to all the parties to the respective treaty. Thus Art. 2 (7) Single Convention spells out that '[s]uch decision shall become fully effective with respect to each Party of such communication, and the parties shall act thereupon as may be required under this Convention'.

Almost identical provisions can be found in Art. 3 (7) 1971 Convention and Art. 2 (6) 1988 Convention.[70] Regarding the scheduling of substances, this means that the UN Drug Conventions provide the 53 members of the CND with the right to bind more than 180 States parties.

On the other hand, however, on all other matters, the UN Drug Conventions do not allow the CND to take any binding decisions. To the contrary, the CND is only provided with the authority 'to consider all matters' pertaining to the aims of the UN Drug Conventions. More precisely under the 1971 Convention and the Single Convention the CND may make 'recommendations' on their provisions (Art. 8 (c) Single Convention; Art. 17 (1) 1971 Convention). Thus, the CND may guide States parties on how to implement the provisions of the UN Drug Conventions.[71] It is obvious, however, that States parties have not assigned the CND with the authority to interpret and develop *ex officio* the provisions of the UN Drug Conventions.[72]

69 S. K. Chatterjee, *Legal Aspects of International Drug Control*, p. 253; cf. also Stefanie Klinger, *Die Implementationssicherungsmechanismen der UN-Drogenkonventionen von 1961, 1971, und 1988*, p. 134.

70 As to the differences between the Single Convention and the 1971 Convention with regard to scheduling procedure cf. *infra* 5.2.1.

71 Art. 21 (b) 1988 Convention likewise allows the CND to 'make suggestions and general recommendations based on the examination of the information of the parties'; cf. as to this assessment United Nations, Commentary on the United Nations Convention against Illicit Traffic in Narcotic Drugs and Psychotropic Substances 1988 done at Vienna on 20 December 1988, 1998, UN Doc. E/CN.7/590 [hereinafter referred to as Commentary 1988 Convention], Art. 21, MN 21.6. Similar to the earlier UN Drug Conventions and the 1972 Protocol, the impetus for writing a Commentary on the 1988 Convention came from the ECOSOC. In Resolution 19993/42, 1993, UN Doc. E/Res/1993/42, the Council 'requested' the Secretary General to prepare such a commentary (preambular para. 5).

72 It seems worth pointing in that regard that Art. 10 (2) of the Third Draft of the Single Convention contained a clause on the entry into force of the recommendations and decisions of the CND, whereby

> [e]ach decision or recommendation of the Commission shall come into force in respect of each party upon the receipt of a notification of the Secretary General that the provisions of this article have been satisfied and of a copy the final text of the decision or recommendation in question.

Thus CND resolutions are first and foremost political statements, even when references to the stipulations of the UN Drug Conventions are made. This does not suggest, however, that they are without any normative interest. Certainly, once all the States parties to the Drug Conventions accept a certain interpretation contained within a resolution, the CND resolution in question might be considered as an authoritative means of interpretation in accordance with Art. 31 (3) (b) VCLT.

Apart from the question of the formal value of CND resolutions, the CND needs to be considered as an important indicator of how 53 States from all over the globe assess the international drug control system and what solutions they deem viable for the world drug problem. The CND is the most active institution in drug control matters as far as the adoption of resolutions is concerned, and its resolutions cover all the major issues of drug control ranging from demand reduction,[73] to raising the availability of drugs for medical purposes[74] and to new psychoactive substances.[75]

2.2.4 The International Narcotics Control Board: The watchdog of the UN Drug Conventions

In contrast to the CND, the UNGA and the ECOSOC, the INCB is not an institution created by the UN Charter. It is the monitoring body of the UN Drug Conventions, which was created by the Single Convention and started operating on 22 March 1968.[76]

This provision was not retained in the final version of the treaty. It was decided by an ad hoc committee on this issue that the provision was to be deleted; United Nations Conference for the adoption of a Single Convention on Narcotic Drugs New York, 24 January–25 March 1961, Official Records Vol. II, Preparatory Documents, Amendments and Miscellaneous Papers, Proceedings of Committees, Final Act Single Convention and Schedules Resolutions, 1964, UN Doc. E/CONF.34/24/Add.l [hereinafter referred to as OR II Single Convention], p. 275 (16 votes to none with five abstentions). The reasons for this deletion, however, remain obscure since the *procès verbal* of this ad hoc committee is not retained in the official records.

73 Cf. *infra* 6.3.

74 Cf. *infra* 6.1.

75 Cf. *infra* 5.4.4.

76 ECOSOC Resolution 1967/1196 (XLII), 1967, UN Doc. E//RES/1967/1196 (XLII), preambular para. 12. It has also regularly been labelled as carrying out quasi-judicial functions; cf. Mario Bettati, 'Le contrôle international des stupéfiants', *RGDIP* Vol. 78 1974, 170 (183); cf. also the INCB at www.incb.org/incb/en/about.html. Critiques of the international drug control system see the INCB as one of the main obstacles towards substantial reform; cf. in that regard David Bewley-Taylor and Mike Trace, *The International Narcotics Control Board: Watchdog or Guardian of the UN Drug Control Conventions*; Damon Barrett, *Unique in International Relations? A Comparison of the International Narcotic Control Board and the Human Rights Treaty Bodies*; David Bewley-Taylor, *International Drug Control: Consensus Fractured*, pp. 219 et seq. The INCB's secrecy and lack of transparency often is the object of particular criticism, cf. already in that regard Kettil Brunn, Lynn Pan and Ingemar Rexed, *The Gentlemen's Club: International Control of Drugs and Alcohol*, pp. 75 et seq. While it is true that other treaty bodies most notably in the human rights field openly publish their minutes and allow for an active participation of NGOs, such transparency is not always exercised in international fora. Furthermore, the INCB is even required by the 1971 Convention and the Single Convention to react to non-compliance by States parties first of all by opening confidential consultations; cf. Art. 14 (1) (a) Single Convention; Art. 19 (1) 1971 Convention.

2.2.4.1 Membership

The INCB consists of 13 members elected by the ECOSOC (Art. 9 (1) Single Convention) for a period of five years (Art. 10 (1) Single Convention), who 'by their competence, impartiality and disinterestedness, will command general competence' (Art. 10 (2) Single Convention).[77] The members of the INCB do not represent States parties but act as independent experts. According to Art. 9 (2) Single Convention, the ECOSOC shall elect

> (a) [t]hree members with medical, pharmaceutical experience from a list of at least five persons nominated by the World Health Organization and (b) Ten members from a list of persons nominated by the Members of the United Nations and by Parties which are not members of the United Nations.

Furthermore, the ECOSOC has to pay due regard to equitable geographical representation during the election process and has to elect persons with sufficient knowledge of the drug problem in drug-producer, consumer and transit countries (Art. 10 (3) Single Convention).

2.2.4.2 Mandate under the UN Drug Conventions

The INCB, as a treaty body, does not enjoy any functions under the UN Charter; the UN Drug Conventions are its sole and ultimate source of authority.[78] Article 9 (4) Single Convention provides the INCB with a mandate as broad as the aims of the Single Convention. This empowers the INCB to review all aspects of the world drug problem.[79] This broad mandate encompasses the right of the INCB to raise vis-à-vis any government – whether party or not to the UN Drug Conventions – any question related to the world drug problem by offering consultations and other means.[80] More specifically, the UN Drug Conventions vest the INCB with three types of principal functions.[81] First, the INCB can

77 There is possibility of re-election; Art. 10 (1) Single Convention. For more details on the election process of the members of the INCB cf. Commentary Single Convention, Art. 9, para. 1, MN 4 et seq.

78 Cf. as to the sources of authority for treaty bodies in general, Geir Ulfstein, 'Treaty Bodies and Regimes', in: Duncan Hollis (ed.), *The Oxford Guide to Treaties*, 428.

79 Commentary on the Protocol amending the Single Convention on Narcotic Drugs 1961, done at Geneva on 25 March 1972, UN Doc. E/CN.7/588 [hereinafter referred to as Commentary 1972 Protocol], Art. 2, para. 2, MN 1; 3.

80 Commentary 1972 Protocol, Art. 2, para. 2, MN 10.

81 The following remarks cover the main functions of the INCB but are not exhaustive. In practice the country visits of the INCB are considered as a major tool in order to promote its interpretation of the UN Drug Conventions and communicate with the states parties; cf. also David Bewley-Taylor and Mike Trace, *The International Narcotics Control Board: Watchdog or Guardian of the UN Drug Control Conventions*, p. 3. Additionally, the INCB is vested with 'internal powers' such as the competence to adopt rules of procedure (Art. 11 (1) Single Convention) or to convene its meetings (Art. 11 (2) Single Convention); cf. regard to this power of treaty bodies in

take enforcement measures, addressing non-compliance with the provisions of the Single Convention and the 1971 Convention that include as an *ultima ratio*, the recommendation of an embargo (Art. 14 Single Convention; Art. 19 1971 Convention). Second, the INCB administers the international drug control system; it makes an assessment of the global availability of narcotic drugs and psychotropic substances by relying on information submitted by the States parties and thereby ensures that there will no surplus of drugs available (Arts 13 and 20 et. seq. Single Convention; Art. 16 1971 Convention). Third, all three UN Drug Conventions authorize the INCB to prepare an annual report (Art. 15 Single Convention; Art. 18 1971 Convention; Art. 23 1988 Convention). The annual report, on the one hand, shall consist of the (statistical) information at the INCB's disposal (Art. 15 (1) Single Convention; Art. 18 (1) 1971 Convention; Art. 23 (1) 1988 Convention). On the other hand, the INCB is entitled in its annual report to make 'any observations and recommendations it desires to make' (Art. 15 (1) Single Convention; Art. 18 (1) 1971 Convention; Art. 23 (1) 1988 Convention). These annual reports are the starting point in figuring out how the INCB itself interprets the Drug Conventions. The annual reports also contain INCB's observations of a more general nature in a thematic chapter. As the other activities of the INCB are confidential, it is the annual report where the INCB makes its own views on the world drug situation publicly known.[82]

2.2.4.3 Normative value of the drug-related instruments of the INCB

The normative value of the INCB's actions varies. In certain limited cases, the UN Drug Conventions' allow the INCB to make binding decisions. This involves, for example, the request by the INCB for a party to provide additional statistical information (Art. 13 (3) Single Convention; Art. 18 (5) 1971 Convention).

In most cases, however, the INCB does not take any binding decisions; its treaty interpretation is not an authoritative source. Furthermore, its interpretation cannot amount to subsequent practice in accordance with Art. 31 (3) (b) VCLT, since its actions are not attributable to the States parties.[83] This finding has been challenged previously by several authors with regard to human rights treaties' bodies, since human rights treaties can – potentially – be considered

---

general Geir Ulfstein, 'Treaty Bodies and Regimes', in: Duncan Hollis (ed.), *The Oxford Guide to Treaties*, 428 (433).

82 Kettil Brunn, Lynn Pan and Ingemar, Rexed, *The Gentlemen's Club: International Control of Drugs and Alcohol*, pp. 84 et seq.

83 First report on subsequent agreements and subsequent practice in relation to treaty interpretation, Georg Nolte, Report by ILC Special Rapporteur, 2013, UN Doc. A/CN.4/660, Draft Conclusions 3 et seq; cf. for a similar position Laurence Boisson de Chazournes, 'Subsequent Practices, and "Family-Resemblance": Towards Embedding Subsequent Practice in its Operative Milieu', in: Georg Nolte (ed.), *Treaties and Subsequent Practice*, 53 (59).

to be different from 'general' multilateral treaties.[84] his view is hardly convincing. Be it as it may, this question does not have to be resolved for the UN Drug Conventions. The argument in favour of treaty body practice as an authoritative source of treaty interpretation is based on the special status of human rights treaties. This special status consists of providing rights to individuals who are not parties to an international treaty, concluded between States.[85] This line of argumentation is certainly not valid with regard to the UN Drug Conventions that do not foresee any rights or obligations for individuals but merely address the States parties. Nevertheless, the relevance INCB's treaty interpretation cannot be discarded. There is always a possibility that States may subsequently adopt a non-binding interpretation of any treaty body.[86] Others have spoken of the 'catalyst' effect of treaty body publications.[87] However, the main authority of the INCB does not derive from of its formal position. It cannot force States to adopt a certain interpretation of the UN Drug Conventions; the authority of the INCB is informal. It arises out of the weight that the States parties to the UN Drug Conventions accord to its assessments.[88] It is merely by the virtue of 'blaming and shaming' tactics that the INCB may impose its positions on States.[89] As in many other treaty regimes, the INCB has to rely on cooperative forms of 'compliance control', i.e. monitoring, fact finding and cooperation with States parties rather than on coercive sanctions.[90]

84 International Law Association (ILA), Berlin Conference, International Human Rights Law and Practice Final Report on the Impact of Findings of Human Rights Treaty Bodies, 2004, para. 22; Kerstin Mechlem, 'Treaty Bodies and the Interpretation of Human Rights', *Vand. J. Trant'l L.* Vol. 42 2009, 905 (920) and the authorities quoted therein; cf. also Helen Keller and Leena Grover, 'General Comments of the Human Rights Committee and their Legitimacy', in: Geir Ulfstein and Helen Keller (eds), *UN Human Rights Treaty Bodies: Law and Legitimacy*, 116 (130) who leave the question 'open' because of the negative response of States to ILA's findings.

85 ILA, Berlin Conference, International Human Rights Law and Practice Final Report on the Impact of Findings of Human Rights Treaty Bodies, 2004, para. 22.

86 Georg Nolte, Report by ILC Special Rapporteur, UN Doc. A/CN.4/660, 2013, Draft Conclusions 3 et seq., especially 4 (1).

87 cf. in that regard Mechlem, *supra* note 84, 905 (921).

88 It is of course difficult to measure exactly how much weight States parties really subscribe to the assessment of INCB reports. It has been suggested that Denmark refrained from opening drug consumption rooms due to pressure of the INCB; cf. David Bewley-Taylor, *International Drug Control: Consensus Fractured*, p. 246. Many other States have, however, withstood the pressure of the INCB and allow for the operation of drug consumption rooms despite the INCB's criticism; cf. e.g. with regard to Australia, *ibid.*, pp. 252 et seq.

89 Christine Jojarth, *Crime, War and Global Drug Trafficking: Designing International Cooperation*, p. 130. This is of course not a singularity of the international drug control system but applies with regard to many treaty regimes; cf. in that regard Geir Ulfstein, 'Treaty Bodies and Regimes', in: Duncan Hollis (ed.), *The Oxford Guide to Treaties*, 428 (442).

90 Cf. as to this issue Jutta Brunnée, 'Compliance Control', in: Geir Ulfstein, Andreas Zimmermann and Thilo Marauhn (eds), *Making Treaties Work: Human Rights Environment and Arms Control*, 373.

2.2.5 The World Health Organization: Drug control and global health

The WHO is provided with functions related to drug control by its Constitution as well as by the UN Drug Conventions. The WHO to date has 194 member States and thus attains universal membership of the entire international community, including all States parties to the UN Drug Conventions.[91]

2.2.5.1 Mandate with regard to drug control

The WHO was 'established by special agreement'; i.e. the WHO Constitution, as a 'specialized agency' [FN] in accordance with Art. 57 (1) of the Charter.[92] It is tasked with the mandate of the 'attainment by all peoples of the highest possible level of health' (Art. 1 WHO Constitution).[93] It is *the* international organization competent for the protection and improvement of global health.[94] The preamble of the WHO adopts a wide definition of health comprising 'a state of complete physical, mental and social well-being and not merely the absence of disease or infirmity'.

Therefore, the WHO may address all aspects of the world drug problem, as far as health-related aspects are concerned, encompassing most notably the treatment of drug users and the availability of drugs for medical purposes.[95] Article 2 (v) of the WHO Constitution allows the WHO in general to 'take all necessary action to attain the objective'. This role has been filled by the WHO's plenary organ, the World Health Assembly (WHA) (Arts 10 et seq. WHO Constitution); it has adopted numerous resolutions on the health-related aspects of drug control.[96]

Furthermore, the WHO enjoys functions under the 1971 Convention and the Single Convention. It plays a key role in the scheduling of narcotic drugs and psychotropic substances. Although, as will be shown below in greater detail, the role of the WHO in the scheduling process under the 1971 Convention and the

91 https://treaties.un.org/Pages/showDetails.aspx?objid=080000028002d899.

92 A specialized agency is an international organization brought into relationship with the United Nations; Eckart Klein, 'Specialized Agencies', in: Rüdiger Wolfrum (ed.), *MPEPIL*, 2012, MN 1.

93 Constitution of the World Health Organization of 22 July 1946, entered into force 7 April 1948, UNTS Vol. 14, p. 185.

94 Cf. in that regard Werner Meng, 'Art. 57', in: Bruno Simma et al. (eds), *The Charter of the United Nations*, MN 94 et seq.; Yves Beigbeder, 'World Health Organization (WHO)', in: Rüdiger Wolfrum (ed.), *MPEPIL*, 2012, MN 1; ICJ, Legality of the Use by a State of Nuclear Weapons in Armed Conflict, Advisory Opinion of 8 July 1996, para. 20.

95 Cf. also in this regard WHO, 'WHO's Role, Mandate and Activities to Counter the World Drug Problem: A Public Health Perspective', 2014, p. 4.

96 Cf. WHO, 'WHO's Role, Mandate and Activities to Counter the World Drug Problem: A Public Health Perspective', 2014, pp. 8 et seq. for further examples, referring to resolutions on demand reduction, HIV/Aids and availability of drugs for medical and scientific purposes.

Single Convention varies considerably,[97] the expertise of the WHO is decisive as far as the pharmaceutical and scientific assessment of drugs is concerned.[98]

Neither the Single Convention nor the 1971 Convention specify which organ of the WHO should provide such expertise.[99] In practice, although the last word remains with the WHO's Director General, this task is carried out by the WHO Expert Committee on Drug Dependence (ECDD), advising the WHO's Secretary General in this regard.[100] The ECDD was established by the WHO in its first session in 1948, in order 'to act as an advisory body to the [WHO] and the [UN]'.[101]

2.2.5.2 Normative value of World Health Assembly resolutions and ECDD recommendations

The World Health Assembly assembles all 194 member States of the WHO. The WHA, being merely an organ of the WHO, exercises much narrower functions than the UNGA.[102] These differences, however, do not play a role when considering the normative value of drug-related resolutions of the WHA and their potential impact on the interpretation of the UN Drug Conventions. In a similar way to UNGA resolutions, resolutions of the WHA may influence the interpretation of provisions of the UN Drug Conventions in accordance with Art. 31 (3) (b) VCLT. Just as the UNGA, the WHA assembles all States parties to the UN Drug Conventions. Therefore, provided (1) a concrete nexus of WHA resolutions to the UN Drug Conventions can be approved, (2) the resolutions are adopted with consensus of all the States parties and (3) the practice in question

97 Cf. *infra* 5.3 for more details. It suffices here to point out that under the Single Convention, the recommendation of the WHO as far as the assessment of the substances is concerned is final and binds the CND (Art. 3 (3) (iii); (4); (5) Single Convention), whereas under the 1971 Convention, the CND may deviate from the recommendation of the WHO; Art. 2 (5) 1971 Convention. Cf. also in this regard WHO, 'WHO's Role, Mandate and Activities to Counter the World Drug Problem: A Public Health Perspective', 2014, p. 5.

98 Cf. Commentary Single Convention, Art. 3, para. 3 subpara. (iii), MN 18.

99 S. K. Chatterjee, *Legal Aspects of International Drug Control*, p. 277; WHO Expert Committee on Drug Dependence, 36th report, WHO Technical Report Series No. 991, 2015 p. 8.

100 S. K. Chatterjee, 'The WHO Expert Committee on Drug Dependence', *ICLQ* Vol. 28 1979, 27; WHO Expert Committee on Drug Dependence, 36th report, WHO Technical Report Series No. 991, 2015, p. 1.

101 First World Health Assembly, Resolution 25, WHO-Doc. WHA1.25, 1948; quoted in: Chatterjee, *supra* note 100, 27 (28). Art. 18 (e) of the WHO Constitution authorizes the WHA to establish sub-committees. The same competence is accorded to the executive board by Art. 38. The Committee was initially founded as Expert Committee on Habit Forming Drugs. In 1950, it changed its name to Expert Committee on Drugs Liable to Produce Addiction. In 1956, it was renamed into the Expert Committee on Addiction Producing Drugs. From 1964 to 1966 it was named WHO Expert Committee on Dependence Producing Drugs. Since 1966 it is named WHO Expert Committee on Drug Dependence.

102 Cf. as to the special functions of the WHO, ICJ, Legality of the Use by a State of Nuclear Weapons in Armed Conflict, Advisory Opinion of 8 July 1996, paras 18 et seq.

amounts to a certain level of coherence, one can agree that WHO Assembly resolutions influence the interpretation of the UN Drug Conventions.[103]

The recommendations of the ECDD are not binding, but are only considered as scientific expertise on which the WHO's Director General bases its final assessment with regard to the need to schedule a given substance. This assessment will be communicated to the CND.[104]

2.2.6 The United Nations Office on Drugs and Crime

The United Nations Office on Drugs and Crime (UNODC) was created by a merger between the United Nations Drug Control Programme (UNDCP) and the Centre for International Crime Prevention.[105] It is not provided with treaty-based functions by the UN Drug Conventions. Its work is based on three pillars.[106] First, it assumes operational functions, e.g. it advises drug-producing States how to reduce drug supply on the ground. Second, it carries out analytical and research work, of which the most prominent example is the annual World Drug Report. Third, it assists member States on the implementation of the Drug Conventions and serves as a secretariat of the CND and INCB. Despite being a UN Office, 90 per cent of UNODC's budget consists of voluntary contributions from national governments, which entails the risk of stakeholders imposing their agenda on UNODC.[107]

103 Nevertheless, it has to be borne in mind that in contrast to the UNGA, the WHA does not deal with all aspects of the world drug problem but only with regard to its health-related aspects; cf. *supra* 2.2.1.

104 *Supra* note 100.

105 Bernard Levroy, M. Cherif Bassiouini and Jean-François Thony, 'The International Drug Control System', in: M. Cherif Bassiouni (ed.) *International Criminal Law*: Vol. I, 855 (890).

106 UNODC, World Drug Report 2008, UN Publication, Sales No. E.08.XI.1, p. 3.; cf. also www.unodc.org/unodc/en/about-unodc/index.html?ref=menutaop.

107 David Bewley-Taylor, *International Drug Control: Consensus Fractured*, pp. 115 et seq.

2.3 Conclusion

Table 2.1 Overview of drug control's institutional framework

Actor	*Mandate with regard to drug control*		*Normative value of drug-related instruments*			*Relationship with other drug control institutions*
	UN Charter	*UN Drug Conventions*	*Non-binding Recommendations*	*Subsequent practice; Art 31 (3) (b) VCLT*	*Binding decisions vis-à-vis States parties*	
UNGA	Considers all matters within the scope of the UN Charter	Decides on expenses of the INCB and the CND as well as remuneration of INCB members	Yes	Yes	No	Supervises the CND and the ECOSOC
ECOSOC	Specific competence in economic and social issues	Determines whether treaty amendments shall be decided upon by an international conference or by the States parties individually	Yes	No	Decides on appeals of member States against scheduling decisions of the CND	Supervises the CND and elects its members
CND	Subsidiary organ of the ECOSOC for drug control	Considers all matters pertaining to the aims of the UN Drug Conventions	Yes	No	Decides on the scheduling of substances (based on recommendations of the WHO)	
WHO	Specialized agency of the United Nations in health-related matters	Provides for scientific expertise in the scheduling of drugs	Yes	Yes (WHA Resolutions)	No	Gives scientific advice to the CND for the scheduling of substances
INCB	No	Monitors the implementation of the UN Drug Conventions	Yes	No	No (except for the right to propose consultations and the right to demand statistical information)	No
UNODC	No	No	Yes	No	No	No

3 The emergence of the international drug control system

This chapter traces the development of the international drug control system from its origins to the adoption of the contemporary UN Drug Conventions. Instead of recounting in detail negotiations of the 13 multilateral treaties and protocols on drug control adopted between 1912 and 1988, or analyzing the numerous provisions of these treaties, it shows how the contemporary leitmotif of the international drug control system – i.e. the limitation of all the substances to medical and scientific purposes – emerged and developed.[1] To this end the chapter focuses on two aspects: first, the replacement of nineteenth-century uncoordinated bilateralism on drugs by one coherent rule, confining all substances covered to medical and scientific purposes (3.1). Second, the material expansion of the drug control system from opium to other plant-based and synthetic drugs (3.2). The creation of the international drug control system needs to be understood from a wider perspective. The twentieth century saw a gradual emergence of a 'new' international law, i.e. the 'law of cooperation'[2] or *droit institutionel.*[3] This turn towards new horizons in international law has been aptly described by Simma's famous dictum 'from bilateralism to community interests'.[4] It will be shown that the international drug control system is a primary example of this law of cooperation and international law's turn towards the protection of community interests (3.3).[5]

1 The emergence of the international drug control system has been the object of extended study; cf. William McAllister, *Drug Diplomacy in the Twentieth Century: An International History*; David Bewley-Taylor, *The United States and International Drug Control 1909–1997*; Jay Sinha, 'The History and Development of the Leading International Drug Control Conventions', prepared for The Senate Special Committee On Illegal Drugs, Law and Government Division, 21 February 2001; UNODC, 'World Drug Report 2008', UN Publication, Sales No. E.08. XI.1, pp. 173 et seq.; Julia Buxton, 'The Historical Foundations of the Narcotic Drug Control Regime', Policy Research Working Paper 4553; for a historical account of the origins of US drug control, cf. David Musto, *The American Disease: Origins of Narcotic Control.*

2 W. Friedmann, 'General Course in Public International Law', *RdC* Vol. 127 1969 II, 239.

3 Réné-Jean Dupuy, 'Communauté international et disparités de développement: Cours général de Droit International Public', *RdC* Vol. 165 1979 IV, 9.

4 Bruno Simma, 'From Bilateralism to Community Interest in International Law', *RdC* Vol. 250 1994 VI, 217.

5 Cf. also as to the coming into existence of the international drug control and other global prohibition regimes; Ethan A. Nadelmann, 'Global Prohibition Regimes: The Evolution of Norms in International Society', *International Organization* Vol. 44 1990, 479.

3.1 Towards one coherent obligation to confine drugs to medical and scientific purposes

In terms of the endeavour to confine drugs to medical and scientific purposes, three phases may be distinguished.[6] First, uncoordinated bilateralism, where the regulation of opium and other drugs was left to various uncoordinated bilateral commercial treaties (3.1.1). Second, the early stage of the international drug control system, ranging from the International Opium Commission to the early years of the United Nations. This period can be defined as 'flexible multilateralism' (3.1.2). Despite nine multilateral treaties and a high degree of institutionalization, it was impossible for States to agree to universally limit all drugs covered to medical and scientific purposes. Rather, a possibility to opt-out of this rule was preserved for States in which opium smoking was traditional and remained widespread. It was only subsequent to the Single Convention that the contemporary drug control system was established. This third phase can be termed 'inflexible multilateralism' because all substances covered are now universally confined to medical and scientific purposes (3.1.3).

3.1.1 Uncoordinated bilateralism 1858–1908

At the turn of the twentieth century, there was no coherent approach for the control of drugs. International law contained scattered and fragmented rules on opium in bilateral commercial treaties, which can be grouped into two categories. On the one hand, 'no opium clauses' in such treaties prohibited the contracting parties from engaging in the opium trade. Such provisions can be found, for example, in bilateral treaties between the United States and Siam,[7] Japan[8] and Korea,[9] as well as in a commercial treaty between Great Britain and Japan.[10]

On the other hand, China, after defeats in two wars[11] was forced to give up its initial hostile position – relying on moral and legal arguments to denounce the opium trade – towards opium smoking.[12] In 1858, it concluded an agreement

6 Cf. for a different structure, Richard Lines, *Drug Control and Human Rights in International Law*, pp. 16 et seq.

7 Convention of Amity and Commerce of 20 March 1833, entered into force 24 June 1837, reprinted in *AJIL* Supplement Vol. 3 1909, 253 (257).

8 Treaty of Amity and Commerce of 29 July 1858, entered into force 23 May 1860, reprinted in *AJIL* Supplement Vol. 3 1909, 253 (256).

9 Treaty of Peace, Amity, Commerce and Navigation of 22 May 1882, entered into force 4 June 1883, reprinted in *AJIL* Supplement Vol. 3 1909, 253 (257).

10 Regulation 2(8) under which British Trade is to be conducted within Japan, Treaty of Peace, Friendship and Commerce between Great Britain and Japan of 26 August 1858, Annex, entered into force 11 July 1859, CTS Vol. 119, 401.

11 The First Opium War 1840–42; the Second Opium War ('Arrow War') from 1857 to 1859.

12 Cf. for a useful account, UNODC, 'World Drug Report 2008', UN Publication, Sales No. E.08. XI.1, p. 175.

with Great Britain, whereby opium became a tradable good.[13] The legalization of the opium trade forms part of the unequal treaty regime – i.e. a number of treaties between China and 'Treaty Powers' marked by a flagrant imbalance between China and the latter.[14] Thus, up until the International Opium Commission of 1909 there were no universal and coherent rules on how to handle opium. No international drug control system existed. The bilateral treaties on opium – either prohibiting or imposing opium export – were left entirely uncoordinated.[15]

3.1.2 Flexible multilateralism 1909–1960

Following the assembly of the first international opium commission from 1909 onwards, the pre-existing uncoordinated bilateralism was successively replaced with what may be called 'flexible multilateralism'. Thereby, reference is made to a degree of drug control which stands between the initial uncoordinated bilateralism and today's universal reduction of drugs to medical and scientific purposes. As will be seen, however, in the first 50 years of its existence, international drug control – despite all progress – did not achieve a universal reduction of drugs to medical and scientific purposes.

3.1.2.1 The first step towards an international drug control system: The 1909 International Opium Commission

The first attempt to lay out more general rules as to how opium should be handled on a universal level was the International Opium Commission of 1909. This commission was an ad hoc conference, where 13 States assembled upon the invitation of the United States.[16] The work of the International Opium Commission

13 Rule 5 (1) of the Agreement between Great Britain and China, respecting the Revision of the Tariff, made in pursuance of Art. XXVI of the Treaty of June 26 1858, BFSP Vol. 48 1857–1858, p. 58: 'The restriction affecting trade in opium [...] are relaxed under the following conditions: 1. Opium will henceforth pay 30 taels per pecul imported. The importer will sell it only at the port'; for a detailed account, cf. John Wong, *Deadly Dreams Opium and the Arrow War (1858–1860) in China*, pp. 413 et seq. with further details. The legalization of the opium trade in China would be extended to other States subsequently; cf. *AJIL* Supplement Vol. 3 1909, 253 with further references.

14 For more details cf. Anne Peters, 'Treaties, Unequal' in: Rüdiger Wolfrum (ed.), *MPEPIL*, 2012; Dong Wang, *China's Unequal Treaties Narrating National History*; Wang Tieya, 'International Law in China: Historical and Contemporary Perspectives', *RdC* 1990 II Vol. 221, 195 (252 et seq).

15 The legalization of the opium trade, however, seems to have been a Chinese particularity, cf. Opium Agreement between Great Britain and Jawahr of 5 January 1889, CTS Vol. 186, 135; thereby Jawahr – a quasi-sovereign entity in India – consented to only import opium from British sources.

16 These were Austria-Hungary, China, France, Germany, Great Britain, Italy, Japan, the Netherlands, Persia, Portugal, Russia and Siam; cf. as to the Conference in general Hamilton Wright, 'The International Opium Commission', *AJIL* Vol. 3 1909 648; 828.

consisted of reports on the domestic opium situation of every State present and of the adoption of non-binding resolutions on the opium question.[17] Although an emphasis was laid on the opium problem in China, where non-medical opium use had reached epidemic proportions,[18] the Commission also adopted more general principles on the issue, reaching beyond the Chinese situation.[19]

3.1.2.1.1 THE POLITICAL AND ECONOMIC FACTORS LEADING TO THE INTERNATIONAL OPIUM COMMISSION

The International Opium Commission of 1909 became possible because the primary advocate in favour of the legalization of the opium trade had changed its position towards opium. Three years before the assembly of the Commission, Great Britain's decades-long support for the opium trade, which had once played an important role for its economy, finally vanished.[20] On 30 May 1906, the House of Commons adopted a resolution, stating that the Indo-Chinese Opium trade 'is morally indefensible' and requested the British government 'to take such steps as may be necessary for bringing it to a close'. [21] This made it possible to conclude a new Sino-British treaty that allowed the Chinese to cut the imports of opium by 10 per cent per annum *pari passu* the reduction of Chinese consumption and production.[22] It foresaw the termination of the trade within a ten-year period;[23] the treaty was signed in August 1907 and entered into force 1 January 1908 – although at first for a provisional period of three years.[24] Three years later, Great Britain consented to a final termination of the opium trade and by 1913, the Sino-British Opium trade – that had been going on for centuries – was history.[25]

Moreover, the United States had appeared as an actor advocating for an international solution to the opium problem. The devastating opium situation in China was examined with growing interest by the United States.[26] This interest had arisen since the United States was confronted with a domestic opium

17 As to the deliberations cf. International Opium Commission Vol. II Reports of the Delegations, 1909. Cf. also in that regard Peter D. Lowes, *The Genesis of International Narcotics Control*, pp. 121 et seq.; also Wright, *supra* note 16, 648. The resolutions can be found in International Opium Commission Vol. I Reports of the Proceedings, 1909, p. 84; a more easily accessible quotation of the resolutions can be found in *AJIL* Supplement Vol. 3 1909, 275 et seq.
18 It is estimated today that by the turn of the century 23% of the male population were addicted to opium in China; UNODC, 'World Drug Report 2008', UN Publication, Sales No. E.08.XI.1, p. 173.
19 Only four of the nine resolutions adopted concerned specifically the Chinese opium problem.
20 Cf. as to this Carl Trocki, *Opium, Empire and the Global Political Economy*, p. xiii.
21 Resolution of 30 May 1906, quoted, in Peter D. Lowes, *The Genesis of International Narcotics Control*, p. 77.
22 Arrangement between China and Great Britain for restricting the import of opium of 12 August 1907, CTS Vol. 204, p. 346.
23 *Ibid.*
24 For a summary cf. *AJIL* Supplement Vol. 3 1909, 264.
25 Carl Trocki, *Opium, Empire and the Global Political Economy*, pp. 128 et seq.
26 Bertil A. Renborg, 'International Control of Narcotics, Law and Contemporary Problems', *Law and Contemporary Problems* Vol. 22 1957, 86.

problem: opium addiction was widespread among Chinese populations in the newly acquired Philippines and on the US mainland.[27] After having studied the opium problem in the Philippines,[28] it was believed that an international study by interested nations regarding the Chinese opium situation would be beneficial.[29] The lesson that the United States drew from the contemporary Chinese opium malaise was that the opium trade – a problem of transnational scope – could only be resolved through international cooperation. This gave the impetus for convening the International Opium Commission.

3.1.2.1.2 THE RESULTS OF THE INTERNATIONAL OPIUM COMMISSION

The importance of the International Opium Commission lies in the fact that it went beyond settling the Chinese opium question. It set an 'historical precedent'[30] that would be transferred into a binding legal obligation three years later. This precedent is contained in Resolution 4, which stipulates the Commission's view that

> it is [...] the duty of all countries to adopt reasonable measures to prevent at ports of departure the Shipment of Opium, its alkaloids, derivates and preparations, to any country which prohibits the entry of any Opium, its alkaloids derivates and preparations.[31]

This was the first step made by opium-consuming States in trying to control opium supply beyond their borders and preventing the traffic of non-medical opium to their territories. The United States tried to go one step further, and aimed to establish a consensus confining opium use universally to medical purposes. To this end, it proposed a resolution to the Commission, demanding '*to confine the use of opium, its alkaloids, derivates and preparations to legitimate medical practices*'.[32] Such a far-reaching proposal was plainly rejected by the British delegation which considered the implementation of such a rule, in particular in India, to be impossible.[33]

27 The Spanish Crown had ceded the Philippines to the United States after her defeat in the Spanish–American War; Art. III Treaty of Peace between Spain and the United States of 10 December 1898, entered into force 11 April 1899, CTS Vol. 187, p. 100. Cf. as to the report on the opium situation in the Philippines rendered by the Philippine Opium Commission; Thomas Reins, 'Reform, Nationalism and Internationalism: The Opium Suppression Movement in China and the Anglo-American Influence, 1900–1908', *Modern Asian Studies* Vol. 24 1991, 101 (111 et seq.); Peter D. Lowes, *The Genesis of International Narcotic Control*, p. 89; Wright, *supra* note 16, 648 (652).

28 Hamilton Wright, The International Opium Conference, *AJIL* Vol. 6 1912, 648 (670).

29 Peter D. Lowes, *The Genesis of International Narcotic Control*, pp. 107 et seq.

30 Wright, *supra* note 16, 828 (855).

31 International Opium Commission, Resolution 4, International Opium Commission Vol. I Reports of the Proceedings, 1909, p. 84.

32 *Ibid.*, p. 46 (italics added).

33 *Ibid.*, pp. 48 et seq., 50.

The 'American–British compromise'[34] was a resolution, containing a *non liquet* on the question of confining opium solely to medical purposes. Albeit 'the use of Opium in any form otherwise than for medical purposes [was] held [....] to be a matter for prohibition [...] *the International Opium Commission recognise[d] the wide variations between the conditions in different countries*'.[35] The question of the gradual suppression of opium smoking saw a very similar outcome, in that the initial US proposal on opium smoking was watered down.[36]

Thus, the 1909 Commission established consensus with regard to a restriction of the opium trade but failed to carve out a universal paradigm, confining opium to medical purposes. The Commission would hardly be remembered had it not paved the road for the first international drug control treaty, the 1912 Convention.[37] This convention was driven by the '*[d]esir[e] of advancing a step further on the road opened by the International Commission of Shanghai of 1909*'.[38]

3.1.2.2 The first multilateral drug control treaty: The International Opium Convention of 23 January 1912

The International Opium Convention of 1912 turned the pledges made in Shanghai three years earlier into binding obligations under positive international law: States were required to refrain from exporting drugs to States where its importation remained prohibited. This rule was established for all the substances covered by the 1912 Convention, comprising raw opium,[39] prepared opium – opium suitable for smoking[40] – as well as medicinal opium, morphine, cocaine and heroin.[41] It was considered as a 'new principle of international commercial law'.[42] It involved that once an importing State had decided in favour of a drug prohibition, the exporting State would enforce the prohibition by preventing the drug from entering into the territory of the prohibiting State.[43] Thus, the central aim of the United States, when convening the conference to control supply in order to prevent drug

34 Peter D. Lowes, *The Genesis of International Narcotics Control*, p. 152.

35 International Opium Commission Vol. I, Reports of the Proceedings, 1909, p. 84 (italics added); Wright suggests that this resolution 'is a practical condemnation of the illiberal use of opium even in India'; Wright, *supra* note 16, 828 (864). This is most certainly not the way in which the British delegation would have interpreted its content.

36 International Opium Commission Vol. I Reports of the Proceedings, 1909, pp. 46 et seq.

37 The International Opium Convention of 23 January 1912, entered into force 11 February 1915, LNTS Vol. 8, 188 [hereinafter referred to as 1912 Convention].

38 First preambular para., 1912 Convention (italics added).

39 Art. 3 (a) 1912 Convention.

40 Art. 8 (b) 1912 Convention.

41 Arts 13 and 15. The obligation for these substances is somewhat weaker, as is subjected to the 'best endeavours' of the party concerned.

42 Hamilton Wright, 'The International Opium Conference', *AJIL* Vol. 7 1913, 108 (122).

43 *Ibid.*

addiction among its population,[44] was achieved; the international drug trade was subjected to the regulation of the importing State.

Nevertheless, States at the 1912 Conference were unable to erect a universal and stringent system of drug control. Not all the substances covered by the 1912 Convention – which applied to raw opium, prepared opium, medicinal opium, morphine cocaine and heroin[45] – were confined to medical and scientific purposes. It was only in relation to morphine, cocaine and their respective salts that States parties were obligated 'to enact pharmacy laws or regulations to confine to medical and legitimate purposes the manufactures, sale and use'.[46] This obligation also applied *mutatis mutandis* to heroin and medicinal opium as far as their manufacture and sale were concerned.[47]

The production and sale of raw opium, however, was not confined to medical and scientific purposes. States parties were only required to 'enact effective laws or regulations for the control of the production and distribution of raw opium.'[48] Furthermore, the controversial question of whether opium smoking should be prohibited remained unsettled. The 1912 Convention codified the *non liquet* of the 1909 Opium Commission in that regard. Article 6 1912 Convention reads:

> The contracting Powers shall take measures for the *gradual and effective suppression* of the manufacture, of, internal trade in, and use of prepared opium *with due regard of the varying circumstances of each country concerned*, unless regulations on the subject are already in existence.[49]

Article 6 1912 Convention, by leaving a margin of discretion for States parties to either suppress opium smoking or to refrain from doing so, became the safeguard clause for States in possession of territories, where traditional opium use occurred, to refrain from prohibiting opium smoking. This dichotomy between States willing to prohibit opium smoking and States unwilling to do so, marked international drug control matters until the beginning of the United Nations period.

Thus, while it was possible to agree on a restriction of the international opium trade and to confine – then relatively new – drugs to medical and scientific purposes, it was not possible to subject opium smoking and raw opium to this requirement. The divide between those States that were eager to limit raw and prepared opium to medical and scientific purposes and those States that were unwilling to do so was not overcome. States which had possessions in the Far East – with the exception of China – simply considered it impossible to eradicate

44 Cf. with regard to the US viewpoint; Wright, *supra* note 28, 865 (868).

45 As to the expansion of the scope of drug control *ratione materiae*, cf. *infra* 3.2.

46 Art. 9 1912 Convention.

47 Art. 14 *lit.* a and c.

48 Art. 1 1912 Convention.

49 Italics added.

the opium habit. It was not until after World War II that all States were ready to accept the premise that opium should be limited to medical and scientific purposes universally.

3.1.2.3 The international drug control system under the League of Nations: Some progress and continuous discord over a universal limitation of opium to medical and scientific purposes

The interwar period saw a further expansion and institutionalization of the international drug control system. Five treaties came into force during this period and drug control was integrated into the new general system of international cooperation of the League of Nations. By drafting the Covenant of the League, its members decided to 'entrust the League with the general supervision over the execution of agreements with regard to [...] the traffic in opium and other dangerous drugs'.[50]

The League played a central role in international drug control from 1919 onwards. Its functions as far as drug control was concerned, were carried out by the Advisory Committee on Traffic in Opium and Other Dangerous Drugs (OAC),[51] the first permanent international institution for international drug control. It had been established

> in order to secure the fullest co-operation between the various countries in regard to the matter [of supervision of the execution of arrangements on opium and other drugs], and [...] assist and advise the Council in dealing with any question that may arise.[52]

Nevertheless, despite all this progress, no coherent system of international drug control confining all substances covered to medical and scientific purposes was established. The main ambiguities of the 1912 Convention, spelled out by Art. 6 of this treaty, remained unsettled, whereby States were obliged to gradually abolish opium smoking while paying due regard to 'the various circumstances'. Accordingly, during the League of Nations era, raw opium remained unaffected by the obligation to confine drugs to medical and scientific purposes.

Two developments during this period need to be distinguished from each other. First, the agreements concerning opium smoking in the Far East and, second, the developments on a universal level. In both cases it was impossible to limit opium to medical and scientific purposes.

3.1.2.3.1 NO CONSENSUS ON THE ABROGATION OF OPIUM SMOKING IN THE FAR EAST

During the League of Nations period, two treaties were dedicated to opium smoking in the Far East: The Agreement Concerning the Suppression of the

50 Art. 19 (c) Covenant of the League of Nations.

51 For more details, cf. Bertil A. Renborg, 'Principles of International Control of Narcotic Drugs', *AJIL* Vol. 37 1943, 436 (449; 454).

52 First Assembly of the League of Nations Resolution of 15 December 1920 para. 1; quoted in Bertil A. Renborg, 'International Drug Control', 1947, p. 31.

Manufacture of, Internal Trade in, and Use of, Prepared Opium of 11 February 1925[53] and the Agreement Concerning the Suppression for Opium Smoking of 27 November 1931.[54] Contrary to what their titles suggest, both treaties did not provide for a gradual suppression of opium smoking in the Far East.

When the 1925 Agreement was drafted by the Far Eastern Powers and China, the latter was the sole State present that was eager to draft an agreement to confine the use and traffic of prepared opium to medical and scientific purposes.[55] The other States could not accept such far-reaching proposals; the inability of China to control its domestic opium production, according to their view, made it impossible to impose a rigid system suppressing prepared opium in the Far East, for this would only result in promoting illicit traffic.[56]

China, eventually withdrew from the Conference, as it was impossible 'to bring about the effective suppression of the temporarily legalized use of prepared opium to which the Powers had pledged themselves in the 1912 Convention'.[57]

No obligations with regard to the gradual suppression of opium smoking can be found within the final agreement.[58] The remaining signatory States merely promised the adoption of a new agreement entirely eradicating opium smoking once the export of raw opium was sufficiently controlled.[59]

The 1931 Agreement did not overcome these tensions.[60] No progress concerning an abrogation of opium smoking was achieved. The discussion between China and the Far Eastern Powers had stalemated. China believed that the constant demand for opium indulged by the failure of Far Eastern powers to suppress opium smoking in their territories led to growing traffic and cultivation in China.[61] The Far Eastern Powers maintained the position that no effective

53 Entered into force 28 July 1925, LNTS Vol. 51, p. 337 [hereinafter referred to as 1925 Agreement].

54 Entered into force 22 April 1937, LNTS Vol. 177, p. 374 [hereinafter referred to as 1931 Agreement].

55 Sixth Meeting, First Opium Conference Geneva, 3 November 1924–11 February 1925, 1925 Minutes and Annexes, LN Doc. C.684. M. 244. 1924 IX, p. 29:

> To this end, China asks the Powers: 1 That the smoking of prepared opium may be declared in unqualified terms to be a harmful and illegitimate use of opium. 2. That the Importation of opium into their several territories for other than strictly medical and scientific uses be at once forbidden, or where this is not immediately practicable, that such importation be progressively curtailed [...] and be wholly forbidden within a definite and brief period [...] 3. That the exportation of opium for other than strictly medical or scientific purposes be at once forbidden, or where this is not immediately practicable, that such exportation may be progressively curtailed.

56 Cf. Statement by the President of the Conference, Fifth Meeting, First Opium Conference Geneva, 3 November 1924–11 February 1925, 1925 Minutes and Annexes, LN Doc.C.684. M. 244. 1924 IX, pp. 21 et seq.

57 Annex XIV Memorandum of the Chinese Delegation, First Opium Conference Geneva, 3 November 1924–11 February 1925, 1925 Minutes and Annexes, LN Doc.C.684. M. 244. 1924 IX, p. 168.

58 States parties were only required to organize opium distribution by a state-controlled monopoly (Art. I) and prohibit opium smoking of minors (Art. II–Art. III). Furthermore, opium export was prohibited from territories where opium smoking was allowed (Art. VI).

59 Art. II Protocol to the 1925 Agreement, LNTS Vol. 51, 345.

60 William McAllister, *Drug Diplomacy in the Twentieth Century: An International History*, p. 106.

61 Statement by the Chinese Delegate, 11th Meeting, 15th Session of the Advisory Committee 15 April–4 May 1932, Minutes of the 15th Session, LN Doc. C. 575. M. 282. 1932. XI., p. 37.

agreement with regard to the suppression of opium smoking in the Far East could be reached as long as there was massive Chinese supply. Trying to prohibit this habit too early would only result in stimulating the illicit traffic.[62] Thus, China did not attend the Conference as it was unlikely to achieve any results towards the suppression of opium smoking.

3.1.2.3.2 PERSISTING DISAGREEMENT OVER A LIMITATION OF PLANT-BASED DRUGS TO MEDICAL AND SCIENTIFIC PURPOSES ON A UNIVERSAL LEVEL

Despite the drafting of three drug treaties with universal scope during the League of Nations period (the International Opium Convention of 19 February 1925,[63] the Convention for Limiting the Manufacture and Regulating the Distribution of Narcotic Drugs of 13 July 1931[64] and the Convention for the Suppression of the Illicit Traffic in Dangerous Drugs of 26 June 1936[65]) it was impossible to agree on a universal limitation of raw and prepared opium to medical and scientific purposes.

3.1.2.3.2.1 Disagreement within the Opium Advisory Committee Already in the early years of the League, intensive debates within the OAC exposed the continuous discord among States regarding the viability to universally subject opium to medical and scientific purposes. These controversies became apparent when the United States joined the OAC, despite its status as a non-member to the League. The United States was eager to intensify international drug control efforts due to its conviction that drug control on a domestic level would be impossible without establishing an effective international system.[66] However, it would not participate in international cooperation that would weaken the 1912 Convention and subjected its participation in the OAC to the acceptance of two resolutions.[67] The first resolution suggested an interpretation of the 1912 Convention that denied

62 Cf. e.g. for this position Statement by the British Delegate, 11th Meeting, 15th Session of the Advisory Committee 15 April–4 May 1932, Minutes of the 15th Session, LN Doc. C. 575. M. 282. 1932. XI, pp. 43 et seq.; with great sympathy for the approach of the Far Eastern Powers cf. statement by the Belgian delegate, *ibid.*, p. 39; First Meeting General Statement of the French Delegation Conference on the Suppression of Opium Smoking convened under Article XII of the [1925 Agreement], 9–27 November 1931, LN Doc. C.577.M.284.1932.XI, pp. 16 et seq.

63 Entered into force 25 September 1928, LNTS Vol. 81, p. 319 [hereinafter referred to as 1925 Convention].

64 Entered into force 9 July 1933, LNTS 139, p. 303 [hereinafter referred to as 1931 Convention].

65 Entered into force 26 October 1939, LNTS Vol. 198, p. 301 [hereinafter referred to as 1936 Convention].

66 Cf. in that regard H.J.Res., 453 451 Stat. 1431:

> the imperative duty of the United States Government to safeguard its people from the persistent ravages of habit-forming narcotic drugs; the effective control of these drugs can only be obtained by limiting their production to the quantity required for strictly medicinal and scientific purposes.

67 Quincy Wright, 'The Opium Question', *AJIL* Vol. 18 1924, 281 (290).

the legitimacy of opium use for other than scientific and medical purposes.[68] The second resolution intended to confine the production of raw opium to medical and scientific purposes.[69]

The US proposal provoked intensive debate within the OAC.[70] The American delegate to the OAC argued that both resolutions merely clarified the existing *lex lata* of the 1912 Convention.[71] The interpretation of the 1912 Convention suggested by this proposal was firmly objected to by the Indian,[72] Japanese[73] and Dutch delegations.[74] After a lengthy debate, a resolution was adopted whereby the limitation of opium use to medical and scientific purposes embodied 'general principles'.[75] Seven States,[76] however, made a reservation whereby the use of prepared opium and the import of raw opium was 'legitimate', as long as it was carried out in accordance with Chapter II of the 1912 Convention – which meant that raw and prepared opium were not limited to medical and scientific purposes.[77] This resolution did not move drug control beyond the status quo of the 1912 Convention; opium smoking still had to be regarded as legitimate in places where it was traditional.[78]

3.1.2.3.2.2 The 1925 Convention: No limitation of plant-based drugs to medical and scientific purposes The status quo was also not overcome by the 1925 Convention, which failed to confine raw products of drugs to medical and

68 '1. If the purpose of the Hague Opium Convention is to be achieved according to its spirit and true intent, it must be recognized that the use of opium products for other than medical and scientific purposes is an abuse and not legitimate', Advisory Committee on Traffic in Opium and Other Dangerous Drugs, Report on the Work of the Fifth Session 24 May–7 June 1923, LN Doc. C.399.1923. XI; *League of Nations Official Journal* Vol. 4 1923, 1019 (1020)

69 '2. In order to prevent the abuse of these products it is necessary to exercise the control of the production of raw opium in such a manner that there will be no surplus available for non-medical and non-scientific purposes', Advisory Committee on Traffic in Opium and Other Dangerous Drugs, Report on the Work of the Fifth Session, 24 May–7 June 1923, LN Doc. C.399.1923. XI; *League of Nations Official Journal* Vol. 4 1923, 1019 (1020).

70 For a detailed account cf. Commission consultatif de l'opium et autres drogues nuisibles, Procès-verbal de la cinquième session, 1923, LN Doc. C.418.M.184.1923.XI, pp. 15–24; 81–119. For a pertinent summary cf. Wright, *supra* note 67, 281 (289 et seq.). The present author will use the quotations of the French version of this document, as he had exclusively access to the documents in this language.

71 Commission consultatif de l'opium et autres drogues nuisibles, Procès-verbal de la cinquième session, 1923, LN Doc. C.418.M.184.1923.XI, pp. 15 et seq.

72 *Ibid.*, pp. 18 et seq.

73 *Ibid.*, p. 24.

74 *Ibid.*, p. 145.

75 The resolution is quoted in Wright, *supra* note 67, 281 (291 et seq); The representative of the Government of India associates himself with the foregoing resolution, subject to the following reservation regarding para. I, 'The use of raw opium, according to the established practice in India, and its production for such use, are not illegitimate under the Convention'; *ibid.*

76 France, Germany, Great Britain, Japan, the Netherlands, Portugal and Siam.

77 Wright, *supra* note 67, 281 (291).

78 William McAllister, *Drug Diplomacy in the Twentieth Century: An International History*, p. 53; Olof Hoijer, *Le trafic de l'opium et d'autres stupéfiants*, 1925, pp. 51 et seq.

scientific purposes. The treaty only required States to exercise an 'effective control'[79] over raw opium and thereby simply reiterated a similar provision to the 1912 Convention.[80] The US proposal to supplement this provision by the words '*so that there will be no surplus available for the purposes not strictly medical and scientific*'[81] was rejected. A majority of States was not ready to subject raw opium to medical and scientific purposes, thus the status quo of the 1912 Convention was left unmodified.[82] The president of the conference rightly concluded, 'The American principle for a limitation of production to medical and scientific purposes [...] has not been included by the Convention as a contractual obligation.'[83]

As the *conditio sine qua non* for US participation in international drug control of the reduction of raw opium to medical and scientific purposes was not contained in the final treaty, the US decided to withdraw from the conference.[84]

Accordingly, the obligation 'to limit exclusively to medical and scientific purposes the manufacture, import, sale, distribution and use' – as in the 1912 Convention – only applied to medicinal opium, morphine, heroin and cocaine.[85] Thus, the double standard that was already contained in the 1912 Convention was perpetuated. On the one hand, manufactured drugs – cocaine, heroin and medicinal opium – were confined to medical and scientific purposes. On the other hand, plant-based narcotic drugs – coca leaf, cannabis and raw opium – were not subjected to medical and scientific purposes.[86] The Far Eastern Powers as well as other drug producing States were unwilling to subject these substances to medical and scientific purposes.[87]

However, major advancements were nevertheless achieved as far as the control of international trade was concerned. In particular, a treaty body, the Permanent Central Board (PCB), was set up in order to 'watch the course of the international trade'.[88] In case of an unjustified massive failure of a State party to comply with its obligations under the 1925 Convention, the PCB would be entitled to recommend an embargo.[89] By comparing the estimates to the statistics, the PCB was enabled to see whether unreasonable quantities of drugs were to be imported into one State.[90] Thus, although the 1925 conferences foresaw a further institutionalization in drug control matters, it was, despite all efforts, impossible to subject plant-based narcotic drugs to the 'medical and scientific purposes constraint'.

79 Art. 2 1925 Convention.
80 Art. 1 1912 Convention.
81 Quincy Wright, 'The Narcotics Convention of 1931', *AJIL* Vol. 28 1934, 475 (480) (italics added).
82 Quincy Wright, 'The Opium Conferences', *AJIL* Vol. 19 1925, 559 (560).
83 Quoted in UNODC, 'World Drug Report 2008', UN Publication, Sales No. E.08.XI.1, p. 193.
84 Letter of the American Delegation to the 1925 Conference of 6 February 1925, quoted in *AJIL* Vol. 19 1925, 380.
85 Chapter III 1925 Convention.
86 Cf. for the same conclusion, Wright, *supra* note 81, 475 (480).
87 Wright, *supra* note 82, 559 (561); as to the position of the Far Eastern Powers with regard to opium cf. *supra* 3.1.2.3.1.
88 Art. 24 (1) 1925 Convention.
89 Art. 24 (2) 1925 Convention.
90 Renborg, *supra* note 52, p. 100.

3.1.2.3.2.3 The 1931 Convention: Enhancing the control of manufactured drugs It had become clear during the negotiations of the 1925 Convention that a universal agreement involving the reduction of raw and prepared opium to medical and scientific purposes was impossible to achieve. Thus, control of drug supply would need to be enhanced by confining manufactured drugs to medical and scientific purposes. This gave the impetus for the 1931 Convention. In 1929, the Assembly requested the OAC to call a conference on the limitation of manufacture of narcotic drugs.[91] The outcome was the 1931 Convention for limiting the Manufacture and Regulating the Distribution of Narcotic Drugs.[92]

In the words of its preamble, the 1931 Convention intended to 'supplement the provisions' of the previous drug conventions '*by rendering effective by international agreement the limitation of the manufacture of narcotic drugs to the world's legitimate requirements for medical and scientific purposes*'.[93] Limitation of the manufacture of drugs was to be achieved by ensuring that no State party would manufacture more drugs than required for medical and scientific needs.[94] Each State was required to limit its own manufacture of narcotic drugs to the amount that was sufficient to guarantee availability of drug use for medical and scientific purposes in its own territory or for the purposes of export.[95] The stringency of the system was to be guaranteed by ensuring supervision of the States. Therefore, a new institution – the Supervisory Body (SB) – was set up in order to verify the accuracy of the estimates.[96]

3.1.2.3.3 THE 1936 CONVENTION: A FIRST ATTEMPT TO SUPPRESS THE ILLICIT DRUG TRAFFIC

The League of Nations period saw no further progress in achieving a universal limitation of drugs to medical and scientific purposes. However, a focus was laid on the suppression of illicit drug traffic. The Convention for the Suppression of the Illicit Traffic in Dangerous Drugs aimed to strengthen the previous drug control treaties by penalizing the offences contrary their provisions and facilitating prosecution.[97,98] Its practical impact remained very little, as it was only ratified by 14 States.[99]

91 1929 Assembly Resolution; quoted in Sixth Meeting, Records of the Conference for the Limitation of the Manufacture of Narcotic Drugs, 27 May–13 July 1931, LN Doc. C. 509. M. 214. 1 XI, Plenary Meetings and Text of the Debates, Vol. I, p. 57.

92 Of 13 July 1931, entered into force 9 July 1933, LNTS Vol. 139, 303 [hereinafter referred to as 1931 Convention]

93 Italics added.

94 Renborg, *supra* note 26, 86 (91).

95 Arts 6–9 1931 Convention.

96 Art. 5 (6) 1931 Convention; cf. Renborg, *supra* note 52, pp. 38 et seq. with further details.

97 Arts 2, 3 and 7 1936 Convention. For more details as to this issue cf. J. G. Starke, 'The Convention of 1936 for the Suppression of Illicit Traffic in Dangerous Drugs', *AJIL* Vol. 31 1937, 31; Neil Boister, *Penal Aspects of the UN Drug Conventions*, 2001, pp. 32–39.

98 The 1936 Convention hast to be considered against the background of conventions suppressing other transnational criminal activities such as the International Conventions against White Slavery; International Convention for the Suppression of the Traffic in Women and Children of 30 September 1921, entered into force 15 June 1922, LNTS Vol. 9, 415.

99 UNODC, 'World Drug Report 2008', UN Publication, Sales No. E.08.XI.1, p. 196.

Nevertheless, it should not be overlooked for two reasons. First, it started a trend in drug control that continued from the Single Convention onwards.[100] That is, the individual State party is obliged to transfer an obligation to penalize certain conduct into a national penal norm.[101] The effective prosecution of this offence is to be guaranteed by ensuring extradition and extraterritorial prosecution as well as law enforcement measures.[102]

Throughout the era of the League of Nations, the international drug control system was further developed and institutionalized. Despite all this progress, the fundamental divide was unresolved between those States prohibiting opium consumption and those allowing for opium use on territories where its use was traditional. Accordingly, no universal limitation of raw opium and prepared opium use to medical and scientific purposes was achieved. The control of manufactured drugs was, however, considerably strengthened.

3.1.2.4 Drug control during the early UN period: Towards a Single Convention on narcotic drugs (1945–1960)

Albeit that one of the first measures regarding drug control of the newly founded United Nations was to transfer international drug control from the League to the United Nations by adopting the 1946 Lake Success Protocol,[103] the United Nations did not content itself merely with replacing the functions of the League in international drug control efforts. The newly formed organization contributed to a further development of the international drug control system. In the long run it was felt that a comprehensive treaty was needed to merge the existing treaties into one instrument and modernize international drug control: the idea of a Single Convention as a long-term project was born.[104] In the meantime, there were problems with urgency too pressing to await a long-term solution. Rapid measures were needed to cope with the expansion of drug control *ratione materiae* to substances that remained hitherto uncovered by the international drug control system. This problem was dealt with by an entirely new protocol.[105]

100 Neil Boister, *Penal Aspects of the UN Drug Conventions*, p. 39.

101 For this mechanism cf. Neil Boister, 'Transnational Criminal Law?', *EJIL* Vol. 14 2003, pp. 953 (962).

102 Arts 3 and 7 1936 Convention.

103 Protocol signed at Lake Success, New York, Amending the Agreements, Conventions and Protocols on Narcotic Drugs Concluded at The Hague on 23 January 1912, at Geneva on 11 February 1925 and 19 February 1925, and 13 July 1931, at Bangkok on 27 November 1931 and at Geneva on 26 June 1936 of 11 December 1946, entered into force 11 December 1946, UNTS Vol. 12, p. 179 [hereinafter referred to as 1946 Protocol]. This problem had already been recognized previously by Adolf Lande, 'The Adjustments of the International Opium Administration to an Eventual Dissolution of the League of Nations', *CLR* Vol. 45 1945, 392.

104 Cf. as to the run-up process towards the Single Convention; Robert W. Gregg, 'The Single Convention for Narcotic Drugs', *Food, Drug, Cosmetic Law Journal* Vol. 16 1961, 187 (195 et seq.).

105 Cf. as to this issue *infra* 3.2.2.

Additionally, the opium question, which had been left unresolved during the entire League of Nations era, could finally be resolved. The international drug control regime had so far not confined raw opium, opium cultivation and prepared opium to medical and scientific purposes. The opposition of the Far Eastern Powers against the erection of a tight system of control confining raw and prepared opium to medical and scientific purposes had so far prevented such steps. This was considered as a major shortcoming of the drug control system during the League of Nations period.[106] During and after World War II, the political realities in the Far East had changed. On the one hand, the Far Eastern Powers had, during World War II, declared that they were willing to gradually terminate opium smoking and prohibit its non-medical use.[107] On the other hand, the aftermath of the Chinese revolution in 1949 saw an unprecedented and successful campaign to destroy opium supply.[108] The deadlock situation of the inter war period was overcome.[109]

The time seemed ripe to finally erect a tight system in order to control opium supply. The issue should not wait until the long-term project of an entirely new Single Convention on narcotic drugs was completed. Albeit ambitious ideas, such as controlling the international opium trade by an impartial institution, were impossible to achieve,[110] a stricter legal framework to control raw opium remained on the agenda. In 1951, France proposed at the CND to draft an agreement that would extend the scope of control exercised by the 1931 Convention on manufactured drugs *mutatis mutandis* to raw opium.[111] The proposal was the base for the draft submitted to a multilateral conference which crafted the 1953 Protocol.[112] The preamble of this treaty underlines the need to regulate the production of raw material of drugs and to limit them 'to medical and scientific needs'.[113] Accordingly, the 1953 Protocol confined the production,[114] use[115] and trade[116] of opium to medical and scientific purposes. For the first time a multilateral treaty

106 Cf. Adolf Lande, 'The Single Convention on Narcotic Drugs, 1961', *International Organization* Vol. 16 1962, 776 (780).

107 UNODC, 'World Drug Report 2008', United Nations Publication 2008, Sales No. E.08.XI.1, p. 197.

108 *Ibid.*

109 Cf. *supra* 3.1.2.3.1; cf. also https://soundcloud.com/lshtm/american-influence-on-the.

110 Report of the Third Session of the CND, ECOSOC Official Records Supplement No. 9, 1948, UN Doc. E/799; E/RES/1948/159 (VII) IID, 1948; for more details with regard to this issue cf. Robert W. Gregg, 'The United Nations and the Opium Problem', *ICLQ* Vol. 14 1964, 96 (99 et seq.); cf. also *UNYB* 1948–1949, pp. 660 et seq.; *UNYB* 1950, pp. 629 et seq.

111 *UNYB* 1951, pp. 563 et seq.

112 Protocol for Limiting and Regulating the Cultivation of the Poppy Plant, the Production of International Wholesale Trade in, and Use of Opium of 23 June 1953 [hereinafter referred to as 1953 Protocol].

113 Protocol for Limiting and Regulating the Cultivation of the Poppy Plant, the Production of International Wholesale Trade in, and use of Opium of 23 June 1953, entered into force 8 March 1963, UNTS Vol. 456, p. 3 [hereinafter referred to as 1953 Protocol].

114 Art. 4 1953 Protocol.

115 Art. 3 1953 Protocol.

116 Art. 6 1953 Protocol.

recognized the universal limitation of opium to medical and scientific purposes.[117] The sole exception to this limitation was of a transitional nature, allowing for quasi-medical opium use for a limited period of time.[118]

The 1953 Protocol was conceived as an 'interim measure' that prevented the situation from aggravating before the Single Convention, as a final solution on drugs, was adopted.[119] The practical relevance of this protocol was little. When it entered into force in 1963, its abrogation was already foreseen by the Single Convention. This abrogation took place when the Single Convention entered into force in December 1964.[120]

3.1.3 Inflexible multilateralism 1961–the present

The contemporary drug control system – as erected by the Single Convention and developed by the 1971 Convention, the 1988 Convention and the 1972 Protocol – departs from the 'flexible approach' chosen by the earlier treaties in that it universally restricts all drug-related behaviours to medical and scientific purposes.

3.1.3.1 The Single Convention on narcotic drugs and the breakthrough of the universal limitation of drugs to medical and scientific purposes

The Single Convention on narcotic drugs marks the beginning of the contemporary drug control system, as it terminated the previous multilateral drug control treaties.[121] The treaty was drafted in order to unify the existing instruments on drug control into one single treaty, merge the PCB and the Drug Supervisory Body into one single treaty body and limit the production of raw materials for narcotic drugs.[122] It was expected to 'modernize, simplify and generalize the

117 Cf. as to this aspect Harry J. Aislinger, 'The Implementation of Treaty Obligations Regulating the Traffic in Narcotic Drugs', *AmULR* Vol. 8 1959, 108 (115).

118 Art. 19 1953 Protocol.

119 Lande, *supra* note 106', 776 (782).

120 UNODC, 'World Drug Report 2008', UN Publication, Sales No. E.08.XI.1, p. 198. The slow ratification process of the 1953 Protocol was due to the fact that it was difficult to attain the necessary number of three of the seven opium-producing states named by Art. 6 (2) (a) 1953 Protocol, which according to Art. 21 (1) of the same treaty were necessary for its coming into force; Lande, *supra* note 106, 776 (780).

121 Art. 44 Single Convention. The only previous drug control treaty that remained in force is the 1936 Convention; cf. Commentary Single Convention Art. 44, MN 1; cf. for a pertinent analysis of the Single Convention in the light of earlier drug control treaties, David Bewley-Taylor and Martin Jelsma, 'Regime Change: Re-visiting the 1961 Single Convention on Narcotic Drugs', *IJDP* Vol. 23 2012, 72.

122 Salo Engel, 'Integration of International Legislation', *AJIL* Vol. 45 1951, 770 (773). Merging all previous treaties on drug control in one instrument should facilitate its application and interpretation and help to ensure more coherence as differing number of ratifications can be avoided; Leland M. Goodrich, 'New Trends in Narcotics Control', International Conciliation No. 530 1 960, 180 (187 et seq.).

legal bases of the international drug control system',[123] and it was hoped that the instrument was the final solution for international drug control. One of its drafters named it 'the "convention to end conventions" on narcotic drugs'.[124] Bearing these high ambitions in mind, it was no surprise that the drafting process of the instrument proved to be long and difficult. The ECOSOC had already in 1948 requested the Secretary General to begin drafting such an instrument,[125] and it would take three drafts[126] and 13 years before the final treaty was adopted.

Assessing the Single Convention in the light of earlier drug control treaties reveals a mixed picture. The Single Convention contains innovations which had been impossible to negotiate into previous drug control treaties. First, the Single Convention was the first widely ratified drug control treaty to oblige States parties to penalize individuals not complying with its provisions (Art. 36 Single Convention).[127] Second, it was the first treaty to establish control measures with regard to the cultivation of plants necessary for the production of narcotic drugs – the cannabis plant, the opium poppy and the coca leaf (Arts 22–28 Single Convention). Third, an entirely new aspect was introduced into the drug control system by obliging States to adopt measures of treatment for drug users (Art. 38 Single Convention). Fourth, and most importantly, the Single Convention constitutes the final breakthrough in the limitation of all drugs to medical and scientific purposes. Article. 4 (c) Single Convention[128] obliges parties to 'limit exclusively to medical and scientific purposes the production, manufacture, export, import, distribution of, trade in, use and possession of drugs'.

However, the Single Convention – despite more ambitious proposals – contains elements where the preexisting status quo is merely preserved and solidified. First, it does not interfere with the authority of individual States to decide on the implementation of their proper obligations under the treaty. Thus, the proposal to vest the newly created International Narcotics Control Board (INCB) with the authority to impose a 'mandatory' drug embargo on a State party not complying with the obligations of the Single Convention[129] was not retained in

123 *Ibid.* (188).

124 Herbert May, 'The Single Convention on Narcotic Drugs: Comments and Possibilities', *Bulletin on Narcotics* Vol. 7 1955 No. 1, 1 (14).

125 ECOSOC Resolution 1948/159 (VIII) IID, UN Doc. E/Res/1948/159 (VII) IID, 1948, para. 2

126 The detailed history of the negotiation process will not be accounted here; it seems sufficient to illustrate its difficulties, by pointing out that it took three drafts (the first one was elaborated from 1950 to 1955; the second one from 1956 to1957 and the third draft from 1958 to 1960) and 11 years to adopt the final treaty; for a detailed analysis of the Second Draft cf. Adolf Lande, 'La Codification du droit international des stupéfiants', *AFDI* Vol. 2 1956, 557 (562 et seq.).

127 The scarcely ratified 1936 Convention had contained obligations in order to penalize drug-related conduct; cf. *supra* 3.1.2.3.3.

128 The authentic text of the Single Convention refers to Art. 4 para. 1 *lit.* c. As Art. 4 has no para. 2, this book will refer to Art. 4 (c) as meaning Art. 4 (1) (c).

129 Art. 22 (4) Third Draft Single Convention on Narcotic Drugs of 11 September 1958, UN Doc. E/CN.7/AC.3/9 [hereinafter referred to as Third Draft Single Convention].

the final treaty.[130] The drafters considered that the INCB should be a technical body and universal ratification of the treaty should not be jeopardized by creating a too powerful control institution.[131] In the same vein, the idea of reserving the right to cultivate the coca leaf[132] and the opium poppy[133] to a prefixed number of States did not make it into the final treaty. [134] States opposed inflexible solutions as they feared the shortage of controlled substances.[135] Furthermore, a total prohibition of substances considered to be particularly dangerous, e.g. heroin,[136] equally did not make it into the final treaty. Such a clause was rejected by a slim majority,[137] arguing that the matter of total prohibition of a given substance should be left to the individual State party.[138]

The most vivid proponents of a tight system of international drug control – the United States – was therefore disappointed by the final result.[139] The provisions of the 1953 Protocol – an interim measure – were in many respects more ambitious than the final version of the Single Convention. The former treaty had provided for a mandatory drug embargo as well as a fixed number of opium States that were allowed to produce opium for export.[140] The reason for this discrepancy lies in the fact that to achieve universality, the Single Convention had to give away some of the stringency contained in the 1953 Protocol.[141]

3.1.3.2 The 1971 Convention: Expansion of the obligation to reduce drugs to medical and scientific purposes towards psychotropic substances

The 1971 Convention expanded drug control *ratione materiae* to psychotropic substances.[142] These substances were left outside of the Single Convention's scope of control, which was exclusively concerned with narcotic drugs. The 1971

130 Art. 14 (2) Single Convention.
131 Cf. in that regard OR I Single Convention, pp. 80 et seq., espec. p. 82.
132 Art. 37 (1) (a) Third Draft Single Convention.
133 Art. 32 (1) (a) Third Draft Single Convention foresaw that opium should only be exported by Afghanistan, Bulgaria, Greece, India, Iran, Turkey, the Union of Soviet Socialist Republics and Yugoslavia.
134 Art. 22 et seq. Single Convention.
135 Cf. statement by Ghana, OR I Single Convention, p. 38; cf. also critical statements by the United Kingdom, *ibid.*, p. 39; the USSR considered that such a provision would be contrary to the principle of equality of States; *ibid.* p. 40.
136 Art. 2 (1) (e) Third Draft Single Convention
137 OR I Single Convention, p. 22.
138 *Ibid.*
139 Lande, *supra* note 106, 776 (796); cf. also as to the critique regarding the lacking effectiveness of the Single Convention; Jose Cabranes, 'International Law and Control of the Drug Traffic', *Int'l L.* Vol. 7 1973, 761 (764 et seq.).
140 Art. 6 (2) (a) 1953 Protocol; Art. 12 (3) 1953 Protocol.
141 Cf. Lande, *supra* note 106, 776 (795); Ian G. Waddell 'International Narcotics Control', *AJIL* Vol. 64 1970, 310 (321); John Cohrssen and Lawrence Hoover, 'The International Control of Dangerous Drugs', *J. Int'l L. & Econ.* Vol. 9 1974, 81 (85 et seq.).
142 Cf. as to this expansion in detail *infra* 3.2.

Convention constituted a major expansion *ratione materiae* of the obligation to confine drugs to (limited) medical and scientific purposes. Similar to the Single Convention, it also penalizes supply-related offences with regard to psychotropic substances.[143]

3.1.3.3 Consolidation of the international drug control system

The 1972 Protocol and the 1988 Convention – although further developing international drug control – did not depart from the principle of the Single Convention to subject drugs to medical and scientific purposes. Rather they further consolidated the approach chosen by the existing drug control system to confine psychoactive substances – narcotic drugs and psychotropic substances alike – to medical and scientific proposes.

The 1972 Protocol amending the Single Convention on drugs was meant to ameliorate the Single Convention in two ways.[144] On the one hand, the aim was to strengthen the role of the INCB, most importantly by providing it with the possibility to impose a mandatory drug embargo on States.[145] On the other hand, the Single Convention was adjusted and brought into line with the 1971 Convention as far as the treatment of addicts was concerned; a more detailed provision for the treatment of drug users than under the initial Single Convention was adopted.[146] The 1972 Protocol strengthened the Single Convention with regard to a few technical questions,[147] while leaving fundamental principles – i.e. confining drugs to medical and scientific purposes by relying on a universal system of indirect control – of this treaty unmodified. The 1972 Protocol today binds all parties to the Single Convention with the exception of Chad, which merely ratified the Single Convention in 1964 but has so far failed to adhere to the 1972 Protocol.[148]

The 1988 Convention did not modify any fundamental premises of international drug control. It is complementary to the two previous UN Drug Conventions – strengthening the earlier treaties and was meant to 'reinforce and supplement' the Single Convention and the 1971 Convention.[149] The 1988

143 Art. 22 1971 Convention.

144 Cf. as to this Protocol in general Claude-Henri Vignes, 'Les modifications apportées à l'Organe internationale de contrôle par les amendements à la Convention unique sur les stupéfiants', *AFDI* Vol. 18 1972, 629.

145 Amendment Proposal by the United States, United Nations Conference to consider amendments to the Single Convention on Narcotic Drugs, 1961, Geneva – 6–24 March 1972, Official Records Vol. I [hereinafter referred to as OR I 1972 Protocol], pp. 2 et seq.

146 OR I 1972 Protocol, p. 4.

147 E.g. the membership of the INCB was increased from 11 to 13 (Art. 9 (1) Single Convention), the term of office of INCB was extended from three to five years (Art. 10 (1) Single Convention) and the parties were required to submit more detailed estimates to the INCB (Art. 19 (1) Single Convention); cf. as to this, Comparative Table, Annex II OR I 1972 Protocol, pp. 140 et seq.

148 INCB Annual Report 2015, para. 50.

149 Preamble 1988 Convention.

Convention strengthened and reinforced the two earlier treaties by introducing suppressive measures against illicit drug traffic. Thus, the 1988 Convention extended the obligations to adopt penal provisions from the two earlier treaties.[150] Furthermore, it introduced numerous possibilities of transnational cooperation in order to combat illicit drug trafficking, such as extradition,[151] extraterritorial jurisdiction for drug-related offences[152] and measures against illicit traffic in drugs on the high seas.[153] Additionally, it subjected a growing number of 'substances frequently used in the illicit manufacture of narcotic drugs or psychotropic substances' to a number of control measures.[154]

Despite the formal consolidation of the earlier conventions retained within the final instrument, the 1988 Conference also stands as proof for the growing critique to universally reduce drugs to medical and scientific purposes where their use had been traditional.[155] A group of 24 States from Latin and South America suggested to insert a provision into the 1988 Convention, whereby '(1) [Measures to prevent and eradicate illicit cultivation] shall respect fundamental human rights and shall take due account of traditional domestic uses – where there is historic evidence of such use –, as well as the protection of the environment.'[156]

They argued that *'[i]t was particularly important to ensure that the convention did not penalize the licit cultivation of coca bushes and the licit traditional uses of coca leaf and its consumption.*'[157] Furthermore, they held that *'[i]t was important to respect the traditional uses of coca by indigenous inhabitants, which should not be confused with the activities of drug traffickers.*'[158] According to the sponsors, the effect of such a measure, therefore, was to legalize the use of the coca leaf. This proposal was vigorously opposed by proponents of a rigid international drug control system.[159] They were concerned that such a

150 Art. 3 1988 Convention.

151 Art. 6 1988 Convention.

152 Art. 4 1988 Convention.

153 Art. 17 1988 Convention.

154 Art. 12 1988 Convention.

155 Cf. also for a comprehensive account, Sven Pfeiffer, 'Rights of Indigenous Peoples and the International Drug Control Regime: The Case for Traditional Coca Leaf Chewing', *GoJIL* Vol. 5 2013, 287 (322).

156 United Nations Conference for the Adoption of a Convention Against Illicit Traffic in Narcotic Drugs and Psychotropic Substances, Vienna, 25 November–20 December 1988, Official Records Volume I: Preparatory work, Conference documents on organizational matters, Main Conference documents. Final Act and Resolutions, 1994, UN Doc. E/CONF.82/16, [hereinafter referred to as OR I 1988 Convention], p. 150.

157 United Nations Conference for the Adoption of a Convention Against Illicit Traffic in Narcotic Drugs and Psychotropic Substances, Vienna, 25 November–20 December 1988, Official Records Volume II: Summary records of Plenary Meetings, Summary records of Meetings of Committee I, and Committee II, 1994, UN Doc. E/CONF.82/16/Add.l [hereinafter referred to as OR II 1988 Convention], p. 297 (italics added).

158 OR II 1988 Convention, p. 297 (italics added).

159 Cf. OR II 1988 Convention, pp. 298 et seq.

proposal 'would be a step backwards'[160] and argued that it was contrary to provisions of the Single Convention.[161] They managed to negotiate a reference to the Single Convention into the final draft for the 1988 Conference.[162] The result was that the paragraph preceding the reference to traditional licit uses, i.e. Art. 14 (1), clarifies that the 1988 Convention has to be conceived against the background of the previous drug control treaties' efforts to limit all drug-related activities to medical and scientific purposes. This turns into mere symbolism the reference to traditional licit uses retained in Art. 14 (2) 1988 Convention.

3.2 A constant expansion of the international drug control system

During the course of the twentieth century, it was not only drug control's fundamental premise of limiting drugs to medical and scientific purposes that was continuously strengthened. Another notable development occurred during this period. The scope of application of international drug control was gradually expanded from opium to other narcotic drugs and finally to psychotropic substances.

3.2.1 1912–1945: From opium towards a control of plant-based (narcotic) drugs

The international drug control system emerged as a response to the opium epidemic, turning opium into the substance of central concern during drug control's first decades.[163] Already by 1909, however, opium was certainly not the only psychoactive substance worrying policymakers. The potency of opium had been overhauled during the nineteenth century by the creation of opiates, most notably morphine and heroin, whose potency was further increased by the use of hypodermic syringes.[164] Additionally, at the same time it had become possible to isolate cocaine from the coca leaf, thereby notably increasing its potency. The use of cocaine soon became widespread.[165]

These developments were already reflected by the 1909 Opium Commission, where initial pleas were made to bring the derivatives of opium under international

160 Statement US delegate, OR II 1988 Convention, p. 298.

161 Statement French delegate, *ibid.*

162 OR I 1988 Convention, p. 83.

163 Cf. as to this *supra* 3.1.2.1 for more details.

164 Julia Buxton, 'The Historical Foundations of the Narcotic Drug Control Regime', 2008, pp. 5 et seq.

165 David Musto, *The American Disease: Origins of Narcotic Control*, pp. 1 et seq., 6 et seq. Cocaine had been contained in Coca Cola until 1903; cf. as to this issue Paul Gootenberg, 'Secret Ingredients: The Politics of Coca in US–Peruvian Relations, 1915–65', *JLAS* Vol. 36 2004, 233 (239 et seq.).

control.[166] When the 1912 Convention was adopted, this treaty not only applied to raw and prepared opium, it limited medicinal opium, morphine, heroin and cocaine to medical and legitimate purposes (Art. 9 1912 Convention).[167]

The expansion of drug control *ratione materiae* continued with the adoption of the 1925 Convention. This was the first drug control treaty to apply to cannabis – then labelled as 'Indian Hemp'[168] – and the coca leaf.[169] Additionally, the 1925 Convention foresaw the possibility to extend the scope of application to other substances at a later point. Such an extension, however, remained purely recommendatory (Art. 10 (2) 1925 Convention). Under the 1931 Convention it was possible to widen scope of application to 'any product obtained from any of the phenanthrene alkaloids of opium or from ecogine alkaloids of the coca leaf, not in use on this days date' following a mandatory decision of the League's Health Committee and the Office international d'Hygène (Art. 11 (1) 1931 Convention).

3.2.2 The 1948 Protocol: Expanding to synthetic drugs

The scope of application of the international drug control system was not further extended until 1948, when the first new drug control treaty negotiated under the auspice of the newly created United Nations was signed in Paris.[170] This protocol foresaw a further expansion of the obligations of the international drug control system. It aimed to restrict the manufacture of newly discovered drugs – mainly synthetic drugs – to medical and scientific purposes (preambular paras 1 et seq. 1948 Protocol). The protocol did not directly subject such drugs to medical and scientific purposes, but provided for the flexibility to do so. A State party

166 Cf. in this regard Resolutions 3 and 4 1909 Opium Commission. There had already been bilateral treaties prohibiting morphine export prior to the international opium commission. Cf. e.g. Treaty as to Commercial Relations between China and the United States, quoted in *AJIL* Supplement Vol. 3 1909, 255; cf. also Art. XI of the British commercial treaty between China and Great Britain signed in Shanghai 5 September 1902, where Great Britain agreed to the prohibition of morphine in China under certain conditions; quoted in: *ibid.*, 263. This treaty was concluded at a time when the obligation of China to accept the import of British opium was still in force.

167 This created problems in the ratification process, which were only resolved by the adoption of the post-WW1 treaties which obligated States parties to bring the 1912 Convention into force.

168 Chapter IV 1925 Convention; the initiative to include cannabis emanated from the Egyptian delegate; cf. also David Bewley-Taylor, Tom Blickman and Martin Jelsma, 'The Rise and Decline of Cannabis Prohibition: The History of Cannabis in the UN Drug Control System and Options for Reform', TNI, 2014, pp. 14 et seq. with further references.

169 Chapter II 1925 Convention.

170 Protocol bringing under international control drugs outside the scope of the Convention of 13 July 1931 for limiting the manufacture and regulating the distribution of narcotic drugs, as amended by the Protocol signed at Lake Success on 11 December 1946 of 19 November 1948, entered into force 1 December 1949, UNTS Vol. 44, p. 277 [hereinafter referred to as 1948 Protocol]. For more details cf. S. K. Chatterjee, *Legal Aspects of International Drug Control*, pp. 327 et seq.

concerned with a substance not covered by the 1931 Convention but 'liable to the same kind of abuse and productive of the same kind of harmful effects' could refer this to the CND and the World Health Organization (WHO) (Art. 1 (1) 1948 Protocol). The WHO would examine the merits of this notification and could place the substance under the regime of the 1931 Convention in case 'that the drug in question is capable of producing addiction or of conversion into a product producing addiction' (Art. 1 (2) 1948 Protocol).

3.2.3 The narrow scope of application of the Single Convention and the need to adopt a treaty on psychotropic substances

It is rather curious that the Single Convention created a gap within the control of many synthetic drugs. This gap subsequently made the adoption of a new treaty on psychotropic substances necessary. The Single Convention – despite some initial wishes of its drafters[171] – was not of similar flexibility to the 1948 Protocol, which was terminated by the Single Convention's entry into force (Art. 44 (1) (h) Single Convention). As will be shown in greater detail below (5.2), albeit that its scope of application can be modified, only substances with similar properties to the initial plant-based drugs covered by the Single Convention (i.e. cannabis, opiates and the coca leaf/cocaine) can be added to its schedules. This explains the need to draft an entire treaty for substances not sharing these attributes, i.e. psychotropic substances. The final outcome of these developments is the 1971 Convention on psychotropic substances.

3.3 The international drug control system as a prime example of the law of cooperation

Having outlined the emergence of the international drug control system, the following section anchors this development within the wider context of international law's evolution during the twentieth century. The gradual erection of institutionalization in the field of drug control has to be considered against the background of other fields of international law – such as international human rights protection or international environmental law – where States have yielded their sovereignty in order to achieve a common goal. These fields of international law have been referred as the 'law of international cooperation',[172] *droit institutionnel*[173] or the 'law of coordination'.[174] The term is a counterpart to the 'law of coexistence'[175] or *droit relationnel*.[176] The latter describes classical, Westphalian, international law during the times of the *concert européen* where States

171 Cf. in this regard statement by the French delegate, OR I Single Convention, p. 9.

172 Friedmann, *supra* note 2, 47 (91 et seq.).

173 Dupuy, *supra* note 3, 9 (55 et seq.).

174 Georg Schwarzenberger, *Power Politics: A Study of International Society*, p. 212.

175 Friedmann, *supra* note 2, 47 (91 et seq.).

176 Dupuy, *supra* note 3, 9 (49 et seq.).

viciously protected their own sovereignty, unwilling to corporate or to integrate into any permanent international form of organization whatsoever.[177] The law of cooperation, however, refers a higher stage in the social relationship of States: States that are ready to cooperate in permanent structures on various sectors in order to achieve common goals unified by shared values.[178] This cooperation derives from of a necessity posed by the magnitude of a problem whose solution cannot be achieved unilaterally.[179]

Although international drug control was unnoticed by many,[180] it perfectly fits the category of the law of cooperation. Contemporaries considered that the Single Convention in particular and drug control in general would serve humanitarian and social objectives.[181] International drug control was included in the category of treaties for the protection of minorities and the status of refugees.[182] The first international meeting in order to gain control over opium, the International Opium Commission in Shanghai of 1909, is considered a classic example of Ppre-1914 social internationalism.[183] The anti-opium movement, which eventually would succeed in establishing a universal drug control system, consisted out of missionaries and other 'moral entrepreneurs' of the late nineteenth and early twentieth centuries[184] who shared similarities to the anti-slavery and other humanitarian movements of that time.[185]

Additionally, the relatively high level of institutionalization that the international drug control system achieved at a fairly early stage suggests considering this system as part of the law of cooperation. As has been shown, the drug control system was 'governed' already during the League of Nations period by an Opium Advisory Committee and two treaty bodies.[186] This made the international drug control system a primary example of how a modern cooperation

177 Simma, *supra* note 4, 217 (229 et seq.); Georges Abi Saab, 'Whither the International Community', *EJIL* Vol. 9 1998, 248 (250 et seq).
178 For a definition of treaties establishing community interests cf. Simma, *supra* note 4, 217 (233).
179 Abi Saab, *supra* note 177, 248 (252 et seq).
180 See *supra* Introduction, note 36.
181 Paul Reuter, 'The Obligations of the States under the Single Convention on Narcotic Drugs, 1961', *Bulletin on Narcotics* Vol. 20 No. 4 1968, 3; cf. in that regard Bettati Mario, 'Le contrôle international des stupéfiants', *RGDIP* Vol. 78 1974, 170 (173): 'Or, dans cette matière [de contrôle international des stupéfiants], comme dans toutes les questions de droit humanitaire et social.'; cf. also Georg Schwarzenberger, *Economic World Order: A Basic Problem of International Economic Cooperation*, p. 54 referring to the control of drugs as a 'humanitarian tradition'.
182 Cf. eg. George Schwarzenberger, *Power Politics: A Study of International Society*, p. 212 who includes these treaties into the International Law of Coordination.
183 Peter D. Lowes, *The Genesis of International Narcotics Control*, pp. 1 et seq., 194.
184 Nadelmann, *supra* note 5, 479 (503 et seq.); David Courtwright, 'Foreword: Drug Use and Prohibition: Three Reform Traditions', in: Beatriz Caiuby Labate and Clancy Cavnar (eds), *Prohibition, Religious Freedom, and Human Rights: Regulating Traditional Drug Use*, 2014, v.
185 Nadelmann, *supra* note 5, 479 (503). Cf. also in this regard, Peter D. Lowes, *The Genesis of International Narcotics Control*, pp. 2 et seq., 58 et seq.
186 Cf. *infra* 3.1.2 for more details.

could resolve problems of true international magnitude. Thus, after the adoption of the 1931 Convention,[187] the Assembly of the League of Nations remarked:

> The Convention marks an entirely new and highly important development in international cooperation, since this is the first time an industry has been brought under international regulation, and that manufacture in its economic aspect has been wholly subordinated to higher humanitarian and moral aims.[188]

The international drug control system was considered as 'one of the most successful activities of the League'[189] and perceived as 'one of the most highly developed instrumentalities for enforcement of decisions of the international community'.[190] Thus, international drug control was seen as a successful example of how international cooperation could bring a problem of international magnitude under control; it showed that 'international law can offer satisfactory remedies'.[191] This narrative was prevalent until very recently; thus, the 1988 Convention was considered as exemplary for how a transnational criminal activity could be countered by international cooperation.[192]

Today, the bulk of analysis on the UN Drug Conventions is less positive.[193] The UN Drug Conventions are even considered by many as inhuman and – albeit indirectly – causing human rights violations on a domestic level.[194] What seems to have remained unnoted by scholars concerned with the international drug control system to date, is that it is not merely the international drug control

187 Convention for Limiting the Manufacture and Regulating the Distribution of Narcotic Drugs of 13 July 1931, entered into force 9 July 1933, LNTS Vol. 139, 303 [hereinafter referred to as 1931 Convention].

188 Quoted in J. W. Samuels, 'International Control of Narcotic Drugs and International Economic Law', *Can. Y. B. Int'l* Vol. 7 1969, 192 (202).

189 Bertil A. Renborg, 'The Grand Old Men of the League of Nations: What They Achieved and Who They Were, *Bulletin on Narcotics* Vol. 15 1964 Issue 4, 1. Cf. for a similar assessment Renborg, *supra* note 51, 436 (459).

190 Leland M. Goodrich, 'New Trends in Narcotics Control', International Conciliation No. 530 1960, 180; cf. for a similar conclusion William McAllister, *Drug Diplomacy in the Twentieth Century: An International History*, p. 132; cf. for a similar conclusion Cohrssen and Hoover, *supra* note 141, 81 (84) 'a high level of international cooperation'.

191 S. K. Chatterjee, *Legal Aspects of International Drug Control*, p. 540.

192 D. W. Sproule and Paul St-Denis, 'The UN Drug Trafficking Convention: An Ambitious Step' *Can. Y. B. Int'l* Vol. 27 1989, 263 (291). The 'pattern' of the 1988 Convention has been followed by subsequent conventions penalizing and prosecuting transnational criminal activity such as the Transnational Crime Convention; Neil Boister, 'Human Rights Protections in the Suppression Conventions', *Human Rights Law Review* Vol. 2 2002, 199 (211).

193 Damon Barrett et al., 'Recalibrating the Regime: The Need for a Human Rights-based Approach to International Drug Policy', The Beckley Foundation Drug Policy Programme, 2008; Richard Lines, *Drug Control and Human Rights in International Law*, *passim*.

194 Damon Barrett and Manfred Nowak, 'United Nations and Drug Policy: Towards a Human Rights-based Approach', in: Aristotle Constantinides and Niko Zaikos (eds), *Essays in Honour of Kalliopi Koufa*, 2009, 449.

system, but a myriad of fields of the contemporary law of cooperation, that is undergoing a profound identity crisis.[195] Describing, let alone understanding, this identity crises which today touches upon such a variety of fields of international cooperation, ranging from investment treaty arbitration to the international criminal court, goes beyond the scope of this book. However, understanding the international drug control system as part of the law of cooperation allows for the establishment of a framework in which this legal system is operating and a point of reference for understanding the similarities and particularities of the international drug control system from a more general perspective.

3.4 Conclusion

This chapter has traced the development of the international drug control system from its origins to the adoption of the 1988 Convention. It has shown that it took more than 50 years to agree on a universal limitation of drugs to medical and scientific purposes by drafting the Single Convention. This rule was further consolidated by the 1971 Convention, the 1972 Protocol and the 1988 Convention. In short, the world drug problem, and more precisely illicit drug use, was viewed as an 'evil' whose complete eradication seemed essential and achievable by tight international cooperation;[196] nonmedical drug use was to be curtailed and be subjected to as few exceptions as possible.[197] Meaningful results were possible if States would yield their carefully guarded sovereignty and cooperate in good faith in order to preserve humanity from the scourge of drug trafficking and drug use.[198] This would be possible by ensuring universal commitment to the UN Drug Conventions and the effective implementation of these treaties.[199] However, the drafting of the 1988 Convention stands as proof of early doubts that all substances covered by the Single Convention should in fact be limited universally to medical and scientific purposes. Some States within Latin America opposed the limitation of the coca leaf to medical and scientific purposes.

195 See Jose Alvarez and Benedict Kingsury, *AJIL* at 111, *AJIL* Vol. 111 2017, 1 (2 et seq.).

196 S. K. Chatterjee, *Legal Aspects of International Drug Control*, pp. 523 et seq.

197 Courtwright, *supra* note 184', v.

198 Cf. in that regard S. K. Chatterjee, *Legal Aspects of International Drug Control*, 1981, pp. 523 et seq.; although it was recognized that a complete eradication would not be possible; *ibid.*; Adolf Lande and Geleitwort in: Walter von Wartburg (ed.), *Drogenmissbrauch und Gesetzgeber, Methodik und Möglichkeit einer optimalen Kontrolle des Missbruachs von Drogen und Arzneimitteln*, Experentia Supplementum Vol. 21 1974, pp. V et seq.

199 Lande and Geleitwort, *supra* note 198, pp. V et seq.

4 The objective of the international drug control system

Limitation of drugs to medical and scientific purposes

Having outlined that the emergence of the international drug control system means the coming into existence of a multilateral effort to restrain a growing number of substances to medical and scientific purposes, this chapter elaborates in detail on the meaning of the limitation of drugs to medical and scientific purposes.

4.1 The need to understand the limitation of drugs to medical and scientific purposes

The UN Drug Conventions have established a highly elaborate and complex system. They contain 118 articles on such various issues as the control of drug production and trade, penal sanctions and treatment of drug abuse. The international drug control system, as any normative system, is not a simple addition of the numerous rules contained in its various instruments, but follows an inherent logic that deserves to be made transparent: it is based on the premise to limit drugs to medical and scientific purposes.

Trying to understand the current drug control system without reference to this norm means to put the cart before the horse. Albeit that scholarship in general accepts that the limitation of drugs to medical and scientific purposes forms the heart of the international drug control system, nobody has so far carried out an in-depth analysis of what this limitation really means.[1]

1 Cf. e.g. Melissa T. Ayoagi, 'Beyond Punitive Prohibition: Liberalizing the Dialogue on International Drug Policy', *NYU JILP* Vol. 37 2005, 555 (587); David Bewley-Taylor and Martin Jelsma, 'Regime Change: Re-visiting the 1961 Single Convention on Narcotic Drugs', *IJDP* Vol. 23 2012, 72 (76); David Bewley-Taylor, *International Drug Control: Consensus Fractured*, p. 248; S. K. Chatterjee, *Legal Aspects of International Drug Control*, p. 357; Bernard Levroy, M. Cherif Bassiouini and Jean-François Thony, 'The International Drug Control System', in: M. Cherif Bassiouni (ed.) *International Criminal Law: Vol. I, Sources, Subjects, and Contents*, 855 (872); J.W. Samuels, 'International Control of Narcotic Drugs and International Economic Law', *Can. Y. B. Int'l* Vol. 7 1969, 192 (201 et seq.); Richard Lines, *Drug Control and Human Rights in International Law*, pp. 115 et seq.

4.1.1 The limitation of drugs to medical and scientific purposes as the point of reference for all drug-related activities

Opponents of the international drug control system have labelled the international drug control system as 'prohibitionist'[2] and defenders of the system have argued that the true objective of international drug control is the preservation of mankind's health and welfare.[3]

Both characterizations, however, fail to reveal entirely the premises on which the international drug control system is based. The reference to health and welfare within all three preambles of the UN Drug Conventions merely outlines their long-term goal. However, this reference cannot be understood without considering the limitation of drugs to medical and scientific purposes. A close reading of the preambles shows that the drugs are limited to medical and scientific purposes due to the States parties' concern for the health and welfare of mankind. This derives from, in particular, the authentic French and Spanish wording: the States parties were '*soucieux*' or '*preocupadas*', i.e. worried, by the diametrical effects that drugs posed to mankind's health and welfare and, therefore, were eager to limit drugs to medical and scientific purposes.[4]

By the same token, conceiving the UN Drug Conventions as merely prohibitionist fails to provide an in-depth understanding of their approach to drugs. This is true despite the fact that States do prohibit psychoactive substances on a domestic level in order to comply with their obligations arising out of these treaties. However, as already results from the Single Convention's second preambular paragraph, the drafters of the UN Drug Conventions did not opt for a total prohibition of drugs, but considered their medical use 'indispensable' for the relief of pain. Conversely, drug addiction is recognized by the preceding paragraph of the Single Convention's preamble as an 'evil' that States need to eradicate. This dualism between drugs for medical and scientific needs, on the one hand, and drugs for other purposes, on the hand, is inherent across the drug control system. The entire regulation of the production and trade of drugs[5] is only required because of the need to establish a controlled economy for drugs to satisfy the world's demand for drugs for medical and scientific purposes. Therefore, the terminology of a 'legal' or 'illegal' drug is misleading. Rather, one needs to ask whether a given drug-related activity – production, trade and use – is carried

2 Damon Barrett et al., 'Recalibrating the Regime: The Need for a Human Rights-based Approach to International Drug Policy', The Beckley Foundation Drug Policy Programme, 2008, p. 5.

3 INCB Annual Report 2014, paras 3 and 5. Cf. for a similar conclusion, INCB Annual Report 2015, para. 1. See as to the *telos* of protecting mankind's health and welfare, Richard Lines, *Drug Control and Human Rights in International Law*, pp. 122 et seq.

4 Under the Single Convention (Art. 30 (1)) as well as the 1971 Convention (Art. 33) the Chinese, English, French, Russian and Spanish versions of the text are equally authentic. The 1988 Convention adds to these languages, Arabic as being equally authentic (Art. 40 (1)). In accordance with Art. 33 (1) VCLT all texts in one of those languages are equally authoritative.

5 Cf. *infra* 6.1.

out for medical and scientific purposes and is, therefore, licit, or is carried out for any other purposes and is, therefore, illicit. Thus, whether a drug-related activity corresponds with medical and scientific needs distinguishes the fine line between an allowed and a prohibited activity under the UN Drug Conventions.[6]

As has been rightly observed, '[t]he difficulties in defining the scope of the expression "medical and scientific purposes"' are many'.[7] States have not clarified further the meaning of drug use for medical purposes.[8] A comprehensive definition is also not provided by the *travaux préparatoires*, although during the conference on the Single Convention, some States asked for a definition and clarification of the terminology in this regard.[9] Adolf Lande – acting in the capacity of Deputy-Executive Secretary – explained that '[i]t would hardly be possible in a treaty to use wording which coincided with the legal terminology of every single country.'[10]

Thus, the parties agreed that drug use for medical purposes should remain open for differing meanings in differing contexts. Consensus was reached that the term 'medical purposes' should comprise the use of drugs for veterinary and dental medicines.[11] Furthermore, the States parties agreed that indigenous medicine could also be subsumed under medical purposes.[12] Likewise, the commentaries to the Single Convention and the 1971 Convention do not define the meaning of 'medical purposes', but underline the temporal and cultural relativity of the term.[13]

The same is true for the term 'scientific purposes'. The States parties did not provide for a definition of drug use for scientific purposes when drafting the Single Convention and the 1971 Convention.[14] By the same token, the commentaries have not elucidated the meaning of drug use for scientific purposes.[15] So far as can be seen, what may be subsumed under drug use for scientific purposes was not discussed among the doctrine.

6 As to eventual exceptions to this rule cf. *infra* 4.3.
7 S. K. Chatterjee, *Legal Aspects of International Drug Control*, pp. 356 et seq.
8 Albeit there has been substantial disagreement among States parties regarding the compatibility of certain forms of treatment of drug users with the limitation of drugs to medical purpose, it is not clear whether this discord results from differing interpretations of the term 'medical purposes' or incompatible conceptions regarding their treatment; cf. *infra* 6.3 for more details. See, however, a definition for international purposes, INCB Annual Report 2003, paras 233 et seq., which was never adopted by the CND.
9 Cf. statement of the Dutch delegate, OR I Single Convention, p. 123; statement of the delegate from Ghana, *ibid.*, p. 124.
10 OR I Single Convention, p. 124; cf. in this regard statement of the Canadian delegate, *ibid*; statement of the Israeli delegate, *ibid.*
11 OR I Single Convention, p. 124.
12 *Ibid.*
13 Commentary Single Convention, Art. 4 para. 1, MN 12;
14 The only exception was the statement by the Peruvian delegate, whereby 'in his country, the word "scientific" referred to theory and research', OR I Single Convention, p. 32.
15 Cf. Commentary Single Convention, Art. 4, MN 9 et seq.; Commentary 1971 Convention, Art. 5 paras 2 and 3, MN 1 et seq.

The will of the States parties in this regard needs to be respected. However, it needs to be resolved how drug use for medical and scientific purposes can be distinguished practically from drug use for other ends. Drawing a clear line between illicit and licit drug use is inherent to the task of the international drug control system establishing a global restriction on drugs, otherwise a State legalizing the sale of a drug could simply assert that this legalization was complying with medical purposes. This would counter the objective of building a coherent and universal drug control system that aims to limit drug use. An interpretation of the UN Drug Conventions that leaves the classification of drug use for medical purposes entirely to the disposal of the States parties would deprive international drug control of an objective normative core, and should therefore be discarded. This is backed up by the cardinal principle of treaty interpretation, of good faith (Art. 31 (1) VLCT). This principle commands in the first place to interpret any treaty term as 'intended to mean something, rather than nothing',[16] or, in the other words, an interpretation depriving a 'treaty of a great part of its value, is inadmissible'.[17]

The need to understand the limitation of drugs to medical and scientific purposes also follows from its important position as the objective of the international drug control system.

4.1.2 The limitation of drugs to medical and scientific purposes as the object and purpose of the international drug control system

The fundamental importance of the limitation of drugs to medical and scientific purposes for the entire international drug control system can be deduced simply from the UN Drug Conventions, as well as related soft law instruments.

Indeed, Art. 4 (c) Single Convention spells out the limitation of drugs to medical and scientific purposes as the 'general obligation' of the treaty.[18] The importance of the limitation of drugs to medical and scientific purposes as the central

16 Mark E. Villiger, 'Art. 31', *Commentary to the 1969 Vienna Convention on the Law of Treaties*, MN 6.

17 PCIJ, *Acquisition of Polish Nationality*, Advisory Opinion No. 7 of 15 September 1923, Series B, p. 17. Mark E. Villiger, 'Art. 31', *Commentary to the 1969 Vienna Convention on the Law of Treaties*, MN 12; this consideration is known as the 'principle of effective interpretation'; cf. also Richard Gardiner, *Treaty Interpretation*, p. 148; Oliver Dörr, 'Art. 31', in: Oliver Dörr and Kirsten Schmalenbach (eds), *Vienna Convention on the Law of Treaties: A Commentary*, MN 57; Luigi Crema, 'Disappearance and New Sightings of Restrictive Treaty Interpretation', *EJIL* Vol. 21 2010, pp. 681 (691 et seq.). The principle of effective treaty interpretation, which predates the VCLT, had already been characterized by Fitzmaurice as early as 1951, as a 'well known and valuable rule of treaty interpretation'; Gerald Fitzmaurice, 'The Law and Procedure of the International Court of Justice: Treaty Interpretation and other Treaty Points', *BYBIL* Vol. 28 1951, 1 (8). Cf. also as to this issue Hersch Lauterpacht, 'Restrictive Interpretation and the Rule of Effectiveness in the Interpretation of Treaties', *BYBIL* Vol. 29 1949, 48 (56 et seq.); cf. also Lord McNair, *The Law of Treaties*, pp. 383 et seq.

18 The central importance of Art. 4 (c) also derives from the drafting history of this provision. Initially it was foreseen to include the limitation of drugs to medical and scientific purposes into the Single Convention's Art. 30. The Danish delegate requested, however, that this provision should be placed in a 'prominent position' in the treaty as it constituted 'the heart of the Convention'; cf. OR II Single Convention, p. 80.

leitmotif for drug control, is further underlined by the concluding paragraph of the Single Convention's preamble, stipulating that earlier drug control treaties should be replaced with a coherent approach of limiting drugs to medical and scientific purposes.[19] The limitation of drugs to medical and scientific purposes as the central pillar of the Single Convention is also shared by the Commentary, prescribing it as the 'object of the international narcotics system'.[20] In sum, the conclusion that the limitation of drugs to medical and scientific purposes is the fundamental core and *raison d'être* of the Single Convention seems universally shared.[21]

The same result can be approved for the 1971 Convention. Although no 'general obligation' of limiting all psychotropic substances to medical and scientific use exists under the 1971 Convention, a general requirement of limiting the use of all substances to these ends results from the *chapeau* of Art. 5. Additionally, several statements clarify the objective of this treaty to limit psychotropic substances to medical and scientific purposes.[22]

The 1988 Convention does not reiterate the limitation of drugs to medical and scientific purposes. However, it is built around the same normative core as the two earlier drug conventions. This can be seen with regard to preambular para. 13 of the 1988 Convention, whereby the 1988 Convention was meant to 'reinforce and supplement' the measures contained in the Single Convention and the 1971 Convention.[23] The consideration to strengthen more

19 Preambular para. 8 reads: 'Desiring to conclude a generally acceptable international convention replacing existing treaties on narcotic drugs, limiting such drugs to medical and scientific use, and providing for continuous international cooperation and control for the achievement of such aims and objectives.' The central importance of the limitation of drugs to medical and scientific purposes also results from the Single Convention's operative provisions. It appears *inter alia* within the mandate of the INCB (Art. 4 (c) Single Convention), the administration of the estimate system through the INCB (Art. 12 (5) Single Convention) and the limitation of manufacture and import (Art. 21 (1) (a) Single Convention).

20 Commentary Single Convention, Art. 4, MN 9.

21 Cf. for a similar conclusion, cf. also in this regard, Daniel Heilmann, 'Narcotic Drugs and Psychotropic Substances', in: Rüdiger Wolfrum (ed.), *MPEPIL*, 2012, MN 15, referring to Art. 4 (c) as 'the central operational provision' of the Single Convention; Bernard Levroy, M. Cherif Bassiouini and Jean-François Thony, 'The International Drug Control System', in: M. Cherif Bassiouni (ed.), *International Criminal Law: Vol I, Sources, Subjects, and Contents*, 855 (872); Sven Pfeiffer, 'Rights of Indigenous Peoples and the International Drug Control Regime: The Case for Traditional Coca Leaf Chewing', *GoJIL* Vol. 5 2013, 287 (310); Cody T. Mason, 'Coca Leaves and Colorado: International Law and the Shifting Landscape of Drug Reform', *Md. J. Int'l L.* Vol. 29 2014, 238 (243); David Bewley-Taylor, Tom Blickman and Martin Jelsma, 'The Rise and Decline of Cannabis Prohibition: The History of Cannabis in the UN Drug Control System and Options for Reform', TNI, 2014, p. 8.

22 Cf. e.g. of the Australian delegate, OR II 1971 Convention, p. 87; statement Ghanaian delegate, *ibid.*, p. 89. Cf. in this regard Daniel Heilmann, 'Narcotic Drugs and Psychotropic Substances', in: Rüdiger Wolfrum (ed.), *MPEPIL*, 2012, MN 21; S. K. Chatterjee, *Legal Aspects of International Drug Control*, p. 456; D.W. Sproule and Paul St-Denis, 'The UN Drug Trafficking Convention: An Ambitious Step', *Can. Y. B. Int'l* Vol. 27 1989, 266.

23 Cf. also for this idea, Commentary 1988 Convention, Art. 25, MN 25.4.

firmly the approach to limit drugs to medical and scientific purposes is spelled out by preambular para. 12 of the 1988 Convention which '*[r]eaffirm[s] the guiding principles of existing treaties in the field of narcotic drugs and psychotropic substances and the system of control which they embody.*'"[24] The delegates of the 1988 Conference were well aware of the fact that the guiding principles would be the limitation of drugs to medical and scientific purposes. It was explicitly held that the 'objective' of the international drug control regime 'was to limit the use of narcotic drugs and psychotropic substances to medical and scientific purposes'.[25]

Additionally, an abundance of UNGA resolutions have spelled out the goal of eradicating illicit drug supply, demand and traffic.[26] This goal to resolve the world drug problem by eradicating or reducing significantly and measurably illicit drug production, traffic and demand for narcotic drugs and psychotropic substances is nothing but another formula for the limitation of drugs to medical and scientific purposes. This is true because the determination of any drug-related activity as illicit or licit will be determined by the Single Convention and the 1971 Convention. These Conventions assess all drug-related activities by their compliance with the limitation to medical and scientific purposes.[27] Thus, the limitation of drugs to medical and scientific purposes is the common objective of all three UN Drug Conventions, reinforced by subsequent UNGA resolutions on the world drug problem.[28] This in itself explains the need to understand the meaning of

24 Italics added.

25 OR I 1988 Convention, p. 60.

26 Cf. in this regard the goals spelled out by UNGASS 1990 and 1998 as well as the CND Action Plan passed subsequent to the high-level segment. UNGA, Plan of Action, 1990, UN Doc. A/Res-17/2, para. 1: 'We resolve to protect mankind from the scourge of drug abuse and illicit trafficking in narcotic drugs and psychotropic substances'; cf. for a similar consideration, UNGA, Political Declaration Annex, 1998, UN Doc. S-20/2, Annex, para. 1: 'Reaffirm our unwavering and commitment to overcoming the world drug problem though domestic and international strategies to reduce illicit supply of and the demand for drugs.' The first footnote of this very declaration defines 'world drug problem' as the '[t]he illicit cultivation, production, manufacture, sale, demand, trafficking and distribution of narcotic drugs and psychotropic substances, including amphetamine-type stimulants, the diversion of precursors and related criminal activities.' Cf. also CND, Plan of Action on International Cooperation towards an Integrated and Balanced Strategy to Counter the World Drug Problem, 2009, UN Doc. E/2009/28, 37; here, the CND affirmed the goal of tackling the world drug problem; *ibid*., preamble. The world drug problem was defined as: 'The illicit cultivation, production, manufacture, sale, demand, trafficking and distribution of narcotic drugs and psychotropic substances, including amphetamine-type stimulants, the diversion of precursors and related criminal activities.' The goal of achieving measurable results of reducing illicit drug demand and supply was formulated for 2018; *ibid*., para. 36.

27 Cf. as to the exceptions to this rule *infra* 4.3.

28 This result is also shared by scholarship; cf. Francisco E. Thoumi, 'The International Drug Control Regime's Straight Jacket: Are There Any Policy Options?', *Trends Organ. Crim.* Vol. 13 2010, 75 (77); for a similar view cf. P. von Wartburg, 'Drogenmissbrauch und Gesetzgeber, Methodik und Möglichkeit einer optimalen Kontrolle des Missbruachs von Drogen und Arzneimitteln', Experentia Supplementum Vol. 21 1974, p. 200; David Bewley-Taylor,

this norm. What is more, however, is that a deeper understanding of what the limitation of drugs to medical and scientific purposes means is a prerequisite for understanding the current tensions surrounding this system.

4.1.3 The limitation of drugs to medical and scientific purposes as the key to understanding drug control's current tensions

First of all, the harm reduction issue exemplifies the need to understand the meaning of the limitation of drugs to medical and scientific purposes. States, the INCB and civil society have for quite a while quarreled around the permissibility of such health related interventions – including *inter alia* providing drug users with clean syringes (needle exchange programmes) or rooms where they can consume drugs under supervision (drug consumption rooms) – under the UN Drug Conventions. This question will be treated in greater detail later in this book (*infra* 6.3.4). Suffice it to outline at this point that it is simply impossible to determine the permissibility of such measures under a legal regime based on the assumption of limiting drugs to medical and scientific purposes, without understanding *in concreto* what this assumption entails (see *infra* 4.2).

Establishing the meaning (see *infra* 4.2) and, perhaps more pertinently, the boundaries of the limitation of drugs to medical and scientific purposes will allow us to assess whether States can rely on exceptions to justify non-medical and non-scientific drug use on their territory. The question is particularly relevant to the legalization of cannabis (see *infra* 4.3). Can States rely on exceptions contained in the UN Drug Conventions to justify such policies or is there at least enough leeway to enlarge existing exceptions in this regard?

Moreover, Bolivia did test the possibility to enlarge existing exceptions to the limitation of drugs to medical and scientific purposes for the coca leaf (*infra* 4.4).[29] Having been unable to achieve a treaty amendment freeing the coca leaf from international control measures, Bolivia resorted to a creative step of denouncing the Single Convention and subsequently re-entering the Single

---

International Drug Control: Consensus Fractured, p. 3; Daniel Heilmann, 'The International Control of Illegal Drugs and the UN Treaty Regime: Preventing or Causing Human Rights Violations?', *Cardozo J. Int'l & Comp. L.* Vol. 19 2011, 237 (241; 247); Bernard Levroy, M. Cherif Bassiouni and Jean-François Thony, 'The International Drug Control System', in: M. Cherif Bassiouni (ed.), *International Criminal Law: Vol. I, Sources, Subjects, and Contents*, 2008, 855 (868); cf. for a similar approach Damon Barrett and Manfred Nowak, United Nations and Drug Policy: Towards a Human Rights-based Approach, in: Aristotle Constantinides and Niko Zaikos (eds), *Essays in Honour of Kalliopi Koufa, 2009*, 449, p. 7; cf. for a similar conclusion Neil Boister, *Penal Aspects of the UN Drug Conventions*, pp. 2 et seq.; *id.*, *An Introduction to Transnational Criminal Law*, pp. 50 et seq. As to the issue of whether international drug control, besides imposing the goal of limiting drugs to medical and scientific purposes, inscribes the goal of ensuring drugs for medical and scientific purposes, cf. *infra* 6.1.

29 Cf. *supra* Introduction.

Convention in order to bring its international obligations into line with its domestic policy on the issue.

The third question regarding the limitation of drugs to medical and scientific purposes concerns the relationship with international human rights law (*infra* 4.5). It tries to define how problematic the objective of universally confining drugs to medical and scientific purposes can be considered. This question is equally of practical relevance. In particular, with regard to traditional drug use by indigenous peoples, it is highly pertinent to ask whether a cultural right to drug use exists.

4.2 The meaning of the limitation of all drug-related activities to medical and scientific purposes

4.2.1 Three obligations, one rule

The absence of one single obligation, limiting both psychotropic substances as well as narcotic drugs to medical and scientific purposes, makes the task of giving a meaning to these terms complex. Such a single obligation is lacking because narcotic drugs and psychotropic substances are treated by two different treaties, the Single Convention and the 1971 Convention.

Three different provisions, Art. 4 (c) Single Convention, Art. 5 (2) 1971 Convention and Art. 7 (a) 1971 Convention, limit drugs to medical and scientific purposes. It will be shown that these provisions embody one coherent rule limiting all drug-related activities to medical and scientific purposes.

Article 4 (c) Single Convention – entitled 'General Obligation'– reads: 'The Parties shall take such administrative and legislative measures [...] subject to the provisions of this Convention, to limit exclusively to medical and scientific purposes the production, manufacture, export, import, distribution of, trade in, use and possession of drugs.'

The general obligation of Art. 4 (c) Single Convention applies to all narcotic drugs. Such a 'general obligation' is missing under the 1971 Convention. The 1971 Convention does not contain one single provision limiting all psychotropic substances to medical and scientific purposes. The treaty differentiates between substances classed into Schedules[30] II, III and IV, on the one hand, and those substances subjected to Schedule I, on the other hand. Whereas Schedules II, III and IV fall under Art. 5 (2) 1971 Convention, Schedule I is regulated by Art 5 (1) in conjunction with Art. 7 (a) of the same treaty (Art. 5 (1) 1971 Convention).

30 The Single Convention and the 1971 Convention class all substances covered into various schedules; see *infra* 5.1 for further details.

Article 5 (2) 1971 Convention stipulates: 'Each Party shall [...] limit by such measures as it considers appropriate the manufacture, export, import, distribution and stocks of, trade in, and use and possession of, substances in Schedules II, III and IV to medical and scientific purposes.'

Article 7 (a) 1971 Convention obligates that States parties

> [i]n respect of substances in Schedule I, (a) Prohibit all use except for scientific and very limited medical purposes by duly authorized persons, in medical or scientific establishments which are directly under the control of their Governments or specifically approved by them.

Despite their different wording, both provisions embody the same underlying rule of limiting all drug-related activities to medical and scientific purposes. This follows from reading Art. 5 1971 Convention as a whole. The *chapeau* of Art. 5 – entitled 'Limitation of Use to Medical and Scientific Purposes'– applies to all the schedules. It clarifies that the substances of all four schedules shall be coherently limited to medical and scientific purposes.

Additionally, the *travaux préparatoires* also show the clear will of States parties to subject psychotropic substances to the very same limitation to medical and scientific purposes as narcotic drugs. Thus, it was outlined at the opening of the 1971 Conference, where the president of the conference stated that the 1971 Convention should confine the application of psychotropic substances to medical and scientific uses.[31]

In this light, it is appropriate to interpret these three provisions as spelling out one single rule, which is to limit all drug-related activities to medical and scientific purposes.

4.2.2 Drug-related actions comprised

Elucidating the meaning of the limitation of drugs to medical and scientific purposes requires, as a first step, an understanding of the very scope of this limitation. In other words, it needs to be assessed which drug-related activities actually have to be limited to medical and scientific purposes.

The international drug control system limits the entire drug supply chain to medical and scientific needs. This covers the process from a drug's manufacture

31 United Nations Conference for the Adoption of a Protocol on Psychotropic Substances, Vienna, 11 January–19 February 1971, Official Records Volume II Summary Records of Plenary Meetings, Minutes of the meetings of the General Committee and the Committee on Control Measures, 1973, UN Doc. E/CONF.58/7/Add.1 [hereinafter referred to as OR II 1971 Convention] p. 2. Cf. also in this regard, statement by the Mexican delegate, OR II 1971 Convention, p. 10; statement by the Danish delegate, *ibid.*, p. 10; statement by the French delegate, *ibid.*, p. 13; Statement by the Iranian delegate, *ibid.*, pp. 14 et seq.; statement by the Argentinian delegate, *ibid.*, p. 15; statement by the Indian delegate, *ibid.*, p. 16.

to the domestic and international trade, and finally to the possession and use of a drug.[32] Albeit the entire drug supply chain is covered by the limitation of drugs to medical and scientific purposes, it will be the destined or actual use that is decisive in order to assess whether drug-related activities comply with the limitation to medical and scientific purposes.

There are no objective criteria that allow distinguishing supply-related activities with regard to psychoactive substances into (a) deviating from or (b) complying with the limitation to medical and scientific ends. It is only as far as the use of drugs is concerned that a distinction may be drawn between use that is carried out for medical and scientific purposes and use that is not carried out for such ends.[33]

This should not cause the impression that the international drug control system does not require States parties to adopt additional measures, ensuring that the drugs produced and trafficked will not feed the demand for non-medical drug use. However, these special measures – subjecting licit drug production and trade to licences and providing the INCB with the competence to review their effective implementation – have to be distinguished from the general requirement to reduce drugs to medical and scientific purposes.[34] As far as this general requirement is concerned, it is only the intended or actual use of a drug that allows drawing of the line between actions complying with or failing to comply with the limitation to medical and scientific purposes.

4.2.3 'Limit'

The Parties are required to 'limit' drugs to medical and scientific ends. This means that drugs should only be available, as far as required, for medical and scientific purposes and should only be used to satisfy those needs. It has been suggested that this obligation would involve an imperative to provide drugs for medical and scientific ends (positive obligation).[35] This interpretation has to be rejected, as to set a limitation does not necessarily mean that all activities below this threshold are guaranteed

32 Albeit the wording of Art. 7 (a) 1971 Convention only refers to use, it becomes clear when considering Art. 7 as a whole that this provision, similar to Art. 5 (2) 1971 Convention and Art. 4 (c) Single Convention, limits all drug-related activities to medical and scientific purposes.

33 Cf. in this regard Commentary Single Convention Art. 4, MN 11 et seq. The Commentary exclusively refers to 'use' when fleshing out the meaning of medical purposes; cf. also for an identical approach Commentary 1971 Convention, Art. 5 paras 2 and 3, MN 2 et seq.

34 The Single Convention and the 1971 Convention subject drugs destined for medical and scientific purposes to additional requirements of a controlled economy in order to ensure that the produced drugs will be used only for licit medical and scientific purposes; cf. as to this issue *infra* 6.1.

35 Cf. in this regard Husain Asra, Marty Skemp Brown and Martha A. Maurer, 'Do National Drug Control Laws Ensure the Availability of Opioids for Medical and Scientific Purposes?', *Bulletin of the World Health Organization* Vol. 92 2014, 108 (109); as to the issue of ensuring availability of drugs for medical and scientific purposes, cf. *infra* 6.1.

The obligation to limit drug-related activities to medical and scientific purposes entails the requirement to suppress non-medical and non-scientific drug manufacture, traffic and use. It is not clear from the wording of Art. 4 (c) Single Convention, Art. 5 (2) 1971 Convention and Art. 7 (a) 1971 Convention what means a State has to employ in order to ensure such a limitation.

Article 4 (c) Single Convention does not instruct that States are specifically obligated to penalize non-medical drug use. An obligation to penalize acts contravening the limitation of drugs to medical and scientific purposes is only contained in Art. 36 of the same treaty on 'Penal Provisions'. In other words, whereas the status of non-medical and non-scientific drug use as a domestic offence is not prescribed by Art. 4 (c), the requirement that non-medical and non-scientific drug use has to remain illegal is mandatory.[36] The same applies *mutatis mutandis* to psychotropic substances. States are obligated to prevent the manufacture, traffic and use of psychotropic substances by adopting a broad range of administrative measures. The specific obligation to penalize acts contravening the limitation of psychotropic substances to medical and scientific purposes is provided for by Art. 22 1971 Convention.

4.2.4 *Drug use for medical purposes*

4.2.4.1 *The ordinary (and very broad) meaning of 'drug use for medical purposes'*

According to the Oxford English Dictionary, 'medical' means 'relating to the science or practice of medicine',[37] which in turn is defined as '[t]he science or practice of the diagnosis, treatment, and prevention of disease.'[38] Therefore, medical drug use is carried out for the treatment and prevention of a disease. Additionally, the respective drug use has to be carried out for medical 'purposes'. Thus, drug use for medical purposes denotes drug use initiated in order to diagnose, prevent or treat a disease and objectively suited for these ends.

4.2.4.2 *A formal characterization of 'drug use for medical purposes'*

4.2.4.2.1 MEDICAL PRESCRIPTIONS ARE NOT CONSTITUTIVE FOR DRUG USE FOR MEDICAL PURPOSES

It has been argued that, in spite of the absence of a recognized definition of medical use, 'medical prescription is medical use'.[39] This would mean that the decisive criterion of medical drug use is whether the drug use is carried out in

36 Cf. for a similar view Krzysztof Krajewski, 'How Flexible are the United Nations Drug Conventions?', *IJDP* Vol. 10 1999, 329 (332).

37 Concise Oxford English Dictionary, 11th edn 2006, p. 887.

38 *Ibid.*

39 Cindy S. J. Fazey, The Commission on Narcotic Drugs and the United Nations International Drug Control Programme: Politics, Policies and Prospects for Change', *IJDP* Vol. 14 2003, 155 (161).

accordance with medical prescriptions. The wording of Art. 4 (c) Single Convention does not precondition medical drug use to the fulfilment of formal requirements in the form of prescriptions. The Single Convention only requires medical prescriptions when narcotic drugs in Schedules I and IV (Art. 30 (2) (b) (i); Art. 2 (2)– (4) Single Convention) are 'dispensed'. Conversely, narcotic drugs in Schedule II are not subjected to this requirement.[40] Thus, there is no general requirement of prescription for all narcotic drugs. This may be invoked against the conclusion that prescriptions are constitutive for medical drug use within the meaning of Art. 4 (c) Single Convention.[41] The requirement for medical prescription only concerns *ratione materiae* those narcotic drugs in Schedules I and IV Single Convention. All narcotic drugs can – at least theoretically from a purely legal perspective – be consumed for medical purposes. Article 4 (c) Single Convention, being a 'general obligation', applies to all narcotic drugs, including those covered by Schedule II. Hence, prescriptions cannot *e contrario* be understood as a general requirement for medical drug use. In other words, according to the conception of the Single Convention, medical prescription and drug use for medical purposes are separate issues.[42]

This result equally applies to the 1971 Convention, in accordance with the general conception outlined above that medical drug use under this treaty has the same meaning as under the Single Convention.[43] Furthermore, likewise to the Single Convention, the 1971 Convention equally does not make medical prescriptions mandatory for all psychotropic substances. Article 9 (1) 1971 Convention requires the States parties to subject dispensing psychotropic substances of Schedules II, III and IV to prescriptions. However, in accordance with Art. 9 (3) 1971 Convention, States may deviate from this requirement for those substances classed into Schedules III and IV under certain conditions. Thereby, prescriptions are only mandatory for those substances classed into Schedule II. Thus, under both treaties, medical drug use does not need to be conducted in accordance with medical prescriptions.[44] Neither the Single Convention nor the

40 Commentary Single Convention, Art. 30 para. 2 subpara. (b) clauses (i) and (ii), MN 5.

41 For a different opinion, at least with regard to medical cannabis, see INCB, 'The Therapeutic Use of Cannabis', para. 5 (available online at: www.incb.org/documents/News/Alerts/Alert_on_Control_of_Narcotic_Drugs_June_2017.pdf).

42 Cf. as to the differentiation between drug use for medical purposes and prescription, Commentary Single Convention, Art. 33, MN 4.

43 Cf. *supra* 4.2.1; Commentary 1971 Convention, Art. 5 paras 2 and 3, MN 2: 'It may be assumed that the phrase ["medical purposes"] has in the [1971] Convention the same meaning as in the Single Convention.'

44 A specific requirement in this regard is laid out by Art. 7 (a) 1971 Convention for drugs contained in Schedule I. It requires drug use to take place in the following context: 'by duly authorized persons, in medical or scientific establishments which are directly under the control of their Governments or specifically approved by them'; see as to this Commentary 1971 Convention, Art. 7, introductory para., paras (a) and (e). This requirement concerns those substances classed in Schedule I which according to Article 7 (a) are prohibited with the exception of scientific and very limited medical purposes.

1971 Convention requires medical drug use to be carried out in accordance with prescriptions.

4.2.4.2.2 'DRUG USE FOR MEDICAL PURPOSES' REQUIRES MEDICAL ASSISTANCE

Although drug use for medical purposes does not require a prescription, it may be questioned whether medical drug use is subjected to less restrictive requirements. Arguably, drug use for medical purposes requires a formal approval of a person carrying out medical functions. The wording 'medical purposes', does not forcibly lead to such a conclusion. It seems noteworthy in this regard that medical drug use under the 1953 Protocol required drug use under the authority of a person assuming medical functions. In Resolution XI of the 1953 Conference, quasi-medical drug use denotes 'the use of opium *without medical aid* for relief of pain other than that caused by addiction to opium or to other narcotic drugs'.[45]

Thus, arguably, under the 1953 Protocol the distinctive criterion between quasi-medical and medical opium use was whether opium use occurred with *medical aid*. The authentic French wording is even more explicit in this regard since it refers to '*assistance medical*'.[46] Accordingly, the 1953 Protocol defines medical use of opium as use of opium for pain relief that occurs with medical aid or assistance being the decisive criterion in order to distinguish medical from quasi medical opium use. The considerations of the 1953 Conference are not per se of relevance to the characterization of drug use under the current drug control system. Nevertheless, when taking a close look at the Single Convention and the 1971 Convention, those treaties reveal that drug control requires that drug use for medical purposes is to be controlled and administered to a certain extent. In other words, it is not at the disposition of the individual drug user to decide on the medical utility of the intended drug use. This underlying idea appears in Art. 33 Single Convention, whereas the parties are required to not permit the possession of drugs except under legal authority.[47] By the same token, Art. 5 (3) 1971 Convention recommends that parties do not permit the possession of psychotropic substances classed in Schedules II–IV except under legal authority.

This formal characterization of the term 'medical purposes', to denote drug use under the aid and authority of a person exercising medical functions also stems from effective interpretation of 'drug use for medical purposes'. This requires the establishment of a clear-cut criterion that differentiates medical from non-medical drug use. This criterion may only be found within the formal medical assistance.

45 Resolution XI, UNTS Vol. 456, p. 34.

46 Art. 16 1953 Protocol.

47 This provision had been included into the Single Convention 'because there would have been a lacuna in the control system without a provision of the kind'; OR I Single Convention, p. 210.

Thus, due to the open meaning of medical drug use, the main criterion for drug use for medical purposes is not *what* medical drug use actually involves but *who* gets to decide on what medical drug use constitutes in a concrete case. Drug use for medical purposes requires that the drug use occurs with the assistance of a person exercising medical functions. Furthermore, in order to prevent abuse of these medical functions, it is necessary to require that this assistance was given in accordance *de lege artis* medical practice

This medical assistance – although requiring some form of medical authority over the intended drug use – can be distinguished from medical prescriptions. Whereas a prescription is the formal – written or oral – explicit *a priori* approval of the intended drug use, medical assistance for drug use can take less formal means.

4.2.4.2.3 DRUG USE FOR MEDICAL PURPOSES DOES NOT REQUIRE ABSTINENCE BY INDIVIDUALS WHO ARE DEPENDENT ON DRUGS

The question arises as to whether drug use by individuals who are dependent on drugs can constitute drug use for medical purposes. This is doubtful in light of the negative context in which the word 'addiction' is used by the Single Convention. Preambular para. 3 condemns addiction in the most rigid manner. Thus, the parties recognized 'that addiction to narcotic drugs constitutes a serious evil for the individual and is fraught with social and economic danger to mankind'.

This terminology is taken up by a resolution adopted at the 1972 Conference without, however, clarifying the parties' definition of addiction.[48]

The question of whether these terms are the direct opposite of 'drug use for medical purposes' needs to be pursued. This would involve *in concreto* that the mitigation withdrawal symptoms could not be considered medical drug use, as in such a scenario of drug-dependent people using drugs. Such a conception, however, fails to recognize the pathological character of drug dependence as a mental disorder. In other words, drug dependence is a disease. Drugs have to be used in order to treat this disease. This is – although only very cautiously and ambiguously – recognized by the Commentary to the Single Convention, noting that 'a number of countries have permitted consumption by persons whose addiction proves to be incurable of the minimum quantities required to prevent painful withdrawal symptoms and to enable them to lead a normal life'.[49]

The Commentary to the 1971 Convention is clearer in this regard:

> In the view of the fact that it seems now to be rather generally accepted that the Single Convention's limitation of the use of drugs to medical and scientific purposes does not prevent the use of 'narcotic' drugs [...] for a medically justified maintenance of drug addiction, it must be assumed that [the 1971 Convention] does not prohibit the use of psychotropic substances

48 Cf. Resolution III, preambular para. 3, adopted by the United Nations Conference for the Adoption of a Single Convention on Narcotic Drugs, quoted in OR I 1972 Protocol, p. 129.

49 Commentary Single Convention, Art. 4, MN 11.

in Schedules II, III and IV for a medically justified maintenance of dependence on such substances.[50]

The highly cautious statements of the commentaries on this issue may be explained by the fact that during the time of the drafting of both treaties, abstinence for addicted drug users was still considered the best form of treatment. The idea can be seen with regard to Resolution II adopted at the 1961 Conference where it is 'declared' that '*one of the most effective methods of treatment for addiction is treatment in a hospital institution having a drug free atmosphere*'[51] This resolution, which in accordance with Art. 31 (2) (b) VCLT has to be taken into account when interpreting a treaty, shows that although the parties considered abstention to be the most effective method of treatment, it is not the case that the parties considered abstention to be the *exclusive* way in which drug dependence should be treated.

Thus, although abstinence of drug use by drug addicts was regarded as a desirable long-term goal, the parties to the Single Convention do not seem to have considered that abstinence of drug addicts was universally compulsory at all stages of addiction, most notably during the withdrawal symptoms.[52]

4.2.5 Drug use for scientific purposes

Article 4 (c) Single Convention, Art. 5 (2) 1971 Convention and Art. 7 (a) 1971 Convention limit drug use to 'scientific purposes'. Despite the fact that drug use for scientific purposes is equally mentioned with drug use for medical purposes, hardly anyone seems to have elaborated on the meaning of drug use for scientific purposes. Presumably this lack of attention is due to the fact that drug use for scientific purposes is carried out very infrequently when compared to drug use for medical purposes. This may explain why it is not deemed necessary to distinguish drug use for scientific purposes from drug abuse. Despite all this, a sound definition of drug use for scientific purposes can be found. The starting point is the wording of the term 'drug use for scientific purposes' (Art. 31 (1) VCLT).

4.2.5.1 The ordinary meaning of 'drug use for scientific purposes'

The meaning of the term 'scientific', according to the Oxford English Dictionary, is 'related to or based on science'.[53] Science in turn refers to '[t]he intellectual and practical activity encompassing the systematic study of the structure

50 Commentary 1971 Convention, Art. 5 paras 2 and 3, MN 2.

51 Resolution II adopted by the United Nations Conference for the Adoption of a Single Convention on Narcotic Drugs, Treatment of Drug Addicts, quoted in OR II Single Convention, p. 316, para. 1 (italics added).

52 Cf. in this regard statement by the US delegate on Resolution II: 'The institution concerned, would be a hospital in which the patient, after the completion of the withdrawal state, would be deprived of the further use of drugs.' OR I Single Convention, p. 196.

53 Concise Oxford English Dictionary, 11th edn 2006, p. 1287.

and behaviour of the physical and natural world through observation and experiment.'[54] Likewise to medicine, the term is variable with regard to its cultural and temporal context.[55] Furthermore, drug use has to be carried out for scientific purposes and thus has to be initiated from the motivation to obtain scientific results.[56]

4.2.5.2 Subsequent practice

A further clarification of the terminology was not achieved in the aftermath of the adoption of the UN Drug Conventions by subsequent practice of the States parties. The INCB – whose instruments do not form part of authentic treaty interpretation in accordance with Art. 31 (3) (b) VCLT – adopts a rather narrow definition of scientific drug use:

> The designation of the use of a drug for 'scientific purposes' is appropriate when it is used as a tool for investigating mechanisms of health or disease or when investigating the use of a product as a medicine. In patients, the investigation would be done as part of a clinical trial, which requires prior approval from the research ethics committee.[57]

In other words, the INCB asserts that scientific drug use only occurs when psychoactive substances are used in order to obtain insights on the medical utility of a substance involved.

This restrictive interpretation however seems to be at odds with the broad wording of scientific purposes. As has been shown, the wording 'scientific purposes' comprises all forms of drug use in accordance with a scientific methodology. It cannot be deduced from the treaties or otherwise that the parties were eager to confine scientific drug use to use for the science of medicine. To the contrary, as the distinction between medical and scientific purposes shows, the States parties considered both ends – scientific and medical – to be distinguishable from each other. As the *travaux préparatoires* show, the parties clearly separated scientific research from medical practice.[58] This result is also supported by the Commentary to the 1971 Convention, which clarifies that scientific purposes cover scientific research for medical 'and other purposes'.[59]

54 *Ibid.*

55 ICJ, Whaling in the Antarctic (*Australia v. Japan*) Memorial of Australia Vol. I, 9 May 2011, para. 4.4.7.

56 Thus, the expression 'purposes' has the same meaning in conjunction with medical as well as scientific; as to medical purposes cf. *supra* 4.2.4.1.

57 INCB Annual Report 2003, para. 236.

58 Cf., e.g. statement by the British delegate, OR I Single Convention, p. 4; statement by the Peruvian delegate, *ibid.*, p. 41; statement by the Swiss delegate, OR II 1971 Convention, p. 7; statement by the Iranian delegate, *ibid.*, p. 14.

59 Commentary 1971 Convention, Art. 7 paras (a) and (e), MN 2.

4.2.5.3 A formal characterization of 'drug use for scientific purposes'

In accordance with the approach given to 'drug use for medical purposes', it is held that scientific drug use may be primarily characterized by its occurrence under scientific authority. Similar to a clear delimitation of medical purposes, the principle of effective treaty interpretation requires a clear-cut definition of drug use for scientific purposes. This criterion must be formal in nature, i.e. depending on the personal qualification of the individual deciding on the scientific nature of the intended drug use. Thus, scientific drug use occurs under the authority of a person exercising scientific functions. This decision will have to be exercised *de lege artis* in accordance with well recognized scientific principles. The decision of whether the actual drug use occurs for scientific purposes, is not taken by the drug user himself. Thus, as has been outlined with regard to medical drug use, the idea of drug control inherently requires such a restrictive criterion for scientific drug use.

It may be concluded that drug use for scientific purposes denotes drug use carried out under the authority of individuals exercising scientific functions, in accordance with recognized scientific principles.

4.2.6 Excurse: The limitation of raw materials for narcotic drugs and psychotropic substances to medical and scientific purposes

It has been shown so far that the limitation of drugs reduces all substances covered across the entire drug supply chain to medical and scientific purposes, regardless of whether the substances are covered by the Single Convention or the 1971 Convention. The following will show that despite this finding, the scope of this limitation differs considerably as far as its application towards plant-based drugs are concerned.

Moreover, it is not always easy to determine from which stage within the drug supply chain the limitation of drugs to medical and scientific purposes applies, as the case of hoasca/ayahuasca shows.

4.2.6.1 Cultivation, production and manufacture of psychotropic substances

In contrast to the Single Convention (see *infra* 4.2.6.2), the 1971 Convention does not extend its scope of control to the plants necessary for obtaining psychotropic substances.[60] No provisions on cultivation are contained in the 1971 Convention. Additionally, the 1971 Convention, in contrast to the Single Con-

60 Cf. also in this regard Commentary 1971 Convention Art. 32, MN 12; in its 2010 Annual Report, the INCB urged states to enhance the control of those plants in order to prevent their abuse; cf. INCB Annual Report 2010, paras 328 et seq.; critical in this regard Kenneth Tupper and Beatriz Labate, 'Plants, Psychoactive Substances and the International Narcotics Control Board: The Control of Nature and the Nature of Control', *Human Rights and Drugs* Vol. 2 2012, 17 (28 et seq.).

vention, is silent on 'production'. Initially, it had been foreseen to extend the 'limitation to medical and scientific purposes' to the 'production' of psychotropic substances – which would have comprised 'the obtaining by planting, cultivation or harvesting of natural material which constitutes a psychotropic substance or from which such a substance may readily be obtained'.[61]

The decision to delete 'production' from the 1971 Convention was made in order to avoid difficulties caused by controlling the biologic origins of psychotropic substances. It was considered impossible to restrict the abundant number of psychoactive species – ranging from mushrooms, cacti and fish to plants grown for ornamental purposes – to medical and scientific purposes.[62] This line of argumentation was accepted by the conference and the production of psychotropic substances was omitted from the 1971 Convention.[63]

Thus, the plant-based materials that are subsequently used in order to obtain psychotropic substances are not restricted to medical and scientific purposes. This limitation only applies subsequent to the 'manufacture' of a psychotropic substance, i.e. once the substance is 'obtained' (Art. 1 (1i) 1971 Convention). Thus, once the psychotropic ingredient is separated from the rest of the plant-based material, the 1971 Convention applies.

This moment is not always easy to determine. This can be shown with regard to hoasca, a brew made from two plants that originate in the Amazon region, i.e. *Banisteriopsis caapi* (containing harmala alkaloids) and *Psychotria viridis* (containing dimethyltryptamine (DMT) a substance covered by Schedule I of the 1971 Convention).[64]

The INCB considers that hoasca does not fall under the 1971 Convention's scope because the plants from which the brew is made are not covered by this treaty.[65] The US Supreme Court, however, held in *Alberto R. Gonzales v. O Centro Espirita Beneficente Uniao Do Vegetal* that hoasca was indeed covered by the 1971 Convention.[66] Because the preparation of hoasca

61 Art. 1 (l) revised draft 1971 Convention, OR I 1971 Convention, p. 24.

62 Cf. statement of the Australian delegate, OR II 1971 Convention, p. 78.

63 Cf. statement of the French delegate, *ibid.*, p. 79.

64 Cf. INCB, List of Psychotropic Substances under International Control (available online at: www.incb.org/documents/Psychotropics/greenlist/Green_list_ENG_V17–06834.pdf). For a detailed account cf. e.g. Stefanie Küfner, Drew Rabe and Barbara Sonczyk, 'The Santo Daime Church: The Protection of Freedom of Religion Under International Law', Amsterdam International Law Clinic, 2007, pp. 4 et seq.

65 Cf. also for such a line of argumentation INCB Annual Report 2010, paras 284 et seq.; INCB Annual Report 2012, paras 328 et seq.; cf. for this opinion also Tupper and Labate, *supra* note 62, 17 (28 et seq.); unclear in this regard Beatriz Labate and Kevin Feeny, 'Ayahuasca and the Process of Regulation in Brazil and Internationally: Implications and Challenges', *IJDP* Vol. 23 2012, 154 (156).

66 546 U.S. 418 (2006); see for a similar assessment Arrondissements Rechtbank Te Amsterdam (District Court of Amsterdam) Parketnummer: 13/067455-99, Judgment of 21 May 2001 (available online at: http://uitspraken.rechtspraak.nl/inziendocument?id=ECLI:NL:RBAMS:2001:AB1739&keyword=13%2f067455-99); cf. for an account Stefanie Küfner, Drew Rabe and Barbara Sonczyk, 'The Santo Daime Church: The Protection of Freedom of Religion Under International Law', Amsterdam International Law Clinic, 2007, pp. 8 et seq.

was a solution or mixture containing DMT, the 1971 Convention applied, as this mixture was a preparation within the meaning of the 1971 Convention.[67] The Supreme Court suggests that because hoasca consists out of a plant-based brew that in turn contains DMT, the 1971 Convention applies. This automatism cannot be approved. Rather a distinction between plants containing psychotropic substances and psychotropic substances needs to be drawn.[68] As has been shown, plants containing psychotropic substances or parts thereof are deliberatively excluded from the scope of application of the 1971 Convention. The result would only be different once the psychotropic substance is 'obtained' through being separated from its plant of origin. This, according to the Commentary, requires some procedure – albeitI entirely simple – of manufacturing.[69] The process of producing a brew, however, in itself does not per se seem sufficient in this regard. In order to be a psychotropic substance in accordance with the 1971 Convention, the plant-based material – *in casu Psychotria viridis* – has to be separated from – DMT – while hoasca is prepared. This, however, is not the case. The definition of psychotropic substances of the 1971 Convention, leaves open the possibility for the States parties to subject such plant-based raw materials containing psychotropic substances to the 1971 Convention in the future.[70] This results from Art. 1 (e) 1971 Convention, defining psychotropic substance as 'any substance natural or synthetic, or any natural material in Schedules I, II, III and IV'.

4.2.6.2 Cultivation, production and manufacture of narcotic drugs

Narcotic drugs are of a plant-based or synthetic nature (Art. 1 (1) (j) Single Convention). Plant-based narcotic drugs are opium, coca leaves and cannabis. The limitation of drugs to medical and scientific purposes applies to these substances from the moment that they are produced, i.e. once separated from their plant of origin (Art. 4 (c) Single Convention; Art. 1 (1) Single Convention). Before this moment, the cultivation of narcotic plants, i.e. the cannabis plant, the opium poppy and the coca bush, is subjected to an entirely different regime laid out by Arts 22 et seq. Single Convention. Article 4 (c) Single Convention is not applicable to the cultivation of those plants. This clearly derives from out of the wording of the Single Convention. Article 1 (1) (j) Single Convention defines a 'drug' as a substance classed in Schedules I and II. Although Schedule I contains plant-based materials, the plants themselves are not contained within Schedules I and II. Additionally, Art. 4 (c), while referring to drug production and manufacture, omits drug cultivation.

Hence, the control of plant-based ingredients for drugs differs considerably between the Single Convention and the 1971 Convention. Whereas the former

67 546 U.S. — (2006), p. 17.

68 Commentary 1971 Convention, Art. 34, MN 5; 12, with further examples.

69 *Ibid.*, Art. 1 para. (e), MN 2.

70 *Ibid.*

defines such plant-based substances as the coca leaf expressively as narcotic drugs and controls the cultivation of the plants necessary for obtaining narcotic drugs, the latter treaty does not extend its scope of control to plants containing psychotropic substances.

4.2.7 Conclusion

The above has given a meaning to the limitation of drugs for medical and scientific purposes. As has been pointed out, leaving this issue open by admitting entire indeterminacy of these terms contradicts the *telos* of the UN Drug Conventions to establish a system of control that effectively confines and limits drug use. However, the will of the parties to adopt a wide understanding of drug use for medical and scientific purposes has to be taken into account equally. Resolving this dilemma has been attempted, by giving an effective meaning of these two terms, and respecting their ordinary wording of, and the intention of, the parties to leave open the possibility of differing medical approaches in various regions and States. Nevertheless, the task of giving a similarly wide and concise meaning of the limitation of drugs to medical and scientific purposes has proven feasible, and will be relied on for the remainder of this book.

4.3 Exceptions to the limitation of drugs to medical and scientific purposes within the international drug control system

In order to grasp the real impact of the limitation of drugs to medical and scientific purposes, it is necessary to go one step further than merely outlining the origins and meaning of this obligation. The true margin of manoeuvre for States parties with respect to the limitation of drugs to medical and scientific purposes can only be assessed once the eventual exceptions to this norm are clearly identified.

This question is particularly timely. States have recently begun to openly challenge the objective of the UN Drug Conventions to reduce drug use to medical and scientific purposes. For instance, a regulatory market for cannabis has been established in Uruguay and several jurisdictions within the United States.[71]

71 Cf. in general Bewley-Taylor, Blickman and Jelsma, *supra* note 21, pp. 52 et seq.; Bennett Wells and John Walsh, 'Marijuana Legalization is an Opportunity to Modernize International Drug Treaties', Center for Effective Public Management at Brookings, 2014. For more details on the legalization of cannabis in Colorado, cf. John Hudak, 'Colorado's Rollout of Legal Marijuana is Succeeding: A Report on the State's Implementation of Legalization', Center for Effective Public Management at Brookings, July 2014. For more information with regard to Washington cf. Phillip Wallach, 'Washington's Marijuana Legalization Grows Knowledge, Not Just Pot: A Report on the State's Strategy to Assess Reform', August 2014. Cf. also for a pertinent overview Robin Room, 'Legalizing a Market for Cannabis for Pleasure: Colorado, Washington, Uruguay and Beyond', *Addiction* Vol. 109 2014, 345. For later developments cf. INCB Annual Report 2016, para. 445; thus, voters in California, Maine, Massachusetts and Nevada approved the legalization of Cannabis for non-medical and non-scientific purposes.

Other States including Canada[72] are currently considering similar steps. These developments, of which exact outcome cannot be predicted at this date, need to be aligned with the overall imperative of the international drug control system to limit drugs to medical and scientific purposes. It needs to be examined whether the UN Drug Conventions provide for any flexibility to deviate from this limitation.

4.3.1 The very narrow exceptions to the limitation of drugs to medical and scientific purposes under the Single Convention and the 1971 Convention

Derived from the wording of Art. 4 (c) Single Convention – 'subject to the provisions of this Convention' – the limitation of drugs to medical and scientific purposes is not absolute.[73] There are two exceptions to the limitation of drugs to medical and scientific purposes.

First, there is a general exception to the limitation of drugs to medical and scientific purposes contained in Art. 2 (9) Single Convention. This provision was included to enable the use of drugs within industrial processes other than the pharmaceutical industry.[74] Apart from this general exception, which applies to all substances, there is one specific exception for the coca leaf. States retain the ability to allow for the use of coca leaves for the preparation of a flavouring agent that does not contain any alkaloids (Art. 27 (2) Single Convention).[75] This provision, which has been referred to as the 'Coca Cola joker', helped to secure the predominantly (if not exclusively) US interests of the Coca Cola Company to obtain the coca leaf for the purpose of producing this drink.[76]

Similarly, the 1971 Convention contains exceptions to the limitation of drugs to medical and scientific purposes. The parties are allowed to exempt substances

72 INCB Annual Report 2016, MN 223; cf. in this regard the announcement of Canada's new government to legalize cannabis, 'Canada's New Liberal Government Repeats Promise to Legalize Marijuana', *The Guardian*, 4 December 2015 (available online at: www.theguardian.com/world/2015/dec/04/canada-new-liberal-government-legalize-marijuana).

73 Cf. already in this regard Commentary Single Convention, Art. 4, MN 10.

74 Cf. Commentary Single Convention, Art. 2 para. 9, MN 1 et seq. with further references. The same rationale underlies Art. 28 (2) Single Convention which allows for the cultivation of the cannabis plant for industrial purposes. This, however, is no exception to the limitation of drugs to medical and scientific purposes for this limitation does not apply to cultivation in the first place; cf. *supra* 4.2.6.2.

75 Cf. for a similar view Commentary Single Convention, Art. 4, MN 10.

76 Cf. in this regard Paul Gootenberg, 'Secret Ingredients: The Politics of Coca in US–Peruvian Relations', 1915–65, *JLAS* Vol. 36 2004, 233 (260). Gootenberg, who has reviewed formerly classified material from the US Federal Bureau of Narcotics concludes that: 'Coca-Cola [...] was active in every major draft of the Single Convention', *ibid.* In spite of this evidence one could also label Art. 27 (1) Single Convention as the Lex 'Coca Cola'; cf. for a similar conclusion with regard to Art. 27, Francisco E. Thoumi, 'A Modest Proposal to Clarify the Status of Coca in the United Nations Conventions', *Crime, Law & Social Change* Vol. 42 2004, 297 (299).

classed in Schedules II–IV from the limitation of drugs to medical and scientific purposes in three types of constellations under Art. 4 of this treaty.

First, Art. 4 (b) 1971 Convention allows a State to use psychotropic substances in the pharmaceutical industry for the production of non-psychotropic substances. Second, in accordance with Art. 4 (a), a party may permit the carrying of small quantities of preparations by travellers. Third, Art. 4 (c) allows States to provide for psychotropic substances for the capture of animals. The provision was inserted into the 1971 Convention in order to allow States to use psychotropic substances to catch wild animals, as well as to anaesthetize livestock during the slaughter process for meat production.[77]

4.3.2 The 1988 Convention: Providing for further exceptions?

It has been argued repeatedly that Art. 14 (2) 1988 Convention would exempt traditional drug uses from the limitation of drugs to medical and scientific purposes.[78] The argument is rooted in an isolated reading of the second sentence of Art. 14 (2) which requires States to 'take due account of traditional licit uses' of plants containing narcotic drugs, including the coca bush.

This argument needs to be discarded in light of the first sentence of Art. 14 (2). It obligates States parties to eradicate plants containing narcotic drugs and it is only when such plants are eradicated that the imperative to take due account of licit uses comes into play. Additionally, the preceding paragraph to Art. 14 (2) spells out that the measures adopted under Art. 14 shall not be less stringent than under the previous drug conventions. It follows also out of the title of this provision – 'Measures to eradicate illicit cultivation of narcotic plants and to eliminate illicit demand for narcotic drugs and psychotropic substances' – that Art. 14 (2) was not meant to allow for traditional drug uses for other than medical or scientific purposes. Indeed, by referring to illicit cultivation of and illicit demand for drugs, the drafters of the 1988 Convention re-emphasized the link to the Single Convention and the 1971 Convention, which assess the licity of any drug-related activity by its compliance with the limitation of drugs to medical and scientific purposes. Rather, the term 'traditional licit uses' has to be understood as ensuring that measures against illicit crop cultivation do not run counter traditional uses that are in accordance with the limitation to medical and scientific purposes.[79]

In sum, the limitation of drugs to medical and scientific purposes is subjected to narrow caveats which concern the industrial use of drugs, coca use as a

77 OR II 1971 Convention, p. 46.

78 Cf. *supra* 3.1.3.3; cf. for the historical roots of this argument; cf. also for such a line of argumentation Luciana Boiteux, Luciana Peluzio Chernicharo and Camila Souza Alves, 'Human Rights and Drug Conventions: Searching for Humanitarian Reason in Drug Laws', in: Beatriz Caiuby Labate and Clancy Cavnar (eds), *Prohibition, Religious Freedom, and Human Rights: Regulating Traditional Drug Use*, 1 (15); cf. already for this argument Neil Boister, *Penal Aspects of the UN Drug Conventions*, p. 435.

79 Cf. also in this regard Commentary 1988 Convention, Art. 14 para. 1, MN 14.3 et seq.; *ibid.*, Art. 14 para. 2, MN 14.15 et seq.

flavouring agent and psychotropic substances for the capture of animals. There are no additional exceptions of the UN Drug Conventions from this norm.

4.3.3 Legal assessment of the creation of a regulatory market for cannabis

The creation of a regulatory market is not in compliance with the limitation of drugs to medical and scientific purposes. The customers use cannabis for recreational purposes. No one ensures that cannabis will be solely used for medical needs or scientific needs. There is no one to decide on whether the drug use carried out is medically required or needed because of scientific reasons. Nevertheless, the United States suggests that the creation of a legal market on their territories would be compatible with the UN Drug Conventions. The same position is advanced by Uruguay. Their legal arguments for the creation of such a market, therefore, have to be critically analysed.

The United States is currently advancing the position that a flexible interpretation of the treaties would allow for the creation of a regulatory market for cannabis on a State level.[80] President Obama held, 'The U.N. drug-control conventions allow sovereign nations the flexibility to develop and adapt the most appropriate policies and programs in keeping with their own national circumstances, while also achieving the conventions' aims.'[81]

The United States fails, however, to specify, where this flexibility should come from. It is arguing that it would comply with the UN Drug Conventions on a federal level.[82] It could not, however, enforce effectively its obligations under the UN Drug Conventions on a State level and was barred by constitutional law from ensuring that States effectively comply with these treaties.[83] In other words, its constitution would not enable enforcing the limitation of drugs to medical and scientific purposes on a State level.

This argument is not persuasive from a legal perspective. While there are indeed some provisions – most notably the obligation to penalize drug use – of the

80 Cf. for a good account of the US position, then Ambassador William R. Brownfield, Assistant Secretary of State for International Narcotics and Law Enforcement, Center for International and Strategic Studies, 31 March 2014 (see www.csis.org/events/focus-international-drug-policy-debate).

81 'Presidential Determination – Major Drug Transit or Major Illicit Drug Producing Countries for Fiscal Year 2016', 14 September 2015 (available online at: www.whitehouse.gov/the-press-office/2015/09/14/presidential-determination-major-drug-transit-or-major-illicit-drug).

82 Cf. in this regard US Department of Justice Office of the Deputy Attorney General, James M. Cole, Memorandum for all United States Attorneys of 29 August 2013 (available online at: www.justice.gov/iso/opa/resources/3052013829132756857467.pdf). The memorandum clarifies that cannabis remains illegal under the federal Controlled Substances Act. Federal attornies and law enforcement agencies will enforce this prohibition by adopting certain law enforcement priorities in order to protect minors and prevent diversion of cannabis to States where it remains illegal, etc. States and local governments that are authorizing the sale of cannabis are required to address the threats of this legalization for public safety and, most notably, have to ensure that the above-mentioned federal enforcement priorities are respected.

83 US position by Ambassador William R. Brownfield, Assistant Secretary of State for International Narcotics and Law Enforcement, Center for International and Strategic Studies, 31 March 2014 (available online at: www.youtube.com/watch?v=gtOLegzeEoQ).

UN Drug Conventions that are subject to a party's constitution, the limitation of drugs to medical and scientific purposes is not subjected to such loopholes. The well recognized principle of international law that a State cannot rely on its own constitution in order to deviate from its international obligations applies to the limitation of drugs to medical and scientific purposes (Art. 27 VCLT).[84] This limitation, albeit it does not involve the obligation for States to penalize non-medical and scientific drug use, means that States are required to prevent and terminate non-medical drug use.[85]

Establishing a regulatory market for cannabis – or any other narcotic drug or psychotropic substance – is incompatible with this requirement, even when this decision is taken on a State level. It is also well-known that federal States are liable for the actions of their federal entities on an international level.[86] The true rationale of the US argument, so it seems, is to create the impression to be still based on the current legal framework, while in reality deviating from its most fundamental premises.[87] This, however, cannot be taken into account legally.[88]

84 Cf. as to this, Annemie Schaus, 'Art. 27', in: Olivier Corten and Pierre Klein (eds), *The Vienna Convention on the Law of Treaties: A Commentary*, MN 1 et seq.; cf. already in this regard PCIJ, *Treatment of Polish Nationals and other Persons of Polish Origin or Speech in the Danzig Territory:* Advisory Opinion, 4 February 1932, Series A/B No. 44 p. 24:

> It should however be observed that, while on the one hand, according to generally accepted principles, a State cannot rely, against another State, on the provisions of the latter's Constitution, but only on international law and international obligations duly accepted, on the other hand and conversely, a State cannot adduce as against another State its own Constitution with a view to evading obligations incumbent upon it under international law or treaties in force.

85 Cf. *supra* 4.2.3.

86 Cf. in this regard, e.g. James Crawford, *State Responsibility: The General Part*, pp. 123 et seq.; cf. also ICJ, LaGrand Case (*Germany v. United States of America*) Request for the Indication of Provisional Measures, Order of 3 March 1999, para. 28:

> Whereas the international responsibility of a State is engaged by the action of the competent organs and authorities acting in that State, whatever they may be; [...] whereas the Governor of Arizona is under the obligation to act in conformity with the international undertakings of the United States.

Cf. for the same consideration *id.*, Request for Interpretation of the Judgment of 31 March 2004 in the case concerning Avena and other Mexican Nationals (*Mexico v. United States of America*) Request for the Indication of Provisional Measures, Order of 16 July 2008, para. 77.

87 Cf. for the same view, Rick Lines, Damon Barrett and Patrick Gallahue, 'Guest Post: Has the US Just Called for Unilateral Interpretation of Multilateral Obligations?', 18 December 2014 (available online at: http://opiniojuris.org/2014/12/18/guest-post-us-just-called-unilateral-interpretation-multilateral-obligations/); cf. also Damon Barrett, Martin Jelsma and David Bewley-Taylor, 'Fatal Attraction: Brownfield's Flexibility Doctrine and Global Drug Policy Reform', *Huffington Post*, 18 November 2014 (available online at: www.huffingtonpost.co.uk/damon-barett/drug-policy-reform_b_6158144.html?utm_hp_ref=tw).

88 Cf. also for the same result Wells and Walsh, *supra* note 72, pp. 14 et seq.; Rick Lines, Barrett and Gallahue, *supra* note 88.

The case of Uruguay is hardly more convincing. Uruguay argues that it would adopt an interpretation of the UN Drug Conventions that is in accordance with its human rights obligations and its constitution.[89] Uruguay fails to clarify, however, why these instruments would allow, let alone require, the creation of a regulatory market for cannabis. What is more, is that even when *arguendo*, these instruments would require for a legalization of cannabis in one form or another,[90] one cannot see how it follows therefrom that such a step was allowed under the Single Convention. Thus, the assessment of the INCB that the legalization of cannabis is not permissible under the current legal framework, is correct.[91]

4.4 Options to deviate from the limitation of drugs to medical and scientific purposes in the international drug control system

In spite of this narrow leeway for domestic policies derogating from the limitation of drugs to medical and scientific purposes, it seems viable to examine the options for States to deviate from this obligation by modifying their obligations. Thus, it is pertinent to examine whether the Single Convention or the 1971 Convention foresee procedures allowing States to deviate from the limitation of drugs to medical and scientific purposes by modifying their obligations under those treaties.[92] Two options can be discussed in this regard: first, the possibility of States to modify their own obligations under the Single Convention respectively the 1971 Convention by making reservations (4.4.1).[93] Second, the modification of the treaties for all States parties by treaty amendment (4.4.2).[94]

89 Cf. for the position of Uruguay, 'Presentacion de Uruguay ante la 4 de febero 2014' (available online at: www.mrree.gub.uy/frontend/page?1,embajada-eeuu,ampliacion-embajada,O,es,0,PAG;CONC;442;5;D;presentacion-de-uruguay-ante-la-jife;4;PAG).

90 Cf. as to this *infra* 4.5.

91 Cf. with regard to the United States, INCB Annual Report 2012, paras 80 et seq.; *id.* Annual Report 2014, paras 138 et seq.; cf. with regard to Uruguay *id.* Annual Report 2012, para. 257, *id.* Annual Report 2013, para. 429; *id.* Annual Report 2014, paras 144 et seq.; cf. more generally against the legalization of cannabis *id.* Annual Report 2013, paras 169 and 700; *id.* Annual Report 2016, para. 223; cf. for the same result that this policy is not legal under the UN Drug Conventions, Bewley-Taylor, Blickman and Jelsma, *supra* note 21, pp. 58 et seq.

92 Modifying the obligations under the 1988 Convention would seem irrelevant. The 1988 Convention does not extend the limitation of drugs to medical and scientific purposes to further substances and only foresees complementary measures in order to enforce this limitation as spelled out by the Single Convention and the 1971 Convention.

93 Art. 2 (1) (d) VCLT.

94 A treaty amendment can be distinguished from a reservation by its scope. An amendment modifies the treaty as a whole for all the parties or a number of parties *inter se*, whereas a reservation only pertains the reserving State, while leaving the rights and obligations of the other States parties unaffected (Art. 21 (2) VCLT).

4.4.1 Reservations: A viable option in order to deviate from the limitation of drugs to medical and scientific purposes?

A State aiming to allow for the use of controlled substance(s) for other than medical or scientific purposes could try to attain this goal by making a reservation that exempts one or more substances from the scope of the Single Convention and the 1971 Convention. It will be assessed how far such procedures of modification could be used, in order to create leeway for national drug policies that do not restrict certain psychoactive substances to medical and scientific purposes. This question had been discussed within the literature for a long time[95] and was recently put into practice by Bolivia for the coca leaf.[96]

The idea to deviate from the limitation of drugs to medical and scientific purposes may be rooted in an assessment contained in the Commentary on Art. 50 (3) Single Convention, suggesting that a State could allow for the non-medical and non-scientific use of a certain substance by making a reservation.[97] In reality, things are not as simple but the legality of reservations in general, and in particular under the both the Single Convention and the 1971 Convention, is of 'baffling complexity'.[98]

There are three different possibilities to make a reservation under the Single Convention. First, there are transitional reservations foreseen by Art. 49 Single Convention that allowed for the traditional use of certain substances within a transitional period. Second, there is a possibility to formulate permanent reservations under Art. 50 (2); these reservations are limited *ratione materiae* to seven provisions and cannot be used to deviate from the limitation of drugs to medical and scientific purposes.[99] Third, a State may formulate a permanent reservation on questions not regulated by Art. 49 or Art. 50 (2), by the virtue of Art. 50 (3). In contrast to the reservations contained within Art. 49 or Art. 50 (2), the entry into force of this reservation can be precluded by an objection of more than one third of the States parties.

95 Cf. for a very early proposal in this regard Mark A. Leinwand, 'The International Law of Treaties and United States Legalization of Marijuana', *Colum. J. Transnat'l L.* Vol. 10 1971, 413 (420 et seq.); cf. also for a more recent example Robin Room and Sarah Mackay, 'Roadmaps to Reforming the UN Drug Conventions', A Beckley Foundation Report, 2012, pp. 33 et seq. 54 et seq.; Wells and Walsh, *supra* note 72, pp. 21 et seq.). Cf. also with regard to a positive assessment of the Bolivian 'inside out', Mason, *supra* note 21, 238 (251 et seq.); for a more differentiated view cf. Pfeiffer, *supra* note 21, 287 (299 et seq., especially 306); cf. also TNI press release, www.tni.org/pressrelease/bolivia-wins-rightful-victory-coca-leaf.

96 Pien Metaal, 'Coca in Debate: The Contradiction and Conflict between the UN Drug Conventions and the Real World', in: Beatriz Caiuby Labate and Clancy Cavnar (eds), *Prohibition, Religious Freedom, and Human Rights: Regulating Traditional Drug Use*, 25 (34 et seq.).

97 Commentary Single Convention, Art. 50, MN 3.

98 Cf. as to this assessment under general international law, Sir Hersch Lauterpacht quoted, in D. R. Anderson, Reservations to Multilateral Conventions: A Re-examination, *ICLQ* Vol. 13 1964, 450.

99 Art. 50 (2) mentions provisions on the settlement of disputes – including an optional clause of compulsory jurisdiction for the ICJ (Art. 48) – on estimates (Art. 12), statistics (Art. 13), measures of the INCB to ensure the execution of this convention (Art. 14) and the control of persons engaged in the export of drugs (Art. 31 (3) (b)).

The three-layered system of reservations contained within the Single Convention is also incorporated within the 1971 Convention. First, Art. 32 (2) 1971 Convention allows a State to make reservations with regard to seven provisions which are not related to the limitation of psychotropic substances to medical and scientific purposes.[100] Second, Art. 32 (4) 1971 Convention allows for reservations on the traditional use of plants containing psychotropic substances. Third, Art. 32 (3) 1971 Convention allows for reservations 'other than those made under paragraphs two and four' of Art. 32, provided that they are not objected to by more than one third of the States parties.

It is against this background that the possibility for States to deviate from the limitation of drugs to medical and scientific purposes with regard to particular substances covered by the international drug control system by the means of reservations is evaluated. In a first step, the possibility to deviate from this norm by relying on the provisions on reservations 'specifically related to traditional drug use', as spelled out by Art. 49 Single Convention and Art. 32 (4) 1971 Convention will be discussed (4.4.1.1). In a second step, the possibility to allow for non-medical or non-scientific drug use by invoking the general provisions on reservations will be examined (4.4.1.2). Finally, it will be outlined whether a State already bound by the Single Convention or the 1971 Convention is legally allowed to denounce one of these treaties in order to re-accede with a reservation exempting a substance from drug control's control regime ('inside out') (4.4.1.3).

4.4.1.1 Specific reservations allowing for traditional drug use for other than medical or scientific purposes

The Single Convention and the 1971 Convention contain(ed) options for States to allow for the use of drugs for other than medical and scientific purposes in areas where this use has been traditional. However, whereas this possibility under Art. 49 Single Convention is no longer prevalent, as its applicability *ratione temporis* has expired, Art. 32 (4) 1971 Convention allows for the traditional use of psychotropic substances for an indeterminate period of time.

In accordance with Art. 49, a party was vested with the possibility to allow drug use for other than medical or non-scientific purposes for a transitional period. This possibility concerned '*[t]he quasi-medical use of opium, [o]pium smoking, [c]oca leaf chewing, [t]he use of cannabis, cannabis resin, extracts and tinctures of cannabis for non-medical purposes*' (Art. 49 (1) Single Convention). [101] The possibility was limited to '*the extent that they were traditional in the territories in respect of which the reservation [was] made, and were there permitted on 1 January 1961*' (Art. 49 (2) (a) Single Convention).[102]

100 Those reservations concern the settlement of disputes (Art. 31) – including an optional clause of compulsory jurisdiction of the ICJ, the application of the 1971 Convention to non-metropolitan territories (Art. 27) and the measures of the INCB to ensure the execution of this convention (Art. 19).

101 Italics added.

102 Italics added.

Despite its unclear wording, Art. 49 pertains to traditional drug-related activities not carried out for medical or scientific purposes. Article 49 (1) has to be considered as *lex specialis* to Art. 4 (c). The former provision – serving as a temporal exception to the limitation of drugs to medical and scientific purposes – would be meaningless if the limitation to medical and scientific purposes applied to the drug-related acts mentioned therein.[103]

Article 49 (2) lays out the limited period of time for which the practices stipulated within Art. 49 (1) could be authorized. The transitional period after which the non-medical and non-scientific drug use should vanish varied: Coca leaf chewing and non-medical cannabis use had to be abolished within a 25-year period after the Single Convention's entry into force (Art. 49 (2) (e) and (f) Single Convention), whereas the quasi-medical use of opium should be eradicated 15 years after this date (Art. 49 (2) d Single Convention). The Single Convention entered into force on 13 December 1964, thus, the temporal reservation for quasi-medical opium expired on 12 December 1979 and for coca leaf chewing and cannabis use on 12 December 1989.[104] No fix date of termination was foreseen for opium smoking. However, the parties considered that opium smoking would eventually be terminated over time, as opium smoking should only be permitted to those persons, which had been registered by 1 January 1964 (Art. 49 (2) (c) Single Convention).

It seems notable – especially against the background of today's controversies concerning the coca leaf – that the practical relevance of those temporal reservations was little. Not all States where coca, opium and cannabis had been used traditionally, made reservations and many States that had done so withdrew these reservations before the transitional period expired.[105] Given the rather unfavourable light in which traditional drug use was perceived during this time, this may not come as a surprise.

In contrast to the Single Convention, the 1971 Convention is less rigid as far as the traditional use of hallucinogens is concerned. Article 32 (4) 1971 Convention reads:

> 4. A State on whose territory there are plants growing wild which contain psychotropic substances from among those in Schedule I and which are traditionally used by certain small, clearly determined groups in magical or religious rites, may, at the time of signature, ratification or accession, make

103 Cf. also Commentary Single Convention, Art. 4, MN 10; cf. also for the particular case of the Coca leaf, Pfeiffer, *supra* note 21, 287 (311).

104 INCB Annual Report 1989, para. 40.

105 Neither Peru nor Bolivia and Colombia made a reservation allowing for traditional coca use; INCB Annual Report 1989, para. 41. Peru initially had made a reservation – cf. UNTS Vol. 576, 376 – but eventually decided to withdraw it; *ibid.*, p. 414. It was only Argentina that allowed coca chewing for a transitional period; cf. Argentinian reservation of 31 July 1961, UNTS Vol. 576, p. 353. Myanmar had permitted opium smoking and quasi-medical opium use, furthermore, India, Bangladesh, Nepal and Pakistan had inserted provisional reservations allowing for opium and cannabis use; INCB Annual Report 1989, para. 41.

> reservations concerning these plants, in respect of the provisions of article 7, except for the provisions relating to international trade.

Thus, under the 1971 Convention, a State is not required to limit psychoactive plants to medical and scientific purposes. Article 32 (4) was inserted in order to preserve this status quo, in spite of possible modifications of the scope of applicability of the 1971 Convention.[106] A reservation under Art. 32 (4) was made by the United States,[107] Mexico[108] and Peru.[109] Article 32 (4) 1971 Convention differs from the regulation of traditional drug use under Art. 49 Single Convention. Whereas the latter only applies for a transitional period of time and thus reflects the logic that traditional drug use can and should be eventually eradicated, Art. 32 (4) 1971 Convention, in contrast, allows States to create an exception from the limitation of drugs to medical and scientific purposes, which is valid for an indeterminate period of time. The provision is so far deprived of any practical impact. As has been shown above, the limitation of drugs to

106 As to the modification *ratione materiae* cf. *infra* 5.3; Commentary 1971 Convention, Art. 32, MN 13.

107 Cf. Reservation of the United States made upon ratification of 30 April 1980, Depositary Notification of the Secretary General of 30 April 1980, C.N.118.1980.TREATIES-4 (available online at: https://treaties.un.org/doc/Publication/CN/1980/CN.118.1980-Eng.pdf):

> That in accord with paragraph 4 of Article 32 of the Convention, peyote harvested and distributed for use by the Native American Church in its religious rites is excepted from the provisions of Article 7 of the Convention on Psychotropic Substances.

108 Cf. Reservation of Mexico made upon accession, UNTS Vol. 1019, p. 352:

> The Government of Mexico, in acceding to the Convention on Psychotropic Substances adopted on 21 February 1971, makes, pursuant to the provisions of article 32, paragraph 4, of the Convention, an express reservation with regard to the application of the said international instrument, since there still exist in its territory certain indigenous ethnic groups which, in magical or religious rites, traditionally make use of wild plants which contain psychotropic substances from among those in Schedule I.

109 Cf. in this regard Communication of Peru of concerning the Reservation to Article 7 Made upon Accession, 31 December 1981, Depositary Notification of the Secretary General, C.N.388.1981.TREATIES-9 (available online at: https://treaties.un.org/doc/Publication/CN/1981/CN.388.1981-Eng.pdf):

> The reservation referred to was motivated [sic.] by the following two wild plant species: Ayahuasca, a liana which grows in the Amazon region and which contains the active element N, N-dimethyltryptamine, and a columnar cactus known as San Pedro which grows in the desert coastal regions and in the Andean region and contains mescaline. Ayahuasca is used by certain Amazon ethnic groups in magical and religious rites and rites of initiation into adulthood; San Pedro is used in magical rites by indigenous medicine men or shamans. Because of their psychotropic content, both plant species are included in the reservation option made possible by article 32, paragraph 4, of the Convention.

The initial instrument of ratification to which the communication relates is Accession by Peru to the 1971 Convention of 25 February 1980, Depositary Notification of the Secretary General, C.N.N.44.1980.TREATIES-1 (available online at: https://treaties.un.org/doc/Publication/CN/1980/CN.44.1980-Eng.pdf).

medical and scientific purposes under the 1971 Convention does not extend to plants containing psychotropic substances.[110]

4.4.1.2 *Admissibility of 'general reservations' deviating from the limitation of drugs to medical and scientific purposes*

Assessing the possibility to rely on Art. 50 (3) Single Convention and Art. 32 (3) 1971 Convention for making reservations allowing for the use of narcotic drugs, respectively psychotropic substances, for other than medical or scientific purposes, requires, in the first place, determining whether those provisions apply *ratione materiae* to reservations deviating from the medical and scientific purposes constraint.

4.4.1.2.1 APPLICATION OF 'GENERAL RESERVATIONS' TO THE MEDICAL AND SCIENTIFIC PURPOSES CONSTRAINT

Article 50 (3) Single Convention applies to 'reservations other than those made in accordance with paragraph 2 of this article or Art. 49'. It has been argued by the Russian Federation and Portugal that Art. 50 (3) would not apply *ratione materiae* to those acts, which according to Art. 49 Single Convention had to be abrogated within a transitional period. Accordingly, Art. 49 would be the sole and only provision of the Single Convention, allowing 'temporarily' for non-medical and non-scientific drug use and precluded as *lex specialis* the application of Art. 50 (3) to non-medical and non-scientific use of the coca leaf and opium.[111] According to this line of argumentation, those acts contained within Art. 49 could not be subjected to a reservation of Art. 50 (3).

The wording of Art. 50 (3) Single Convention does not settle this question. It is unclear whether by referring to 'reservations other than those made' under Art. 49, the parties meant to express that reservations allowing for non-medical drug use could exclusively be made for a transitional period of time in accordance with Art. 49 and, therefore, be excluded from Art. 50 (3). The parties, when drafting the provisions of the Single Convention on reservations, were eager to treat the question of 'permanent' reservations contained within Art. 50 distinctively from 'transitional' reservations contained in Art. 49. Several delegates argued against the initial conception of the Single Convention to have

110 Cf. *supra* 4.2.6.1.

111 Russian Federation: Objection to the Reservation contained in the Communication by the Plurinational State of Bolivia, Depositary Notification of the Secretary General, C.N.88.2013. TREATIES-VI.18, 18 January 2013 (available online at: http://treaties.un.org/doc/Publication/CN/2013/CN.88.2013-Eng.pdf). Cf. also for a similar consideration Portugal, Objection to the Reservation contained in the Communication by the Plurinational State of Bolivia, Depositary Notification, C.N.93.2013.TREATIES-VI.18 of 16 January 2013 (available online at: http://treaties.un.org/doc/Publication/CN/2013/CN.93.2013-Eng.pdf).

only one single provision on reservations[112] and favoured two distinct and independent provisions on transitional reservations and permanent reservations.[113] In the view of the parties, reservations under Art. 49 should be subjected to an entirely distinctive legal regime from Art. 50 (3). Much speaks in favour of the conclusion that the scope of application of Art. 50 (2) and Art. 49 overlap. Had the parties considered that Art. 49 would regulate exclusively all reservations that allow for drug use for other than medical and scientific purposes, one would assume that they would have made this more explicit.

The same result applies to the relationship between paras 2 and 4 of Art. 32 1971 Convention. Article 32 (3) 1971 Convention – by allowing for reservations 'other than those made under' Art. 32 (2) and (4) – does not involve that reservations allowing for traditional drug use can exclusively made under Art. 32 (4). This also derives from of the subsequent practice of these provisions by the States parties. When acceding to the 1971 Convention, Canada exempted the traditional use of the psychedelic peyote cactus from the limitation to medical and scientific purposes.[114] Rather than relying on Art. 32 (4) 1971 Convention, Canada invoked Art. 32 (3). This move did not see any objection.

Therefore, under the Single Convention as well as the 1971 Convention the general provision of reservations apply to reservations deviating from the medical and scientific purposes constraint. This in itself does not mean that such reservations are allowed by those treaties. Serious doubts of the legality of such reservations are raised by the fact that they are incompatible with the overarching backbone of both treaties to limit drugs to medical and scientific purposes.

4.4.1.2.2 A RESERVATION ALLOWING FOR NON-MEDICAL OR NON-SCIENTIFIC DRUG USE CONTRADICTS THE OBJECT AND PURPOSE OF THE SINGLE CONVENTION OR THE 1971 CONVENTION

It has been shown above that the objective of the entire international drug control system is to limit drugs to medical and scientific purposes. It has been

112 Art. 56 Third Draft of the Single Convention.

113 Cf. statement by the Soviet delegate (OR I Single Convention, p. 178):

> Legally the [transitional] reservations contained in paragraph 2 to 6 [of Art. 50 of the Third draft] were not true reservations. They were provisions which would cease to apply after a certain time. They should therefore be placed in a separate article, […].

Cf. also statement by the Canadian delegate: '[who] agreed with the USSR representative that several provisions of article 56 [Third Draft Single Convention] were transitional. He was quite willing to agree that they should be separated from the reservations proper."; *ibid.*, p. 179. Cf. also similar statement by the Indian delegate; *ibid.*, p. 180.

114 Accession by Canada of 9 September 1987, Depositary Notification of the Secretary General, C.N.191.1987.TREATIES-2 (available online at: https://treaties.un.org/doc/Publication/CN/1987/CN.191.1987-Eng.pdf). It is remarkable that Canada relied on para. 3 of Art. 32 to this end and not on parag. 4, though that would have been possible.

argued conversely for the case of cannabis that exempting one single substance from the Single Convention's scope of control would have a rather marginal impact and leave the integrity of this treaty unaffected, which today covers more than 100 substances.[115] This idea, however, is based on a misconception of the Single Convention's control regime. This treaty aims to reduce all the substances covered universally to medical and scientific purposes. The reaction of States with regard to Bolivia's re-accession of the Single Convention with a reservation to the coca leaf is particularly indicative.[116] Numerous objections of various State parties to the Single Convention were based on the assumption that the Bolivian reservation would violate the Single Convention's object and purpose.[117]

It has to be considered in this regard that the parties made specific provisions on how the scope of application of the Single Convention can be modified, which requires concerted action by the WHO and CND as well as the ECOSOC.[118] It is not foreseen that States parties may unilaterally single out the narcotic drugs to which they deem that the limitation of drugs to medical and scientific purposes should be applicable. To suggest otherwise would mean to argue in favour of a Single Convention à la carte, where each State could unilaterally decide on the applicability of the Single Convention to individual substances. This contradicts the idea of a universal system of control limiting all substances covered to medical and scientific purposes. Thus, a reservation allowing for the non-medical and non-scientific use of a narcotic drug – and be it only a single one – would contradict the Single Convention's object and purpose. The same result applies to the 1971 Convention. The treaty is based on the premise to limit all psychotropic substances to medical and scientific purposes. It

115 Leinwand, *supra* note 96, 413 (429).

116 Cf. *supra* 1.1.

117 Cf. e.g. objection of Japan to the Reservation of the Plurinational State of Bolivia, 10 January 2013, Depositary Notification of the Secretary General, C.N.84.2013.TREATIES-VI.18 (available online at: http://treaties.un.org/doc/Publication/CN/2013/CN.84.2013-Eng.pdf); cf. also objection of Ireland to the Reservation of the Plurinational State of Bolivia of 18 January 2013, Depositary Notification of the Secretary General, C.N.101.2013.TREATIES-VI.18 (available online at: http://treaties.un.org/doc/Publication/CN/2013/CN.101.2013-Eng.pdf); cf. also earlier negative responses to Bolivia's proposal to amend the Single Convention so as to exempt the coca leaf from the international drug control system in accordance with Art. 47 (1) (b) of the Single Convention; United States, note verbale, 19 January 2011, Depositary Notification of the Secretary General, C.N.15.2011.TREATIES-3 (available online at: http://treaties.un.org/doc/publication/CN/2011/CN.15.2011-Eng.pdf); Canada, note verbale, 26 January 2011, Depositary Notification of the Secretary General, C.N.33.2011.TREATIES-6 (available online at: http://treaties.un.org/doc/publication/CN/2011/CN.33.2011-Eng.pdf); Italy, note verbale, 28 January 2011 Depositary Notification of the Secretary General, C.N.38.2011.TREATIES-11 (available online at: http://treaties.un.org/doc/publication/CN/2011/CN.38.2011-Eng.pdf); as to the Bolivian inside out cf. *supra* 1.1.

118 As to the modification of the Single Convention's scope of control, cf. *infra* 5.3.

also foresees specific procedures of modification of the substances covered (Art. 2 1971 Convention).

The key question here, however, is not whether a reservation permitting for the non-medical and non-scientific drug use of a narcotic drug is incompatible with the object and purpose of these treaties, but whether under the regime of reservations as erected by these two conventions the prohibition or reservations that do not comply with a treaty's object and purpose apply in the first place.

4.4.1.2.3 APPLICABILITY OF THE OBJECT AND PURPOSE CRITERION FOR RESERVATIONS UNDER THE SINGLE CONVENTION OR THE 1971 CONVENTION

While today the rule that a reservation has to comply with a treaty's object and purpose is accepted under positive international law,[119] the Single Convention was adopted during a time when the law governing reservations was in midst of a fundamental paradigm shift and this rule was not established as *lex lata*.[120] In 1951, the International Court of Justice (ICJ) had adopted by a narrow seven to five margin its Advisory Opinion on the *Reservations to the Convention on Genocide*, and replaced the old unanimity rule – subjecting the entry into force of a reservation to the tacit approval of 'all' the States parties – by a more flexible approach.[121] This flexible approach requires that a valid reservation has to comply with a treaty's object and purpose.[122] Article 50 (3) Single Convention, by subjecting the entry into force of a reservation to the tacit approval of two thirds of the States parties, stands in between this new flexible approach and the old unanimity rule.

The *travaux préparatoires* do not provide for a clear-cut answer whether Art. 50 (3) requires a reservation to be compatible with the Single Convention's object and purpose. Some parties thought the object and purpose of a treaty should have a role to play within the Single's Convention's reservations regime. The Turkish delegate held that reservations '*should be admissible only if not contrary to the purposes of the Convention*'.[123] This view was also shared by the

119 ILC, Guide to Practice on Reservations to Treaties with Commentaries, 2011, UN Doc. A/66/10 Add. 1, Guideline 3.1.1 (c).

120 Cf. as to this problem Lord McNair (writing in 1961): 'If it is asked whether the criterion of compatibility [with the treaty's object and purpose] now is part of international law, the answer is difficult'; Lord McNair, *The Law of Treaties*, p. 168.

121 ICJ, *Reservations to the Convention on the Prevention and Punishment of the Crime of Genocide*, Advisory Opinion of 28 May 1951.

122 *Ibid.*, pp. 18 et seq.; cf. for a comprehensive account Alain Pellet, 'Art. 19', in: Olivier Corten and Pierre Klein (eds), *The Vienna Convention on the Law of Treaties: A Commentary*, MN 3 et seq. with further references.

123 OR I Single Convention, p. 178 (italics added).

Indian,[124] Soviet[125] and Hungarian delegations.[126] Others were of a different view: the Brazilian delegate, considered the two-thirds majority rule, as later encapsulated in Art. 50 (3), to be a 'satisfactory compromise' given that 'the criterion of the compatibility of a reservation with the object and purpose of a multilateral convention [...] was not suitable for application to multilateral conventions'.[127]

What is more is that that the *telos* of Art. 50 (3), i.e. subjecting the existence of a reservation to the will of the parties, means to introduce a subjective criterion for the validity of reservations. This subjective assessment of a reservation's validity clearly deviates from the idea of the object and purpose as announced by Art. 19 (c) VCLT. The object and purpose criterion aims to prevent multilateral treaties from fragmentizing into multiple but distinct bilateral contractual obligations. In contrast, the Single Convention allows the majority of the parties to decide themselves on reservations.

The fact that the parties to the Single Convention adopted a reservation regime which is different from the one contained within the VCLT also results out of the *travaux préparatoires* to the 1971 Convention. The Swiss delegation opposed a Turkish proposal incorporating a similar provision to Art. 50 (3) Single Convention into the 1971 Convention on the ground that the VCLT could serve as a guide.[128] The Turkish delegate responded that the Single Convention 'should inspire much more confidence' than the VCLT.[129]

This shows that the parties considered the Single Convention's provisions on reservation to deviate from the premises of the general regime of reservations as laid out by the VCLT. Thus, the prohibition to deviate from the treaty's object and purpose as encapsulated by Art. 19 (c) VCLT does not apply to Art. 50 (3) Single Convention. This line of argumentation may be applied *mutatis mutandis* to Art. 32 (3) 1971 Convention. The above-mentioned statements show the general will of applying the same regime as reservations as under the Single Convention. Hence, Art. 50 (3) Single Convention as well as Art. 32 (3) 1971 Convention impose the sole condition that a reservation has to fulfil, i.e. that it is not objected to by more than one third of the States parties irrespectively whether the reservation complies with the object and

124 *Ibid.*, p. 180.

125 *Ibid.*, p. 181:

> It was of course true that the reservations in question should be compatible with the object and purpose of the Convention; that was an accepted rule in international law and there was no need to reaffirm it in the Convention. Such reservations could deal only with certain specific points.

126 Cf. statement of Hungary, OR I Single Convention, p. 181, suggesting that the advisory opinion was 'categorical' as to the question that reservations could only be made when being in accordance with a treaty's object and purpose.

127 *Ibid.*, p. 182.

128 *Ibid.*, p. 108.

129 *Ibid.*

purpose of those treaties, i.e. the limitation of all substances to medical and scientific purposes.

This conclusion is based on a purely material assessment of reservations deviating from the limitation of drugs to medical and scientific purposes. The material admissibility of reservations deviating from the limitation of drugs to medical and purposes under the Single Convention and the 1971 Convention does not mean that all States are effectively allowed by international law to make such a reservation. The simple fact has to be borne in mind that a reservation is in general made when ratifying, signing or acceding to a treaty (Art. 2 (d) VCLT). However, 186 States are today bound to the provisions of the Single Convention and 183 States are parties to the 1971 Convention. If a State party intends to submit a reservation on a narcotic drug or psychotropic substances, it has to denounce the Single Convention (Art. 46) or the 1971 Convention (Art. 29) in the first place and re-accede to it with a reservation. The legality of a procedure to denounce a treaty in order to re-enter it with a reservation is highly controversial.[130]

4.4.1.3 Formal considerations: Denouncing the Single Convention or the 1971 Convention in order to re-accede to one of those treaties with a reservation requires consent of all States parties

Bolivia's 'inside out' to the Single Convention caused a number of objections invoking a violation of the principle of good faith and *pacta sunt servanda*.[131] The Secretary General – acting as the Single Convention's depositary – *in fine* deposited the Bolivian reservation and communicated the Bolivian accession; this communication in itself, however, cannot be seen as determining authoritatively the legality of such a procedure.[132]

130 Cf. for a detailed account of various cases in which cases opted for an 'inside out'; Björn Arp, 'Denunciation Followed by Re-accession with Reservations to a Treaty: A Critical Appraisal of Contemporary State Practice', *NILR* Vol. 61 2014, 141.

131 Objection of Italy to the Reservation contained in the Communication by the Plurinational State of Bolivia of 2 January 2013, Depositary Notification of the Secretary General, C.N.750.2012. TREATIES-VI.18 (available online at: http://treaties.un.org/doc/Publication/CN/2012/CN.750.2012-Eng.pdf); Objection of Finland to the Reservation contained in the Communication by the Plurinational State of Bolivia of 8 January 2013, Depositary Notification of the Secretary General, C.N.95.2013.TREATIES-VI.18 (available online at: http://treaties.un.org/doc/Publication/CN/2013/CN.95.2013-Eng.pdf); Objection of Ireland to the Reservation contained in the Communication by the Plurinational State of Bolivia of 9 January 2013, Depositary Notification of the Secretary General (available online at: http://treaties.un.org/doc/Publication/CN/2013/CN.101.2013-Eng.pdf); Objection of the Netherlands to the Reservation contained in the Communication by the Plurinational State of Bolivia of 8 January 2013, Depositary Notification of the Secretary General, C.N.102.2013.TREATIES-VI.18 (available online at: https://treaties.un.org/doc/Publication/CN/2013/CN.102.2013-Eng.pdf).

132 Bolivia Communication of 10 January 2013, Depositary of the Secretary General (available online at: https://treaties.un.org/doc/Publication/CN/2011/CN.829.2011-Eng.pdf).

Despite these legal controversies such a procedure is not without precedent.[133] In 1998, Trinidad and Tobago had denounced the first protocol to the International Covenant on Civil and Political Rights (ICCPR) and subsequently re-acceded to this treaty, while making a reservation that would exclude the competence of the Human Rights Committee (HRC) for any individual communications of prisoners serving a death sentence.[134] In the famous *Rawle Kennedy* case, the HRC held that said reservation would violate the ICCPR's object and purpose,[135] but failed to make a statement regarding the legality of the 'inside out' procedure to which Trinidad and Tobago had resorted. Several States objected to this re-accession because they considered that re-acceding to a treaty with the sole purpose of making a reservation that had not been made at the initial accession would seem incompatible with the law of treaties.[136]

Whether the law of treaties per se prohibits such a procedure is unclear. Aust considers that denouncing a treaty and re-entering it with a reservation as '*a single transaction*'[137] and equates it with a 'late reservation', i.e. a reservation that, contrary to Art. 2 (1) (d) and Art. 19 VCLT, is not formulated while signing, ratifying, approving or acceding to a treaty, but after this point.[138] This approach seems to have been shared by the ILC.[139] According to the latter, late reservations are deemed accepted by other States parties if not objected to 'by any' State party within a one-year period following the accession.[140] This is

133 Arp, *supra* note 131, 141 (163 et seq.); Laurence Helfer, 'Not Fully Committed? Reservations, Risk and Treaty Design', *YJIL* Vol. 31 2006, 367 (371 et seq.); Palitha Kohona, 'Some Notable Developments in the Practice of the UN Secretary General as Depositary of Multilateral Treaties: Reservations and Declarations', *AJIL* Vol. 99 2005, 433 (439); cf. also as to this issue Yogesh Tyagi, 'The Denunciation of Human Rights Treaties', *BYBIL* Vol. 67 2008, 87 (175 et seq.).

134 Cf. Trinidad and Tobago, Accession to the Optional Protocol to the International Covenant on Civil and Political Rights of 26. May 1998, Depositary Notification of the Secretary General C. N. 230.1998.TREATIES (available online at: https://treaties.un.org/doc/Publication/CN/1998/CN.230.1998-Eng.pdf).

135 HRC, *Mr. Rawle Kennedy v. Trinidad and Tobago*, Communication No. 845/1998, View of 26 March 2002, UN Doc. CCPR/C/74/D/845/1998.

136 Arp, *supra* note 131, 141 (155) with further references; cf. also Kohona, *supra* note 134, 433 (438).

137 Anthony Aust, *Modern Treaty Law and Practice*, 2007, p. 160 (italics added).

138 *Ibid.*, p. 158 (italics added).

139 The commentaries to the Guide to Practice mention as an example for late reservations, the French denunciation followed by re-accession of the Convention providing for a uniform law of cheques; cf. in this regard ILC, Guide to Practice on Reservations to Treaties with Commentaries, 2011, UN Doc. A/66/10 Add. 1, Guideline 2.3, MN 11. For a different view cf. Glenn McGrory, 'Reservations of Virtue? Lessons from Trinidad and Tobago's Reservation to the First Optional Protocol', *HRQ* Vol. 23 2001, 769 (811 et seq.) who considers that such a procedure may be, nevertheless, illegal under Art. 44 VCLT, since it has the fact of suspending a part of a treaty.

140 ILC, Guide to Practice on Reservations to Treaties with Commentaries, 2011, UN Doc. A/66/10 Add. 1, Guideline 2.3; cf. for a detailed account on late reservations Daniel Müller, 'Reservations and Time: Is There Only One Right Moment to Formulate and to React to Reservations?', *EJIL* Vol. 24 2013, 1113 (1120 et seq.); cf. as to the practice of the Secretary General, Kohona, *supra* note 134, 433 (435 et seq.).

sound because the interests of the other States parties to the treaty are similar in both constellations. In the case of late reservations and an 'inside out' procedure, the reserving State unilaterally modifies its obligation vis-à-vis the other States parties.

Moreover, the interests of the other parties can be invoked in favour of requiring universal approval by all States parties of a reservation followed by an 'inside out' procedure. They have subjected themselves to a treaty regime on the expectation that the other parties also faithfully abide by their obligations. Assuming international obligations in the first place, without formulating any reservations and subsequently modifying these obligations unilaterally seems incompatible with the cardinal principles of the international legal order, *pacta sunt servanda* and *bona fide*, as enshrined by Art. 26 VCLT. All States have to abide by the obligations that they themselves have assumed in the first place. The principle of good faith is complied with as long as the States parties to the treaty have not objected to the re-accession after an 'inside out' procedure.

Thus, a State party to the Single Convention may only denounce this treaty and re-access to it while making a reservation provided that *no* State party objects to this reservation. The same is true for the 1971 Convention. Given that almost all States are bound by these treaties, the fact that Art. 50 (3) Single Convention and Art. 30 (3) allow States parties to deviate from drug control's object and purpose by making a reservation allowing for non-medical or non-scientific drug use of a substance is deprived of practical effect if such a step is not approved by all States parties.

4.4.2 Deviating from the limitation of drugs to medical and scientific purposes by treaty amendment

The Single Convention and the 1971 Convention provide the possibility to modify their obligations by amendments. The amendment procedure is not subjected to the same inherent limitations as the reservation procedure. Amendments do not have to comply with a treaty's object and purpose and they can be made after accession. Thus, States could exempt singular substances from the scope of application of the Single Convention or the 1971 Convention by the form of treaty amendment.

The threshold, however, for amending a treaty is high. Consensus of all States parties – in one form or another – is mandatory for successfully modifying the provisions of a convention.

The Single Convention contains two possibilities for treaty amendment. On the one hand, an international conference can be called in accordance with Article 62 (4) of the UN Charter by the ECOSOC in order to 'consider the proposed amendment' (Art. 47 (1) (a) Single Convention). Article 47 (1) (a) Single Convention is silent, however, on the instrument by which such an amendment is adopted and how it enters into force.

The sole successful amendment of the Single Convention occurred by adopting a protocol.[141] This, however, is not compelling. Article 39 VCLT lays out the relative informality of treaty amendments; they only have to take the form of agreements. The term 'agreement' is not clarified by the VCLT. An agreement may take less formal means then the adoption of an entirely new protocol. States can directly modify the terms of the treaty by adopting memoranda of understandings, resolutions, etc.[142] No particular form is required, it is only necessary to make explicit the intention of the parties to amend the treaty.[143]

The exact modalities on the adoption of such an agreement – including the required majority for the amendment – would depend on the modalities agreed upon by the respective conference. Thus, in future, States could resort to Art. 47 (1) (a) Single Convention in order to modify the Single Convention by means other than adopting a protocol. It should be kept in mind, however, that the possibility for States disagreeing with such an amendment would have the possibility of opting out of the modified treaty (Art. 40 (4) VCLT) and preserve the anterior status quo.

The other possibility for States parties to amend the Single Convention would be to submit the amendment proposal to the parties directly. Accordingly, 'the Parties shall be asked whether they accept the proposed amendment' (Art. 47 (1) (b) Single Convention). If such an amendment proposal 'has not been rejected by any party within 18 months after it has been circulated, it shall thereupon enter into force' (Art. 47 (2) Single Convention). This means an amendment of the Single Convention may be achieved by tacit approval of all the States parties. If this approval is not achieved, the ECOSC may nevertheless decide to call for a conference (Art. 47 (2) Single Convention).

Article 30 1971 Convention follows the wording of Art. 47 1971 Convention and could be used in order to exempt substances from their limitation to medical and scientific purposes. In sum, treaty amendment seems a viable means in order to deviate from the limitation of drugs to medical and scientific purposes.

4.4.3 Conclusion

The above-mentioned consideration show that the current drug control system does not provide for any notable leeway in order to deviate from the limitation of drugs to medical and scientific purposes. There are no notable exceptions within the UN Drug Conventions under which States could allow for non-medical or

141 Statement of the Mexican delegate, OR II 1972 Protocol, p. 5; cf. also statement the Brazilian delegate, *ibid.*

142 Philippe Sands, 'Art. 40', in: Olvier Corten and Pierre Klein (eds), *The Vienna Convention on the Law of Treaties: A Commentary* Vol. II 2011, MN 22 et seq.; ILC, Second Report on Subsequent Agreements and Subsequent Practice in relation to the Interpretation of Treaties (Georg Nolte), 2014, UN Doc. A/CN.4/671, pp. 51 et seq.

143 ILC, Second Report on Subsequent Agreements and Subsequent Practice in relation to the Interpretation of Treaties (Georg Nolte), 2014, UN Doc. A/CN.4/671, pp. 67 et seq.

non-scientific drug use. Likewise, deviating from this norm, whether by making reservations or by demanding treaty amendment, without universal consensus of all States parties is impossible; in this light, and when considering the legal uncertainties relating to reservations, the most viable option for a State in order to modify legal obligations to which it is bound, is an amendment procedure.[144]

Exceptions for the benefit of traditional drug use under the Single Convention were merely of temporal scope (Art. 49). This is no accident, but rooted in the assessment of the Single Convention's drafters that such practices would be overcome over time. There was consensus among the States parties in this regard. Even the Bolivian delegate considered that 'Coca leaves had presented a huge social problem'.[145] The situation is different as far as the 1971 Convention intersects with the traditional drug use of plant-based hallucinogens by indigenous peoples. States have been provided with the possibility to allow for such uses without any time constraints. Thus, whereas the 1971 Convention disposes some amount of flexibility to avoid a conflict between traditional drug use and the limitation of psychotropic substances to medical and scientific purposes, under the Single Convention there is no room for manoeuvre whatsoever to allow for the traditional use of the coca leaf by indigenous peoples.

Other global systems of international cooperation, most notably international environmental law, foresee certain exceptions to their objectives in order to allow for more flexibility for the States parties concerned. Some multilateral environmental agreements striving for the universal protection of certain species do contain exceptions for the benefit of indigenous practices of hunting and fishing, etc.[146] These multilateral environmental treaties are comparable to the UN Drug Conventions, in that they establish a universal goal that is coherently pursued by leaving as few exceptions as possible. By providing for such flexibility they ensure that their obligations remain coherent with cultural indigenous rights.

There are other examples of how even advanced systems of multilateral cooperation balance global solutions with the needs of States parties for sufficient flexibility. Thus, the GATT agreement (General Agreement on Tariffs and Trade), whilst providing for a general framework which liberalizes trade in goods, foresees exceptions on which States can rely in order to restrict international trade. Article XX GATT thus allows States to adopt trade restrictions *inter alia* for

144 Cf. also in this regard Allison E. Don, 'Lighten Up: Amending the Single Convention on Narcotic Drugs', *Minn. J. Int'l L.* Vol. 23 2014, 213 (234).

145 OR I Single Convention, p. 57.

146 Cf. in this regard Art. VIII Interim Convention on Conservation of North Pacific Fur Seals of 9 February 1957, entered into force 30 October 1958, UNTS Vol. 314, p. 105; Art. III (d) Agreement on the Conservation of Polar Bears of 15 November 1973, entered into force 26 May 1976, ILM Vol. 13, 13; Art. 5 (c) Convention on the Conservation of Migratory Species of Wild Animals ILM of 23 June 1979, entered into force 1 November 1983, ILM Vol. 19, 15; cf. also ILA, The Hague Conference (2010), Rights of Indigenous Peoples, Interim Report, fn 281 with further references and examples.

the protection of public morals.[147] By the same token, human rights treaties foresee the possibility of temporal derogations, e.g. Art. 15 (1) of the European Convention on Human Rights (ECHR) allows for a State to derogate from its obligations during the time of emergency.[148] The Single Convention lacks any such possibilities. This is noteworthy as rigid obligations without any exceptions are rare in public international law. They usually pertain to rules of outstanding importance for the international legal system as a whole as the prohibition of slavery or torture which are of *ius cogens.*

The limitation of drugs to medical and scientific purposes is not a rule of similar magnitude. Arguably, it is not the rule of this limitation itself which is responsible for the current tensions within the international drug control system but the fact that this rule is not subjected to any exceptions which explains the current discontent. The temporal reservation of Art. 49 allows for the conclusion that States when adopting this treaty were guided by the naïve assessment that traditional drug use would be eradicated by modern societies. This proved to be wrong, not only for traditional drug use. The failure of the Single Convention to allow for exceptions from the limitation of drugs to medical and scientific purposes, in particular with regard to traditional drug use, creates potential for normative conflicts for international human rights law that will be examined in the following section.

4.5 Does international human rights law conflict with the limitation of drugs to medical and scientific purposes?

4.5.1 Setting the stage: International human rights law and the legitimacy of the international drug control system

International human rights law has been used for a long time to discredit the legitimacy of drug control.[149] It has been invoked to argue that some kind of right to recreational drug use exists. The claim was made earlier that such a right could be affirmed morally[150] or found in domestic constitutions.[151] Authors have subsequently relied on international human rights law in order to invoke some kind of right to recreational drug use. It has been argued that such a right would be grounded in the international protection of privacy as *inter alia* recog-

147 General Agreement on Tariffs and Trade of 15 October 1947, entered into force 1 January 1948.

148 Convention for the Protection of Human Rights and Fundamental Freedoms of 4 November 1950 as amended by Protocol No. 14 (CETS No. 194), entered into force 1 June 2010. See for further examples regarding flexible treatment of States parties in various contexts, Lavanya Rajamani, *Differential Treatment in International Environmental Law*, pp. 13 et seq.

149 The aim of the following is merely to lay out the relationship of the limitation of drugs to medical and scientific purposes and not to broadly examine the relationship between the international drug control system and international human rights law as a whole; cf. as to this issue *infra* 6.2.

150 Cf. as to this issue Douglas Husak, *Drugs and Rights*, *passim*; David A.J. Richards, 'Drug Use and the Rights of the Person: A Moral Argument for Decriminalization of Certain Forms of Drug Use', *Rutgers L. Rev.* Vol. 33 1981, 607.

151 Cf. as to this issue and more generally as to constitutional questions of the United States involving a right to privacy and recreational drug use; Douglas Husak, *Drugs and Rights*, p. 37.

nized by Art. 12 of the Universal Declaration of Human Rights.[152] A right to non-medical drug use has also been relied upon in the context of the protection of indigenous rights.[153] Additionally, the idea to add to the universal declaration of human rights a new right to recreational drug use, has been proposed.[154]

Such claims are, of course, controversial; other authors have quite vividly disputed the existence of any human right to use drugs for other than medical or scientific purposes.[155] The existence of such a right would indeed conflict with the categorical imperative of the UN Drug Conventions to reduce drugs to medical and scientific purposes. This explains the need to discuss the existence of a normative conflict between the limitation of drugs to medical and scientific purposes and international human rights law. Thus, some brief preliminary remarks regarding the interplay of obligations from various treaty regimes – *in casu* international human rights law and the UN Drug Conventions – seem necessary, as the respective human rights norms will be considered against the background of the imperative to limit drugs to medical and scientific purposes.

4.5.2 Systemic integration and a presumption against normative conflict

The wide expansion of international law bears the inherent risk of the appearance of normative conflicts, i.e. of a situation where two norms applying to the same facts would obligate a State to take two incompatible actions.[156] This well-known problem concerns the interplay of various treaty regimes, e.g. international human rights law and international humanitarian law.[157] The primitive

152 Simon Flacks, 'Drug Control, Human Rights, and the Right to the Highest Attainable Standard of Health: A Reply to Saul Takahashi', *HRQ* Vol. 33 2011, 855 (874); Neil Hunt, 'Public Health or Human Rights: What Comes First?', *IJDP* Vol. 15 2004, 231 (235 et seq.).

153 Cf. in that regard James Kirk, 'Coca, Cocaine and the Rights of Indigenous Peoples', *TCLR* Vol. 10 2007, 77 (93); Tupper and Labate, *supra* note 61, 17 (26); Martin Jelsma, 'Lifting the Ban on Coca Chewing: Bolivia's Proposal to Amend the 1961 Single Convention', Transnational Institute, Series on Legislative Reform of Drug Policies No. 11 2011, p. 4; Luciana Boiteux, Luciana Peluzio Chernicharo and Camila Souza Alves, 'Human Rights and Drug Conventions: Searching for Humanitarian Reason in Drug Laws', in: Beatriz Caiuby Labate and Clancy Cavnar (eds), *Prohibition, Religious Freedom, and Human Rights: Regulating Traditional Drug Use*, 2014, 1 (15 et seq.).

154 Erik van Ree, 'Drugs as a Human Right', *IJDP* Vol. 10 1999, 89 (92).

155 Saul Takahashi, 'Drug Control, Human Rights, and the Right to the Highest Attainable Standard of Health: By No Means Straightforward Issues', *HRQ* Vol. 31 2009, 748; *id.*, *Human Rights and Drug Control: The False Dichotomy*, 2016, *passim*; Stephan Dahlgren and Roxana Stere, 'The Protection of Children from Illicit Drugs – A Minimum Human Rights Standard: A Child-Centered vs. a User-Centered Drug Policy', 2012, *passim*.

156 This is a restrictive definition of a norm conflict; ILC, Fragmentation of International Law: Difficulties arising from the Diversification and Expansion of International Law, Report of the Study Group of the International Law Commission Finalized by Martti Koskenniemi, 2006, UN Doc. A/CN.4/L.682, MN 24; see as to this issue with regard to drug control, Richard Lines, *Drug Control and Human Rights in International Law*, pp. 80 et seq., 86 et seq., 101 et seq.

157 Cf. as to the relationship between international humanitarian law and international human rights Law, Marko Milanovic, *Extraterritorial Application of Human Rights Treaties*, 2011, pp. 229 et seq.

status quo of the international legal order, being – with the sole exception of *ius cogens* and Art. 103 of the UN Charter – of a purely horizontal nature, without a priority of norms that we know from more elaborated domestic legal systems, makes it difficult, if in some cases impossible, to resolve such tensions and frictions.

This may explain why, when interpreting norms of differing treaty regimes, the first instinct of the interpreter will be to avoid such normative conflicts. This can be achieved in most cases by connecting the different obligations from various regimes. As the ILC has noted, legal rules do not 'apply in a vacuum' and the international legal system is more than a random accumulation of numerous rules and different legal regimes but has to be considered as a whole.[158] Therefore, it is important to contextualize the different rules contained in the various legal regimes; an idea that was also embodied within Art. 31 (3) (c) VCLT. Thereby, when interpreting an obligation, '[a]ny relevant rules of international law applicable in relations between the parties' have to be taken into account. This contextualization takes place by the virtue of 'systemic integration' that embodies 'a strong presumption against normative conflict'.[159] In order to provide for a smooth coexistence of the various legal regimes, the interpreter will first of all rely on 'harmonious interpretation'. This means to interpret two legal obligations contained in two separate regimes as one single set of rules.[160]

Thus, obligations of the UN Drug Conventions will have to be interpreted in light of other applicable obligations of States under international human rights law.[161] It also means, however, that when international human rights norms are interpreted, the limitation of drugs to medical and scientific purposes comes into play. This speaks *prima facie* against assuming that international human rights

158 ILC, 'Fragmentation of International Law: Difficulties Arising from the Diversification and Expansion of International Law', Report of the Study Group of the International Law Commission, finalized by Martti Koskenniemi, 2006, UN Doc. A/CN.4/L.682, MN 120; cf. also in this regard for the relationship between human rights law and the UN Drug Conventions; Damon Barrett and Manfred Nowak, 'United Nations and Drug Policy: Towards a Human Rights-based Approach', in: Aristotle Constantinides and Nikos Zaikos (eds), *Essays in Honour of Kalliopi Koufa*, 2009 (available online at: http://papers.ssrn.com/sol3/papers.cfm?abstract_id=1461445), pp. 12 et seq.; cf. also for the same consideration as far as the relationship between WTO law and general international law is concerned; United States – Standards for Reformulated and Conventional Gasoline, Report of the Appellate Body of 29 April 1996, p. 17 recognizing that the GATT is not to be read in "clinical isolation from public international law".

159 ILC, Fragmentation of International Law: Difficulties arising from the Diversification and Expansion of International Law, Report of the Study Group of the International Law Commission Finalized by Martti Koskenniemi, 2006, UN Doc. A/CN.4/L.682, MN 37 (italics added).

160 *Ibid.*, MN 14 Conclusion 4.

161 Cf. also for this, Damon Barrett and Manfred Nowak, 'United Nations and Drug Policy: Towards a Human Rights-based Approach', in: Aristotle Constantinides and Nikos Zaikos (eds), *Essays in Honour of Kalliopi Koufa*, 2009, 449 (available online at: http://papers.ssrn.com/sol3/papers.cfm?abstract_id=1461445), *passim*.

law derogates from the obligation to limit drugs to medical and scientific purposes. When States forged norms under international human rights law, they did this against the background of – mostly – pre-existing rules of the international drug control treaties and, therefore, in the normative context of an obligation to limit drugs to medical and scientific purposes. This presumption of coherence of the obligations under international human rights law with the obligations of the UN Drug Conventions can be rebutted. It is well recognized that a State theoretically can assume a new obligation under international law that is incompatible with its previous obligations.[162]

It is against this background that it will be determined whether a right to use drugs for other than medical or scientific purposes can be derived from of international human rights law. Four human rights will be examined in this regard:

- First, the right to religion;
- Second, the right to privacy;
- Third, cultural rights of minorities;
- Fourth, cultural rights of indigenous peoples.

4.5.3 The right to manifest one's religion and a right to use drugs for religious purposes?

It has been argued that the right to manifest religious belief would encapsulate a right to use drugs in connection with religious rituals.[163] The right to have religious beliefs (*forum internum*) and to practice and manifest such beliefs (*forum externum*) is protected by regional and universal human rights instruments.[164] This right to *manifest* religious beliefs is wide, comprising all sorts of ritual practices, ranging from worship to missionary activities and to the conduct of religious rituals.[165]

In many religious communities drug use connected with religious rituals can be subsumed under the right to manifest religious beliefs. Resorting to mind-stimulating practices for religious rituals seems to be familiar, even compulsory, in various religions, ranging from the drinking of wine for the Christian

162 Alexander Orakhelashvili, 'Art. 30', in: Olivier Corten and Pierre Klein (eds), *The Vienna Convention on the Law of Treaties: A Commentary*, 2011, MN 19; cf. also *ibid.*, MN 3 et seq. for examples prior to the adoption of the VCLT.

163 Cf. e.g. Charlotte Walsh, 'Drug and Human Rights: Private Palliatives, Sacramental Freedoms and Cognitive Liberty', *IJHR* Vol. 14 2010, 425 (430 et seq.).

164 Cf. e.g. Art. 18 (1) ICCPR, Art. 9 ECHR and Art. 12 (1) American Convention on Human Rights of 22 November 1969, entered into force 18 July 1978, UNTS Vol. 1144, p. 123 [hereinafter referred to as ACHR]; Walter Kälin, Jörg Künzli, *The Law of International Human Rights Protection*, pp. 413 et seq.

165 HRC, General Comment No. 22, The Right to Freedom of Thought, Conscious and Religion, 1994, UN Doc. HRI/GEN/1/Rev.1, para. 4; Christoph Grabenwarter, *European Convention on Human Rights: Commentary*, 2014, Art. 9, MN 9 et seq.

communion to rituals connected with psychotropic plants of indigenous peoples. The 'official standing' of the religion or practice at stake within the State or the society at large is as irrelevant as the numerical size of the religious group in question or its age.

Therefore, it is plausible to subsume religious drug use under the right to exercise religious beliefs. The HRC, however, was initially sceptical in this regard. In *M.A.B., W.A.T., and J.-A.Y.T. v. Canada*, the HRC had to consider a communication resulting from three individuals, who had been part of the Assembly of the Church of the Universe. The religious rites of this group were mainly connected with cannabis use. The applicants had claimed a violation of their right to liberty by the imprisonment following a raid at their church where cannabis had been detected.[166] The HRC rejected the admissibility of the claim, since the communication would not even *prima facie* raise issues under the ICCPR. It considered that

> a belief consisting primarily or exclusively in the worship or the distribution of a narcotic drug cannot conceivably brought within the scope of the [...] freedom of religion and conscience.[167]

The case law of the HRC has developed, however. In *Gareth Anver Prince v. South Africa*, a member of the Rastafari religion submitted that the failure of South African authorities to let him perform a period of community service would be incompatible with his right to practice his Rastafari religion that requested the use of cannabis. This time, in contrast to *M.A.B*, the Committee considered that drug use in connection with religious rituals could be subsumed under the scope of protection of the right to manifest one's religion. This right protected drug use by members of the Rastafarian religion, for whom cannabis use was an essential part of their religious faith.[168]

However, the Committee

> recalle[d] that the freedom to manifest one's religion or beliefs is not absolute and may be subject to limitations which are prescribed by the law and are necessary to protect public safety, order, health, or morals or the fundamental rights and freedoms of others.[169]

166 HRC, M.*A.B., W.A.T., and J.-A.Y.T. v. Canada*, Communication No. 570/1993, Decision of 8 April 1994, UN Doc. CCPR/C/50/D/570/1993, para. 4.2.

167 *Ibid.*, para. 4.

168 HRC, *Gareth Anver Prince v. South Africa*, Communication No. 1474/2006, View of 31 October 2007, UN Doc. CCPR/C/91/D/1474/2006, para. 7.2; the result to include cannabis use for religious purposes within the scope of protection of Art. 18 is widely shared within the literature; Walter Kälin and Jörg Künzli, *The Law of International Human Rights Protection*, p. 413; Sarah Joseph and Melissa Castan, *The International Covenant on Civil and Political Rights*, MN 17.05 et seq.

169 HRC, Gareth Anver Prince v. South Africa, View of 31 October 2007, Communication No. 1474/2006, UN Doc. CCPR/C/91/D/1474/2006, para. 7.2.

The Committee observed that the restriction of the right to practice religion was prescribed the law. Furthermore, this law 'was designed to protect public safety, order, health, morals or the fundamental rights and freedoms of others, based on the harmful effects of cannabis'.[170] This justified the South African prohibition of cannabis and an exemption from this prohibition for religious purposes was not required.

Indeed, Art. 18 (3) ICCPR allows a State party to subject the right to manifest one's religion to such limitations as are prescribed by law and are necessary to protect public safety, order, health, or morals or the fundamental rights and freedoms of others.[171] The HRC by invoking this provision – without relying on the UN Drug Conventions and the limitation of drugs to medical and scientific purposes prescribed therein – seems to have come to a correct conclusion.[172]

When interpreting the right to manifest one's religion against the background of the obligation to limit drugs to medical and scientific purposes, harmonizing these two obligations means to rely on a possible restriction of the right to manifest one's religion for the benefit of drug control. As Art. 18 (3) ICCPR and parallel provisions *expressis verbis* allow for restrictions to the manifestations of the right to religion for the sake of public health, invoking the UN Drug Conventions – and their national measures of implementation – in order to justify a restriction seems appropriate. The approach by the UN Drug Conventions is to protect public health by restricting drugs to medical and scientific purposes. This seems to be a legitimate aim in accordance with Art. 18 (3) ICCPR.

Additionally, a restriction of the right to manifest one's religion would have to be proportionate. This means that besides pursuing a legitimate aim, the restriction in question has to be necessary, i.e. the least restrictive means available and, additionally, has to be proportionate *stricto sensu*, i.e. the aim in question is not unduly encroached by the respective measure.[173] The proportionality of a restriction of the right to manifest one's religion by using drugs will depend on the national drug control measure at stake. It may solely be concluded that restricting this right on the basis of drug control would seem to pursue a legitimate aim.

This line of argumentation was also adopted by national courts.[174] In *R. v. Taylor*, a conviction of a member of a Rastafari group for possessing 40g of

170 *Ibid.*, para. 7.3.

171 This is also true for both, the ACHR (Art. 12 (3)) as well as the ECHR (Art. 9 (2)).

172 For a more critical view however, cf. Melissa Bone, 'From the Sacrilegious to the Sacramental: A Global Review of Rastafari Cannabis Case Law', in: Beatriz Caiuby Labate and Clancy Cavnar Caiuby (eds), *Prohibition, Religious Freedom, and Human Rights: Regulating Traditional Drug Use*, 89 (100).

173 Emily Crawford, 'Proportionality', in: Rüdiger Wolfrum (ed.), *MPEPIL*, 2012, MN 2.

174 Cf. also for a similar conclusion the judgment of the South African Supreme Court in the Prince case which gave rise to the communication of the latter to the HRC; Prince v President of the Law Society of the Cape of Good Hope (CCT36/00) [2002] ZACC 1; 2002 (2) SA 794; 2002 (3) BCLR 231 (25 January 2002), paras 131 et seq.; the majority within the South African Supreme Court was narrow. The right of Mr. Prince to use cannabis for religious purposes was denied by a slim 5 to 4 majority. For a similar view cf. also German Federal Administrative Court, Judgment of 21 December 2000, quoted, in: *NJW* Vol. 54 2001, 1365.

cannabis was upheld by a British Court of Appeal.[175] The judgment assessed whether the convicted could validly invoke the freedom to manifest his religion as guaranteed by Art. 9 (1) ECHR. The Court relied on the possibility to restrict the right to manifest one's religion as prescribed Art. 9 (2) ECHR. Thereby, a restriction to the right to practice one's religion has to be prescribed by the law, be necessary in a democratic society (i.e. proportionate) and taken for the interests of public safety, for the protection of public order, health or morals. The ruling upheld the assessment of the trial judge that the restriction of religious drug use was in accordance with Art. 9 (2) ECHR. It would be justified as the British Misuse of Drugs Act had been adopted in order to fulfil the obligations under the Single Convention and the 1988 Convention. These treaties showed an international consensus that banning cannabis use would be necessary for the protection of public health and welfare.[176]

It cannot be excluded, however, that in the future one might see normative development with regard to the issue. This can be exemplified with cases by the US Supreme Court and the District Court of Amsterdam that involved the spiritual use of hoasca/ayahuasca by a religious group from Brazil.[177] Hoasca is used by members of this group for obtaining a 'communion', consisting of drinking hoasca and experiencing the psychoactive effects of this brew. Both judgments – in contrast to the conclusion of this book – considered that hoasca would be subjected to Schedule I of the 1971 Convention.[178]

The US Supreme Court held in *Alberto R. Gonzales v. O Centro Espirita Beneficente Uniao Do Vegetal* that the United States government could not prohibit the import of hoasca for the benefit of a religious group. The Court considered that the 1971 Convention applied, but held that this 'does not automatically mean that the Government had a compelling interest in applying the Controlled Substances Act, which implements the [1971] Convention, to the [...] sacramental use of [hoasca]'.[179]

Such a compelling interest would have been required under the Religious Freedom Restoration Act, adopted by the US Congress to ensure that First Amendment Rights were adequately safeguarded.[180]

A similar line of argumentation was pursued by the District Court of Amsterdam. It relied on the right to manifest one's religion as laid out in Art. 9 (1) ECHR. The Court, however, considered that the condition of proportionality as contained within para. 2, Art. 9 ECHR was not fulfilled and that the restriction

175 [2001] EWCA Crim 2263; for a critical view, Walsh, *supra* note 164, 425 (430 et seq.).

176 [2001] EWCA Crim 2263.

177 Cf. as to these judgments, Kirk, *supra* note 154, 77 (94 et seq.); Gabrielle Raemy Charest, The Visionary Vine: When Domestic Religious Freedom and International Law Conflict, *TJICL* Vol. 12 2004, 435; Stefanie Küfner, Drew Rabe and Barbara Sonczyk, 'The Santo Daime Church: The Protection of Freedom of Religion Under International Law', Amsterdam International Law Clinic, 2007, pp. 8 et seq.; cf. with regard to hoasca, *supra* 4.2.6.1

178 Cf. *supra* 4.2.6.1 for further references.

179 546 U.S. __ (2006), p. 17.

180 Walsh, *supra* note 164, 425 (431).

of the right to manifest one's religion was not necessary in a democratic society. This was true because of the integral importance of hoasca for the religious group involved, and the fact that the substance was strictly controlled by the religious group itself in order to prevent its use for other than religious purposes.

Thus, two tendencies may be highlighted from the above-mentioned case law.

First, there seems to be growing recognition that the right to manifest one's religion comprises the right to use drugs for religious and ritual purposes. Second, this does not mean that this right could not be restricted. Courts have relied on the possibility to justify restrictions of this right for the benefit of public health. This has the effect of prohibiting the individual from effectively carrying out his or her right to use drugs for religious purposes. Such a result seems to be in accordance with the interplay of the right to freely exercise one's religion with the obligation to limit drugs to medical and scientific purposes. In order to comply with the latter obligation, States rely on the possibility to restrict the right to manifest religious beliefs.[181]

Second, for the case of hoasca, it has been concluded that a prohibition of this substance would be disproportionate, if not leaving exceptions allowing for its religious use. There seems to be a tendency to consider the degree of control that the religious group exercises on the drug use of its members. Several courts justified the restriction of the right to manifest one's religion for members of Rastafari communities by the fact that these communities do not restrict or control the cannabis use of their members.[182] In cases, however, such as hoasca, peyote or mushroom use for religious purposes, where the drug use for religious purposes is controlled by the group itself, domestic courts seem to be more willing to grant the religious drug use in question.[183]

Whether these rulings, may be invoked in favour of a right to drug use for religious purposes that would effectively deviate from the limitation of psychotropic substances to medical and scientific purposes, is far from certain. In the case of hoasca, this obligation is not applicable *ratione materiae* in the first place. The same is true for mushrooms and cactuses. All these substances are plant-based material to which the 1971 Convention does not apply.[184] Case law approving an effective right to religious drug use for substances subjected to the limitation of

181 Cf. e.g. Prince v President of the Law Society of the Cape of Good Hope (CCT36/00) [2002] ZACC 1; 2002 (2) SA 794; 2002 (3) BCLR 231 (25 January 2002).

182 Cf. Prince v President of the Law Society of the Cape of Good Hope (CCT36/00) [2002] ZACC 1; 2002 (2) SA 794; 2002 (3) BCLR 231 (25 January 2002), para. 129:

> Cannabis, unlike peyote, is a drug in which there is a substantial illicit trade which exists within South Africa and internationally. Moreover, the use to which cannabis is put by Rastafari is not simply the sacramental or symbolic consumption of a small quantity at a religious ceremony. It is used communally and privately, during religious ceremonies when two or more Rastafari come together, and at other times and places.

183 Cf. in this regard State v. McBride 24 Kan.App.2d 909, 955 P.2d 133; here, the Court of Appeals of Kansas rejected the claim of the defendants that cannabis use for religious purposes deserved equal protection to the use of peyote for ritual purposes by indigenous people within the US, *ibid.*, p. 919.

184 Cf. *infra* 4.2.6.1.

drugs to medical and scientific purposes has so far not been found. This does not mean that such practice could come into existence *de lege ferenda* in the future and a conflict with the limitation of drugs to medical and scientific purposes could thus arise.

4.5.4 The right to privacy and a right to use drugs as an exercise of personal autonomy?

The right to privacy is protected by several regional human rights instruments, as well as the ICCPR.[185] Although there are no explicit cases known where international courts or treaty bodies have concluded that recreational drug use would be encompassed by the right to privacy, it seems highly plausible to argue that this is the case.[186] Indeed, the scope of protection of the right to privacy is wide, 'guaranteeing the right of everyone to personal autonomy'.[187] This entails the freedom for every individual to take autonomous decisions on personal matters.[188] Such personal matters comprise decisions relating to the own body, including a decision to consume a psychoactive substance. The fact that drug use is potentially harmful to the body is irrelevant in this regard. International jurisprudence has recognized that harmful activities such as sadomasochistic sexual practices or suicide can be subsumed under the right of privacy.[189] It is also well recognized within the literature that personal autonomy extends to potentially harmful activities, as long as others remain unaffected.[190] Thus, it seems hardly deniable that consensual use of a psychoactive substance by a mature and capable individual human being could be subsumed under the scope of protection of the right to privacy. Whether this comprises drug uses in all settings or is confined to drug use by individuals in a clear separation from the public sphere is unclear. The European Court of Human Rights (ECtHR showed doubts whether such sadomasochistic practices carried out by a high number of people, while being videotaped, could be subsumed under the right to private life as protected under Art. 8 ECHR.[191]

However, as it is the case with the right to manifest one's religion, the right to privacy may be restricted. For instance, Art. 17 (1) ICCPR only prohibits *unlawful*

185 Art. 17 ICCPR; Art. 8 (1) ECHR; Art. 11 (2) ACHR.

186 Flacks, *supra* note 153, 855 (874 et seq.); Hunt, *supra* note 153, 231 (234).

187 Walter Kälin and Jörg Künzli, *The Law of International Human Rights Protection*, p. 381.

188 Ineta Ziemele, 'Privacy, Right to, International Protection', in: Rüdiger Wolfrum (ed.), *MPEPIL*, 2012, MN 1.

189 ECtHR, *Laskey and Others v. United Kingdom*, Judgment of 19 February 1997 (Application No. 21627/93; 21628/93; 21974/93), paras 35 et seq.; ECtHR, *Pretty v. United Kingdom*, Judgment of 29 July 2002 (Application No. 2346/02), para. 62.; cf. for a similar parallel between Laskey and drug use, Tom Obokata, 'Illicit Cycle of Narcotics from a Human Rights Perspective', *NQHR* Vol. 25 2007, 159 (172 et seq., esp. 176).

190 Cf. in this regard Ineta Ziemele, 'Privacy, Right to, International Protection, in: Rüdiger Wolfrum (ed.), *MPEPIL*, 2012, MN 7; Sarah Joseph and Melissa Castan, *The International Covenant on Civil and Political Rights*, para. 16.01; Walter Kälin and Jörg Künzli, *The Law of International Human Rights Protection*, pp. 382 et seq.; cf. explicitly with regard to drug use, Manfred Nowak, *U.N. Covenant on Civil and Political Rights*, Art. 17, MN 24 et seq.

191 ECtHR, *Laskey and Others v. United Kingdom*, Judgment of 19 February 1997, Application No. 21627/93; 21628/93; 21974/93, para. 36.

or *arbitrary* interferences with the right to privacy.[192] This threshold is not particularly high. The HRC has lined out that interference can take place on the basis of a law which has to comply with the aims and objectives of the Covenant.[193] It is held that a law protecting a common good may well be deemed a lawful interference provided that it is not to be considered 'overly far-reaching'.[194] States have to rely on a legitimate aim in order to be able to justify a restriction.[195] Domestic drug control laws, which have been adopted in order to implement the provisions of the UN Drug Conventions into national law and thereby prevent non-medical and non-scientific use do not per se fall short of this threshold. In order to comply with the obligation of the UN Drug Conventions to restrict drugs to medical and scientific purposes, States may restrict the right to privacy.

The possibility to restrict the right to privacy for the sake of drug control is shared mostly by domestic courts. The right to privacy has been invoked before national courts in conjunction with drug use. In 1975, the Supreme Court of Alaska rejected the argument that the right to privacy, as guaranteed by Section 1.22 of the Constitution of Alaska, would encompass the right to possess and use cannabis.[196] In 1994, in a well-known judgment, the German Federal Constitutional Court had to consider whether the penalization of cannabis was compatible with the right to personal self-determination (*Recht auf allgemeine Handlungsfreiheit*) as protected under Art. 2 (1) of the German Constitution.[197] The Court – while relying on the unlimited scope of protection of

192 A similar possibility of restriction can be found within the ECHR (Art. 8 (2)) and the ACHR (Art. 11 (2)).

193 HRC, General comment No. 16: Article 17 (Right to privacy), 1988, UN Doc., HRI/GEN/1/Rev.1, para. 4:

> The introduction of the concept of arbitrariness is intended to guarantee that even interference provided for by law should be in accordance with the provisions, aims and objectives of the Covenant and should be, in any event, reasonable in the particular circumstances.

194 Manfred Nowak, *U.N. Covenant on Civil and Political Rights*, Art. 17, MN 25.

195 Ineta Ziemele, 'Privacy, Right to, International Protection, in: Rüdiger Wolfrum (ed.), *MPEPIL*, 2012, MN 6.

196 Supreme Court of Alaska, *Ravan v. State*, 537 P.2d 494 of 27 May 1975, p. 502: 'Therefore, if we were employing our former test, we would hold that there is no fundamental right, either under the Alaska or federal constitutions, either to possess or ingest marijuana.' The Court, however, found that the right to privacy – due to the special relationship of the citizens of Alaska with their home – would encompass the right to possess and use cannabis within their own home; *ibid.*, p. 511:

> Thus we conclude that no adequate justification for the state's intrusion into the citizen's right to privacy by its prohibition of possession of marijuana by an adult for personal consumption in the home has been shown. The privacy of the individual's home cannot be breached absent a persuasive showing of a close and substantial relationship of the intrusion to a legitimate governmental interest. Here, mere scientific doubts will not suffice. The state must demonstrate a need based on proof that the public health or welfare will in fact suffer if the controls are not applied.

This judgment, however, remained isolated within the United States; Jason Brandeis, 'The Continuing Vitality of *Ravin v. State*: Alaskans Still Have a Constitutional Right to Possess Marijuana in the Privacy of their Homes', *Alaska Law Review* Vol. 29 2012, 175.

197 This right encompasses the right to privacy; cf. in this regard Horst Dreier, 'Art. 2 I', in: Horst Drier (ed.), *Grundgesetz Kommentar*, 2013, MN 11 et seq.

Art. 2 (1) – subsumed the smoking of cannabis under Art. 2 (1), but simultaneously underlined the possibility to restrict this right in accordance with the German Constitution.[198]

However, in a judgment dating from 4 November 2015, Mexico's *Suprema Corte de Justicia de la Nacion* went one step further. While concurring with the above-mentioned judgments that the right to personal self-determination (*Derecho al libre desarrollo de la Personalidad*) comprised a right to use cannabis for other than medical purposes, it decided that this right of the plaintiffs had been violated.[199] The Court reasoned that a blanket prohibition of cannabis use was not necessary for protecting public health, because as the regulation of alcohol and tobacco showed, there were possibilities to regulate cannabis in a way that was less intrusive to the right of personal self-determination.[200] Whether this assessment will be shared by other constitutional or international courts in the future remains to be seen.

4.5.5 *A cultural right to drug use for members of minorities in accordance with Art. 27 ICCPR and Art. 15 (1) (a) ICESCR?*

Both Covenants protect the free participation of individuals in cultural life (Art. 15 (1) (a) ICESCR; Art. 27 ICCPR).[201] The use of various psychoactive substances plays a primordial role for ethnic and religious groups. One example being the use of khat by inhabitants of East Africa and Yemen.[202] The question arises, whether such collective practices may be subsumed under the protection of 'culture'.

Under both Covenants the term 'culture' has a dual meaning. On the one hand, there exists a narrow and individualistic conception of 'culture' as an observable product – irrespective whether as a piece of art, music, film, etc. – whose

198 German Federal Constitutional Court Judgement of 9 March 1994, MN 136.

199 Primera Sala de la Suprema Corte de Justicia de la Nación, Amapro en Revsion 237/2014; Andrés Aguinacoa and Aram Barra, 'Cannabis for Personal Use in the Supreme Court of Mexico: Legal Case and Potential for Policy Change', *IJDP* Vol. 50 2017, 9.

200 Primera Sala de la Suprema Corte de Justicia de la Nación, Amapro en Revsion 237/2014, pp. 65 et seq., in particular pp. 76 et seq. The Court considered the UN Drug Conventions but held that these treaties were not violated in the present case because States were not required to penalize drug use; *ibid.*, pp. 86 et seq. and thus confuses the obligation to penalize illicit drug use, which as will be shown is subjected to notable loopholes, with the limitation of drugs to medical and scientific purposes, which, as has been shown, is mandatory.

201 Art. 15 (1) (a) ICESCR reads: '1. The States Parties to the present Covenant recognize the right of everyone: (a) To take part in cultural life'; Art. 27 ICCPR stipulates:

> In those States in which ethnic, religious or linguistic minorities exist, persons belonging to such minorities shall not be denied the right, in community with the other members of their group, to enjoy their own culture, to profess and practise their own religion, or to use their own language.

202 Axel Klein, Pien Metaal and Martin Jelsma, 'Chewing over Khat prohibition: The Globalization of Control and Regulation of an Ancient Stimulant', TNI Series on Legislative Reform of Drug Policies January 2012, p. 2.

creation and enjoyment is protected by international human rights law.[203] Understood in this narrow sense, drug use could not be considered to fall under the scope of protection of international human rights law. However, it is well recognized today that, on the other hand, the term 'culture' has similarly a wide and collectivistic meaning. Thus, the protection of culture under both covenants aims at preserving a characteristic lifestyle of minorities and groups (anthropological meaning).[204] In a nutshell, this wide understanding of culture aims to protect a collective 'cultural identity' of certain groups and peoples.[205] It is important to stress the collective dimension of 'culture' here. The protection of a certain lifestyle is not to be equated with the protection of an individualistic and isolated way of life by one individual. It is the right of the individual to participate within traditions and lifestyles of minorities and groups that is protected. Although the wording of Art. 27 ICCPR, by referring to the right of persons belonging to minorities to enjoy their culture in community with the other members of such a group, makes the collective dimension of culture more clear, the collective dimension of culture is also recognized for Art. 15 (1) (a) ICESCR, in that this stipulation posits a group as enjoying the rights laid down therein.[206]

Understood in its wider sense of protecting the cultural identities of certain groups, the claim that an individual right to use drugs with other members of such groups in accordance with well-established practices of the group falls under the protection of culture, cannot *prima facie* be excluded. It cannot be denied that drug use as a collective experience has played, and continues to play, a primordial role within the collective life of groups and peoples. The HRC shares

203 Cf. e.g. Ben Saul, David Kinley and Jaqueline Mowbray, *The International Covenant on Economic, Social and Cultural Rights*, pp. 1180 et seq.

204 Cf. already in this regard Lyndel Prott, 'Cultural Rights as Peoples' Rights in International Law', in: James Crawford (ed.), *The Rights of Peoples*, 93 (94 et seq.). This was not always unequivocally shared; cf. for a narrow definition of culture; Yoram Dinstein, 'Cultural Rights', *Isr.Y.B.Hum.Rts* Vol. 9 1979, 58 (70). However, today, it would seem the prevailing view; Roger O'Keefe, 'The "Right to Take Part in Cultural Life" under Article 15 of the ICESCR', *ICLQ* Vol. 47 1998, 904 (917); *id.*, 'Cultural Life, Right to Participate in, International Protection', in: Rüdiger Wolfrum (ed.), *MPEPIL*, 2012, MN 12; Alexandra Xanthaki, 'Indigenous Cultural Rights in International Law', *Eur. J.L. Reform* Vol. 2 2000, 343 (355 et seq.); CESCR, General Comment No. 21, Right of Everyone to Take Part in Cultural Life (art. 15, para. 1 (a), of the International Covenant on Economic, Social and Cultural Rights), 2008, UN Doc. E /C.12/GC/21, para. 13; this wide meaning of culture had already been adopted by the HRC much earlier, HRC, General Comment No. 23 (Art. 27), 1994, UN Doc. CCPR/C/21/Rev.1/Add.5, para. 7; cf. also with regard to the transformation of the meaning of culture, Alexandra Xanthaki, 'Indigenous Cultural Rights in International Law', *Eur. J.L. Reform* Vol. 2 2000, 343 (355 et seq.); cf. also S. James Anaya, 'International Human Rights and Indigenous Peoples: The Move toward the Multicultural State', *AJICL* Vol. 21 2004, 13 (22).

205 Roger O'Keefe, 'Cultural Life, Right to Participate in, International Protection', in: Rüdiger Wolfrum (ed.), *MPEPIL*, 2012, MN 12.

206 O'Keefe, supra note 205, 904 (917); cf. in this regard also CESCR, No. 21, Right of Everyone to Take Part in Cultural Life (Art. 15, para. 1 (a), of the International Covenant on Economic, Social and Cultural Rights), 2008, UN Doc. E/C.12/GC/21, paras 11 et seq.

the assumption made above and has subsumed traditional practices of minorities – ranging from fishing[207] to reindeer herding[208] under Art. 27 ICCPR. The possibility to subsume drug use of members of minorities with their fellow members under Art. 27 ICCPR was recognized by the HRC in the above-mentioned *Prince* case. The HRC considered that a member of a Rastafarian community smoking cannabis fell under the scope of Art. 27 ICCPR.[209] By the same token, however, the HRC pointed out the fact that the rights enjoyed under Art. 27 ICCPR could be restricted: 'Certain limitations on the right to practice one's religion through the use of drugs are compatible with the exercise of the right under article 27 of the Covenant.' [210]

However, the wording of Art. 27 ICCPR – 'nobody shall be denied the right' – seems to argue against the possibility of restrictions of the rights laid out by this article. It has been argued that Art. 27 could only be restricted when cultural practices affect human rights of individuals and minorities inherent to the Covenant itself.[211] This debate cannot be fully recaptured here, but it seems safe to argue that Art. 27 ICCPR can be restricted for a legitimate aim.[212] When considering the ICCPR as a whole, it becomes obvious that Art. 27 cannot have been intended to apply without any restrictions. This would lead to manifestly incoherent results for practices similarly protected by Art. 27 and other human rights. For instance, it would mean that the same religious practice that can be restricted under Art. 18 (3) ICCPR could not be restricted under Art. 27.[213] This was not the intention of the drafters of the ICCPR.[214]

207 HRC, *Apirana Mahuika et al. v. New Zealand*, View of 27 October 2000, Communication No. 547/1993, UN Doc. CCPR/C/70/D/547/1993, para. 9.3.

208 HRC, *Ivan Kitok v. Sweden*, View of 27 July 1988, Communication No. 197/1985, UN Doc. CCPR/C/33/D/197/1985, para. 24.

209 HRC, *Gareth Anver Prince v. South Africa*, View of 31 October 2007, Communication No. 1474/2006, UN Doc. CCPR/C/91/D/1474/2006, para. 7.4.

210 *Ibid.*, para. 7.4.

211 Cf. for such an argumentation Manfred Nowak, *U.N. Covenant on Civil and Political Rights*, Art. 27, MN 52 et seq.

212 Cf. in this regard Louis B. Sohn, 'The Rights of Minorities', in: Louis Henkin (ed.), *The International Bill of Rights*, 270 (285); Christian Tomuschat, 'Protection of Minorities under Article 27 of the International Covenant on Civil and Political Rights', in: Rudolf Bernhardt, Wilhelm Karl Geck, Günther Jaenicke and Helmut Steinberger (eds), *Völkerrecht als Rechtordnung Internationale Gerichtsbarkeit Menschenrechte Festschrift für Hermann Mosler*, 950 (976 et seq.); Sarah Joseph and Melissa Castan, *The International Covenant on Civil and Political Rights*, MN 24.55; cf. also Ana Filipa Vrdojak, 'Self-determination in Cultural Rights', in: Francesco Franoini and Martin Scheinin (eds), *Cultural Human Rights*, 41 (63).

213 The possibility to restrict Art. 27 is also recognized by HRC, which considers that States may curtail the rights protected under Art. 27 for the sake of economic development; cf. HRC, *Länsman et al. v. Finland*, View of 26 October 1994, Communication No. 511/1992, UN Doc. CCPR/C/52/D/511/1992, para. 9.4; cf. also Individual Opinion submitted by Mr. Nisuke in the *B. Ominayak and the Lubicon Lake Band v. Canada*, View of 26 March 1990, Communication No. 167/1984, UN Doc. A/45/40.

214 Cf. in this regard statement within the *travaux préparatoires*, reprinted in: Marc Bossuyt, *Guide to the Travaux Préparatoires of the International Covenant on Civil and Political Rights*, p. 497.

Therefore, the line of argumentation pursued for Art. 18 (3) ICCPR can be *mutatis mutandis* applied to Art. 27 ICCPR. Although drug use may be subsumed under Art. 27, as constituting a cultural practice within the scope of protection of this provision, a State is allowed to restrict this cultural practice and thereby complies with the limitation of drugs to medical and scientific purposes. The same is true for Art. 15 (1) (a) ICESCR; here the right to participate in cultural life can be restricted in accordance with Art. 4 ICESCR.[215] Accordingly, the cultural right to drug use of a member of a religious or ethnic community may be restricted by a State in order to comply with its obligation to limit drugs to medical and scientific purposes.

4.5.6 A right of indigenous peoples to traditional drug use?

The fact that indigenous peoples differ most notably from minorities by being able to invoke the right of self-determination,[216] justifies examining their claim for a right to traditional drug use separately from the rights of members of minorities to use drugs.

4.5.6.1 A universal protection of traditional drug use as a cultural practice of indigenous peoples by international law?

In the last years and decades, a body of law has developed that aims for a specific protection of indigenous peoples. This body of law consists most notably out of International Labour Organization (ILO) Convention No. 169[217] and the United Nations Declaration on the Rights of Indigenous Peoples (UNDRIP).[218] The protection of cultural identity plays a primordial role in this regard due to the particular vulnerability of indigenous peoples. As was noted by one scholar, the 'cultural integrity norm [...] has developed remedial aspects particular to indigenous peoples in light of their historical and continuing vulnerability'.[219]

215 General Comment No. 21, Right of Everyone to Take Part in Cultural Life (Art. 15, para. 1 (a), of the International Covenant on Economic, Social and Cultural Rights), 2008, UN Doc. E /C.12/GC/21, para. 19; cf. also Ben Saul, David Kinley and Jaqueline Mowbray, *The International Covenant on Economic, Social and Cultural Rights*, p. 240.

216 Benedict Kingsbury, 'Indigenous Rights', in: Rüdiger Wolfrum (ed.), *MPEPIL*, 2012, MN 54.

217 Convention (No. 169) concerning Indigenous and Tribal Peoples in Independent Countries of 27 June 1989 entered into force 5 September 1991, UNTS Vol. 1650, p. 384 [hereinafter referred to as ILO Convention No. 169].

218 UNGA Resolution 61/295, 2004, UN Doc. A/Res/61/295; such cultural rights and rights to traditional medicine can be found in arts. The declaration had been negotiated for 22 years. The resolution had initially been adopted with four dissenting votes by Canada, New Zealand, Australia and the United States. All four States, however, shifted their position subsequently; cf. for more details Benedict Kingsbury, 'Indigenous Rights', in: Rüdiger Wolfrum (ed.), *MPEPIL*, 2012, MN 11.

219 Anaya, *supra* note 205, 13 (26); cf. for a comprehensive account S. James Anaya, *Indigenous Peoples in International Law*, pp. 98 et seq.

This fundamental role of the cultural protection for indigenous rights in general was aptly highlighted by then International Law Association's (ILA) rapporteur on the Rights of Indigenous Peoples, Federico Lenzerini:

> Indigenous peoples have the right to recognition and preservation of their cultural identity. This includes [...] the right to be free from ethnocide. The [right to be free from ethnocide] presupposes that all the prerogatives that are essential to preserve the cultural identity of indigenous peoples according to their own perspective must be preserved, including, e.g., the right to use ancestral lands and natural resources according to their own tradition, the right to profess and manifest their religion in community with the other members of the group, the right to pursue their traditional medicines and burial traditions, etc.[220]

It is, therefore, no coincidence that numerous provisions of ILO Convention No. 169 – voicing the aspirations of the indigenous people to gain control over their own way of life – aim at protecting ancient cultural practices of indigenous communities.[221] Most notably, Art. 2 (2) (b) of this convention obligates States parties to adopt systematic action, including measures 'promoting the full realisation of the social, economic and cultural rights of these peoples with respect for their social and cultural identity their customs and traditions and their institutions'.

In 2008, indigenous rights – including rights to exercise indigenous culture, a 'predominant theme throughout the whole text'[222] – were further strengthened by the adoption of UNDRIP. In particular, Art. 11 (1) UNDRIP recognizes the right for indigenous peoples 'to practise and revitalize their cultural traditions and custom'.[223]

In spite of the above-mentioned conclusions regarding the protection of drug use as a cultural right, it seems fairly safe to conclude that indigenous practices involving the use of psychoactive substances are encompassed by the protection of cultural indigenous rights as enshrined in UNDRIP and ILO Convention No. 169. However, it has to be kept in mind in this regard that both UNDRIP and ILO Convention No. 169 are not universal binding *lex lata*. ILO Convention No. 169 was ratified by merely 22 States.[224] Furthermore, the rights stipulated by UNDRIP are only enshrined in an UNGA resolution, which as such has no binding force per se.[225] Albeit that UN Special Rapporteur on Indigenous

220 ILA, The Hague Conference (2010), Rights of Indigenous Peoples, Interim Report, pp. 43 et seq.; *ibid.*, p. 51: This preliminary conclusion was retained within the final report of the study group; cf. *id.*, Sofia Conference (2012) Rights of Indigenous Peoples, Final Report, p. 29.

221 Preambular para. 5; cf. as to this treaty in general, S. James Anaya, *Indigenous Peoples in International Law*, pp. 48 et seq. Provisions relating to indigenous culture are also contained in Arts 4 (1), 5 (a), 7 (1), 7 (3), 10 (1), 13 (1), 22 (3), 25 (2), 27 (1) and 30 (1).

222 ILA, Sofia Conference (2012) Rights of Indigenous Peoples, Final Report, p. 16.

223 Arts 12 and 13 also protect indigenous rights.

224 https://treaties.un.org/pages/showDetails.aspx?objid=08000002800c0136.

225 Cf. as to the normative impact of UNGA resolutions *supra* 2.2.1.2.

Issues, James Anaya[226] and the ILA Committee on the Rights of Indigenous Peoples considered that some 'key parts' of UNDRIP[227] would be enshrined within customary international law, their precise status remains unclear. It is all the more unclear as to how far indigenous rights protect traditional drug use of indigenous peoples globally. There is no State practice or jurisprudence that would support such a far-reaching conclusion to date.

4.5.6.2 A cultural right to traditional coca use in South America

4.5.6.2.1 A LEGAL PROTECTION OF INDIGENOUS COCA LEAF CHEWING IN SOUTH AMERICA

The inexistence of a global protection of traditional drug use by indigenous peoples does not mean that traditional drug-related indigenous practices are also unprotected on a regional level. In South America, indigenous rights in general and the chewing of the coca leaf in particular enjoy a specific protection.

The legal status of indigenous rights, including the rights contained within ILO Convention No. 169 and UNDRIP is well-recognized within the particular normative environment of South America: ten out of 12 States in South America have ratified ILO Convention No. 169.[228] Furthermore, it is in this regional context where ILO Convention No. 169 is often cited by domestic and regional jurisprudence, in particular the Inter-American Courts of Human Rights (IACHR).[229] The latter has recognized a right to 'cultural particularism' of indigenous communities.[230] In spite of these normative developments one may conclude that at least within the region of South America, indigenous rights – including cultural rights – have become part of (regional) international law.[231]

226 HRC, Report of the Special Rapporteur on the Situation of Human Rights and Fundamental Freedoms of Indigenous People James Anaya, 2008, UN Doc. A/HRC/9/9 S., para. 41.

227 ILA, Resolution No. 5/2012 Rights of Indigenous Peoples, para. 2.

228 Cf. https://treaties.un.org/pages/showDetails.aspx?objid=08000002800c0136; French Guiana is part of the French territory and therefore not considered as a South American State.

229 Cf. in this regard, Benedict Kingsbury, 'Indigenous Rights, in: Rüdiger Wolfrum (ed.), *MPEPIL*, 2012, para. 20: 'ILO Convention 169 has become a significant part of the rapid juridification of indigenous issues in Latin America'; cf. also Anthanasios Yupsanis, 'The International Labour Organization and Its Contribution to the Protection of the Rights of Indigenous Peoples', *Can. Y. B. Int'l L.* Vol. 49 2011, 117 (136; 163 et seq.).

230 Laurence Burgorgue-Larsen and Amaya Úbeda de Torres, *The Inter-American Court of Human Rights*, 2011, p. 516.

231 The ICJ has noted in several cases that norms of customary international law do not necessarily have to be universal but can emerge in a limited geographical context of a particular region or even bilaterally between two States; ICJ., Rights of Nationals of the United States of America in Morocco (*France v. United States of America*), Judgment of 27 August 1952, pp. 199 et seq.; *id.*, Asylum (*Colombia v. Peru*) Judgment of 20 November 1950, pp. 276 et seq.; cf. also *id.*, Right of Passage over Indian Territory (*Portugal v. India*), Judgment of 12 April 1960, p. 39; cf. also as to this issue, Patrick Daillier, Mathias Forteau and Alain Pellet (Nguyen Quoc Dinh †), *Droit International Public*, MN 211.

What is more, is that the claim that the protection of these cultural rights would extend to drug use was made expressively with regard to the ancestral practice of traditional coca leaf chewing, prevalent within the cultures of indigenous tribes within the Andes region of South America.[232] This claim has transcended into Art. 384 of the Constitution of the Plurinational State of Bolivia of 2008, where it is recognized that 'The State protects the native and ancestral coca as cultural patrimony, as a renewable natural resource of the biodiversity of Bolivia, and as a factor of social unity. In its natural state coca is not a narcotic.'[233]

Albeit other constitutions in this region do not provide for similar guarantees with regard to the coca leaf, a general high level of protection for cultural patrimony of indigenous peoples can be found within the legal systems of all States within the Andes region.[234] Such guarantees have been interpreted as comprising a right to traditional coca use. In the case *C-SY/2011*, the Colombian Supreme Court had to consider a petition against an amendment of the Colombian Constitution. The amendment involved the prohibition of the possession and use of narcotic drugs and psychotropic substances, with the sole exception of their use in accordance with medical prescriptions. The Colombian Supreme Court considered that the amendment – in order to be constitutional – had to be interpreted as not applying to members of indigenous communities and within their territories, as long as the possession and use of narcotic drugs and psychotropic substances was associated with ancestral practices.[235]

232 Cf. for a similar view, Kirk, *supra* note 154, 77 (81 et seq.; 94); Pfeiffer, *supra* note 21, 287 (313 et seq.).

233 Constitution of the Plurinational State of Bolivia, entered into force 7 February, 2009 (English translation available online at: www.constituteproject.org/constitution/Bolivia_2009.pdf).

234 Cf. Art. 89 of the Constitution of Peru, entered into force 29 December 1993 (English translation available online at: www.congreso.gob.pe/Docs/files/CONSTITUTION_27_11_2012_ENG.pdf); Art. 57 of the Constitution of Ecuador of 28 September 2008, entered into force 20 October 2008 (English translation available online at: http://pdba.georgetown.edu/Constitutions/Ecuador/english08.html); Art. 7 et seq. of the Constitution of Colombia of 4 July 1991 (available online at: www.constituteproject.org/constitution/Colombia_2005.pdf); Art. 75 (17) of Argentina of 1 May 1853 (English translation available online at: www.parliament.am/library/sahmanadrutyunner/argentina.pdf); Art. 119 et seq. of the Constitution of the Bolivarian Republic of Venezuela of 15 December 1999 (English translation available online at: wwwl.umn.edu/humanrts/research/venezuela-constitution.html). The Chilean Constitution does not guarantee for indigenous rights. However, Ley Indígena Ley N.° 19.253 D. of 5 October 1993 guarantees for a comprehensive protection of indigenous rights. Additionally, the Chilean Supreme Court has granted Convention No. 169 constitutional status; cf. Yupsanis, *supra* note 230, 117 (168). Cf. also more generally, Pfeiffer, *supra* note 21, 287 (296).

235 Supreme Court of Colombia, Judgment of 23 November 2011, Sentencia C-882/11 para. 2.8:

> La Sala observa [que] en todo caso, la prohibición no es aplicable dentro de los territorios indígenas ni a los miembros de las comunidades cuando el porte y consumo está asociado con prácticas ancestrales, pues el artículo 49 superior, sobre el derecho a la salud y en el que se insertó la reforma, no hace parte de los derechos que limitan la autonomía de las comunidades indígenas, en los términos de la jurisprudencia constitucional.

Additionally, UNDRIP has been interpreted specifically to protect the traditional use of the coca leaf. Ecuador supported the Bolivian proposal to amend the Single Convention and exempt the coca leaf from the scope of control of this treaty, by relying on the rights spelled out by Arts 11, 12 and 13 UNDRIP.[236] This result was also shared by the Permanent Forum on Indigenous Issues. This forum – consisting of individual experts – held that the provisions of the Single Convention on the coca leaf were inconsistent with the rights of indigenous peoples to maintain their traditional health and cultural practices as spelled out by UNDRIP.[237,238]

This does not mean that indigenous peoples per se universally have a positive right to use traditional drugs in accordance with their ancestral practices. The existence of such a right with regard to the traditional practice coca leaf chewing of indigenous peoples within South America hardly can be denied, in spite of this evolving practice. Thus, the question arises how to reconcile such a right to traditional coca use with the obligation of the Single Convention to limit the coca leaf to medical and scientific purposes.

4.5.6.2.2 A POSSIBILITY TO RECONCILE THE RIGHT TO TRADITIONAL COCA USE WITH THE LIMITATION OF COCA TO MEDICAL AND SCIENTIFIC PURPOSES?

There are two possibilities in order to resolve the normative conflict of an indigenous right to traditional coca use with the limitation of drugs to medical and scientific purposes as spelled out by the Single Convention. One way would be to provide for more flexibility within the Single Convention, in order to allow for traditional drug use of indigenous peoples. As has been outlined above, the Single Convention lacks such flexibility.

Another option for reconciling the right to traditional coca use with the limitation of the coca leaf to medical and scientific purposes would be to restrict this right. It is true that as any other human right, the right of indigenous peoples to

236 Ecuador, note verbale of 31 January 2011, Depositary Notification of the Secretary General, C.N.48.2011.TREATIES-18.

237 Permanent Forum on Indigenous Issues, 2009, UN Doc E/2009/43, para. 89:

> The Permanent Forum recognizes the cultural significance and medical importance of the coca leaf in the Andean and other indigenous regions of South America. It also notes that coca leaf chewing is specifically banned by the United Nations Single Convention on Narcotic Drugs (1961). The Permanent Forum recommends that those portions of the Convention regarding coca leaf chewing that are inconsistent with the rights of indigenous peoples to maintain their traditional health and cultural practices, as recognized in articles 11, 24 and 31 of the Declaration, be amended and/or repealed.

This recommendation was reiterated twice; *id.*, 2010, UN Doc. E/2010/43, para. 35; *id.*, 2011, UN Doc. E/2011/43, para. 54. The Permanent Forum on Indigenous Issues was established as a subsidiary organ of the ECOSOC by ECOSOC Resolution E/2000/22, 2000, UN Doc. E/2000/22 E/2000/22, 2000.

238 Pfeiffer, *supra* note 21, 287 (315).

maintain their cultural traditions is not absolute.[239] ILO Convention No. 169, far from stipulating clear-cut and universally applicable obligations, allows for flexibility. It subjects many of the rights contained to the compliance of these rights with recognized human rights standards.[240] By the same token, Art. 46 of UNDRIP allows for a restriction of indigenous rights – including cultural rights. In particular, Art. 46 (2) subjects the exercise of indigenous rights to the respect for human rights or requires the restriction to be determined by the law, in accordance with international human rights law, non-discriminatory and 'strictly necessary solely for the purpose of securing due recognition and respect for the rights and freedoms of others and for meeting the just and most compelling requirements of a democratic society'.

While the first three conditions do not seem to pose particular problems when cultural rights of indigenous peoples are restricted for the purpose of complying with the limitation of drugs to medical and scientific purposes, the fourth condition poses difficulties. Preventing drug use by indigenous peoples will not be necessary in order to secure the rights of others. There is no human right to be free from drug abuse. Although States under human rights law are required to handle psychoactive substances, including the coca leaf, restrictively, they do not have to limit this to medical and scientific purposes. There is no right for members of indigenous communities to be protected from non-medical and non-scientific drug use. Therefore, restricting a right to traditional coca use in accordance with Art. 46 (2) of UNDRIP does not seem possible.

It has been argued that a right to traditional coca use could be reconciled with the limitation of the coca leaf to medical and scientific purposes by relying on the concept of free, prior and informed consent. Hence, according to this argument States could restrict traditional coca use to medical and scientific purposes in accordance with indigenous rights, provided that they consult indigenous communities over the exact implementation of this restriction.[241] This line of argumentation seems doubtful. The right for indigenous peoples to give free, prior and informed consent developed in order to preserve indigenous claims for lands and natural resources.[242] An application of the concept of restricting indigenous rights in accordance with their free prior and informed consent to cultural practices is not viable as far as traditional drug use is concerned. In contrast to indigenous rights to land and natural resources which can be compensated

239 Pfeiffer, *supra* note 21, 287 (315). This why it has been held that UNDRIP would have renounced to a strong form of self-determination; Karen Engle, 'On Fragile Architecture: The UN Declaration on the Rights of Indigenous Peoples in the Context of Human Rights', *EJIL* Vol. 22 2011, 141.

240 Cf. in this regard the provisions that subject the exercise of these rights to their compatibility with human rights; Art. 8 (2) and Art. 9 (1) ILO Convention No. 169; cf. also in this regard Art. 34 providing for flexibility for the conditions of each country concerned when implementing this treaty.

241 Pfeiffer, *supra* note 21, 287 (315 et seq.).

242 Tara Ward, 'The Right to Free, Prior, and Informed Consent: Indigenous Peoples' Participation Rights within International Law', *NUJIHR* Vol. 10 2011, 54.

when taken away from indigenous peoples, cultural practices once they have perished will be lost eternally. Such a fundamental interference within indigenous cultural rights only seems justified when required for the protection of human rights of members of indigenous peoples.

The Colombian Supreme Court, in the *C-SY/2011* case, likewise, did not rely on the possibility to restrict indigenous drug use by relying on the free, prior and informed consent of indigenous groups; the Court plainly refrained from applying the prohibition of drug possession to indigenous peoples, thereby circumventing the problem of having to decide whether the constitutional amendment required a consultation of indigenous communities.[243]

Thus, the right to traditional coca use by indigenous peoples cannot be restricted in accordance with indigenous rights. The divergence between indigenous rights and cultural rights in this regard[244] can be justified by the crucial fact that minorities, in contrast to indigenous peoples, do not enjoy the right to self-determination.[245] Indeed, indigenous rights are particular when compared to other human rights guarantees. Indigenous rights have developed throughout the last decades of the twentieth century in order to overcome old assimilationist structures.[246] Cultural rights are essentially important in this regard. Given that indigenous peoples, despite their accepted claim for self-determination, under the present state of affairs do not have a right to their own State,[247] their survival as peoples is dependent on the recognition that they are different from the rest of the societies where they dwell, and that this difference as a general rule will be protected.

Therefore, at least in the case of traditional coca use, the clash of cultural rights for indigenous peoples with the obligation to limit the coca use to medical and scientific purposes is inevitable. The cultural rights of indigenous people to coca leaf chewing cannot be reconciled with the limitation of drugs to medical and scientific purpose. The presumption against normative conflict which in this case is a presumption against the existence of a right to use drugs for other than medical or scientific purposes is rebutted. The question, therefore, becomes

243 Supreme Court of Colombia, Judgment of 23 November 2011, Sentencia C-882/11 para. 2.8; cf. for a similar conclusion, Thoumi, *supra* note 77, 297 (307).

244 See *supra* 4.5.5.

245 Cf. to the lack of the right to self-determination of minorities; Louis B. Sohn, 'The Rights of Minorities', in: Louis Henkin (ed.), *The International Bill of Rights The Covenant on Civil and Political Rights*, 270 (276).

246 Within the middle of the twentieth century, the idea of assimilation of indigenous peoples and communities was prevalent; cf. in this regard the Convention concerning the Protection and Integration of Indigenous and other Tribal and Semi-Tribal Populations in Independent Countries (ILO Convention No. 107 of 26 June 1957, entered into force 2 June 1959) UNTS Vol. 328, p. 24. This idea was finally overcome with the adoption of ILO Convention No. 169; cf. as to this development, S. James Anaya, *Indigenous Peoples in International Law*, pp. 44 et seq.

247 Cf. in this regard Art. 46 (1) UNDRIP; cf. as to the gradual shift of claims of indigenous peoples and groups from self-determination towards framing their rights into an accepted human rights framework, Engle, *supra* note 240, 141.

crucial for this right of how to resolve the conflict between these two obligations under general international law.

4.5.6.2.3 THE IMPOSSIBILITY TO RESOLVE THIS NORMATIVE CONFLICT IN ACCORDANCE WITH GENERAL INTERNATIONAL LAW

International law is ill-equipped to resolve these kinds of situations. None of the rules, neither the limitation of drugs to medical and scientific purposes nor the right of indigenous people to use coca in accordance with their ancestral traditions, can claim superiority. This is true because *ius cogens* norms – which in accordance with Art. 53 VCLT could claim superiority – remain of limited number and certainly do not comprise any of the rules that conflict here.

The same is true for the principle of *lex specialis derogat legi generali*. It is impossible in the present type of constellation – where the right of members of indigenous peoples to traditional coca leaf use conflicts with the limitation of the coca leaf to medical and scientific purposes – to assess which norm would be special and which one would be general.[248] It could be argued that the right for indigenous peoples to exercise the cultural right of ancestral coca use is more special than the general obligation to limit drugs to medical and scientific purposes. However, the converse line of argumentation can also be pursued: the Single Convention, by regulating all drug-related activities and by specifically aiming for the eradication of non-medical coca use within a certain timeframe, excluded the possibility to deviate from the limitation to medical and scientific purposes, which cannot be circumvented by a general cultural right of indigenous peoples.

The third rule of how to resolve a normative conflict, i.e. *lex posterior derogat legi priori*, also will not resolve the present type of constellation.[249] A schematic application of the *lex posterior* rule for two different rules belonging to two different sets of regimes – *in casu* international human rights law and the UN Drug Conventions – hardly seems plausible. As was rightly held by the ILC 'in case of conflicts or overlaps between treaties in different regimes' the point of time at which treaties have been adopted 'does not necessarily express any presumption of priority between them'.[250]

248 Cf. ILC, 'Fragmentation of International Law: Difficulties arising from the Diversification and Expansion of International Law', Report of the Study Group of the International Law Commission, finalized by Martti Koskenniemi, 2006, UN Doc. A/CN.4/L.682, MN 58.

249 The rule is encapsulated within Art. 30 (3) and (4) VCLT.

250 ILC, 'Fragmentation of International Law: Difficulties arising from the Diversification and Expansion of International Law, 2006', UN Doc. A/CN.4/L.702, para. 26; ILC, 'Fragmentation of International Law: Difficulties arising from the Diversification and Expansion of International Law', Report of the Study Group of the International Law Commission, finalized by Martti Koskenniemi, 2006, UN Doc. A/CN.4/L.682, para. 272; 323 for a similar view cf. Christopher Borgen, 'Treaty Conflicts and Normative Fragmentation', in: Duncan Hollis (ed.), *The Oxford Guide to Treaties*, 448 (469).

4.5.7 Conclusion

It has been argued that no general right to use drugs for other than medical or scientific purposes exists. Universal human rights such as the right to privacy and the right to religion do not encompass a right to drug use for other than medical or scientific purposes. By the same token there is no right for members of minorities to use drugs for other than medical or scientific purposes in accordance with ancestral tradition. In contrast to these universal rights it was concluded that indigenous communities in South America enjoy a right to traditional coca use. Whether such a right exists for all indigenous peoples and all substances used by indigenous communities cannot be entirely resolved. It is unclear, whether indigenous rights as contained within UNDRIP and ILO Convention No. 169 gained a similar stance in other regions of the world as in South America. The existence of a normative conflict between the limitation of the coca leaf to medical and scientific purposes as spelled out by the Single Convention and the right for indigenous peoples to use the coca leaf in accordance with ancestral traditions is, of course, far from satisfying and needs to be addressed.

4.6 Conclusion

This chapter has shown that the current international drug control system is a system of rules and obligations based on a normative core – the limitation of drugs to medical and scientific purposes.

It was shown that the UN Drug Conventions embody a formal understanding of medical drug use. Medical drug use is drug use in accordance with medical assistance that has been carried out de *lege artis*. The same is true for scientific use, which is drug use under scientific authority that is in accordance with scientific principles. The limiting notion of medical and scientific purposes applies to the entire drug supply chain. It restricts all drug-related activities, i.e. not only drug production and trade but also use. Compliance with or deviation from drug-related activities with the limitation to medical and scientific purposes can only be assessed with regard to the actual or intended drug use: is this use carried out for medical or scientific purposes? It is against this background that the UN Drug Conventions assess all drug-related activities as either licit (as allowed) or illicit (as prohibited). The international drug control system in its present form leaves rather narrow leeway to deviate from the limitation of drugs to medical and scientific purposes. The creation of a regulatory market for cannabis or any other substance covered by the Single Convention or the 1971 Convention is incompatible with the limitation of drugs to medical and scientific purposes.

The chapter has concluded that the most viable way for States to deviate from this limitation is to amend the 1971 Convention and the Single Convention. Reservations were, however, not considered as a viable solution for States to deviate from the limitation of drugs to medical and scientific purposes as long as not met by tacit approval of all States parties. This judgment could be questioned in the light of the dilemma caused between a right to indigenous peoples of traditional coca leaf use, on the one hand, and the rigorous limitation of the very same coca leaf to medical and scientific purposes by the Single Convention, on the other hand. In spite of this dilemma, the question comes up whether an 'inside out' procedure, i.e. denouncing the Single Convention in order to re-accede to this treaty with a reservation allowing for traditional coca leaf, is not, after all, a sound option.

This, however, has to be discarded. The reason why this chapter has argued against resorting to reservations in order to deviate from the limitation of drugs to medical and scientific purposes is purely formal. Almost all States are today a party to the Single Convention and the 1971 Convention and reservations thus can only be made to the treaties, when they are denounced and re-acceded to. Resorting to such a procedure without the tacit approval of all States parties sets a very poor precedent for other fields of international law. Multilateral treaties rely on the premise that a treaty to which consent has been given can only be modified by procedures to which all parties have previously consented. Arguing otherwise would imperil multilateral treaties as instruments that ensure global cooperation. The 'inside out' option appears as a tempting route to unilaterally alter what has been part of a whole package deal that was once agreed upon. Applied regularly, such a modus operandi, would be a Pandora's box, imperilling the institutions of multilateral treaties which remain until this day indispensable 'workhorses of community interests'.[251]

Changing such treaties requires consensus and goes by treaty amendment. Consensus may not always be easy to obtain. When a State does not achieve consensus to obtain the desired results and does not want to comply with its obligations, the correct instrument is the denunciation of a treaty. The peril of denunciations would certainly, at the very least if exercised by a group of States, press for changes. However, these changes seem required in the long term. The contemporary legal order of the twenty-first century recognizes cultural plurality as a benefit and not as an obstacle that has to be overcome. The Single Convention should reflect this reality. This does not mean that the limitation of drugs to medical and scientific purposes as the ultimate cornerstone of the drug control system has to be entirely abrogated. Small modifications would be sufficient: balancing this overall limitation with local concerns would seem sufficient. The 1971 Convention, which allows for traditional-use hallucinogens could set the example in this regard. States should be left with the possibility to allow for the traditional use of narcotic drugs for other than medical or scientific purposes.

251 Bruno Simma, 'From Bilateralism to Community Interest in International Law', *RdC* Vol. 250 1994 VI, 217 (322 et seq.).

5 The material scope of the international drug control system

This chapter examines the scope *ratione materiae* of the international drug control system, analysing which substances this system applies to. This question is important because the limitation to medical and scientific purposes only applies to *drugs* in the first place. Additionally, the scope of application of the international drug control system is also at the heart of the global drug control debate.

To the author's knowledge it is not suggested that it would be per se wrong to limit drugs to medical and scientific purposes. Rather, it is argued that the international drug control system would somehow comprise the 'wrong' substances. The scope of application of the limitation to medical and scientific purposes would be arbitrary in covering certain substances, while leaving other psychoactive substances with negative health effects, such as alcohol, uncovered. It is held, that there has never been a risk-assessment of the covered substances, but that they were only subjected to the drug control system due to moral convictions of a small numbers of States, mainly from North America and Europe.[1] In particular, the applicability of the drug control system to cannabis and the coca leaf – substances whose danger to public health would seem to be manageable – would appear arbitrary.[2]

Conversely, some conceive that the scope of application of the international drug control system should be enlarged and extended to include even more substances hitherto left outside its scope of control. According to this narrative, the international drug control system would be too inflexible in order to swiftly react to changing patterns of recreational drug use and drug abuse. Indeed, the

1 Cf. with a heavy emphasis on the United States, Ethan A. Nadelmann, 'Global Prohibition Regimes: The Evolution of Norms in International Society', *International Organization* Vol. 44 1990, 479 (502 et seq.).

2 Cf. with regard to the coca leaf, Francisco E. Thoumi, 'The International Drug Control Regime's Straight Jacket: Are There Any Policy Options?', *Trends Organ. Crim.* Vol. 13 2010, 75 (77 et seq.); Pien Metaal, 'Coca in Debate: The Contradiction and Conflict Between the UN Drug Conventions and the Real World', in: Beatriz Caiuby Labate and Clancy Cavnar (eds), *Prohibition, Religious Freedom, and Human Rights: Regulating Traditional Drug Use*, 25 (26 et seq.); cf. with regard to cannabis David Bewley-Taylor, Tom Blickman and Martin Jelsma, *The Rise and Decline of Cannabis Prohibition The History of Cannabis in the UN Drug Control System and Options for Reform*, pp. 8 et seq.

flexibility of the system to adjust to the quick appearance and multiplication of so-called 'new psychoactive substances' is under a heavy constraint.[3] Those substances are *per definitionem* not within the scope *ratione materiae* of the UN Drug Conventions. Although this scope can be modified, the procedures in this regard are considered by some as being too time consuming in order to keep pace with these rapid developments.[4] As a consequence, domestic regulations on 'new psychoactive substances' would remain uncoordinated and their trade flourish.[5]

Hence, a detailed examination of the material application of the international drug control system is necessary. What needs to be addressed is the inflexibility of this system to either subject new substances to its scope of application or conversely to exempt substances thereof.

This chapter starts by outlining the actual and potential scope of application of the international drug control system. Hence, it identifies more closely the substances limited to medical and scientific purposes – narcotic drugs and psychotropic substances (5.1) – and shows in detail how the scope of application of the system can be modified, and which criteria govern such modifications (5.2). In light of this, it will be exemplified with regard to cannabis and the coca leaf how much leeway there is in reality to exempt substances from the international drug control system whose limitation to medical and scientific purposes causes controversy (5.3.). The chapter concludes by examining whether the international drug control system is of adequate flexibility to react swiftly to the appearance of 'new psychoactive substances' which have hitherto remained outside its scope of control (5.4).

5.1 Substances limited to medical and scientific purposes

There are two different groups of substances which the international drug control system limits to medical and scientific purposes. First, narcotic drugs which are covered by the Single Convention and, second, psychotropic substances come under the 1971 Convention.[6]

The term 'narcotic drug' is not defined by the Single Convention. Albeit mainly designed to control plant-based drugs – cannabis, opiates, the coca leaf and cocaine – in accordance with the approach of the earlier drug control convention, the treaty does not encapsulate a static conception of the substances covered.[7] It defines 'drugs' as substances classed into Schedules I, II and IV

3 Cf. as to this issue UNODC, 'The Challenge of New Psychoactive Substances, A Report from the Global SMART Programme', 2013.

4 EMCDDA, *Perspectives on Drugs: Controlling New Psychoactive Substances*, 2013, p. 1.

5 H.R. Sumnall, M. Evans-Brown and J. McVeigh, 'Social, Policy and Public Health Perspectives on New Psychoactive Substances', *Drug Testing and Analysis* Vol. 3 2011, 515.

6 The international drug control system does not only comprise substances which are subjected to medical and scientific purposes but also substances that do not have to be limited to medical and scientific purposes. These are first 'preparations' containing psychotropic substances or narcotic drugs but from which these substances are not easily recoverable (Schedule III Single Convention; Art. 3 1971 Convention) and 'precursors' which are used in the production of narcotic drugs or psychotropic substances (Art. 12 1988 Convention).

7 See as to the expansion *ratione materiae* of the international drug control system, *supra* 3.2.

of the Single Convention (Art. 1 (1) (j) Single Convention). The schedules are annexed to the Single Convention and contain a list of the individual substances (Art. 1 (1) (u) Single Convention).[8] Because of the Single Convention's referral to 'narcotic drugs' in its title, these substances are referred to as narcotic drugs.

The Single Convention does not lay out the criteria which governed the initial composition of the schedules.[9] An earlier draft of the Single Convention's schedules had been prepared by a technical committee[10] in which it clarified that there were two 'main considerations' governing the placing of the substance in the schedule, i.e. '(a) its degree of liability to abuse, and (b) its risk to public health and social welfare'.[11] However, no scientific review by the WHO was carried out during this stage.[12] The result is that three of the four most prominent substances falling under the scope of control of the Single Convention – cocaine, opium and morphine – have never been scientifically reviewed by the WHO.[13]

A psychotropic substance is any substance covered by Schedules I, II, III or IV of the 1971 Convention.[14] The 1971 Convention does not lay bare the initial criteria that were employed for scheduling a substance during the 1971 Conference. The final scheduling was made by a Technical Committee, guided by criteria that the ECDD had previously adopted for classifying psychotropic

8 Schedule IV contains the most restrictive control regime of the Single Convention. The entirety of the Single Convention applies to these substances and, additionally, States may adopt special measures of control with regard to these substances (Art. 2 (5) (a) Single Convention). Such special measures encompass a total prohibition of the substance in question, 'if in opinion [of the party] the prevailing conditions in its country, render it the most appropriate means of protecting the public health and welfare' (Art. 2 (5) (b) Single Convention). All substances contained in Schedule IV are also contained in Schedule I. All obligations of the Single Convention apply to drugs classed in Schedule I (Art. 2 (2) Single Convention) – with the sole exception of the special measures reserved for the substances classed in Schedule IV. Schedule II drugs are subjected to all drug control measures, except for two obligations, regarding the retail trade (Art. 2 (4) Single Convention): States do neither have to require prescription for these substances (Art. 30 (2) (b) Single Convention), nor do they have to impose labels indicating the exact drug content and weight (Art. 30 (5) Single Convention). Schedule III contains preparations consisting out of narcotic drugs, but which cannot be readily be recovered into narcotic drugs (Art. 3 (4) Single Convention) and thus are not subjected to medical and scientific purposes.

9 As to the modification of the schedules cf. *infra* 5.2.2.1.

10 Cf. on the appointment of such a committee, Organization of the Work of the Conference Note by the Secretary-General, OR I Single Convention, p. xxi; for the actual appointment cf. OR I p. 47.

11 Report of the Technical Committee, OR II Single Convention, p. 263.

12 The ECDD never reviewed thoroughly the composition of the Schedules in the run-up to the Single Convention, E. Danenberg et al., 'Modernizing Methodology for the WHO Assessment of Substances for the International Drug Control Conventions', *Drug and Alcohol Dependence* Vol. 131 2013, 175 (176 et seq.).

13 *Ibid.* (176). It seems doubtful that they have ever been reviewed scientifically before being subjected to the 1912 Convention's scope of control; *ibid.* (180).

14 Schedule I contains the most restrictive regime of the entire UN Drug Conventions (Art. 7 1971 Convention; cf. I. Bayer and H. Ghodse, 'Evolution of International Drug Control, 1945–1995', *Bulletin on Narcotics* Vol. 51 1999, 1 (11). The scope of control imposed on substances in Schedule I differs considerably from the control of substances contained in Schedules II, III and IV. The difference of control between the substances classed into Schedules II, III and IV is only a difference in degree. Thus, Arts 8, 9, 10, 13 (1) and 14 (1) apply to all schedules; the degree of control of Schedules II, III and IV varies in Arts 11, 12 and 16 (4).

substances.[15] The ECDD considered that two main characteristics should be taken into account, when deciding whether a substance should be subjected to international control: '(a) the degree of risk to public health and (b) the usefulness of the drug in medical therapy.'[16] Accordingly, it proposed individual substances that should be included into the 1971 Convention's schedules. The conference drafting the 1971 Convention complied – one exception notwithstanding – with these proposals.[17]

5.2 Modification of the scope of application of the international drug control system (scheduling)

Under the UN Drug Conventions new substances can be added to the schedules, substances can be moved from one schedule to another and substances can, likewise, be removed all together from a schedule and thus the international drug control system as a whole. The modifications of the schedules do not occur by treaty amendment, but are subject to particular procedures carried out by drug control's institutions.

5.2.1 The procedure for modifying the schedules

The procedure for modifying a schedule under the Single Convention is regulated by Arts 3 (3) (iii), 3 (4), 3 (5) and 3 (6) Single Convention. A modification of the schedules is either initiated by the WHO *motu proprio* or by a State party (Art. 3 (1) Single Convention).[18] Subsequently, the WHO examines the substance and issues a recommendation (Art. 3 (4)–(6) Single Convention) upon which the CND makes its final decision (Art. 3 (7) Single Convention). The recommendation of the WHO is mandatory in the sense that any modification of the schedule by the CND has to be in accordance with the recommendation of the WHO.[19] The CND may, likewise, decide not to concur with the recommendation of the WHO. In this case, however, no successful modification of the schedules takes place and the initial status quo is retained.

The modification of the schedules becomes effective for all the States parties once the Secretary General has notified them of the CND's decision (Art. 3 (7) Single Convention). The decision of the CND, however, is subject to review by the ECOSOC upon the request by a party up until 90 days after the receipt of the Secretary General's notification (Art. 3 (8) Single Convention). The

15 Commentary 1971 Convention, Art. 2 para. 4, MN 50.

16 ECDD, 17th Report, 1970, WHO Technical Report Series No. 437, pp. 9 et seq.

17 Commentary 1971 Convention, Art. 2 para. 4, MN 50.

18 In most cases the procedure for scheduling seems to have been initiated by the WHO and not by the States parties; cf. in this regard United Kingdom, Background Paper Related to its Notification Submitted on 23 January to the Secretary General on the Review of the Scope of Control of Mephedrone, 2014, UN Doc. E/CN.7/2014/CRP.11, p. 1. This seems to be true for the Single Convention and the 1971 Convention.

19 Cf. for a similar view S. K. Chatterjee, 'The WHO Expert Committee on Drug Dependence', *ICLQ* Vol. 28 1979, 27 (48).

ECOSOC is free to reverse or confirm the decision of the CND and takes the final decision (Art. 3 (8) (c) Single Convention).

The procedure for modifying the schedules under the 1971 Convention bears similarities to the Single Convention. It is initiated by the WHO *moto proprio* or a State party (Art. 2 (1) 1971 Convention). The decision of placing a substance within a schedule lies with the CND and is preceded by a recommendation of the WHO. Moreover, a party may request the ECOSOC to review this decision (Arts 2 (5) and 2 (7) 1971 Convention). There is, however, a difference between the 1971 Convention and the Single Convention as far as the legal effects of the amendment are concerned. Under the Single Convention, the decision of the CND to amend the schedules becomes effective for *all the States parties* once a notification of this decision has been made by the Secretary General (Art. 3 (7) Single Convention).[20] The 1971 Convention grants the possibility for the parties to opt out of such a decision (Art. 2 (7) 1971 Convention). Within a 180-day period, States parties may formulate a notice to the Secretary General that '*in view of exceptional circumstances*' individual provisions of the 1971 Convention cannot be applied to the substance in question (Art. 2 (7) 1971 Convention).[21] Additionally, as will be shown in greater detail below under the 1971 Convention, the recommendation of the WHO is not binding for the CND in every aspect.[22]

5.2.2 The material criteria for modifying the schedules

5.2.2.1 The criteria for modifying narcotic drugs covered by the Single Convention: Convertibility and similarity

The Single Convention lays out the criteria that govern the recommendation of the WHO,[23] but does not stipulate the criteria for the final (political) decision of the CND.

20 There is, however, a possibility to request the ECOSOC to alter such a decision in accordance with Art. 2 (8) 1971 Convention.

21 Notwithstanding this notification, the party will be required to apply a number of control measures for the substance in question (Art. 2 (7) (a)–(d) 1971 Convention). The degree of control which is required will depend on the Schedule in which the substance has been placed.

22 See *infra* 5.2.2.2.

23 The WHO relies on the ECDD in the scheduling process; cf. as to the mandate of the ECDD, *supra*, 2.2.5.1 In practice, the ECDD schedules substances in accordance with revised Guidelines on the WHO Review of Psychoactive Substances for International Control that have been adopted by WHO's Executive Board in 2010, which apply both to the scheduling under the Single Convention and the 1971 Convention; WHO, Guidance on the WHO Review of Psychoactive Substances for International Control, 2010, para. 1. While the final recommendation of the WHO will be made by its Director-General, the latter acts on the advice of the ECDD; *ibid.*, para. 10. The WHO review procedure consists out of two steps. First, the pre-review, whose sole purpose is for the ECDD to determine, whether current information on an individual substance justifies critical review; *ibid.*, para. 14. Second, the critical review, where the ECDD will assess the 'the dependence-producing capability, the likelihood of abuse and of causing public health and social problems, and usefulness in medical therapy of each substance'; *ibid.*, para. 32; for a brief account cf. Danenberg et al., *supra* note 12, 175 (177 et seq.).

With regard to a substance which is not contained in Schedules I and II, the WHO will determine whether the substance is 'liable to similar abuse and productive of similar ill effects to the drugs in Schedule I or Schedule II or is convertible into a drug' (Art. 3 (3) (iii) Single Convention). Thus, there are two criteria – similarity and convertibility – that have to be distinguished from each other.

The criterion of 'convertibility' had been defined prior to the adoption of the Single Convention by the WHA, as to refer to 'the ease of conversion and the yield obtained constitute a risk to public health',[24] which is also used by the Commentary.[25] The chemical structure of the substance is irrelevant; what counts, however, is that its properties allow it to be transformed into narcotic drugs with '*relative ease*'.[26]

However, similarity of a substance means that a substance has to be either 'morphine-like, cannabis-like or cocaine-like'.[27] This view was unsuccessfully challenged by a group of States within the WHA in 1968. They advanced a draft resolution recommending the inclusion of six substances (including various amphetamines) into Schedule I of the Single Convention.[28] According to them, 'similarity' in the sense of Art. 3 (3) (iii) related to the diametrical effects on human health and danger of abuse of the individual substance concerned, irrespective whether the substance in question had comparable characteristics to the other substances covered by the Single Convention. [29] The resolution, however, was not adopted by the WHA. The view among States parties, the PCB, the INCB as well as the Office of Legal Affairs of the United Nations Secretariat prevailed that it was not legally possible to widen the scope of the Single Convention to such (psychotropic) substances. They referred *inter alia* to the *travaux préparatoires* as excluding such a possibility.[30]

Additionally, a substance classed into Schedule I will be simultaneously added into Schedule IV, and thus subjected to the most restrictive regime foreseen by

24 WHA Resolution 7.7., quoted in Official Records of the World Health Assembly No. 5, Seventh World Health Assembly Part. I, 1954, pp. 19 et seq.

25 Commentary Single Convention, Art. 3 para. 3, sub-para. (iii), MN 11.

26 *Ibid.*, MN 10.

27 *Ibid.*, MN 5; Claude-Henri Vignes, 'La Convention sur les Substances Psychotropes', *AFDI* Vol. 17 1971, 641 (643).

28 Cf. draft WHA resolution introduced by Sweden, Denmark, Finland, Iceland, Norway and Yugoslavia, Official Records of the World Health Organization No. 169 21st World Health Assembly Part II, 1968, pp. 393 et seq.; cf. also for an account Kettil Brunn, Lynn Pan and Ingemar Rexed, *The Gentlemen's Club: International Control of Drugs and Alcohol*, pp. 17; 246 et seq.

29 Cf. in this regard the statement by the Sweden, Official Records of the World Health Organization No. 169 21st World Health Assembly Part II, 1968, p. 394, describing the deplorable effects of amphetamines to the users.

30 Cf. for the view of the INCB, Official Records of the World Health Organization No. 169 21st World Health Assembly Part II, 1968, pp. 400 et seq.; cf. for the view of the Legal Office quoted by the United Division on Narcotic Drugs, *ibid.*, p. 398; PCB, Rapport final du Comité central permanent des stupéfiants et de l'Organe de contrôle des stupéfiants, UN Doc. E/OB/23-E/DSB-25, 1967, paras 146 et seq.; see for a negative view of the States parties, statement by the US delegate, Official Records of the World Health Organization No. 169 21st World Health Assembly Part II, 1968, p. 396; cf. also the views of the Austrian delegate; *ibid.*, p. 398, and the New Zealand delegate, *ibid.*, p. 398, and the view of the Dutch delegate, *ibid.*, p. 399. For a similar conclusion cf. Kettil Brunn, Lynn Pan and Ingemar Rexed, *The Gentlemen's Club: International Control of Drugs and Alcohol*, pp. 247 et seq.

the Single Convention, provided that the WHO determines that it 'is particularly liable to abuse and to produce ill effects', which are 'not offset by substantial therapeutic advantages not possessed by substances other than drugs in Schedule IV'(Art. 3 (5) Single Convention). The transfer of a substance from one schedule to another or the deletion of a substance from the schedules all together as spelled out by Art. 3 (6) is based on the same criteria of 'similarity' and 'convertibility'.[31]

Hence, when the WHO assess that a substance is similar to cannabis, cocaine, the coca leaf and opiates or convertible into such a drug, it will recommend the scheduling of such a substance. In the alternative it will advise against scheduling it.

5.2.2.2 *The criteria for modifying psychotropic substances under the 1971 Convention: Similarity, capacity to produce dependence and the viability of international control*

The criteria for modifying the schedules of the 1971 Convention are different from the Single Convention. Although similarity plays an important role for modifying the schedules, a substance can also be added to the scope of the 1971 Convention because of its capacity to cause dependence and its health-related risks.

5.2.2.2.1 THE RECOMMENDATION OF THE WHO

Article 2 (4) 1971 Convention lays bare the criteria that the WHO has to consider when recommending the appropriate schedule to the CND. These criteria apply to the addition of new substances to the schedules, as well as the deletion and transfer of psychotropic substances from one schedule to another (Art. 2 (5) and (6) 1971 Convention).

Likewise, to the Single Convention, the WHO in accordance with Art. 2 (4) (a) (ii) will determine, whether a substance 'has the capacity to produce similar abuse and similar ill effects as a substance in Schedule I, II, III and IV'. This will be approved for substances 'similar to the barbiturates and to the tranquillizers already controlled by the [1971 Convention'.[32] In the alternative, the WHO will determine whether 'the substance has the capacity to produce (1) A state of dependence, and (2) Central nervous system stimulation or depression, resulting in hallucinations or disturbances in motor function or thinking or behaviour or perception or mood' (Art. 2 (4) (a) (ii) 1971 Convention).

In order to distinguish psychotropic substances from other mind-altering substances, including tobacco or alcohol,[33] the WHO will, in addition to the assessment made under Art. 2 (4) (a) (i) or (ii), examine whether the substance is 'being or is likely to be abused' and thereby 'constitute a public health and social

31 Cf. for a similar line of argumentation Commentary Single Convention, Art. 3 para. 6, MN 3.

32 Commentary 1971 Convention, Art. 2 para. 4, MN 15; in contrast to the Single Convention, the 1971 Convention, however, fails to cover substances merely because they are convertible into psychotropic substances; *ibid.*, Art. 2 General Comments, MN 7

33 See Commentary 1971 Convention, Art. 2 para. 4, MN 15; cf. also Comment, 'The Convention on Psychotropic Substances: Domestic Consequences of Ratification', *Iowa L. Rev.* Vol. 63 1978, 950 (955); see with regard to tobacco, ECDD, 31st Report, 1999, WHO Technical Report Series, No. 887, p. 13.

problem warranting the placing of the substance under international control' (Art. 2 (4) (b) 1971 Convention). This requires examining whether the substance causes problems of a transnational nature: the failure of one State to control the substance in question has to result in a lack of control in another State.[34] The last paragraph of Art. 2 (4) contains additional aspects to consider, namely the 'extent or likelihood of abuse', 'the degree of seriousness of the public health and social problem' and 'the degree of usefulness of the substance in medical therapy'.

5.2.2.2.2 THE DECISION OF THE CND

The final decision of the CND is based on two components. On the one hand, the Commission is required to 'take into account the communication of the [WHO] whose assessment shall be determinative as to medical and scientific matters' (Art. 2 (5) 1971 Convention). These medical and scientific matters cover the similarity of a substance (Art. 2 (4) (a) (ii) 1971 Convention) as well as its dependence-producing potential and mind-altering capacities (Art. 2 (4) (i) 1971 Convention). The binding part of the WHO's communication also extends to the likelihood of abuse and the degree of usefulness of a substance in medical therapy, mentioned by the last paragraph of Art. 2 (4) 1971 Convention. As far as these factors are concerned, the CND has to accept the scientific assessments of the WHO as a given. It can neither question their correctness, nor would the CND be able to replace them by other scientific expertise.

This is very different from the other part of the WHO's communication laid out by Art. 2 (4) (b) and the last paragraph of Art. (2 (4) 1971 Convention. This part considers the assessment of the WHO that is not related to medical and scientific purposes. It comprises the WHO's view of whether a substance requires international control (Art. 2 (4) (b)), as well as the determination of the seriousness of the public health and social problem (last para., Art. 2 (4)). As far as these factors are concerned, the communication of the WHO will not be binding upon the CND. Here it may effectively replace the WHO's findings with its own and deviate from the WHO's assessment.[35] Additionally, the CND makes its own assessment with regard to factors that have not previously been considered by the WHO. The Commission has to bear in mind the 'economic, social, legal and all other factors it may consider relevant' when it places a substance into one of the schedules (Art. 2 (5) 1971 Convention). The assessment that the CND enjoys here is wide, but it is not allowed to act arbitrarily.[36]

5.3 Prospects for exempting cannabis and the coca leaf from drug control's scope of application

In light of the flexible scope of application of the UN Drug Conventions, the question arises concerning whether it would be possible to ease tensions surrounding

34 Commentary 1971 Convention, Art. 2 para. 4, MN 8; cf. also; WHO, Guidance on the WHO Review of Psychotropic Substances for International Control, 2010, para. 57.

35 Commentary 1971 Convention, Art. 2 paras 5 and 6, MN 19.

36 *Ibid.*

the international drug control system by freeing certain substances from international control.[37] In particular, the limitation of two substances to medical and scientific purposes – the coca leaf and cannabis – has proven controversial.[38] Why this is the case and why those two substances are of such particular interest and controversy cannot be satisfactorily resolved here.[39] The following remarks on cannabis and the coca leaf can, in any event, be taken as exemplary for other narcotic drugs. It, therefore, seems relevant to discuss if and how these substances could be exempted from the international drug control system by relying on the scheduling procedure.

5.3.1 Modifying the scope of control for cannabis

Cannabis is currently listed in Schedules I and IV of the Single Convention and thus subjected – together with substances like heroin – to the most restrictive measures of control under this treaty. [40] This scheduling occurred without any scientific review by the WHO.[41]

5.3.1.1 Delisting cannabis from Schedule I

In order to be exempted from the Single Convention's scope of control, cannabis would have to be removed from Schedule I of the Single Convention. The

37 This ideas has already been discussed before; cf. e.g. Robin Room and Sarah Mackay, 'Roadmaps to Reforming the UN Drug Conventions', A Beckley Foundation Report, 2012, p. 11.

38 Bewley-Taylor, et al., *supra* note 2, pp. 60 et seq.; Mark A. Leinwand, 'The International Law of Treaties and United States Legalization of Marijuana', *Colum. J. Transnat'l L.* Vol. 10 1971, 413 (420 et seq.); cf. also Martin Jelsma, 'UNGASS 2016: Prospects for Treaty Reform and UN System-Wide Coherence on Drug Policy', 2016, p. 22.

39 It has recently been noted that the effects of cannabis would warrant more research. This concerns both the abuse potential of cannabis as well as its suitability for medical purposes; Daniel Cressey, 'The Cannabis Experiment', *Nature* Vol. 524 2015, 280.

40 Art. 1 (1) (b) Single Convention defines cannabis as 'the flowering or fruiting tops of the cannabis plant (excluding the seeds and leaves when not accompanied by the tops) from which the resin has not been extracted, by whatever name they may be designated'. It has rightly been remarked that this definition excludes the cannabis leaf, which has psychoactive effects minor to the cannabis resin and the tops; Bewley-Taylor et al., *supra* note 2, p. 25 with further references. The main psychoactive ingredient of cannabis, tetrahydrocannabinol (THC), is also covered by Schedule I of the 1971 Convention. Additionally, a stereochemical variant of THC, dronabinol, is contained in Schedule II of the 1971 Convention. The fact that those two substances are scheduled under the 1971 Convention seems to be without practical relevance to contemporary non-medical cannabis use. Cannabis itself is not covered by the 1971 Convention. The application of the 1971 Convention is only triggered once dronabinol or THC are separated from cannabis; cf. as to this *supra* 4.2.6.1. THC and dronabinol in their pure form are only very rarely consumed; cf. as to dronabinol, ECDD, 34th Report, 2006, WHO Technical Report Series No. 942, p. 3; cf. for proposals to reschedule dronabinol within Schedule III of the 1971 Convention; Bewley-Taylor et al., *supra* note 2, pp. 25 et seq.

41 The ECDD only considered that cannabis was of no medical use; cf. ECCDD, 14th Report, 1965, WHO Technical Report Series No. 312, p. 11; *id.*, 11th Report, 1961, WHO Technical Report Series No. 211, p. 11; *id.*, 3rd Report, 1952, WHO Technical Report Series No. 57, p. 11.

removal from Schedule I would have the effect of *ipso iure* removing the substance simultaneously from Schedule IV.[42]

In 2015, the ECDD made known that it would carry out a review on cannabis – comprising but not limited to its toxicity, dependence potential as well as its medical use.[43] In 2017, the ECDD requested the WHO's Secretariat to prepare the relevant documentation for a pre-review.[44] The ECDD dedicated its 40th meeting (held from 4 to 7 June 2018) to the pre-review, but no final report has so far been issued at the time of writing. A possible next step for the WHO would be to carry out a more holistic critical review, which in turn could result in the WHO issuing a recommendation to the CND.[45]

Such a review will hardly lead to the result of exempting cannabis from Schedule I of the Single Convention. The main reason is the political majorities within the CND that make a delisting of this drug highly improbable.[46] Moreover, even *if* the ECDD arrived at the conclusion that cannabis has a very low potential for dependence and high therapeutic value, it seems unlikely that it could recommend deleting this substance from the Single Convention's scope. The reason for this lies with the normative framework for the WHO's recommendation laid out by Art. 3 (3) (iii) and Art. 3 6 (b) Single Convention.

As has been shown above, the assessment of a substance by the WHO under the Single Convention is *not* an independent scientific assessment. Article 3 (3) (iii) Single Convention does not require the WHO to examine the abuse potential and therapeutic properties of a substance. The recommendation of the WHO to schedule a substance under the Single Convention depends on the likeness or resemblance of a substance with drugs that were contained in the original schedules to the Single Convention or its convertibility into such substances. Cannabis had been contained within the initial version of Schedules I and IV of the Single Convention. This means that as long as the WHO acts in accordance to the letter and spirit of Arts 3 (3) (iii) and 6 (b) – even when *arguendo* that new evidence suggested that cannabis would not be dependence producing and of high therapeutic value – it could not recommend the deletion of cannabis from Schedule I.

5.3.1.2 Delisting cannabis from Schedule IV

The result may be different, however, with regard to the prospects of deleting cannabis from Schedule IV of the Single Convention. Recommending the removal of a substance from Schedule IV in accordance with Arts 3 (6) and 3 (5) Single Convention differs notably from the assessment carried out under Arts 3 (6) and 3 (3) (iii) Single Convention. When carrying out an assessment under Art. 3 (5), the WHO is not bound by the similarity of cannabis with substances classed into Schedule IV. Rather, the WHO will determine whether a substance

42 Art. 28 Single Convention on the cannabis plant, however, would remain in force.

43 ECDD, 36th Report, 2015, WHO Technical Report Series No. 991, pp. 48 et seq.

44 ECDD, 38th Report, 2015, WHO Technical Report Series No. 1005, pp. 48; with regard to the scope of the pre-review see *supra* note 23.

45 See *ibid.* for the scope of the critical review.

46 Bewley-Taylor et al., *supra* note 2, pp. 60 et seq.

is particularly liable to abuse and whether it produces ill effects which are not offset by substantial therapeutic advantages possessed by substances other than drugs in Schedule IV (Art. 3 (5) Single Convention).

It has been argued by a peer-reviewed article to which one member of the ECDD contributed that it could not today be maintained that cannabis would fulfil the requirements for drugs contained within Schedule IV.[47] This is not the place to contribute to the debate concerning the effects of cannabis on human health.[48] It suffices to conclude, however, that should the recommendation of the WHO involve that cannabis needs to be delisted from Schedule IV of the Single Convention, the final decision would lie with the CND in this regard. Although, for political reasons the latter can decide not to comply with the WHO's recommendations, it would have to invoke good reasons for deviating from the WHO's views in order to be able to justify its decision.

It has to be kept in mind, however, that in this case cannabis would still be subjected to the Single Convention's Schedule I. The measures of control reserved for substances contained in Schedule IV – ranging up to a total prohibition (including for medical and scientific purposes) of Schedule IV substance – are merely recommendatory (Art. 2 (5)). The rest of the Convention, including the limitation to medical and scientific purposes would remain in force with regard to cannabis. Thus, deleting a substance from Schedule IV would mostly have a symbolic effect. In this case the substance would still be covered by Schedule I of the Single Convention and remain a narcotic drug limited to medical and scientific purposes.

5.3.2 Freeing the coca leaf from international control

The coca leaf is currently listed in Schedule I of the Single Convention. It is thus subjected to the same measures of control as cocaine, despite the fact that cocaine is considerably more potent than the coca leaf.[49] As has already been shown, its status as a controlled substance under the UN Drug Conventions has caused numerous tensions and frictions. Its scheduling under the Single Convention can be attributed to a report of a commission of enquiry dating from 1950.[50]

The ECDD carried out a pre-review on the coca leaf in 1992. It considered that 'the coca leaf was appropriately scheduled under the Single Convention [...]

47 Cf. for a similar conclusion Danenberg et al., *supra* note 12, 175 (180); Bewley-Taylor et al., *supra* note 2, p. 61.

48 Cf. as to this Cressey, *supra* note 39, 280.

49 Francisco E. Thoumi, 'A Modest Proposal to Clarify the Status of Coca in the United Nations Conventions', *Crime, Law & Social Change* Vol. 42 2004, 297.

50 Report of the Commission of Enquiry on the Coca Leaf, May 1950, Official Records of the Economic and Social Council, May 1950. This report is viewed today by many as biased; cf. in this regard, e.g. Sven Pfeiffer, 'Rights of Indigenous Peoples and the International Drug Control Regime: The Case for Traditional Coca Leaf Chewing', *GoJIL* Vol. 5 2013, 287 (302) with further references.

since cocaine is readily extractable from the coca leaf'.[51] Thus the ECDD, far from basing its assessment on the threats of the abuse of the coca leaf itself, seems to have considered that the coca leaf was appropriately scheduled, due to its convertibility into cocaine – for which it is the main ingredient. This assumption seems to be correct under the present legal framework. Articles 3 (6) and 3 (3) (iii) of the Single Convention enable the WHO to recommend to schedule a substance within Schedule I if the substance is convertible into another drug covered by Schedule I. The coca leaf is the main ingredient for cocaine and this is sufficient in order to place it within Schedule I of the Single Convention.

Additionally, the same argument against de-scheduling cannabis from Schedule I could be invoked with regard to the coca leaf. Thus, notwithstanding the convertibility of the coca leaf and even if the WHO were to conclude that the coca leaf has a low potential for abuse and high therapeutic value, one can hardly see how the WHO could recommend to free the coca leaf from international control. The coca leaf was covered within the initial Schedules of the Single Convention. Delisting a substance requires that the ECDD concludes that similarity with a substance contained in the initial Schedules can be denied (Arts 3 (6); 3 (3) (iii) Single Convention). The coca leaf, however, was classed in the initial schedules of the Single Convention and one may hardly conceive how the WHO could come to a recommendation in favour of delisting this substance.

5.3.3 Conclusion

The prospects for freeing the coca leaf and cannabis from the Single Convention are slim. The main criterion for scheduling a substance – its comparability to the substances initially contained in the Single Convention's schedules – does not allow for an adequate amount of flexibility. A substance that was initially scheduled under the Single Convention cannot subsequently be freed from its scope of control by a modification of the schedules; what counts is whether the substance has cannabis-, opium- or cocaine-like effects. This is the case for the coca leaf and cannabis. This result cannot be altered, even if the WHO concluded that such a substance does not pose a threat to human health and is of high therapeutic value. Cannabis and the coca leaf are merely exemplary in this regard. The Single Convention's scope of application with regard to plant-based narcotic drugs is inflexible. This is no coincidence. This instrument was drafted in order to specifically subject these drugs to medical and scientific purposes and no provisions were foreseen allowing subsequent exemption of these substances from its scope of control.

This material inflexibility of the Single Convention is at odds with the very idea of providing for a flexible legal framework by introducing schedules. Instead of

51 ECDD, 28th report 1992, pp. 38 et seq. The initial scheduling of the coca leaf has been based on different grounds Pien Metaal, 'Coca in Debate: The Contradiction and Conflict Between the UN Drug Conventions and the Real World', in: Beatriz Caiuby Labate and Clancy Cavnar (eds), *Prohibition, Religious Freedom, and Human Rights: Regulating Traditional Drug Use*, 25 (32 et seq.).

leaving the fate of the composition of the schedules to the WHO's scientific assessment regarding the therapeutic usefulness and the health-related risks of the individual substance concerned, the criterion of similarity perpetuates the Single Convention's initial status quo. Other multilateral treaties that rely on the same technique of schedules or annexes provide more flexibility in this regard. For example, the UNESCO World Heritage Convention allows its treaty body – the Cultural Heritage Committee – to modify the sites, monuments and buildings protected as cultural and ecological heritage 'which it considers as having outstanding universal value in terms of such criteria as it shall have established'.[52] It is not bound by the initial assessment of the States parties in this regard. Similar techniques can be found in the International Whaling Convention[53] and Convention on Migratory Species.[54] The schedules or annexes of these treaties can be modified without being limited to the scientific knowledge that applied when these instruments were adopted. Obviously these treaties have hardly anything in common with the UN Drug Conventions. They are employed in this analysis to illustrate that the 'material inflexibility' of the Single Convention is without parallel in multilateral treaty making. The result is different for the 1971 Convention. Here, the WHO effectively may assess the potential of a substance to produce dependence and its effects on the central nervous system (Art. 2 (4) (a) 1971 Convention). If new scientific evidence suggests that this is no longer the case, the WHO may recommend that the substance in question should be freed from international control.

5.4 The challenge of regulating uncertainty: the rise of new psychoactive substances and the international drug control system

The inflexible scope of application of the international drug control system is not only deplored by those who claim that certain substances should not be limited to medical and scientific purposes, it is also argued that many substances currently outside drug control's scope of application should be limited to medical and scientific purposes. This concerns so-called 'new psychoactive substances'.

5.4.1 Definition of new psychoactive substances

New psychoactive substances are used in order to obtain psychoactive effects, similar to those of psychotropic substances or narcotic drugs, while circumventing

52 Art. 11 (2) Convention Concerning the Protection of the World Cultural and Natural Heritage of 23 November 1972, entered into force 15 December 1975, UNTS Vol. 1037, 151.

53 Art. V (1) International Convention for the Regulation of Whaling of 2 December 1946, entered into force 10 November 1948, UNTS Vol. 161. p. 72.

54 Art. XI Convention on the Conservation of Migratory Species of Wild Animals of 23 June 1979, entered into force 1 November 1983 UNTS Vol. 1651, p. 356.

their control measures.[55] A new psychoactive substance is a substance that (a) is neither controlled by the Single Convention nor the 1971 Convention ***and*** (b) due to its psychoactive effects poses a threat to public health that is at least comparable to psychotropic substances or narcotic drugs.[56] 'New' in this regard does not necessarily mean that the substance in question has been produced or discovered lately, but that it has only recently become available.[57] This definition is of course very wide and the UNODC subsumes different substances ranging from khat – a plant-based stimulant, used in certain parts of Eastern Africa and the Arabian Peninsula for centuries[58] – to 'spice' – synthetic cannabinoids, having similar effects to cannabis – under this label.[59] The intended use of new psychoactive substances, is often – albeit only very superficially – disguised by marketing them as 'bath salts' or 'aromatic potpourri'.[60]

New psychoactive substances seem to have proliferated with unprecedented speed in the last years.[61] The European Monitoring Centre on Drugs and Drug Addiction (EMCDDA) reported that more than 100 new substances were detected in 2014 alone.[62] These figures are impressive; new psychoactive substances today outnumber all substances covered by the 1971 Convention and the Single Convention.[63] The proliferation of new psychoactive substances, or 'legal highs',[64] is spurred by their sale and marketing via the Internet.[65] Although the exact dynamics driving their use are not entirely identified, drug control measures seem to play a relevant part in this regard. Once a substance is subjected to drug control measures, those users which are eager to remain within a legal

55 One example of new psychoactive substances are synthetic cannabinoids, known as 'spice' which are used in order to replace cannabis; cf. also for further examples, UNODC, 'The Challenge of New Psychoactive Substances, A Report from the Global SMART Programme', 2013, pp. 3 et seq.

56 Cf. in this regard, the definition by the INCB; INCB Annual Report 2012 MN 260; UNODC, 'The Challenge of New Psychoactive Substances, A Report from the Global SMART Programme', 2013, p. iv; EMCDDA, Monitoring New Drugs, 2005.

57 UNODC, 'The Challenge of New Psychoactive Substances, A Report from the Global SMART Programme', 2013, p. iv.

58 Cf. in this regard ECDD, 13th Report, 1962, WHO Technical Report Series No. 273, pp. 10 et seq.

59 Cf. UNODC, 'The Challenge of New Psychoactive Substances, A Report from the Global SMART Programme', 2013, pp. 3 et seq. for further examples.

60 Cf. e.g. Kathryn Seely, Jeff Lapoint, Jeffery Moran and Liana Fattore, 'Spice Drugs are More than Harmless Herbal Blends: A Review of the Pharmacology and Toxicology of Synthetic Cannabinoids', *Progress in Neuro-Psychopharmacology & Biological Psychiatry* Vol. 39 2012, 234 (235).

61 These proliferation seems to be caused inter alia by the decrease of the quality of controlled drugs; Colin Davidson, 'New Psychoactive Substances', *Progress in Neuro-Psychopharmacology & Biological Psychiatry* Vol. 39 2012, 219, as well as the availability of new psychoactive substances on the Internet; UNODC, Expert Consultation on New Psychoactive Substances, 3–5 September 2013, 2014, UN Doc. E/CN.7/CRP.1, para. 10.

62 EMCDDA, Drug Report 2014, p. 16.

63 UNODC and WHO, Expert Consultation on New Psychoactive Substances, Vienna 9–11 December 2014, UN Doc. E/CN.7/2015/CRP.2, para. 2. In 2012 alone, UNODC identified 251 new psychoactive substances, whereas the number of substances covered by the Single Convention and the 1971 Convention stood at 234; UNODC, World Drug Report 2008, UN Publication, Sales No. E.08.XI.1, p. 106 with further references.

64 Carolyn Coulson and Jonathan P. Caulkins, 'Scheduling of Newly Emerging Drugs: A Critical Review of Decisions over 40 Years', *Addiction* Vol. 107 2011, 367.

65 The Internet also serves as a guide where users share their experiences with regard to their effects; cf. e.g. Sumnall et al., *supra* note 5, 515 (516).

market will try to circumvent these very control measures by resorting to psychoactive substances legally available.[66]

Thus, forcibly, regulatory measures aiming to control such substances will lag behind the actual developments. States have sought to close some gaps, by introducing generic or dynamic schedules, in order to be able to cover substances before they actually appear on the market.[67] Furthermore, the European Union has taken measures on a regional level.[68] These responses, however, are insufficient in order to tackle a problem that has already become of transnational extent – new psychoactive substances are traded on a global market.[69] In spite of all this, it has been concluded that the problem is so serious that 'the model on which drug control policies have been historically based appears to be, if not broken then at least in need of serious repair'.[70] This requires in the first place to identify the deficits of the scheduling process of the UN Drug Conventions with regard to new psychoactive substances.

5.4.2 Deficits of the scheduling process with regard to new psychoactive substances

The emergence of new psychoactive substances potentially challenges the scheduling process of the Single Convention and the 1971 Convention in two ways. First, the scheduling process may be too slow to react quickly to modifying patterns of recreational drug use (5.4.2.1). Second, it may be the case that the evidence required for a successful modification of the schedules of both treaties, is simply unavailable (5.4.2.2).

5.4.2.1 Time-constraint posed by the appearance of new psychoactive substances

The fact that the procedures for modifying the schedules would be time-consuming was already recognized by the drafters of the Single Convention.[71] A modification of the schedules of the Single Convention and the 1971 Convention requires a recommendation of the WHO and a decision of the CND. The CND meets annually in March. The ECDD has no permanent staff but

66 CND 'Making Drug Control "Fit for Purpose" Building on the UNGAS's Decade Report by the Executive Director of the UN Office on Drugs and Crime as a Contribution to the Review of the Twentieth Special Session of the General Assembly' of 7 March 2008, UN Doc. E/CN.7/2008/CRP.17, p. 10.

67 UNODC, Expert Consultation on New Psychoactive Substances, 3–5 September 2013, UN Doc. E/CN.7/CRP.1, 2014, para. 37; cf. also Coulson and Caulkins, *supra* note 64, 367 with further references; the CND has encouraged national legislation in this regard; CND Resolution 55/1, 2012, UN Doc. E/2012/28 paras 4 et seq.; cf. also UNODC, World Drug Report 2008, UN Publication, Sales No. E.08.XI.1, pp. 109 et seq.

68 Council Decision 2005/387/JHA of 10 May 2005, *OJEC* L 127/32.

69 Cf. for this idea Paul Griffiths, Michael Evans-Brown and Roumen Sedefov, 'Getting Up to Speed with the Public Health and Regulatory Challenges Posed by New Psychoactive Substances in the Information Age,' *Addiction* Vol. 108 2013, 1700 (1701); UNODC, 'The Challenge of New Psychoactive Substances, A Report from the Global SMART Programme', 2013, pp. 33 et seq.

70 Griffiths et al., *supra* note 69, 1700 (1701).

71 Cf. in this regard a warning already by the British delegate; OR I Single Convention, p. 22.

experts that will contribute to its work; it meets on an ad hoc basis every two years.[72] Thus, especially since the ECDD usually carries out the pre-review and the critical review separately,[73] a modification of the schedules of the Single Convention and the 1971 Convention may easily take up to five years from the initial notification of a State party or the WHO until the final decision of the CND. However, this is not forcibly the case.

The WHO can carry out the pre-review and critical review in one step,[74] and the synchronization of the decision-making procedures of the CND and WHO is also considered in order to save time.[75] Timely responses to new psychoactive substances are possible.

This can be shown with regard to the scheduling of 'mephedrone' – a substance bearing similarities to amphetamine-type stimulants. In January 2014, the United Kingdom had notified the Secretary General that a procedure under Art. 2 1971 Convention should be initiated, in order to bring mephedrone under the scope of control of the 1971 Convention (Art. 2 (1) 1971 Convention).[76] Subsequently, the Secretary General informed the parties, the CND and the WHO (Art. 2 (2) 1971 Convention).[77] The ECDD – meeting in the same year from 16 to 24 June – carried out the pre-review and the critical review in one step for mephedrone.[78] It recommended the inclusion of mephedrone in Schedule II of the 1971 Convention, due to the substantial risk for public health and dependence potential.[79] Only nine months later, in March 2015, the CND decided to include mephedrone in Schedule II of the 1971 Convention.[80] Thus, it was possible to schedule a new psychoactive substance within a period of roughly 13 months. In order to allow for such quick responses on a regular basis, the ECDD would have to meet annually. The example of mephedrone shows that *if* the CND and the WHO act in coordination and reach a common assessment with regard to a substance in question, quick modifications of the schedules are possible.

5.4.2.2 Unavailability of evidence on new psychoactive substances

A more substantial problem of 'major concern' posed by new psychoactive substances to the scheduling process is the lack of scientific evidence.[81] All too often

72 Christopher Hallam, David Bewley-Taylor and Martin Jelsma, 'Scheduling in the International Drug Control System', TNI Series on Legislative Reform of Drug Policies, June 2014, p. 2.

73 See with regard to the review practice by the ECDD, *supra* note 24.

74 UNODC, Expert Consultation on New Psychoactive Substances, 3–5 September 2013, 2014, UN Doc. E/CN.7/CRP.1, para. 49.

75 *Ibid.*, para. 52.

76 Cf. for this, United Kingdom, Background Paper Related to its Notification Submitted on 23 January to the Secretary General on the Review of the Scope of Control of Mephedrone, 2014, UN Doc. E/CN.7/2014/CRP.11, p. 1.

77 *Ibid.*

78 ECDD, 36th Report, 2014, WHO Technical Report Series No. 991, p. 26.

79 *Ibid.*, pp. 25 et seq. The recommendation seems to be predominantly grounded in the similarity of mephedrone to MDMA; *ibid.*

80 CND, Decision 58/1, 2015, UN Doc. E/2015/28.

81 ECDD, 36th Report, 2014, WHO Technical Report Series No. 991, p. 9.

their potential for dependence and their effects on human health, remain an unknown.[82] This lack of knowledge is related to a substantial paucity of data for new psychoactive substances.[83] This is no coincidence, given that new psychoactive substances are multiplying so quickly that it is difficult to keep pace with analysing their chemical structure.[84] In some cases, such substances may even be more harmful than the controlled substances they are replacing.[85] In other cases, new psychoactive substances might also have medical uses.[86] The problem caused by a paucity of data is exacerbated by the substances' 'diverse chemical structure'.[87] This makes it particularly difficult to analyse the risk of new psychoactive substances for human health and their ability to produce dependence.[88] The lack of data has practical consequences. When evidence is insufficient, the ECDD in accordance with its guidelines will not be able to recommend scheduling of a substance.[89] Thus, the ECDD in 2014 recommended against scheduling a substance in almost 50 per cent of the substances reviewed due to the absence of reliable evidence.[90]

The problem could possibly be mitigated to a certain extent by basing a decision to schedule a substance on its similarity to other controlled substances rather than on its dependence-producing potential and threat to human health. Indeed, both Conventions allow the WHO to recommend the scheduling of a substance due to its similar effects to other controlled substances (Art 3 (3) (iii) Single Convention; Art. 2 (4 (a) (ii) 1971 Convention). When mephedrone was scheduled, the WHO focused on similarity as outlined by Art. 2 (4) (a) (ii) 1971 Convention than on the characteristics of a substance as mentioned by Art. 2 (4) (a) (i) of the same treaty.[91] Focusing on similarity in times of limited evidence was also considered as a possibility by experts when dealing with limited evidence available.[92]

82 Griffiths et al., *supra* note 69, 1700 (1701); Sumnall et al., *supra* note 5, 515 (516); cf. more concretely with regard to 'spice' Seely et al., *supra* note 60.

83 UNODC, 'The Challenge of New Psychoactive Substances, A Report from the Global SMART Programme', 2013, p. 3; UNODC and WHO, Expert Consultation on New Psychoactive Substances, Vienna 9–11 December 2014, UN Doc. E/CN.7/2015/CRP.2, paras 15 et seq.

84 L.A. King and A.T Kickman, 'A Brief History of "New Psychoactive Substances"', *Drug Testing and Analysis* Vol. 3 2011, 401 (402).

85 Cf. in this regard for 'spice' Maren Hermanns-Clausen et al., 'Acute Toxicity due to the Confirmed Consumption of Synthetic Cannabinoids: Clinical and Laboratory Findings', *Addiction* Vol. 108 2013, 534 (540): 'Altogether, the synthetic cannabinoids appear to be more toxic than cannabis products.' However, the converse result is also possible; King and Kickman, *supra* note 84, 401 (403).

86 Davidson, *supra* note 61, pp. 219 et seq.

87 King and Kickman, *supra* note 84, 401 (402).

88 *Ibid.*

89 WHO, Expert Consultation on New Psychoactive Substances, Vienna 9–11 December 2014, UN Doc. E/CN.7/2015/CRP, para. 15.

90 Cf. in this regard ECDD, 36th Report, 2014, WHO Technical Report Series 991, where the WHO advised against the scheduling of 11 substances; 23 substances where reviewed *in toto* in the session.

91 ECDD, 36th Report, 2014, WHO Technical Report Series No. 991, pp. 25 et seq.

92 UNODC and WHO, Expert Consultation on New Psychoactive Substances, Vienna 9–11 December 2014, UN Doc. E/CN.7/2015/CRP, para. 43.

Nevertheless, at least for the 1971 Convention, the WHO will require sufficient evidence that a substance effectively possess similar ill-effect as the controlled substances.

Conversely, as the examples of the coca leaf and cannabis show, the decision to subject an individual substance to the international drug control system can lead to great controversy; scheduling is not a decision that should be taken too lightly.[93] Hence, the recommendation for adding a substance to the scope of application of the drug control system should be taken with great scrutiny and be based on scientific evidence. In spite of the poor evidence on the health-related effects of many new psychoactive substances, the adoption of provisional control measures for their control might seem a promising solution.

5.4.3 Provisional control measures as a possible solution?

The drug control treaties foresee two types of provisional measures of control. On the one hand, the Single Convention and the 1971 Convention contain obligations for States parties to assess the adoption of provisional control measures, as long as the scheduling procedure is pending (Art. 3 (3) (i) Single Convention; Art. 2 (3) 1971 Convention) (5.4.3.1). On the other hand, the Single Convention provides the possibility for the CND to provisionally subject a substance to Schedule I during this period (Art. 3 (3) (ii) Single Convention) (5.4.3.2).

5.4.3.1 An obligation for States parties to examine the provisional application of control measures

Both under the 1971 Convention as well as under the Single Convention, States parties are required to examine the application of provisional control measures for substances while the recommendation of the WHO is pending (Art. 3 (3) (i) Single Convention and Art. 2 (3) 1971 Convention).[94]

The obligation applies from the moment that a State party receives a notification that the scheduling process has been initiated by a party or by the WHO (Art. 3 (2) Single Convention; Art. 2 (2) 1971 Convention). Subsequently, a party has to assess whether provisional drug control measures are required. In other words, it has to examine whether to provisionally subject the substance in question to its domestic system of drug control. The content of this obligation is rather vague. This obligation is not an obligation of result to effectively take drug control measures for such substances, but a mere obligation of conduct to examine the application of provisional control measures to such substances. Thus, a party only has to assess bona fide whether provisional drug control measures should be taken. Various States parties may of course adopt diverging views on the viability of adopting

93 Peter Reuter, 'The Dangerous Charm of the Unknown', *Addiction* Vol. 107 2012, 1902 (1903).

94 Art. 3 (3) (i) Single Convention has been overlooked by some; cf. UNODC, World Drug Report 2013, UN Publication, Sales No. E.13.XI.6, p. 109.

provisional measures of control with regard to one similar substance; a refusal to adopt such measures cannot in itself amount to a breach of this obligation.[95] Hence, these provisional measures taken on a domestic level will hardly lead to uniform drug control measures while the scheduling process is pending.

However, as has been rightly noted by the United Kingdom, relying on this obligation has several benefits.[96] Awareness with regard hitherto unknown substances can be raised. Moreover, and perhaps more crucially, States will – by carrying out the assessment under these articles in accordance with their domestic drug control systems – possibly collect more evidence on the health impact of these substances.[97] These insights may be valuable, in turn, on the international level, when the WHO carries out its critical review. It has been held that despite its long-time existence within the legal framework, 'provisional control has never been explored fully'.[98] It may be time for States parties to use this obligation in order to create more knowledge with regard to new psychoactive substances.

Thus, the obligation of States to conduct a preliminary assessment of drug control measures for substances not yet under international control, may well enhance reactions on an international level by creating insights that the WHO can subsequently use.[99] More uniform responses could be provided for, by allowing provisional scheduling as long as the procedure for modifying the schedules is pending.

5.4.3.2 Provisional scheduling

Provisional scheduling is foreseen for narcotic drugs by the Single Convention (Art. 3 (3) (ii) Single Convention). No comparable obligation is imposed on psychotropic substances by the 1971 Convention.

Provisional scheduling differs notably from the obligations to examine provisional drug control measures that were just described. Whereas the latter merely require States to consider which provisional measures they would deem appropriate, provisional scheduling effectively obligates States to apply the entire regime of the Single Convention under international law (obligation of result). This obligation applies as long as the final decision on the status of the substance under the Single Convention is pending.[100]

95 Commentary 1971, Convention, Art. 2 para. 3, MN 3; for a similar view, see United Kingdom, Background Paper related to its Notification Submitted on 23 January to the Secretary General on the Review of the Scope of Control of Mephedrone, 2014, UN Doc. E/CN.7/2014/CRP.11, p. 2.

96 United Kingdom, Background Paper related to its Notification Submitted on 23 January to the Secretary General on the Review of the Scope of Control of Mephedrone, 2014, UN Doc. E/CN.7/2014/CRP.11, p. 2.

97 *Ibid.*

98 *Ibid.*

99 Cf. for a more critical view, however, Hallam et al., *supra* note 72, p. 15.

100 The Commentary to the Single Convention differentiates between a 'discretionary provision' and a 'mandatory provision' for provisional scheduling; Commentary Single Convention, Art. 3 para. 3, subparas 1 and 2, MN 2.

Once the procedure of scheduling a substance under the Single Convention is initiated by the WHO or a State party and the recommendation of the WHO is pending, it is possible for the CND authoritatively to decide to include the substance provisionally into Schedule I. Article 3 (3) (ii) Single Convention has so far remained *lettre morte* but could be activated any time by the CND.[101] Whether the application of this procedure is well suited to enhance the control of new psychoactive substances may well be questioned. Provisional scheduling can occur without any scientific input by the WHO. This creates a risk of limiting substances to medical and scientific purposes, whose viability of scheduling will be *in fine* denied.

5.4.4 *New psychoactive substances, the institutional framework and the limits of the international drug control system*

5.4.4.1 *Possibilities to take measures with regard to new psychoactive substances*

Both the CND and the INCB have already taken measures with regard to new psychoactive substances. Thus, the INCB monitors 'substances not under international control' next to narcotic drugs, psychotropic substances and precursors, as a fourth category within its Annual Report since 2005.[102] Furthermore, the CND has adopted resolutions on new psychoactive substances.[103]

Such practices fall into the mandate of both institutions. As has been shown above, the CND has been provided with a mandate by the UN Charter and the UN Drug Conventions to deal with every aspect of the world drug problem.[104] Drugs in this sense cannot be understood narrowly but

101 UNODC, Expert Consultation on New Psychoactive Substances, 3–5 September 2013, 2014, UN Doc. E/CN.7/CRP.1, para. 24 with further references.

102 Cf. e.g. INCB Annual Report 2005, paras 281, 385 et seq., 431 et seq., 642; *id.* Annual Report 2006, paras 258 et seq., 355 et seq., 457 et seq., 606 et seq., 643 et seq.; *id.* Annual Report 2007, paras 409 et seq., 530 et seq., 727 et seq.; *id.* Annual Report 2008, paras 377 et seq., 465 et seq., 577 et seq., 762; *id.* Annual Report 2009, paras 330, 430 et seq., 505, 552, 604, 724 et seq., 768 et seq.; *id.* Annual Report 2010, paras 330, 426 et seq., 500 et seq., 545, 589, 683, 707, 739 et seq., 789 et seq.; *id.* Annual Report 2011, paras 368, 463 et seq., 561, 575 et seq., 620 et seq., 684, 747 et seq., 795 et seq.; *id.* Annual Report 2012, paras 316 et seq., 389 et seq., 497 et seq., 602 et seq., 644 et seq., 718 et seq., 782 et seq., 833 et seq.; *id.* Annual Report 2013, paras 323 et seq., 363, 401 et seq., 465, 497, 542, 595, 650, 658; *id.* Annual Report 2014, paras 297 et seq., 393 et seq., 446 et seq., 477 et seq., 580 et seq., 640 et seq., 679 et seq.

103 CND Resolution 55/1, 2012, UN Doc. E/2012/28 E/CN.7/2012/18; *id.* Resolution 56/4, UN Doc. E/2013/28 E/CN.7/2013/14, 2013; *id.* Resolution 57/9, 2014, UN Doc. E/2014/28; *id.* Resolution 58/11, 2015, UN Doc. E/2015/28. Resolutions on individual new psychoactive substances were adopted earlier, however, cf. in this regard, e.g. CND Resolution 53/13, 2010, UN Doc. E/2010/28 on poppers or CND Resolution 53/11, 2010, UN Doc. E/2010/28 on synthetic cannabinoids.

104 Cf. as to the mandate of the CND *supra* 2.2.3.1.

comprises all sorts of mind-altering substances, including psychoactive substances which are currently left outside of the scope of the international drug control system.[105]

The same seems true with regard to the INCB. This body is allowed to make any recommendation it desires within the Annual Report.[106] This margin is of course very wide and concerns any question related to the world drug problem.[107] The INCB is not confined to substances covered by the legal framework. It may also share its views regarding certain questions, where it considers the legal framework to be inadequate – including the fact that certain substances are not covered by the UN Drug Conventions.[108]

The mandate of the INCB and the CND to take measures with regard to substances outside the international drug control system has its limits, however. It is also clear that these two institutions cannot blur the line between substances limited to medical and scientific purposes and those substances to which this obligation does not apply.

5.4.4.2 Limits of the CND and the INCB to take measures with regard to new psychoactive substances

The limits of the mandate of the CND and the INCB with regard to new psychoactive substances will be shown by examining the practice of these institutions with regard to khat and ketamine. In both cases it was concluded that by adopting measures these institutions would have transgressed their mandate.[109]

5.4.4.2.1 THE RECOMMENDATIONS OF THE INCB ON KHAT ARE LEGAL UNDER THE UN DRUG CONVENTIONS

It has been argued that the INCB would have violated its mandate by making recommendations with regard to khat. The plant-based stimulant of khat is neither subjected to the Single Convention nor the 1971 Convention. Its main

105 Cf. for the same result Commentary Single Convention Art. 9, MN 3. This also supported by a long-term practice of the CND to make recommendations with regard to substances hitherto not covered by the UN Drug Conventions; cf. in this regard, e.g. CND Res. 4 (XVII), 1962 (available online at: www.unodc.org/documents/commissions/CND/Drug_Resolutions/1960–1969/1962/CND_Resolution-4_XVII.pdf) on the control of barbiturates that is not covered by the Single Convention; cf. also CND Res.1 (XX), 1965 on new narcotic substances (available online at: www.unodc.org/documents/commissions/CND/Drug_Resolutions/1960–1969/1965/CND_Resolution-1_XX.pdf).

106 Art. 15 (1) Single Convention; Art. 18 (1) 1971 Convention; as to the mandate of the INCB cf. *supra* 2.2.4.2.

107 Cf. also for such a wider understanding Commentary Single Convention, Art. 15, MN 6.

108 Commentary Single Convention, Art. 15, MN 6.

109 With regard to Ketamine cf. Hallam et al., *supra* note 72, p. 8; with regard to Khat cf. *ibid.*, p. 1; cf. also Khat, Axel Klein, Pien Metaal and Martin Jelsma, 'Chewing over Khat Prohibition: The Globalization of Control and Regulation of an Ancient Stimulant', TNI Series on Legislative Reform of Drug Policies, January 2012, p. 4.

psychoactive ingredient, cathinone, is contained within Schedule I of the 1971 Convention.[110] Indeed, the ECDD had carried out review with regard to khat for decades but never recommended the scheduling of this substance.[111] In 2006, during the last critical review, the ECDD concluded that the substance did not warrant international control, since 'the potential for abuse and dependence [was] low [and] the threat to public health [was] not significant enough to warrant international control'.[112]

Nevertheless, the INCB in its Annual Report for the same year stated its 'concern' about khat use in Yemen. It called upon the authorities to take 'appropriate measures to control its cultivation, trade and use' and recommended campaigns 'to raise community awareness regarding the addictive nature of khat and its negative impact on society'.[113]

Such statements in themselves can hardly be seen as transgressing the board's mandate. The INCB did not create the impression that khat would be effectively covered by the international drug control system and that States would be legally required to limit the substance to medical and scientific purposes. Moreover, in most cases, the INCB merely monitors the situation with regard to khat without making any recommendations regarding its abuse whatsoever.[114] One may concur with such statements or be of a different opinion, however, the fact that the INCB merely monitors substances whose scheduling was denied by the ECDD, does not seem to be a violation of its mandate. The INCB's Annual Report is only an account of the INCB's work and has no legal binding value.[115]

The limits of the INCB's and CND's mandate may be transgressed when both institutions collaborate collusively and thereby de facto extend the application of the drug control system, notwithstanding the fact that the WHO has advised against scheduling a substance in question. This was the case with ketamine, a substance both used as a substitute for ecstasy for recreational purposes and as an anaesthetic in human beings for medical reasons.[116]

110 INCB, List of Psychotropic Substances under International Control (available online at: www.incb.org/documents/Psychotropics/greenlist/Green_list_ENG_V17-06834.pdf).

111 Cf. also ECOSOC Resolution 1957/667 (XXIB)D, 1957, UN Doc. E/Res/1957/667(XXIV)D, in which the ECOSOC invited the WHO to study this question; Resolution 1964/1025 (XXXVII), 1964, UN Doc. E/Res/1964/1025/(XXXVII), where it 'not[ed] that medical and social problems connected with the habitual and excessive chewing of khat leaves are at present confined to a limited number of countries in one geographical area'; cf. furthermore, *id.* Resolution 1972/1657(LII), E/1972 where further studies were requested.

112 ECDD, 34th[th] Report, 2006, WHO Technical Report Series No. 942, p. 11 (italics added).

113 INCB Annual Report 2006, para. 556.

114 INCB Annual Report 2010 para. 330; *id.* Annual Report 2011, para. 368; *id.* Annual Report 2012, para. 389; *id.* Annual Report 2013 paras 323 et seq.; *id.* Annual Report 2014, paras 299 et seq.

115 Cf. as to the normative value of INCB Annual Reports, *supra* 2.2.4.3.

116 Cf. also as to this substance UNODC, 'The Challenge of New Psychoactive Substances, A Report from the Global SMART Programme', 2013, p. 8; ECDD, 36th Report, 2014, WHO Technical Report Series No. 991, pp. 42 et seq., p. 43.

5.4.4.2.2 KETAMINE: DE FACTO SCHEDULING BY THE CND AND THE INCB AGAINST SCIENTIFIC EXPERTISE OF THE WHO

The ECDD itself concluded in 2012 that in the case of ketamine:

> de facto over the years a situation of international control has emerged without any scientific assessment of the situation, due to both CND resolutions and the INCB continuous pressure on Member States. It should be mentioned that according to the international drug control conventions the CND has no mandate to conclude to international control [sic.] without a WHO recommendation and the INCB has no mandate at all.[117]

This assessment is rooted on a long-standing quarrel between the ECDD, on the one hand, and the INCB and the CND, on the other hand, with regard to this issue. In 2006, the ECDD had recommended against scheduling ketamine; it decided, however, that another review would be carried out at its next meeting.[118] Despite this, the CND adopted a resolution and 'called upon Member States to place ketamine on the list of substances controlled under their national legislation where their domestic situation so requires'.[119] This resolution was '*welcomed*' by the INCB,[120] and it called '*on all Governments to implement that resolution without delay*'.[121] Neither the CND nor the INCB pointed out the crucial fact that the ECDD had advised against introducing the substance to the 1971 Convention's schedules. The above-mentioned CND resolutions and INCB statements are indeed critical, in that both institutions failed to mention that the ECDD had recommended against scheduling ketamine.

In 2012, when the ECDD finally reconvened,[122] it recommended again not to schedule ketamine within the 1971 Convention.[123] It considered that 'ketamine abuse currently does not appear to pose a significant global public-health risk' and advised against scheduling because its wide use as an 'anaesthetic, especially in developing countries'.[124] In its Annual Report for 2012, the INCB reiterated that States would have to implement CND resolutions on ketamine, but failed to mention that the ECDD again had recommended against placing ketamine under international control.[125] Likewise, in 2014, the CND adopted

117 ECDD, Ketamine Critical Review Report 35th Meeting 2012, p. 35; cf. for the same view Hallam et al., *supra* note 72, p. 9.

118 ECDD, 34th Report, 2006, WHO Technical Report Series No. 942, p. 10.

119 CND Resolution 49/6, 2006, UN Doc. E/2006/para. 2; cf. also *id.* Resolution 50/3, 2007, UN Doc. E/2007/28, preambular para. 2 for a similar consideration.

120 INCB Annual Report 2007, para. 222.

121 *Ibid.*

122 There were no meetings of the ECDD between 2006 and 2012 due to a lack of funding; Hallam et al., *supra* note 72, p. 2.

123 ECDD 35th Report, 2012, WHO Technical Report Series No. 973, p. 9.

124 *Ibid.*

125 INCB Annual Report, paras 316 et seq.

another resolution on ketamine which, as the ECCD's 2012 review noted, failed to clarify the crucial fact that the ECDD repeatedly had recommended against scheduling ketamine.[126]

In the same year, China (re-)initiated the scheduling procedure for ketamine in accordance with Art. 2 (1) 1971 Convention.[127] The Secretary General subsequently notified the member States and the WHO in accordance with Art. 2 (2) 1971 Convention.[128] Thus, in June 2014 the ECDD – for the third consecutive time – carried out a critical review with regard to ketamine, where it once more recommended against scheduling this substance.[129]

The fact that the CND and the INCB have recommended to the States parties to subject ketamine to domestic control measures, despite the ECDD's recommendation to the contrary seems hardly compatible with the scheduling system as foreseen by the UN Drug Conventions.

The problem at hand is not so much related to paucity of evidence, which is mostly problematic in the scheduling process of new psychoactive substance. What causes all the turmoil here is the fact that the CND and the INCB, on the one hand, and the ECDD, on the other hand, differ with regard to the risk assessment of ketamine. The problem of diverging opinions between those institutions, however, is adequately regulated by the international legal framework: the INCB has no role to play in the scheduling process under the 1971 Convention and the Single Convention. It may of course express its non-binding opinions with regard to the need of control for substances but cannot create the impression to somehow monitor resolutions of the CND on substances left outside the UN Drug Convention's scope of application. The WHO, in turn – upon the advice of the ECDD – provides for the scientific input during the scheduling process and disposes of a monopoly as far as the scientific evidence is concerned.

The final decision, however, lies with the CND. The ECDD has – albeit very cautiously – noted that ketamine is liable to abuse and produces dependence, and, therefore, it would seem to fulfil the criteria of Art. 2 (4) (a) (i) 1971 Convention.[130] Its advice against scheduling the substance under the 1971 Convention seems to be based on the assessment that the substance does not warrant international control (Art. 2 (4) (b) 1971 Convention). As was already shown – the CND could well reach a different conclusion in this regard.[131] It could consider that, notwithstanding the ECDD's recommendation to the contrary, the substance effectively does warrant international control in accordance with

126 CND Resolution 57/10, 2014, UN Doc. E/2014/28, preambular paras 8 and 12.

127 CND, Report on the Fifty-seventh Session, 2014, UN Doc. E/2014/28, para. 59.

128 *Ibid.*

129 ECDD, 36th Report 2014, pp. 42 et seq.

130 Overall, the main reason against scheduling for the ECDD seems to be the therapeutic usefulness of this substance; cf. ECDD, 34th Report, 2006, WHO Technical Report Series No. 942, p. 10; *id.*, 35th Report, 2012, WHO Technical Report Series No. 973, pp. 8 et seq.; *id.*, 36th Report, 2014, WHO Technical Report Series No. 991, pp. 42 et seq.

131 Cf. for all this *supra* 5.2.2.2.

Art. 2 (4) (b) 1971 Convention. It is not bound by the assessment of the ECDD in so far, which is only determinative as to medical and scientific matters (Art. 2 (5) 1971 Convention). It may be doubted whether scheduling a substance without the WHO's recommendation would be advisable, given the growing critique that the WHO would tend to be marginalized within the international drug control system.[132] The assessment whether ketamine warrants international control is a question falling into the CND's discretion and for the CND to decide. What seems incompatible with the CND's mandate is to persistently ignore the scientific assessment of the ECDD, and to require the latter again and again to carry out scientific reviews on a matter on which it has already given its scientific expertise. It seems to be the case that the CND waits for the scientific recommendation suiting its own political opinion. This is not the way that the scheduling procedure was designed.

5.4.5 Conclusion

The INCB and the CND dispose of the means in order to deal with new psychoactive substances. They may make recommendations, raise awareness of the States parties in this regard and are allowed to monitor the substances in question. It is not possible, however, to equate uncontrolled substances with narcotic drugs and psychotropic substances. The institutions within the international drug control system cannot obligate States to limit substances outside of drug control's scope to medical and scientific purposes. Extending the limitation of drugs to medical and scientific purposes is possible, but requires an involvement of the WHO. The assessment of the WHO has to be respected and new psychoactive substances should not be used as a pretext for marginalizing its role.

Overall, the rise of new psychoactive substances does not seem to be an unresolvable task for the international drug control system. The schedules of international drug control can be extended quickly and as long as new psychoactive substances are left outside the scope of the drug control system, recommendatory measures for enhancing their control can be taken. Additionally, States are required to assess the viability of provisionally taking control measures of these substances while the scheduling process is pending. This is not to say that the rise of these substances does not put the system under constraint. Indeed, the difficulties regarding the absence of evidence with regard to the effects of these substances can – in many cases – slow down the scheduling process. The slowness caused by the need for scientific evidence to schedule substance is, however, a price worth paying given the far-reaching consequences of limiting universally a substance to medical and scientific purposes.

132 Hallam et al., *supra* note 72, p. 1.

5.5 Conclusion

The international drug control system is of adequate flexibility to subject and add substances with abuse potential of concern to the limitation to medical and scientific purposes. The system, and in particular the Single Convention, seems very inflexible as far as the possibility to exempt substances from this limitation is concerned. The initial decision to subject opiates, the coca leaf, cocaine and cannabis to medical and scientific purposes was not the result of a scientific evaluation process, but the outcome of a political assessment that the threats posed by their (potential) abuse warranted international control.

The current form of the Single Convention, by stipulating similarity and convertibility of substances as the sole criteria for modifying its schedules, makes exemptions of narcotic drugs from the international drug control system almost impossible without treaty amendment. This requires change. A substance with low dependence-producing capabilities and low abuse potential should not remain confined to medical and scientific purposes. In this light, foreseeing a mandatory periodical review of the WHO for all narcotic drugs and psychotropic substances would seem a promising idea.[133] It has to be ensured that it is only when up-to-date scientific expertise suggests that a substance poses a threat to the health and welfare of mankind, it should be limited to medical and scientific purposes.

133 Cf. Danenberg et al., *supra* note 12, 175 (181).

6 Challenges to the implementation of the international drug control system[1]

This chapter examines the means by which the international drug control system attains the goal of limiting drugs to medical and scientific purposes. It is not merely the objective of the international drug control system that is the focus of growing critique, but the premises by which this goal is to be attained are also challenged. In order to examine these challenges, two different sets of obligations have to be outlined.

On the one hand are the obligations concerning the supply of drugs. These obligations have a twofold dimension. First, States are required to control the manufacture and trade of drugs destined for medical and scientific purposes. Their objective is unclear: is it to merely prevent the diversion of drug supply, or is the goal to ensure the availability of drugs for medical and scientific purposes of equal importance?[2] Second, the international drug control system aims to suppress the drug supply that has been produced for other than medical or scientific purposes. This suppressive focus of the international drug control system has been vividly criticized for not taking into account the human rights of the individuals that will be affected by such drug control measures.[3]

On the other hand are the demand-related obligations. Albeit the reduction of supply still forms the bulk of the international drug control system, this system also contains obligations for the reduction of demand. It has been argued that these obligations would prevent States from adopting up-to-date approaches towards addiction and non-medical or non-scientific drug use that support human rights.[4]

1 The arguments advanced in this chapter, have partly already been raised in Robin Geiß and Daniel Wisehart, '"Concerned with the Health and Welfare of Mankind..." The UN Drug Conventions – A Suitable Legal Framework for the 21st Century?', *MPYbUNL* Vol. 19 2014, 368.

2 It has been argued by many that the international drug control system would embrace a dual obligation to limit the availability of drugs to medical and scientific purposes, while at the same time ensuring the availability of drugs for these ends; cf. as to this, e.g. INCB, Availability for Medical and Scientific Purposes 2010, para. 3.

3 Damon Barrett and Manfred Nowak, 'United Nations and Drug Policy: Towards a Human Rights-based Approach', in: Aristotle Constantinides and Nikos Zaikos (eds), *Essays in Honour of Kalliopi Koufa*, 2009, 449, pp. 7 et seq.

4 Human Rights Watch, International Harm Reduction Association, Canadian Aids/HIV Legal Network, Recalibrating the Regime: The Need for a Human Rights Based Approach to International Drug Policy, The Beckley Foundation Drug Policy Programme, 2008, pp. 31 et seq. Cf. also in this regard David Bewley-Taylor, Challenging the UN Drug Conventions: Problems and Possibilities, *IJDP* Vol. 14 2003, 171: 'the United Nations Convention still stand as a major obstacle to the introduction of pragmatic approaches to drug use on a national level'.

Additionally, it has repeatedly been pointed out, that the approach of the international drug control system to reach the underlying goal of limiting drug demand and supply to medical and scientific purposes would overburden a number of States where narcotic drugs are illicitly produced and trafficked. The main load posed by the world drug problem would be carried by these States, whilst States which are – despite all efforts – unable to gain control over drug use by their own population, would be left unaffected.[5]

This chapter tackles these complex issues by adopting a four-step approach. In the first step, it is shown *in concreto* how the system aims to control the licit drug supply chain destined for medical and scientific drug use; the question will be pursued whether these obligations simultaneously limit drugs to medical and scientific purposes and ensure their availability for these ends (6.1). In the second step, the suppressive provisions of the UN Drug Conventions will be displayed (6.2). It will be examined if and how these provisions can be reconciled with international human rights law. The third step investigates whether the demand-related obligations allow for a human rights-conforming treatment of addiction and non-medical drug use (6.3). The fourth and final step examines the claimed overstrain of so-called 'drug-producing' and 'drug-transit' States (6.4). Concepts will be outlined as to how the imbalance of the system towards surpassing illicit supply can be overcome.

6.1 Control of the licit supply chain: achieving a balance between limiting and ensuring an adequate availability of drug supply?

It may come as a surprise that today's world drug problem does not merely consist of a vast surplus of psychoactive substances for other than medical and scientific purposes. However, for many States and regions the unavailability of drugs for medical and scientific purposes is a pressing issue. According to the WHO, 83 per cent of the world's population lives in States with non-existent access to controlled medicines – medicines contained in the schedules of the Single Convention or the 1971 Convention – for pain treatment.[6] In 2009, 93 per cent of the morphine available for medical purposes was consumed in the United States, Europe, Canada and Australia which equalled 17.5 per cent of the world's population during that period.[7] Thus a majority of the world's population does not have access to drugs for medical and scientific purposes.[8] This is even more problematic if one considers the exceptional need for pain treatment in some of these States due to their high mortality rate caused by HIV/Aids or cancer.[9]

5 Cf. Geiß and Wisehart, *supra* note 1, pp. 368 (393), with further references.

6 WHO, Access to Controlled Medications Programme: Improving Access to Medications Controlled under International Drug Conventions, April 2012, p. 1 with further references. Controlled medicines refers to medicines subjected to the drug control system, *ibid.*, p. 6.

7 INCB, Report on the Availability of Internationally Controlled Drugs: Ensuring Adequate Access for Medical and Scientific Purposes, 2010, Figure 1, p. 2.

8 Cf. as to this issue, INCB Annual Report 2011, paras 301 et seq.

9 Ally Taylor, 'Addressing the Global Tragedy of Needless Pain: Rethinking the United Nations Single Convention on Narcotic Drugs', *J. L. Med. & Ethics* Vol. 35 2007, 556 (558); Human Rights Watch, 'Global State of Pain Treatment: Access to Medicines and Palliative Care', 2011, pp. 10 et seq.

In light of this, it seems not without interest to examine if and how the international drug control system embraces to ameliorate the availability of drugs for medical and scientific purposes. The INCB claims today that this control regime would 'serve a dual purpose: to ensure the availability of controlled substances for medical and scientific ends while preventing the illicit production of, trafficking in and abuse of such substances'.[10]

Indeed, the existence of a dual obligation – comprising both the limitation of drugs to medical and scientific purposes as well their availability for such ends – is echoed by many scholars today.[11] It has also been invoked numerous times by the WHO as well as the UNODC.[12] The vast majority of older works on the UN Drug Conventions, however, did not note the existence of such a dual obligation or more generally any legal requirement to ensure the availability of drugs for medical and scientific purposes.[13] By the same token, the UN Commentaries

10 Cf. e.g. INCB, Report on the Availability of Internationally Controlled Drugs: Ensuring Adequate Access for Medical and Scientific Purposes, 2010, p. iii, para. 3.

11 Cf. e.g. Bernad Levroy, M. Cherif Bassiouini and Jean-François Thony, 'The International Drug Control System', in: M. Cherif Bassiouni (ed.), *International Criminal Law: Vol. I, Sources, Subjects, and Contents*, 855 (872); Damon Barrett and Manfred Nowak, 'United Nations and Drug Policy: Towards a Human Rights-based Approach', in: Aristotle Constantinides and Nikos Zaikos (eds), *Essays in Honour of Kalliopi Koufa*, 2009, 449, p. 7; Robin Room and Peter Reuter, 'How Well Do International Drug Conventions Protect Public Health', *The Lancet* Vol. 379 2012, 84 (85); Sven Pfeiffer, 'Rights of Indigenous Peoples and the International Drug Control Regime: The Case for Traditional Coca Leaf Chewing', *GoJIL* Vol. 5 2013, 287 (289).

12 WHO, Access to Controlled Medications Programme: Improving Access to Medications Controlled under International Drug Conventions, April 2012, p. 11; UNODC, Ensuring Availability of Controlled Medications for the Relief of Pain and Preventing Diversion and Abuse: Striking the Right Balance to Achieve the Optimal Public Health Outcome, Discussion Paper based on a Scientific Workshop, 2011, p. 7; *id.*, Drug Policy Provisions from the International Drug Control Conventions, 2014, p. 3.

13 Herbert May, 'The Single Convention on Narcotic Drugs: Comments and Possibilities', *Bulletin on Narcotics* Vol. 7 1955 No. 1, 1 (3 et seq.). After the adoption of the Single Convention one of its drafters, Adolf Lande, while extensively expanding on the limitation of drugs for medical and scientific purposes, failed to include in his analysis the requirement of providing for the availability of drugs for these ends; cf. Adolf Lande, 'The Single Convention on Narcotic Drugs, 1961', *International Organization* Vol. 16 1962, 776 (795). By the same token, Bettati, writing in 1974, concluded:

> Dans l'ordre international comme dans l'ordre interne, le contrôle a principalement pour objet d'empêcher l'usage injustifié de stupéfiants pour la seule satisfaction des toxicomanes, de prévenir les effets nocifs de cet usage pour la santé publique, et d'empêcher l'écoulement par des voies illicites de stupéfiants destiné au commerce légal.
>
> Mario Bettati, 'Le contrôle international des stupéfiants', *RGDIP* Vol. 78 1974, pp. 170 (171)

Similarly, when S. K. Chatterjee wrote his seminal work of 1981, he failed to mention the goal of providing for availability of drugs for medical and scientific purposes, but was only concerned with the limitation of drugs to these ends; cf. e.g. S. K. Chatterjee, *Legal Aspects of International Drug Control*, p. xviii; cf., however, Kettil Brunn, Lynn Pan and Ingemar Rexed, *The Gentlemen's Club: International Control of Drugs and Alcohol*, p. 40:

> There are two sides to controlling drug availability: on the one hand medical and scientific supplies have to be ensured; on the other supply for other kinds of use have to be withheld or restricted [...] the control system is said to have dual goals.

to the Single Convention, the 1972 Protocol and the 1971 Convention do not mention the goal of providing drugs for medical and scientific purposes, but exclusively focus on the limitation of drug supply.[14]

Hence, it seems necessary to resolve whether the control of drugs as imposed by the international drug control system equally involves limiting the availability of drugs to medical and scientific purposes, while ensuring that an adequate amount is available to satisfy medical and scientific needs. It will be shown that the controlled economy of the UN Drug Conventions is exclusively dedicated to *limit* drugs to medical and scientific purposes and not to ensure their availability to these ends (6.1.1). The goal of ensuring drugs for medical and scientific purposes is merely stipulated in the preambles of the Single Convention and the 1971 Convention, but no clear obligations on how this is to be done can be found in the operative part of these treaties (6.1.2). It is only by subsequent practice of drug control's institutions that the goal of ensuring the availability of drugs for medical and scientific purposes has been demonstrated (6.1.3–6.1.4).

6.1.1 A controlled economy limiting the availability of narcotic drugs and psychotropic substances

The Single Convention and the 1971 Convention built an elaborate system that regulates the production, manufacture and trade of narcotic drugs and psychotropic substances. The system imposes a controlled economy on the production, manufacture and trade of narcotic drugs and psychotropic substances that aims to *limit* their availability. There are no obligations foreseen in that regard that require States parties to ensure that a sufficient amount of drugs is available.

6.1.1.1 Limitation of narcotic drugs by the Single Convention

Hence, under the Single Convention the restriction of global drug supply to medical and scientific purposes takes place by estimates and statistics. In accordance with Art. 19 Single Convention, States parties are obligated to provide the INCB with estimates, indicating *a priori* the amount of drugs required for medical and scientific purposes.[15] Conversely, statistics are the figures where a State

14 Cf. Commentary, Single Convention; cf. Commentary, 1971 Convention, *passim*; cf. Commentary, 1972 Protocol, *passim*. It is also noteworthy in this regard that the Commentary on the 1972 Protocol on the sole operative provision within the UN Drug Conventions encapsulating the goal of ensuring availability, i.e. Art. 9 (4), Single Convention, does not spell out this issue in detail; Commentary 1972 Protocol, Art. 2 para. 5, MN 1 et seq.

15 The estimates shall contain the following information (Art. 19 (1) Single Convention): quantities of drugs to be consumed for medical and scientific purposes (Art. 19 (1) (a) Single Convention); quantities of drugs to be utilized for the manufacture of other drugs, preparations (Schedule III) and other substances (Art. 19 (1) (b) Single Convention); stocks of drugs held (Art. 19 (1) (c) Single Convention), including the quantities of drugs necessary for 'special stocks' (Art. 19 (1) (d) Single Convention) (these are stocks of drugs for war time and/or time of natural disasters when a lot of analgesics are required; (Commentary Single Convention,

a posteriori assesses what quantities have effectively been consumed, produced and trafficked (Art. 20 Single Convention). It is by comparing the estimates with the statistics that the INCB is brought into a position to assess whether a State has effectively complied with its obligation to limit drugs to medical and scientific purposes.[16]

The estimates limit the manufacture and import of drugs (Art. 21 (1) Single Convention), as well as the production of opium (Art. 21 bis (1) Single Convention) and the export of drugs (Art. 31 (1) (b) Single Convention).[17] The estimate system indicates that in theory there is a pre-fixed maximum amount of narcotic drugs that may be manufactured, trafficked and produced each year. The purpose of this estimate system is to determine the '*maximum quantities*' each State may manufacture or import.[18] No measures are foreseen that ensure that an adequate amount of narcotic drugs is produced, traded and manufactured in order to satisfy medical and scientific needs.

The INCB both administers the estimate system (Art. 12 Single Convention) as well as the statistical returns system (Art. 13 Single Convention). Article 14 Single Convention vests the INCB with the authority to take measures to ensure the execution of this treaty. In this regard, it may remedy a situation if '[it] has objective reasons to believe that the aims of this Convention are being seriously endangered by reasons of the failure of any party [...] to carry out the provisions of this Convention' (Art. 14 (1) (a)) or when

> without any failure in implementing the provisions of the Convention, a Party or a country or territory has become, or if there exists evidence of a serious risk that it may become, an important centre of illicit cultivation, production or manufacture of, or traffic in or consumption of drugs.

Art. 19 para. 1, sub-para. d, MN 1 with further references); the areas held for the cultivation of the opium poppy (Art. 19 (1) (f) Single Convention), the number of establishments manufacturing synthetic drugs (Art. 19 (1) (h) Single Convention) and the quantities of drugs manufactured therein (Art. 19 (g) Single Convention).

16 Art. 13 (2) Single Convention expressively obligates the INCB 'to examine the [statistical] returns with a view to determining whether a Party or another State has complied with this provisions of this Convention'. This assumption is of course only valid when a State complies with its obligations regarding the estimates and statics reports them to the INCB correctly; Kettil Bruun, Lynn Pann and Ingemar Rexed, *The Gentlemen's Club: International Control of Drugs and Alcohol*, pp. 82 et seq.

17 More generally, Art. 21 (5) Single Convention requires that States not exceed the estimates. It may come as a surprise that the Single Convention only foresaw a specific provision on the limitation of production of opium, rather than requiring States parties to limit the production of narcotic drugs per se. This may be explained by the fact that the drafters of the Single Convention were very well aware that opiates were indispensable as an analgesic for the relief of pain. In contrast, cannabis and the coca leaf were considered to be without any therapeutic value. This explains the absence of any provisions on their production. The States parties considered that no considerable amount of licit supply of these substances would eventually be required. As to the distinction between a production and manufacture of a drug, cf. *supra* 4.2.6.2.

18 Commentary Single Convention, Art. 12, MN 1 (italics added).

It has been argued that this procedure would 'be a powerful tool for encouraging countries to effectively advance the treaty's objective of medical availability'.[19] This seems unconvincing. Provided that confidential consultations and public calls to governments or the ECOSOC have not resolved the situation (Art. 14 (1) Single Convention), the INCB may – as an *ultima ratio* – 'recommend to Parties that they stop the import of drugs, the export of drugs, or both, from or to the country or territory concerned' (Art. 14 (2) Single Convention). The recommendation of an embargo is certainly no adequate tool in order to ensure the availability of drugs for medical and scientific purposes.[20]

Hence, the control of the licit supply chain under the Single Convention involves a limitation of the production, manufacture and trade of narcotic drugs which is monitored by the INCB. Ensuring that drugs are available for medical or scientific purposes, however, is not an element of the controlled drug economy as erected by the Single Convention.

6.1.1.2 Limitation of psychotropic substances by the 1971 Convention

The 1971 Convention is based on the very same idea of the Single Convention to limit all psychotropic substances to medical and scientific purposes. Nevertheless, it lacks one central control element of the Single Convention, the estimate system, and therefore does not require States to limit the manufacture and export to a pre-fixed amount of psychotropic substances.[21] States parties are merely required to furnish the Board with annual statistical reports (Art. 16 (4)) and do not have to *a priori* indicate the amount of psychotropic substances needed for medical and scientific purposes. This lacunae was, however, closed to a certain extent by subsequent soft law measures. The ECOSOC has invited States to provide the INCB with a voluntary assessment of their domestic requirements for psychotropic substances.[22] According to the INCB, all in all, most States would comply with these resolutions in practice.[23] This means de facto the estimate system of the Single Convention has been extended to psychotropic substances and most States, albeit they are not legally obligated to do so. As under the Single Convention, the INCB can resort to measures in order to ensure the execution of the 1971 Convention (Art. 19 1971 Convention) which range from request-

19 Taylor, *supra* note 9, 556 (567).

20 Cf. for a similar view, Christopher Hallam, The International Drug Control Regime and Access to Controlled Medicines, TNI Series on Legislative Reform of Drug Policies, December 2014, p. 11.

21 S. K. Chatterjee, *Legal Aspects of International Drug Control*, p. 480.

22 ECOSOC Resolution 1981/7, 1981, UN Doc. E/Res/1981/7, para. 6. Whereas the latter resolution merely applies to substances in Schedule II, the invitation to communicate information of the INCB for psychotropic substances was subsequently extended for substances in Schedules III and IV; ECOSOC Resolution 1991/44, 1991, UN Doc. E/Res/1991/44.

23 INCB Annual Report 2014, para. 60; cf. also for a positive assessment of the compliance of States with these provisions, et seq.; *id.* Annual Report 2011, paras 150 et seq.; *id.* Annual Report 2012, paras 173 et seq.; *id.* Annual Report 2013, para. 157.

ing consultations to recommending an embargo (Art. 19 (1)–(2) 1971 Convention). Likewise to the Single Convention, the 1971 Convention does not provide for measures to ensure the availability of psychoactive substances for medical and scientific purposes. This is true for all psychotropic substances.

It may safely be concluded that the controlled economy for licit drug supply under both treaties is exclusively focused on limiting the amount of drugs to the amount required for medical and scientific needs. It seems to be based on the unspoken idea that a surplus of drugs is available which simply needs to be curbed to the amount required for medical and scientific needs. In this light, the above-mentioned assessments that the drug control system is based on a dual purpose to limit drugs to medical and scientific purposes, while simultaneously ensuring their availability for these ends, seem rather puzzling. It will be shown that the goal to provide for the availability of narcotic drugs and psychotropic substances can be derived from the preambles of the Single Convention and the 1971 Convention, as well as Art. 9 (4) Single Convention.

6.1.2 Tracing the aim to ensure availability of narcotic drugs and psychotropic substances for medical and scientific purposes in the UN Drug Conventions

6.1.2.1 Preambular provisions of the Single Convention and the 1971 Convention: Outlining the goal of availability

Both, the preamble of the Single Convention and the preamble of the 1971 Convention refer to the need to ensure the availability of narcotic drugs and psychotropic substances. The legal relevance of the Single Convention's preamble has been emphasized by the WHO. It would form a 'legal basis' to make controlled medicines available.[24] As will be shown, such a far-reaching conclusion is neither justified by the material content of this preambular provision nor its formal position within the Single Convention's preamble.

The second preambular paragraph of the Single Convention recognizes that 'the medical use of narcotic drugs continues to be indispensable for the relief of pain and suffering and that adequate provision must be made to ensure the availability of narcotic drugs for such purposes'.

This wording does not suggest that narcotic drugs are per se required for medical purposes, but that they are indispensable for pain treatment and management.[25] The second part of the provision indicates that it is for these purposes – for the relief of pain and suffering – that an adequate provision needs to be made. In contrast to the rather narrow focus of the Single Convention's preamble on

24 WHO, 'Access to Controlled Medicines Programme: Ensuring Balance in National Policies on Controlled Substances – Guidance for Availability and Accessibility of Controlled Medicines', 2011, p. 12.

25 Cf. also in that regard Kettil Brunn, Lynn Pan and Ingemar Rexed, *The Gentlemen's Club: International Control of Drugs and Alcohol*, p. 41.

the utility of narcotic drugs for pain treatment, the preamble of the 1971 Convention contains a more general reference to the availability of psychotropic substances for *all* medical and scientific purposes. [26]

The fifth preambular paragraph of the 1971 Convention recognizes 'that the use of psychotropic substances for medical and scientific purposes is indispensable and that their availability for such purposes should not be unduly restricted'. The provision does not require that the availability of psychotropic substances is guaranteed by taking positive steps, but outlines that psychotropic substances should not be restricted beyond what is required to limit their availability for medical and scientific purposes. The goal of guaranteeing the availability of psychotropic substances for medical and scientific purposes is only very cautiously phrased. Hence, both preambular provisions *do not* require States parties to ensure the availability of psychoactive substances for medical and scientific purposes.

Moreover, given their form as preambular provisions, they have to be distinguished from the operative part of a treaty. Only the latter is obligatory for the States parties.[27] The function of the preamble is rather to highlight the motivation of the parties to the treaty and to determine the treaty's normative context. As recognized by general rules of treaty interpretation encapsulated in Art. 31 (2) VCLT, the preamble is part of a treaty's context which forms the background of treaty interpretation.[28] A preamble is meant to lay out the more general considerations that lead to the conclusion of the treaty.[29] It is of 'theological significance' and of 'textual relevance' and may influence the understanding of the operative provisions.[30]

6.1.2.2 Article 9 (4) Single Convention: The sole operative provision of the UN Drug Conventions spelling out the goal of ensuring availability

In contrast to the above-mentioned preambular provisions that outline the goal to provide for the availability of drugs for medical or scientific purposes, the operative provisions of the Single Convention and the 1971 Convention in general do not contain references to this issue. One operative provision of the Single Convention, however, spells out the goal of providing for the availability of narcotic drugs. Article 9 (4) Single Convention reads:

26 *Ibid.*, p. 41.

27 Patrick Daillier, Matthias Forteau and Alain, Pellet (Nguyen Quoc Dinh †), *Droit International Public*, MN 73; ICJ, South West Africa Cases (*Ethiopia v. South Africa*; *Liberia v. South Africa*), Judgment of 18 July 1966, p. 6 (34).

28 Art. 31 (2) VCLT reads: 'The context of the interpretation of a treaty shall comprise, in addition to the text, including its preamble and annexes'.

29 Makane Moïse Mbenge, 'Preamble', in: Rüdiger Wolfrum, *MPEPIL*, 2012, para. 1.

30 Richard Gardiner, *Treaty Interpretation*, p. 186. Very instructive as to the normative value of preambles in general, Gerald Fitzmaurice, 'The Law and Procedure of the International Court of Justice 1951–4: Treaty Interpretation and Other Treaty Points', *BYBIL* Vol. 33 1957, 203 (227); cf. also ICJ, Case concerning Rights of Nationals of the United States of America in Morocco, Judgment of 27 August 1952, p. 172 (184).

> *The Board, in co-operation with Governments*, and subject to the terms of this Convention, *shall endeavour to limit* the cultivation, production, manufacture and use of drugs to an adequate amount *required for medical and scientific purposes, to ensure their availability for such purposes* and to prevent illicit cultivation, production and manufacture of, and illicit trafficking in and use of, drugs.[31]

Article 9 (4) contains a 'negative part' on the limitation cultivation, production, manufacture and use of narcotic drugs to the amount required for medical and scientific purposes, and a 'positive part' on the availability of drugs for such ends. The content of Art. 9 (4) is wider than para. 2 of the Single Convention's preamble. Whereas the preamble of the Single Convention only recognizes the need to provide for the availability of narcotic drugs in order to alleviate pain and suffering, Art. 9 (4) Single Convention obligates States to ensure the availability of narcotic drugs for all medical and scientific purposes. The means by which this goal has to be ensured are not clarified.

What is more, is that it is unclear whether Art. 9 (4) Single Convention also addresses the States parties or merely lays out a mandate of the INCB. The wording of Art. 9 (4) is somewhat ambiguous in this regard. The reference to the States parties within this provision is indirect. The INCB shall achieve the goals laid out by Art. 9 (4) in 'co-operation with the governments'. This reference, however, seems to indicate that Art. 9 (4) does not exclusively concern the mandate of the INCB, but also creates obligations of the States parties.[32]

Given that the controlled economy erected by the UN Drug Conventions does not operationalize the goal of ensuring availability of narcotic drugs and psychotropic substances, which is merely spelled out in very general terms by these treaties, it seems promising to turn to the subsequent practice of drug control's institutions. Today's high priority of ensuring availability of drugs for medical and scientific purposes does not result from the black letters of the UN Drug Conventions. It was rather innovative practice by drug control's institutions that gradually prioritized the importance of ensuring drugs for medical and scientific purposes.

6.1.3 Prioritizing the availability of drugs for medical and scientific purposes by drug control's institutions

6.1.3.1 A growing emphasis on providing opiates for pain treatment

Eventually drug control institutions highlighted the need to provide for narcotic drugs for medical and scientific purposes. In the beginning the, ECOSOC and the INCB started laying a growing emphasis on the lack of availability of opiates

31 Italics added.

32 Cf. for the same result, Commentary 1972 Protocol para. 2, Art. 2, MN 4; cf. for such an argumentation also Martha Maurer et al., 'Examining Influences on the Availability of and Access to Opioids for Pain Management and Palliative Care', *JPPCP* Vol. 27 2013, 255 (256 et seq.).

for pain treatment. Albeit, before those institutions had been more concerned with a perceived overproduction of opiates than with their lacking availability,[33] in 1988 the INCB expressed its concern regarding the shortage of supply of opiates and conceded that 'there might be legitimate needs hitherto unmet possibly because of insufficient health care, difficult economic situations or other conditions in the countries concerned'.[34]

This consideration was subsequently taken up by the ECOSOC, and the INCB was requested to 'assess legitimate needs of opiates in various parts of the world, hitherto unmet because of insufficient health care, difficult economic situations or other conditions'.[35]

The INCB, therefore, prepared a Special Report on the Availability of Opiates for Medical and Scientific Purposes in 1989. There, the concerns over a lack of availability of opiates for legitimate purposes were reiterated.[36] The ECOSOC endorsed this report and requested the INCB 'to accord priority to monitoring the implementation of the recommendations contained [therein]'.[37] Today, the WHO, the INCB, the UNODC, the CND and the ECOSC all recognize the importance of providing for the availability of drugs for medical and scientific purposes.[38] Accordingly, a balance has to be struck between the opposing goals to limit drugs to medical and scientific purposes, while guaranteeing for

33 Cf. In this regard ECOSOC Resolution 1979/8, 1979, UN Doc. E/Res/1979/8; *id.*, Resolution 1980/20, 1980, UN Doc. E/Res/1980/20; *id.* Resolution 1981/8, 1981, UN Doc E/Res/1981/8; *id.* Resolution 1981/12, 1981, UN Doc. E/Res/1981/12; *id.* Resolution 1982/12, 1982, UN Doc. E/Res/1982/12. These concerns culminated in a request by the ECOSOC to the INCB to prepare a special report on the availability of drugs; *id.*, Resolution 1983/3, 1983, UN Doc. E/Res/1983/3; *id.*, Resolution 1984/21, 1984, UN Doc. E/Res/1984/21, para. 3. The result of this request was INCB, Demand and Supply of Opiates for Medical and Scientific Needs, Special Report pursuant to ECOSOC Resolution 1984/21,1985, UN Doc. E/INCB/1985/1 Supp. This report laid out the fact that Art. 9 (4) Single Convention obligated the INCB to provide for an adequate amount of drugs for medical and scientific purposes; *ibid.*, para. 2. The main focus of this report remained, however, concerns voiced over a perceived overproduction of drugs.

34 INCB Annual Report 1988, para. 40.

35 ECOSOC Resolution 1989/15, UN Doc. E/Res/1989/15, para. 2.

36 INCB, Demand for and Supply of Opiates for Medical and Scientific Purposes, Special Report prepared pursuant to ECOSOC Resolution 1989/15, UN Doc. E/INCB/1989/1/Supp, p. 1; cf. also *ibid.*, para. 38.

37 It 'commended' the INCB for this special report; ECOSOC Resolution 1990/31, 1990, UN Doc. E/Res/1990/31, para. 2.

38 WHO, 'Access to Controlled Medicines Programme: Ensuring Balance in National Policies on Controlled Substances – Guidance for Availability and Accessibility of Controlled Medicines', 2011; UNODC, Ensuring Availability of Controlled Medications for the Relief of Pain and Preventing Diversion and Abuse: Striking the Right Balance to Achieve the Optimal Public Health Outcome, Discussion Paper Based on a Scientific Workshop, 2011; CND, Res. 54/6,2011, UN Doc. E/2011/28; E/CN.7/2011/15, para. 1; ECOSOC Res. 2005/26, 2005, UN Doc. E/Res/2005/26, preambular para. 3; INCB, Report of the INCB on the Availability of Drugs for Medical and Scientific Purposes, 2011, UN–Doc. E/INCB/2010/1/Supp. 1, paras 92 et seq.

their availability for such ends in order to achieve 'the optimal public health outcome'.[39]

6.1.3.2 Anchoring the need to provide for an availability of drugs within the UN Drug Conventions

Subsequently, a link between the above-mentioned growing prioritization of the availability of drugs for medical and scientific purposes and the UN Drug Conventions' obligations was established. At the outset, rather than invoking obligations of the States parties to provide for an adequate amount of drugs for medical or scientific purposes, the INCB held that its own mandate would be concerned with ensuring availability for narcotic drugs.[40]

In its above-mentioned 1989 Report, the INCB concluded that '[t]he treaties have aimed at establishing a balance between availability and control of [opiates and certain other substances] so that the latter need not impede the former'.[41] The INCB derived this aim to balance, which it then did not label as an obligation, from the Single Convention's preamble and Art. 9 (4).[42]

Six years later, the INCB for the first time approved the existence of such an obligation under the Single Convention; it held that this treaty spelled out 'a dual drug control obligation for Governments: to ensure adequate availability of narcotic drugs, including opiates, for medical and scientific purposes, while at the same time preventing the illicit production of, trafficking in and use of such drugs'.[43]

This development was perpetuated subsequently; the INCB regularly refers to a dual obligation of the Single Convention to provide for an adequate amount of drugs for medical and scientific purposes, while suppressing the availability for other ends.[44] This existence of an obligation to provide for opiates is also

39 WHO, 'Access to Controlled Medicines Programme: Ensuring Balance in National Policies on Controlled Substances – Guidance for Availability and Accessibility of Controlled Medicines, 2011, p. 4; WHO, Narcotic & Psychotropic Substances, Achieving Balance in National Opioids Control Policy, Guidelines for Assessment, WHO-Doc. WHO/ED;/QSM/2000.4, 2000, p. 11: '[t]he Central Principle of "balance" represents a dual imperative of governments to establish a system of control to prevent abuse, trafficking, and diversion of narcotic drugs while, at the same time, ensuring their medical availability'.

40 Cf. e.g. INCB Annual Report 1980, para. 1; *id.* Annual Report 1981, para. 1; *id.* Annual Report 1982, para. 1; *id.* Annual Report 1983, para. 1; *id.* Annual Report 1984, para. 1; *id.* Annual Report 1985, para. 1.

41 INCB, Demand for and Supply of Opiates for Medical and Scientific Purposes, Special Report prepared pursuant to ECOSOC Resolution 1989/15, UN Doc. E/INCB/1989/1/Supp., para. 39.

42 *Ibid.*

43 INCB, Availability of Opiates for Medical Needs, Special Report prepared pursuant to Economic and Social Council Resolutions 1990/31 and 1991/43, 1995, UN Doc. E/Res/1995/1/Supp., para. 1.

44 Cf. also for similar statements, INCB, Availability for Medical and Scientific Purposes 2010, para. 3; *id.* Annual Report 2013, p. iii; *id.* Annual Report 2014, para. 40 (g).

supported by the WHO; the WHA has adopted a resolution on cancer control in which member States were 'urged to ensure the medical availability of opioid analgesics according to international treaties and recommendations of WHO and the International Narcotics Control Board and subject to an efficient monitoring and control system'.[45] In 2010, the CND, by adopting Resolution 53/4, even more directly linked the need to ensure availability of drugs for medical and scientific purposes with the UN Drug Conventions. The preamble of this resolution recalls the second preambular paragraph of the Single Convention in which the inalienability of narcotic drugs for the treatment of pain is recognized.[46] Furthermore, it 'affirmed' that the UN Drug Conventions would 'seek to achieve a balance between ensuring the availability of narcotic drugs and psychotropic substances under international control for medical and scientific purposes and preventing their abuse'.[47] Thus, the call for enhancing the availability of narcotic drugs was subsequently backed up normatively by the CND and the INCB by developing the concept of a dual obligation to limit narcotic drugs to medical and scientific purposes, while providing for their availability at the same time.

6.1.3.3 From opiates to other substances

The third development that needs to be outlined with regard to the gradual prioritization of ensuring availability of drugs is the gradual extension of the material scope of the substances whose availability needs to be ensured. In the beginning, the ECOSOC and the INCB were exclusively concerned with a lacking availability of opiates.[48] This is no surprise, given the outstanding importance

45 WHA Resolution 58.22, 2005, para. 15; cf. also in that regard WHA Resolution 67.19, 2014, preambular para. 3:

> Acknowledging the special report of the International Narcotics Control Board on the availability of internationally controlled drugs: ensuring adequate access for medical and scientific purposes, and the WHO guidance on ensuring balance in national policies on controlled substances: guidance for availability and accessibility of controlled medicines.

46 CND Resolution 53/4, 2010, UN Doc. E/2010/28, para. 2.

47 *Ibid.*

48 ECOSOC Resolution 1979/8, 1979, UN Doc. E/Res/1979/8; *id.* Resolution 1980/20, 1980, UN Doc. E/Res/1980/20; *id.* Resolution 1981/8, 1981, UN Doc. E/Res/1981/8; *id.* Resolution 1981/12, 1981, UN Doc. E/Res/1981/12; *id.* Resolution 1982/12, 1982, UN Doc. E/Res/1982/12; *id.* Resolution 1983/3, 1983, UN Doc. E/Res/1983/3; *id.* Resolution 1984/21, 1984, UN Doc. E/Res/1984/21; *id.* Resolution 1985/16, 1985, UN Doc. E/Res/1985/16; *id.* Resolution 1986/9, 1986, E/Res/1986/9 UN Doc. 1986/9; *id.* Resolution 1987/31, 1987, UN Doc. E/Res/1987/31; *id.* Resolution 1988/10, 1988, UN Doc. E/Res/1988/10; *id.* Resolution 1989/15, 1989, UN Doc. E/Res/1989/15; *id.* Resolution 1990/31, 1990, UN Doc. E/Res/1990/31; *id.* Resolution 1991/43, 1991, UN Doc. E/Res/1991/43 paras 2 et seq.; *id.* Resolution 1992/30, 1992, UN Doc. E/Res/1992/30, paras 2 et seq.; *id.* Resolution 1993/37, UN Doc. E/Res/1993/37, para. 2 (a); *Id.*, Resolution 1994/5, 1994, UN Doc. E/Res/1994/5; *id.* Resolution 1995/19, 1995, UN Doc. E/Res/1995/19; *id.* Resolution 1996/19, 1996, UN Doc. E/Res/1996/19; *id.* Resolution

of opiates for the treatment of pain. The INCB would soon blur the distinction between opiates and other narcotic drugs, on the one hand, and psychotropic substances, on the other hand.

In its 1999 Annual Report, the INCB implicitly held that no difference could be made between the 1971 Convention and the Single Convention as far as the need to ensure the availability of drugs and psychotropic substances was concerned. The INCB concluded that 'States recognized in the Convention on Psychotropic Substances of 1971 that the availability of psychotropic substances for medical and scientific purposes should not be unduly restricted.'[49]

Additionally, the INCB in its 2010 Report on the Availability of Internationally Controlled Drugs concluded that the two 'conventions established a control regime to serve a dual purpose'.[50] This development was supported by the CND.[51] Albeit the INCB holds that psychotropic substances and narcotic drugs have to be made available for medical or scientific purposes due to one common aim or principle, it has so far not spoken of a clear-cut obligation for States to ensure the availability of psychotropic substances for medical and scientific purposes. This seems to be correct in light of the fact that the 1971 Convention does not contain an obligation to make psychotropic substances available.

6.1.3.4 The growing emphasis on providing for the availability of drugs by the UNGA

The growing priority which the issue of ensuring availability of drugs for medical and scientific purposes had been accorded to by the INCB and the CND was for a long time not reflected by UNGA practice. In contrast to other institutions, the UNGA was silent with regard to the issue. This changed in 2009, when the UNGA called for cooperation between member States, the WHO and the INCB to ensure 'adequate availability' of drugs for medical and scientific purposes.[52] In the following years its role was limited to recalling resolutions of the CND on

1997/38, 1997, UN Doc. E/Res/1997/38; *id.* Resolution 1998/25, 1998, UN Doc. E/Res/1998/25; *id.* Resolution 1999/33, 1999, UN Doc. E/Res/1999/33; *id.* Resolution 2000/18, 2000, UN Doc. E/Res/200/18; *id.* Resolution 2001/17, 2000, UN Doc. E/Res/2001/17; *id*, Resolution 2002/20, 2002, UN Doc. E/Res/2002/20; *id.* Resolution 2003/40, 2003, UN Doc. E/Res/2003/40; *id.* Resolution 2004/43, 2004, UN Doc. E/Res/2004/43; *id.* Resolution 2005/26, 2005, UN Doc. E/Res/2005/26; INCB, Demand for and Supply of Opiates for Medical and Scientific Purposes, Special Report prepared pursuant to ECOSOC Resolution 1989/15, UN Doc. E/INCB/1989/1/Supp.

49 INCB Annual Report 1999, para. 1.

50 *Id.* Annual Report 2010, para. 3.

51 Cf. preambular paras 2 and 3, CND Resolution 53/4, 2010, UN Doc. E/Res/53/4 in that regard; cf. also preambular para. 6: in which it is affirmed 'that the international drug control conventions seek to achieve a balance between ensuring the availability of narcotic drugs and psychotropic substances under international control for medical and scientific purposes and preventing their diversion and abuse'.

52 UNGA Resolution 64/182, 2009, UN Doc. A/Res/64/182, para. 19.

the subject.[53] From 2014 onwards, however, the UNGA began to assume a more active role in promoting the availability of drugs for medical and scientific purposes. It repeatedly expressed its 'concern' over the low availability of drugs in many parts and regions of the world and highlighted the need to take measures in order to enhance availability of drugs for medical and scientific purposes.[54]

It was at UNGASS 2016 that the UNGA accorded a high priority to the issue of availability.[55] This is even recognized by harsh critiques of the general outcome of UNGASS.[56] The need to provide for availability of drugs for medical and scientific purposes is the second issue treated by the operative provisions of the outcome document. The 'commitment to improving access to controlled substances for medical and scientific purposes' is further substantiated.[57] Hence, the UNGA is beginning to assume its role as the central actor within the international drug control system with regard to the issue of availability. Further practice with regard to the issue provided could raise political pressure on States and might eventually carve out a coherent subsequent practice in application of the UN Drug Conventions involving an effective obligation of States parties to provide for an availability of narcotic drugs and psychotropic substances.

6.1.4 Ensuring availability of drugs for medical and scientific purposes in practice

Apart from appealing generally to the States parties to enhance the availability of narcotic drugs and psychotropic substances, the CND, WHO and, in particular, the INCB simultaneously are taking measures in order to enhance availability.

6.1.4.1 Monitoring by the INCB

Although conceptualized under the Single Convention and the 1971 Convention as a tool to *limit* the availability of psychotropic substances and narcotic

53 UNGA Resolution 66/183, 2011, UN Doc. A/Res/66/183, preambular para. 18; UNGA Resolution 67/193, 2012, UN Doc. A/Res/67/193, para. 9; UNGA Resolution 68/193, 2013, UN Doc. A/Res/68/193, preambular para. 20.

54 UNGA Resolution 69/201, 2014, UN Doc. A/RES/69/201, para. 14; UNGA Resolution 70/182, 2015, UN Doc. A/Res/70/182, para. 22; UNGA Resolution 71/211, 2016, UN Doc. A/Res/71/211, preamble.

55 See in this regard, speech by then INCB president Werner Sipp at the CND, 16 March 2017 (available online at: www.incb.org/documents/Speeches/Speeches2017/Speech_60th_CND_item_8d_check_against_delivery.pdf).

56 Martin Jelsma, 'UNGASS 2016: Watershed Event or Wasted Opportunity?'; Jamie Bridge, 'The Commission on Narcotic Drugs on the Final Road to UNGASS 2016: Progress Made, but a Long Way Still to Go'.

57 UNGA, Outcome Document UNGASS 2016, 2016, UN Doc. A/Res-S/30/1, para. 2 (b)–(g).

drugs, the INCB also uses estimates with a view to enhance the availability of narcotic drugs and psychotropic substances for medical and scientific purposes. Thus, the INCB uses the estimates provided under the Single Convention in order to monitor the availability of narcotic drugs for medical and scientific purposes.[58] Likewise, and despite the fact that the monitoring obligations under the 1971 are limited, the INCB monitors the availability of psychotropic substances as far as data is available.[59] This practice is backed by the CND.[60]

It is only through this data that the INCB will come to know that drugs for medical and scientific purposes are unavailable and urge States to take measures to improve availability. It uses the unit of 'defined daily doses for statistical purposes (S-DDD) consumed per million inhabitants per day', to measure 'internally, for administrative purposes'[61] if a State party provides for adequate availability. The INCB has invented the unit of defined daily doses in order to measure the availability of drugs for medical purposes. It is impossible to assess in the abstract when an adequate supply of controlled substances exists for medical and scientific purposes. There is no universal agreement as to what amount of drugs can be considered as 'adequate'.[62] This is true because the demand of controlled substances for medical and scientific needs depends on the general health care situation of a State, its morbidity rate, etc.[63]

The sole group of substances where the INCB approves an inadequate amount of availability below a certain threshold are opioids.[64] An inadequate amount of opioids can be approved below a threshold of 200 SDD per million inhabitants;[65]

58 INCB, Report on the Availability of Internationally Controlled Drugs: Ensuring Adequate Access for Medical and Scientific Purposes, 2010, para. 132, Recommendation (a). This is supported by the WHO, see WHA Resolution 67.18, 2014, para. 2 (7).

59 INCB, Report on the Availability of Internationally Controlled Drugs: Ensuring Adequate Access for Medical and Scientific Purposes, 2010, para. 45.

60 CND Resolution 53/4 53/4, 2010, UN-Doc. E/2010/28, para. 8:

> Invites the International Narcotics Control Board, as in previous years, to include in its annual report for 2010, to be presented to the Commission at its fifty-fourth session, information on the consumption of narcotic drugs and psychotropic substances used for medical and scientific purposes worldwide, including an analysis of impediments to their adequate availability and actions to be taken to overcome those impediments and, when available, specific information about the status of and progress made by countries.

61 INCB, Report on the Availability of Internationally Controlled Drugs: Ensuring Adequate Access for Medical and Scientific Purposes, 2010, para. 43.

62 Cf. for the case of opioids, Marie-Josephine Seya et al., 'A First Comparison Between the Consumption of and the Need for Opioid Analgesics at Country, Regional, and Global Levels', *JPPCP* Vol. 25 2011, 6 (7).

63 INCB, Report on the Availability of Internationally Controlled Drugs: Ensuring Adequate Access for Medical and Scientific Purposes, 2010, para. 46. For example, a State party with a high proportion of people suffering from HIV/Aids will need more opiates then a State in which this disease is inexistent.

64 Opioids are opiates, i.e. substances obtained from opium, and substances with similar effects.

65 INCB, Report on the Availability of Internationally Controlled Drugs: Ensuring Adequate Access for Medical and Scientific Purposes, 2010, para. 93. This figure is criticized by some as being too low; cf. in that regard Hallam, *supra* note 20, p. 9.

furthermore a very inadequate level of consumption is to be approved by fewer than 100 SDD per million inhabitants. However, the INCB does not consider that consumption above 200 SDD per million inhabitants is adequate per se.[66] The INCB uses the 100 S-DDD margin for opioid analgesics as the threshold where one can safely assume that a state party is *not* providing for an adequate amount of opioids.

6.1.4.2 Countering undue restrictions

The INCB has demanded States to determine and abrogate 'undue restrictions' which impede the availability and accessibility of narcotic drugs for medical purposes.[67] Likewise, the WHO has requested governments to 'identify and remove impediments to the availability and medical use of opioid analgesics'.[68] This call was also made by the UNGA in UNGASS.[69] However, no institution, including the INCB and the WHO, has so far specified when national restrictions on the availability of drugs for medical purposes would qualify as undue restrictions.[70]

This is far from surprising, given that the goal of ensuring availability lacks concretization by the UN Drug Conventions. The INCB could expand its practice in this regard and lay out precisely when a State would limit the availability of drugs more restrictively than required for medical and scientific purposes. Additionally, the INCB could clarify for more substances than opiates, when their availability has to be considered as inadequate. Lastly, the INCB could use its means of blaming and shaming more openly by naming States parties, not providing for an adequate amount of drugs for medical and scientific purposes.[71]

6.1.5 Conclusion

In sum, control of supply by the international drug control system predominantly means to limit supply to the amount required for medical and scientific purposes. Albeit the aim to ensure the availability of narcotic drugs for medical

66 INCB, Report on the Availability of Internationally Controlled Drugs: Ensuring Adequate Access for Medical and Scientific Purposes, 2010, para. 93.

67 INCB, Availability of Opiates for Medical Needs, Special Report prepared pursuant to Economic and Social Council Resolutions 1990/31 and 1991/43, para. 51 (a): cf. also in that regard, NCB, Report of the INCB on the Availability of Drugs for Medical and Scientific Purposes, 2010, UN-Doc. E/INCB/2010/1/Supp. 1, para. 132, Recommendation (g).

68 WHO, 'Narcotic and Psychotropic Substances: Achieving Balance in National Opioids Control Policy, Guidelines for Assessment', 2000, WHO-Doc. WHO/ED;/QSM/2000.4, p. 11.

69 UNGA, Outcome Document UNGASS 2016, 2016, UN Doc. A/Res-S/30/1, para. 2 (a).

70 Cf. also in that regard INCB, Report of the International Narcotics Control Board for 1989, Demand for and Supply of Opiates for Medical and Scientific Needs, UN Doc. E/INCB/1989/Supp, 1989, p. 1; see also WHO, Access to Controlled Medications Programme: Improving Access to Medications Controlled under International Drug Conventions, April 2012, p. 8.

71 A starting point can be seen within a map, displaying the availability of opioids on a global scale, cf. www.incb.org/incb/en/narcotic-drugs/Availability/availability.html.

and scientific purposes has been gaining ground in the last years and decades, when taking a look at the operative provisions of the Single Convention and the 1971 Convention, the conclusion remains valid that the system is still predominantly focusing on the limitation of availability. A control of licit supply means limiting licit supply, rather than providing for its availability. Nevertheless, this section has demonstrated the considerable legal development on the issue of availability in the last years.

The motivation for the growing emphasis of drug control's institutions on enhancing availability possibly stems outside of the norms and provisions of the UN Drug Conventions.[72] According a priority to the availability of narcotic drugs and psychotropic substances for medical purposes also derives from the right to the highest attainable standard of health (Art. 12 (1) ICESCR (International Covenant on Economic, Social and Cultural Rights)).[73] In accordance with CESCR (Committee on Economic, Social and Cultural Rights) General Comment No. 14 on the Right to the Highest Attainable Standard of Health, this standard comprises an imperative to provide for essential drugs, as from time to time defined under the WHO Action Programme on Essential Drugs,[74] which regularly updates a Model List of Essential Medicines.[75] This list contains narcotic drugs – such as morphine – and psychotropic substances – such as diazepam.[76] The need for States to provide for substances – including narcotic drugs and psychotropic substances – contained in these lists, is considered by the

72 It is noteworthy in this regard that in 1986 – i.e. before the INB had commenced to prioritize the goal of availability – the WHO had issued a report in the aftermath on the WHO Meeting on the Comprehensive Management of Cancer (WHO, Cancer Pain Relief, 1986, p. 27), where it stated the following:

> Of 22 drugs commonly used for cancer relief, eight are covered by the 1961 Convention on Narcotic Drugs and one by the 1971 Convention on Psychotropic Substances. The principal object of these two conventions is to stop trade in, and use of controlled drugs, except for medical and scientific purposes. The conventions are not intended to be an impediment to the use of necessary drugs for the relief of cancer pain.

73 The right to the health is also laid out by other human rights instruments such as Art. 17 CRC; cf. Eibe Riedel, 'Health' Right to, International Protection', in: Rüdiger Wolfrum, *MPEPIL*, 2012, paras 15 et seq.

74 CESCR, General Comment No. 14, The Right to the Highest Attainable Standard of Health, 2000, UN Doc. E/C.12/2000/4, para. 43 (d); cf. also as to this issue, Alma-Ata Declaration adopted by the International Conference on Primary Health Care, 6–12 September 1978, para. VII (3): 'Primary health care: includes at least [...] provision of essential drugs' (available online at: www.who.int/publications/almaata_declaration_en.pdf), as to the normative importance of this declaration cf. John Tobin, *The Right to Health in International Law*, p. 249.

75 WHO, Model List of Essential Medicines, 19th List, April 2015 (available online at: www.who.int/selection_medicines/committees/expert/20/EML_2015_FINAL_amended_AUG2015.pdf?ua=1).

76 According to the WHO, a vast majority of narcotic drugs and psychotropic substances have medical uses; WHO, Access to Controlled Medicines Programme: Ensuring Balance in National Policies on Controlled Substances – Guidance for Availability and Accessibility of Controlled Medicines, 2011, p. 1.

CERSC as a 'core obligation' that cannot be deviated from even by States with low economic resources.[77]

As the international drug control system, and in particular its negative human rights impact, is confronted with growing opposition, the issue of availability arguably is used in order to take the wind from the critiques' sails. By prioritizing the need to provide for availability under the international drug control system, drug control's institutions can demonstrate *in concreto* that this system is in line with human rights obligations.[78] In contrast to other issues, where tensions between the limitation of drugs to medical and scientific purposes and international human rights law arise, ensuring availability of drugs for medical and scientific purposes certainly does not contradict this objective. Therefore, in this field, showing the coherence of the international drug control system with international human rights law does not entail a high risk for these institutions.

6.2 Suppression of illicit supply: the UN Drug Conventions as a punitive and sanction-oriented system of control?

Section 6.1 was concerned with the control of the licit drug supply chain. Exercising control over the licit supply chain, however, leaves the question of how to curb illicit drug supply unresolved. Today, the illicit and the licit drug supply chain seem almost completely separated.[79] The vast amount of drug supply that is manufactured, produced and trafficked for other than medical or scientific purposes is in the hands of transnational drug trafficking cartels. These actors avoid any governmental controls. The drafters of the international drug control system soon became aware of the evident need to counter these tendencies and supress the supply of drugs produced for other than medical or scientific purposes.[80] The UN Drug Conventions – and most notably the 1988 Convention – provide for an extensive set of measures in this regard.

77 CESCR, General Comment No. 14, The Right to the Highest Attainable Standard of Health, 2000, UN Doc. E/C.12/2000/4, para. 43 (d), para. 43. For an extensive critique of core obligations, as being too wide and contrary to the general approach of the ICESCR to subject the guarantee of the rights spelled out to progressive realization (Art. 2 (1), ICESCR); cf. John Tobin, *The Right to Health in International Law*, pp. 232 et seq. Tobin, despite this general critique, also seems to concede that providing essential drugs can be considered a core obligation under the right to the health as outlined by Art. 12, ICESCR; cf. *ibid.*, pp. 250 et seq. Cf. for a similar conclusion, while relying on CESCR's General Comment No. 14, Ben Saul, David Kinley and Jaqueline Mowbray, *The International Covenant on Economic, Social and Cultural Rights*, pp. 1018 et seq.; cf. also Stephen Marks, 'Access to Essential Medicines as a Component of the Right to Health', in: Andrew Clapham and, Mary Robinson (eds), *Realizing the Right to Health*, 82 (94 et seq.).

78 See also for this conclusion, Richard Lines, *Drug Control and Human Rights in International Law*, pp. 84 et seq.

79 Today there is hardly any diversion from licit to illicit channels; UNODC, World Drug Report 2008, UN Publication, Sales No. E.08.XI.1, pp. 205 et seq.

80 The first comprehensive attempt to tackle the illicit traffic in drugs can be traced back to the 1936 Convention; cf. *supra* 3.1.2.3.3.

The negative human rights impact of these measures has been vividly criticized by many.[81] International human rights law and international drug control have been described as 'parallel universes'.[82] The penalization and law-enforcement measures contained in the UN Drug Conventions would lead to domestic drug control measures, imperilling and stigmatizing vulnerable groups. Indeed, excesses like the carrying out of the death penalty for drug-related crimes to commemorate the UN day against drug abuse,[83] the extrajudicial killings of drug traffickers[84] and the marginalization of rural communities growing crops illicitly[85] have provoked outcries. The potential for human rights violations arising out of the UN Drug Conventions can hardly be denied.[86]

Many deny that human rights-abusive drug control measures are merely a product of national drug policies; rather, they argue that human rights violations are 'systemic'.[87] They are related to the way by which the UN Drug Conventions

81 Cf. e.g. already Norbert Gilmore, 'Drug Use and Human Rights: Privacy, Vulnerability, Disability and Human Rights Infringements', *JCHLP* Vol. 12 1996, 335 (403 et seq.); Damon Barrett et al., 'Recalibrating the Regime: The Need for a Human Rights-based Approach to Interynational Drug Policy', The Beckley Foundation Drug Policy Programme 2008, *passim*.

82 Paul Hunt, 'Human Rights, Health and Harm Reduction', An address by the UN Special Rapporteur on the Right to the Highest Attainable Standard of Health, International Harm Reduction Association 19th Conference (available online at www.hri.global/files/2010/06/16/HumanRightsHealthAndHarmReduction.pdf); cf. already in this regard the concern expressed in 1992 by a senior WHO official: 'It is clear [...] that human rights have little or low priority in the [drug control context]'; S.S. Fluss, Human Rights and Responsibilities, Unpublished Paper, quoted in: Gilmore, *supra* note. 81, 355 (401).

83 Cf. e.g. Zachary Keck, Ahead of International Drug Day, China Executes 6 (available online at: http://thediplomat.com/2013/06/ahead-of-international-drug-day-china-executes-6/); as to this issue in general cf. Patrick Gallahue and Rick Lines, 'The Death Penalty for Drug Offences: Global Overview', Harm Reduction International, 2010; Patrick Gallahue, 'The Death Penalty for Drug Offences – Global Overview 2011: Shared Responsibility and Shared Consequences', Harm Reduction International, 2011; Patrick Gallahue and Rick Lines, 'The Death Penalty for Drug Offences: Global Overview 2015 – The Extreme Fringe of Global Drug Policy', 2015.

84 Human Rights Watch, 'Thailand's "War on Drugs", International Harm Reduction Association and Human Rights Watch briefing paper, 2008 (available online at: www.hrw.org/news/2008/03/12/thailands-war-drugs); see also more recently Philippine's 'war on drugs', Human Rights Watch, "Licence to Kill" (available online at: www.hrw.org/report/2017/03/02/license-kill/philippine-police-killings-dutertes-war-drugs); for a critique of the INBC of this policy, see online at: www.incb.org/incb/en/news/press-releases/2016/press_release030816.html.

85 Cf. e.g. Global Commission on Drug Policy, 'War On Drugs', 2011, p. 13; see as to this Geiß and Wisehart, *supra* note 1, 368 (377 et seq.).

86 Cf. Neil Boister, 'Human Rights Protections in the Suppression Conventions', *Human Rights Law Review* Vol. 2 2002, 199 (204) with further references; Daniel Heilmann, 'The International Control of Illegal Drugs and the UN Treaty Regime: Preventing or Causing Human Rights Violations?', *Cardozo J. Int'l & Comp. L.* Vol. 19 2011, 237 (267).

87 Cf. in this regard Damon Barrett, 'Reflections on Human Rights and International Drug Control', in: John Collins (ed.), *Governing the Global Drug Wars Special Report*, LSE Ideas 2012, 55; cf. for the same conclusion Boister, *supra* note 86, 199 (221): 'It is disingenuous to argue that [human rights violations] have nothing to do with the 1988 Convention.'; cf. for the opposing view, Saul Takahashi, *Human Rights and Drug Control: The False Dichotomy*, pp. 84 et seq., p. 92.

unsuccessfully supresses drug supply.[88] In this light, the symbolic references to human rights by drug control's major institutions are seen as mere window dressing, deprived of substance, as long as no credible steps are taken to prevent drug control measures that violate human rights.[89]

This section examines those issues by analysing the UN Drug Conventions within a wider framework of international law of so-called 'suppression conventions' that combat transnational criminal activities. It will be shown that these treaties in general have the potential for human rights violations and it will be questioned whether, from this perspective, the UN Drug Conventions are of a particular 'draconian' character[90] or whether human rights violations occurring in the struggle against transnational crime is in reality a problem of a more general nature. Subsequently, it will be outlined how the UN Drug Conventions can be brought into line with human rights obligations.[91]

6.2.1 Setting the background: The UN Drug Conventions as suppression conventions

In order to assess a possible negative human rights impact of suppressive measures of the UN Drug Conventions, these measures have to be analysed against the backdrop of a category of conventions combatting transnational crime.

The classification of such 'suppression conventions' as transnational criminal law is a rather recent phenomenon.[92] In his groundbreaking 2003 article on 'Transnational Criminal Law', Boister laid out the features of such transnational crimes in order to distinguish them from international crimes *stricto sensu* – aggression, genocide and crimes against humanity. These features are namely: (i) the penalization of a criminal activity with transnational effects; (ii) carried out by private groups or individuals; and (iii) by domestic provisions taken in order to comply with treaty-based international obligations.

88 Barrett et al., *supra* note 81, p. 11.

89 Patrick Gallahue, Roxanne Saucier and Damon Barrett, 'Partners in Crime: International Funding for Drug Control and Gross Violations of Human Rights', 2012, *passim*; cf. also Damon Barrett and Philip Vermann, *Article 33: Protection from Narcotic Drugs and Psychotropic Substances*, p. 2.

90 Commentary 1988 Convention, Art. 5, Implementation Considerations, MN 5.73; cf. also for a discussion of this assessment of the Commentary; Robert J. Currie, 'The Protection of Human Rights in the Suppression of Transnational Crime', in: Neil Boister and Robert J. Currie, *Routledge Companion of Transnational Criminal Law*, 27 (30).

91 This chapter exclusively addresses human rights issues arising on the 'supply side' i.e. out of measures against drug trafficking. The complex human rights issues raised by demand reduction and drug use will be treated below (6.3).

92 Cf. as to the roots of the term transnational crime, Robert J. Currie, 'The Protection of Human Rights in the Suppression of Transnational Crime', in: Neil Boister and Robert J. Currie (eds), *Routledge Companion of Transnational Criminal Law*, 27. The field of transnational criminal law, despite a growing number of publications in the last years, remains inadequately treated by legal scholarship, see Robert J. Currie, book review: 'Neil Boister, *An Introduction to Transnational Criminal Law*', *JICJ* Vol. 13 2015, 1166.

The international penalization of such conduct occurs through 'global prohibition regimes' formed out of the need to cooperate on an international level to suppress a conduct that transgresses domestic borders and moral convictions of 'transnational moral entrepreneurs'.[93] International drug trafficking is a prime example of such a transnational crime and the international drug control system is a prime example of a global prohibition regime.[94] Other examples of such crimes are piracy, human trafficking, corruption, terrorism and transnational organized crime.[95]

Suppression conventions contain a two-step mechanism in order to cope with transnational crimes. First, States are obligated to penalize a certain activity in accordance with their national criminal law.[96] This means that transnational crimes remain domestic criminal offences. A State is under an obligation to penalize a certain activity, but the individual will be prosecuted and tried in accordance with the respective domestic law. Second, States are obliged to cooperate in order to effectively carry out such sanctions. The classical means of cooperation in this regard are extradition and the exercise of extraterritorial jurisdiction. Linking them by obligating States who are captive of a suspected perpetrator to either extradite the individual to the State on whose territory the acts were committed or to exercise extraterritorial jurisdiction (*aut dedere aut iudicare*) – at least in theory – allows for a coherent prosecution of such transborder crimes. [97] Today, however, international cooperation to address such activities goes much further, including *inter alia* mutual legal assistance, cooperation in law enforcement, controlled delivery, etc.

The two-step mechanism inherent to transnational criminal law is apparent within the UN Drug Conventions. Article 36 (1) (a) Single Convention, Art. 21 (1) (a) 1971 Convention and Art. 3 (1) 1988 Convention oblige States parties to penalize illicit traffic in drugs.[98] The offences described in these provisions remain domestic offences (Art. 3 (11) 1988 Convention). No drug trafficker will be tried for a violation of these obligations. The individual will be punished in accordance with domestic law of the respective State carrying out its jurisdiction. The UN Drug Conventions remain an indirect system of control that require implementation of their obligations by the individual State parties.

93 Cf. as to this issue, Ethan Nadelmann, 'Global Prohibition Regimes: The Evolution of Norms in International Society', *International Organization* Vol. 44 1990, 479.

94 Nadelmann, *supra* note 93, 479 (502); Neil Boister, *An Introduction to Transnational Criminal Law*, pp. 50 et seq.

95 See Neil Boister, *An Introduction to Transnational Criminal Law*.

96 *Ibid.*, pp. 16 et seq.

97 Cf. for a good overview of the concept, M. Cherif Bassiouni and Edward M. Wise, Aut Dedere Aut Judicare*: The Obligation to Extradite or Prosecute in International Law*, pp. 3 et seq.

98 Art. 3 (1) 1988 Convention extended the previous provisions of the previous drug control treaties, *inter alia* by removing the subjection of penal obligations to domestic law and including the penalizations of money laundering in the aftermath of drug trafficking as a criminal offence.

Additionally, as with other suppression conventions, the UN Drug Conventions provide for a system of international cooperation allowing for the implementation of these provisions. The 1988 Convention is most relevant in this regard: States are required to counter drug trafficking offences under Art. 3 (1) 1988 Convention in accordance with *aut dedere aut iudicare*, i.e. by establishing extraterritorial jurisdiction for such offences, or extraditing the offenders of such crimes to the territory where the offence occurred.[99] Moreover, the 1988 Convention provides for a framework for mutual legal assistance (Art. 7 (1) 1988 Convention), transfer of proceedings (Art. 8 (1) 1988 Convention) and controlled delivery (Art. 11 (1) 1988 Convention) in order to effectively prosecute the sanctions spelled out in Art. 3 (1).[100]

6.2.2 *Identifying the human rights gap within the UN Drug Conventions*

While laying out the human rights gaps of the UN Drug Conventions, it is shown that the major human rights concern raised by these treaties, i.e. the absence of substantive human rights obligations, is not a singular deficit of these conventions but a general problem of transnational criminal law. However, there are specific deficits of the UN Drug Conventions, inciting abuse by States parties in order to circumvent their human rights obligations.

6.2.2.1 *General problem: absence of substantive human rights obligations*

The negative human rights impact of suppression conventions has been widely recognized.[101] As early as 1974, Bassiouni remarked that these such conventions

99 The 1988 Convention contains a rather weak formula of the aut *dedere aut iudicare* maxim. Thus, a State is only required to exercise extraterritorial jurisdiction over an Art. 3 (1) offence if it rejects extradition on the grounds that the offence was carried out within its jurisdiction or that it does not extradite its nationals (Art. 4 (2) (a) 1988 Convention). Consequently, it is only in these cases – where it fails to extradite because of the nationality of the perpetrator or the fact that the crime was committed on its territory – that a State is legally required to exercise extraterritorial jurisdiction (Art. 6 (9) 1988 Convention). This means that in all other types of constellations there is no effective obligation for a State to extradite or prosecute a perpetrator of Art. 3 (1) offences but a mere possibility to do so; cf. also Neil Boister, *Penal Aspects of the UN Drug Conventions*, pp. 265, 276 et seq.

100 Art. 1 (g) 1988 Convention defines 'controlled delivery':

> the technique of allowing illicit or suspect consignments of narcotic drugs, psychotropic substances, substances in Table I and Table II annexed to this Convention, or substances substituted for them, to pass out of, through or into the territory of one or more countries, with the knowledge and under the supervision of their competent authorities, with a view to identifying persons involved in the commission of offences established in accordance with article 3, paragraph 1, of the Convention.

Other law enforcement measures include confiscation (Art. 5) as well as measures against the illicit cultivation of drugs (Art. 14 (1) 1988 Convention).

101 Cf. for further details, Robert J. Currie, 'The Protection of Human Rights in the Suppression of Transnational Crime', in: Neil Boister and Robert J. Currie (eds), *Routledge Companion of Transnational Criminal Law*, 2015, 27; Boister, *supra* note 86, 199.

'fail[ed] to provide safeguards for those individuals' which are the 'object' of this form of international cooperation.[102]

This is also apparent within the UN Drug Conventions; there are no substantive human rights obligations contained in them. Within all three UN Drug Conventions, there is only one single provision of minor scope, where the words 'human rights' appear:[103] the second sentence of Art. 14 (2) 1988 Convention requires that States, when 'taking appropriate measures to prevent illicit cultivation', adopt measures that 'shall respect fundamental human rights and shall take due account of traditional licit uses, where there is historic evidence of such use, as well as the protection of the environment'.[104] The clause is unclear, as it leaves unmentioned what kind of human rights may be subsumed materially under fundamental human rights.[105]

The absence of human rights obligations remains a general problem of cooperation against transnational crime.[106] States continue to refrain from establishing operative human rights obligations in such treaties. Given the political reality that States indeed want to keep those two bodies of law separated, this is not likely to change soon. Achieving an equilibrium between human rights protection and transnational cooperation in this field is difficult, given 'balance is heavily skewed in favour of suppression'.[107] Even treaties that have been adopted after the 1988 Convention, such as the International Convention for the Suppression of Financing Terrorism,[108] the Convention Against Transnational Crime[109] or the Convention on the Suppression of Unlawful Acts relating

102 M. Cherif Bassiouni, 'An Appraisal of the Growth and Developing Trends of International Criminal Law', *Revue Internationale de Droit Pénal* Vol. 45 1974, 405 (429).

103 Damon Barrett and Philip Vermann, *Article 33: Protection from Narcotic Drugs and Psychotropic Substances*, p. 2.

104 Italics added; it has already been shown above that the reference to traditional licit uses is purely symbolic and does not deviate from the limitation of drugs to medical and scientific purposes; cf. *supra* 4.3.2.

105 Boister, *supra* note 86, 199 (210 et seq.).

106 See with regard to the Transnational Organized Crime Convention, Robert J. Currie, 'The Protection of Human Rights in the Suppression of Transnational Crime', in: Neil Boister and Robert J. Currie (eds), *Routledge Companion of Transnational Criminal Law*, 2015, 27 (32 et seq.).

107 Neil Boister, *Introduction to Transnational Criminal Law*, p. 22.

108 International Convention for the Suppression of the Financing of Terrorism of 9 December 1999, entered into force 10 April 2002, UNTS Vol. 2178, 197.

109 United Nations Convention against Transnational Organized Crime of 15 November 2000, entered into force 29 September 2003, UNTS Vol. 2225, p. 209. The term 'human rights' does not appear once within the entire instrument. However, references to human rights can be found within its Protocol to Prevent, Suppress and Punish Trafficking in Persons, Especially Women and Children, supplementing the United Nations Convention against Transnational Organized Crime, concluded and entered into force on the same date, UNTS Vol. 2227. However, these references only pertain to the human rights of victims of human trafficking and not the human rights of the perpetrators of such crimes which are the object of the penalization and cooperation as laid out by this treaty. See as to the relationship between the 1988 Convention and this treaty, David McClean, *Transnational Organized Crime: A Commentary on the UN Convention and its Protocols*, p. 30, describing the Convention against Transnational Organized Crime as a successor to the 1988 Convention.

to International Civil Aviation[110] do not contain substantive human rights obligations.

Hence, one of the major problems of UN Drug Conventions' obligations against illicit drug supply is in reality a general problem of international cooperation against transnational crime: States are required to penalize a certain activity and cooperate in order to prosecute perpetrators of these crimes, but there are no safeguards for those individuals that will eventually be the object of such a penalization and prosecution. There is, however, a particularity of the UN Drug Conventions that is particularly troublesome from a human rights perspective which cannot be found in other suppression conventions.

6.2.2.2 Particularity of the UN Drug Conventions: 'more severe measures clause'

There is one provision within every Drug Convention which allows State parties to '*adopt more strict or severe measures than those provided by this Convention if, in its opinion, such measures are desirable or necessary for the prevention or suppression of illicit traffic*' (Art. 24 1988 Convention).[111]

States parties rely on these provisions in order to forward a rhetoric that excludes human rights when drug control measures are taken.[112] This can be exemplified by a judgement of the Indonesian Supreme Court in 2007 concerning the legality of the death penalty for drug-related crimes. The Court *inter alia* relied on Art. 24 1988 Convention in order to justify the result that the right to life, as guaranteed by Art. 6 ICCPR, was not violated by such measures. It held:

110 Convention on the Suppression of Unlawful Acts relating to International Civil Aviation of 10 September 2010, not yet entered into force (see online at: www.icao.int/secretariat/legal/Docs/beijing_protocol_multi.pdf)

111 Italics added. Similar clauses can be found within the other UN Drug Conventions. Art. 39 Single Convention reads:

> Notwithstanding anything contained in this Convention, a Party shall not be, or be deemed to be, precluded from adopting measures of control more strict or severe than those provided by this Convention and in particular from requiring that preparations in Schedule III or drugs in Schedule II be subject to all or such of the measures of control applicable to drugs in Schedule I as in its opinion is necessary or desirable for the protection of the public health or welfare.

Art. 23 1971 Convention: 'A Party may adopt more strict or severe measures of control than those provided by this Convention if, in its opinion, such measures are desirable or necessary for the protection of the public health and welfare.' The formulation of Art. 39 Single Convention seems less problematic than the formulation of Art. 23 1971 Convention and Art. 24 1988 Convention. Art. 39 is phrased like a safeguard clause in that the Single Convention does not regulate more restrictive measures. In contrast, the wording of Art. 23 1971 Convention and Art. 24 1988 Convention may create the false impression that more severe measures would be expressively allowed by this treaty.

112 See with regard to this issue, Richard Lines, *Drug Control and Human Rights in International Law*, pp. 106 et seq. and further examples.

> In other words, in relation to the a quo petition, if according to Indonesia, more severe measures are needed to prevent and eradicate such crimes, such measures are not contradictory to but rather are justified and suggested instead by the Convention.[113]

By the same token, when petitioners challenged the constitutionality of the death penalty for drug-related crimes within the High Court of Judicature in Bombay, the Indian government argued this clause could be invoked in order to allow for a State to adopt such a measure as the death penalty for drug-related crimes.[114]

States have also advanced similar lines of argumentation at international fora. Thus, in 2010, Colombia argued in the ICJ *Aerial Herbicide Spraying Case* – which arose out of an application by Ecuador, alleging that Colombia had violated international law by spraying crops next to its border – that:

> Neither under Article 24 [1988 Convention], nor under the 1961 and 1971 Conventions whose effect is preserved by Article 25, is there any provision even arguably incorporating human rights, indigenous rights or environmental obligations. A State accused of disregard for those obligations in taking some measure could simply say that it did so pursuant to the permission in Article 24, or the saving clause in Article 25. Colombia relies on both Article 24 and 25.[115]

Leaving aside the question as to whether Aerial Herbicide Spraying is in conformity with international law, such a reading of the UN Drug Conventions is deeply problematic. If taken for granted, this interpretation would allow for a State to deviate from human rights obligations when taking drug control measures.[116]

Such a 'more severe measures clause' does – to the knowledge of this author – not appear in other suppression conventions. To the contrary, some of them contain 'safeguard clauses', ensuring that human rights obligations remain intact when States implement their obligations. Article 14 (1) of the human trafficking protocol is particularly exemplary in that regard:

> Nothing in this Protocol shall affect the rights, obligations and responsibilities of States and individuals under international law, including international humanitarian law and international human rights law and, in particular, where applicable, the 1951 Convention and the 1967 Protocol relating to the Status of Refugees and the principle of non-refoulement as contained therein.

113 *Sianturi and others v. Indonesia*, Constitutional Review of 23 October 2007, Nos 2, 3/ PUU-V/2007, p. 103.

114 High Court of Judicature at Bombay, *Indian Harm Reduction Network v. Union of India and State of Maharastra*, Judgment of 16 June 2011, para. 25.

115 ICJ, Case concerning Aerial Herbicide Spraying (*Ecuador v. Colombia*), Counter-memorial of Colombia, 29 March 2010, p. 349.

116 Geiß and Wisehart, *supra* note 1, 368 (392).

The provision is not only applicable to victims of human trafficking, but also protects the rights of individuals accused of such acts. Such a provision is useful in that ensures that States cannot rely on this treaty in order to deny the applicability of human rights.

It can be concluded that the general problem of an absence of substantial human rights obligations is exacerbated by the more severe measures clause, which seems to be a particularity of the UN Drug Conventions. Therefore, albeit the human rights gap is inherent to transnational criminal law in general, it is particularly wide in the case of drug control.

6.2.3 Closing the human rights gap

Having established the human rights gap of the UN Drug Conventions, the following examines whether the negative human rights impact of the UN Drug Conventions can be mitigated. It will be discussed whether this can be done by relying on the norms and provisions of the UN Drug Conventions (6.2.3.1) or by contextualizing these treaties within international human rights law 6.2.2–6.2.3.3)

6.2.3.1 Closing the human rights gap by relying on provisions of the UN Drug Conventions

One possibility to balance the obligations of the UN Drug Conventions with human rights would be to rely on domestic law. Indeed, some of the UN Drug Conventions' obligations, in particular the obligations for States parties to adopt penal sanctions, are subjected to the internal law of the party concerned.[117] They seem inadequate to mitigate the severity of drug control measures.[118] In particular, it is unclear which constitutional guarantees trump the obligations to penalize drug-related acts. This is entirely left to the discretion of the respective State party's legal system. A suspected drug trafficker cannot count on the protection of such constitutional safeguards that vary from State to State.

117 The formulation of these safeguard clauses differs somewhat. Whereas Art, 36 (1) (a) Single Convention and Art. 20 (1) (a) 1971 Convention only contained references to States parties constitution, Art. 36 (2) Single Convention and Art. 22 (2) were additionally subjected to a State party's legal system and domestic law. Art. 3 (1) (c) and (2) 1988 Convention subject the obligations contained therein to a party's constitution and basic considerations of its legal system. Additionally, some provisions of the UN Drug Conventions require States to pay due regard to a State party's constitution or domestic law; Art. 35 Single Convention; Arts 10 (2) and 21 1971 Convention. Cf. for a pertinent discussion of these clauses Boister, *supra* note 86, 199 (208 et seq.). Arts 36 (1) (a) and 36 (2) Single Convention; Arts 22 (1) (a) and 22 (2) 1971 Convention; Arts 3 (1) (c) and 3 (2) 1988 Convention.

118 Cf. also in this regard Boister, *supra* note 86, 199 (208): 'these limitation clauses provide no guarantee of constitutional limitation'.

Another provision with potential to mitigate the negative human rights impact of the UN Drug Conventions is Art. 6 (6) 1988 Convention. The provision allows a State to reject an extradition request

> where there are substantial grounds leading its judicial or other competent authorities to believe that compliance would facilitate the prosecution or punishment of any person on account of his race, religion, nationality or political opinions, or would cause prejudice for any of those reasons to any person affected by the request.

The provision is framed narrowly. It is only in cases where a threat of discrimination exists that a State can refuse extradition, but not in other kinds of situations, e.g. when a threat exits that a suspect may be tortured and a State is not required to deny extradition when risks of discrimination arise. Hence, while Art. 6 (6) can potentially be used by individual State parties in order to prevent discrimination caused by an extradition, this provision is not a mandatory human rights safeguard protecting the rights of individuals during the extradition process. Thus, the provisions of the UN Drug Conventions are ill-equipped to restrict the severity of measures implementing their obligations.[119]

A general obligation that would strive for a balance between the legitimate goal of suppressing the illicit drug trade, on the one hand, and the need to ensure the human rights of those that will be affected by the suppression of drug trade, on the other hand, is lacking. This makes it necessary to frame the obligations of the UN Drug Conventions within a broader context.

6.2.3.2 Closing the human rights gap by interpreting the UN Drug Conventions in light of international human rights law

Although the UN Drug Conventions do not contain adequate safeguards for securing the rights of those affected by drug control measures, such safeguards are contained within human rights treaties. Systemic integration of human rights obligations into the interpretation of the UN Drug Conventions is required, and is adequate, in most cases in order to balance the severity of these treaties.[120] Indeed, this systemic integration arises out of the need to understand the international legal order of one integrated system. The risk of fragmentation of this system can only be lowered by interpreting the UN Drug Conventions against the background of international human rights law and relying on Art. 31 (3)

119 The same is also true for Art. 5 (8) 1988 Convention which aims to protect the rights of *bona third parties* when proceeds that are derived from drug trafficking are confiscated in accordance with Art. 5 1988 Convention. This clause aims at the protection of the rights of third parties which may be infringed by confiscation; cf. also Commentary 1988 Convention, Art. 5 para. 8, MN 5.56 et seq. This of course is also only a very fragmented safeguard clause, as the rights of the addressee of a confiscation measure are not taken into account at all.

120 Cf. for a similar view, Heilmann, *supra* note 86, 237 (269 et seq.).

VCLT.[121] This approach is also taken in order to mitigate the severity of other suppression conventions.

The failure of the UN Drug Conventions to spell out substantial human rights obligations does not mean that States would be allowed to deviate from human rights law when they take counter-narcotic measures. They have to abide by their own human rights obligations, whilst curbing the illicit traffic in drugs. This result is not changed by the 'more severe measures clause', spelled out by Art. 39 Single Convention, Art. 23 1971 Convention and Art. 24 1988 Convention. The allowance of the UN Drug Conventions to take more severe measures than those foreseen by these treaties does not involve a right for States to deviate from their human rights obligations.[122] Integrating human rights obligations into the interpretation of the obligations of the UN Drug Conventions to counter the supply for all other than medical or scientific ends is not very complex. This is true because the obligations concerning the suppression of illicit drug supply do not impose any obligation that are clearly contradictory to international human rights law. Therefore, the latter obligations can be read into the UN Drug Conventions.

The effect of this integration can be shown with the following examples:

- When a State extradites a drug trafficker, while relying on the 1988 Convention as an extradition treaty,[123] to another State where the suspected drug trafficker potentially may be tortured, such an extradition violates Art. 3 ECHR, Art. 7 ICCPR and Art. 3 (1) Convention against Torture (CAT);[124]
- A State which is authorized to intersect a vessel on the high seas which is flying the flag of another State party, in accordance with Art. 17 (2) 1988 Convention, violates habeas corpus rights of those on board if they are not presented to a judge within a 'reasonable' time (Art. 9 (3) ICCPR; 5 (3) ECtHR);[125]
- The obligation of a State to make violations of Art. 3 (1) 1988 Convention liable to sanctions 'which take into account the grave nature of such offences' (Art. 3 (4) (a) 1988 Convention) may lead to punishment that is prohibited by international human rights law, such as the death penalty for drug-related crimes, which arguably violates the right to life as guaranteed by Art. 6 ICCPR.[126]

121 See as to this *supra* 4.5.2.

122 Cf. Geiß and Wisehart, *supra* note 1, 368 (392).

123 In accordance with Art. 6 (4) 1988 Convention.

124 Convention against Torture and Other Cruel, Inhuman or Degrading Treatment or Punishment of 10 December 1984, entered into force 26 June 1987, UNTS Vol. 1465, 85 [hereinafter referred to as CAT].

125 Cf. in this regard, ECtHR, *Medvedyev and others v. France*, Judgment of 29 March 2010, Application No. 3394/03. In this case the ECtHR denied that the interdiction of a Cambodian vessel was a lawful deprivation of liberty under Art. 5 (1) ECHR.

126 The issue remains disputed among the States parties; cf. in this regard the two interpretative declarations subsequent to the adoption of the Joint Ministerial Statement of the CND in its

Systemic integration of international human rights law and the UN Drug Conventions is not only required by general international law, it is also the unequivocal will of the States parties of the UN Drug Conventions as a whole. Since 1998, the UNGA has reiterated in its annual resolutions on the World Drug Problem that actions against the world drug problem have to be carried out 'in full conformity with human rights'.[127] This rather open reference to

2014 session. The delegations were unable to agree to a condemnation of the death penalty for drug-related crimes. The outcome were two opposing interpretative declarations with regard to the issue. Whereas a group of 62 States opposed such actions, 17 States underlined that such actions were in conformity with international law; CND, Report of the 57th session, UN Doc. E/2014/28, pp. 61 et seq. Nevertheless, as has been analysed pertinently by others, good arguments can be invoked against the legality of such acts – independently from the question whether the death penalty *per se* violates general international human rights law; cf. e.g. Patrick Gallahue, 'The Death Penalty for Drug Offences – Global Overview 2011'. The following statements can be invoked in favour of the argument that drug-related crimes do not fit the category of most serious crimes: cf. e.g. HRC, Concluding Observations on Thailand, 2005, UN Doc. CCPR/CO/84/THA, para. 14; Concluding Observations on Sudan, 2007, UN Doc. CCPR/C/SDN/CO/3, para. 19; Report of the Special Rapporteur on Extrajudicial, Summary or Arbitrary executions (Asmas Jahangir) Addendum Country Situations, 1999, UN Doc. E/CN.4/1999/39/Add.1, para. 236; Report of the Special Rapporteur on Extrajudicial, Summary or arbitrary Executions (Philip Alston), 2007, UN Doc. A/HRC/4/20, para. 51; Report of the Special Rapporteur on Extrajudicial, Summary or Arbitrary executions (Philip Alston) Addendum Communications to and from Governments, 2010, UN Doc. A/HRC/14/24/Add.1, p. 45 et seq.; Report of the Special Rapporteur on Torture and Other Cruel, Inhuman or Degrading Treatment or Punishment (Manfred Nowak), 2009, UN Doc. A/HRC/10/44, para. 66. The most serious crime requirement is only to be satisfied for crimes for the intentional inflection of grievous bodily harm; cf. e.g. HRC, Concluding Observations on Sri Lanka, 1995, UN Doc. CCPR/C/79/Add.56, para. 14; Roger Hood and Caroline Hoyle, *The Death Penalty:A Worldwide Perspective*, p. 132; Manfred Nowak, *U.N. Covenant on Civil and Political Rights: CCPR Commentary*, MN 37; Niels Petersen, 'Life, Right to, International Protection', in: Rüdiger Wolfrum (ed.), *MPEPIL*, 2012, MN 21; William A. Schabas, *The Abolition of the Death Penalty in International Law*, p. 110; see also Richard Lines, *Drug Control and Human Rights in International Law*, pp. 86 et seq.

127 UNGA, Political Declaration, 1998, UN Doc. A/Res/S-20/2, para. 2.; *id.* Resolution 54/132, 1999, UN Doc. A/Res/54/132, para. 1; *id.* Resolution 55/65, 2000, UN Doc. A/Res/55/65, para. 1; *id.* Resolution 56/124, 2001, UN Doc. A/Res/56/124, para. 1; *id.* Resolution 57/174, 2002, UN Doc. A/Res/57/174, para. 1; *id.* Resolution 58/141, 2003 UN Doc. A/Res/58/141, para. 1; *id.* Resolution 59/163, 2004, A/Res/59/163, para.1; *id.* Resolution 60/178, 2005, UN Doc. A/Res/60/178, para. 1; *id.* Resolution 61/183, 2006, UN Doc. A/Res/61/183, para.1; *id.* Resolution 62/176, 2007, UN Doc. A/Res/62/173, para. 1; *id.* Resolution 63/197, 2008, UN Doc. A/Res/63/197, para.1; *id.* Resolution 64/182, 2009, A/Res/64/182, para. 2; *id.* Resolution 65/233, UN Doc. A/Res/65/233, para. 2; *id.* Resolution 66/183, 2011, UN Doc. A/Res/66/183; *id.* Resolution. 67/193, UN Doc. A/Res/67/193, 2012, para. 2; *id.* Resolution 68/197, 2013, UN Doc. A/Res/68/2013, para. 2; *id.* Resolution 69/200, 2014, UN Doc. A/Res/69/201, para. 2; cf. also CND Resolution 51/12, 2008, UN Doc. E/2009/28. The formulation of these human rights has shifted somewhat. Whereas earlier resolutions required the UNGA States to pursue a solution of the world drug problem, ensuring respect for all human rights, the UNGA nowadays requests States to pursue such solutions in accordance with 'the Universal Declaration of Human Rights and the Vienna Declaration and Programme of Action on human rights'.

international human rights law was strengthened by UNGASS 2016.[128] The UNGA devoted an entire chapter of the outcome document to drugs and human rights. The commitment was made 'to respecting, protecting and promoting all human rights, fundamental freedoms and the inherent dignity of all individuals' when taking drug control measures.[129] Hence, there is unwavering support that international human rights law comes into play when drug control measures are taken. States parties to the UN Drug Conventions by the virtue of UNGA resolutions have unanimously and unequivocally clarified that the UN Drug Conventions' silence on human rights does not mean that human rights are inapplicable when drug control measures are taken.

6.2.3.3 Limits of systemic integration

It must be recognized, however, that systemic integration of human rights obligations has its limits and the absence of substantial human rights obligations remains problematic. These limits concern, first of all the application of human rights obligations to all States parties to the UN Drug Conventions. Not all human rights obligations are universally applicable and, in accordance with the well-established *pacta tertiis* rule (Art. 34 VCLT), do not obligate States which are not parties to the respective treaties. Thus, for instance, States like China or Singapore which are not subjected to the ICCPR are not bound by the right to life as laid down by Art. 6 ICCPR or fair trial guarantees evoked by Art. 9 ICCPR. Whether this means that they do not have any obligations in this regard requires further research on the status of such norms as customary international law. This exceeds the scope of this book. The more general point raised here, is that systemic integration of human rights obligations into the application of the drug control treaties is simply legally not possible in situations in which a State is not bound by the human rights obligation in the first place.

Second, the differing human rights obligations of the States parties become all the more problematic when States need to cooperate to suppress illicit drug supply. In order to comply with the obligations of human rights treaties, States will need to impede international cooperation in suppressing illicit drug supply in cases where cooperation could lead to serious human rights violations. Thus, a State which is bound by the ECHR cannot extradite drug criminals to States where an individual may be subjected to torture or inhuman or degrading treatment which is prohibited by Art. 3 ECHR.[130] By the same token, States which

128 Richard Lines, *Drug Control and Human Rights in International Law*, p. 175.

129 UNGA, Outcome Document UNGASS 2016, 2016, UN Doc. A/Res-S/30/1, para. 4.

130 This principle was announced in the landmark decision of the ECtHR in the Soering case, *Soering v. United Kingdom*, Application No. 14038/88, Judgment of 7 July 1989. The importance of this case for human rights protection in suppression conventions continues until today; Boister, *supra* note 86, 199 (203 et seq.); Robert J. Currie, 'The Protection of Human Rights in the Suppression of Transnational Crime', in: Neil Boister and Robert J. Currie (eds), *Routledge Companion of Transnational Criminal Law*, 27 (36 et seq.).

have abrogated the death penalty are prohibited by Art. 6 ICCPR to extradite individuals to States where a drug trafficker risks being executed.[131] These problems could only be resolved in drug control matters, if the UN Drug Conventions would create a more consistent framework for combatting transnational drug trafficking that would rule out torture or killing of perpetrators of drug trafficking offences.

6.2.4 Conclusion

It has been shown that when the UN Drug Conventions' obligations to supress illicit supply are interpreted against the background of international human rights obligations, this will lead to human rights-conformed drug control measures. This contextualization of drug control within a broader framework of international human rights law should be continuously supported by drug control's institution, the INCB. The condemnation of the death penalty for drug-related crimes by the INCB was a useful starting point.[132] Such recommendations fall into the INCB's rather broad mandate. By the same token, the CND should guide States on adopting human rights-conforming measures to supress illicit drug supply.

The UN Drug Conventions in general, and in the 1988 Convention in particular, by striving for the legitimate goal to suppress illicit drug supply by ensuring international cooperation, failed to balance this goal by protecting the rights of those that may be affected by measures countering and curbing illicit drug supply. Interestingly, this lack of balance is not only problematic for the protection of human rights of the addressees of such measures, but also *in fine* impedes international cooperation in this field.[133] If the system guaranteed minimal human rights standards – including the right to life or prohibition of torture – of international drug traffickers, international cooperation to combat such acts would be facilitated. Extradition, mutual legal assistance and so on could more easily be granted if the guarantees exist that such measures will not facilitate executions or torture and ill treatment.

131 Cf. in this regard the jurisprudence of the HRC, which underlined that States which have abolished the death penalty violate Art. 6 ICCPR when extraditing criminals to States which retain this form of punishment; cf. HRC, *Judge v. Canada*, View of 7 August 1998, Communication No. 829/98, UN Doc. CCPR/C/78/D/829/1998, paras 10.1 et seq. This view deviated from earlier views of the HRC in which the legality of such measures under Art. 6 ICCPR had been recognized; *id.*, *Kindler v. Canada*, View of 30 July 1993, Communication No. 470/1991, UN Doc. CCPR/C/48/D/470/199, paras 13.2 et seq.; *id.*, *Chitat Ng v. Canada*, Communication No. 469/1991, View of 5 November 1993, UN Doc. CCPR/C/49/D/469/1991, paras 15.3 et seq.

132 After years of silence with regard to the issue, the INCB in 2014, 'encouraged' States to consider the abolition of the death penalty for drug-related offences; cf. INCB, Press Release of 4 March 2014 (available online at: www.incb.org/documents/Publications/PressRelease/PR2014/press_release_050314.pdf); see also with regard to later developments, Richard Lines, *Drug Control and Human Rights in International Law*, pp. 177 et seq.

133 Cf. with regard for withdrawal of UNODC support in such cases, UNODC and the Promotion and Protection of Human Rights, 2012, pp. 18 et seq.

These deficits, serious as they are, do not forcibly result in war-on-drugs-like excessive measures against drug supply. States have a responsibility to abide by their human rights obligations when taking counter-narcotic measures. Scholars should remind them of their obligations and should not create the wrong impression that the UN Drug Conventions would involve and allow measures where anything goes. Giving in to the war on drugs terminology, which is not grounded within drug control's legal framework, will not be of great help.

6.3 Demand-reduction obligations providing for a human- and health-oriented treatment of drug users?

It is not only with regard to the supply side that the negative human rights effect of the international drug control system is criticized. It is also the effect of the system on the demand and use of drugs that is a source of controversy. The marginalization and exclusion of drug users from wider society is particularly worrisome.[134] The international drug control system would contribute to their marginalization. It would favour 'zero tolerance approaches' towards illicit drug use[135] and even prevent States from adopting more health-oriented approaches.[136] States would rather criminalize drug users than preventing and reducing the harm that is associated with illicit drug use.[137] The system's exclusive reliance on the control of supply has led to a lack of attention given to comprehensive measures for demand reduction and treatment.[138]

Indeed, the litmus test for a system that repeatedly invokes the protection of mankind's health and welfare seems to be whether it protects the health of those who are directly exposed to drug-related risks. It is well known that these

134 Cf. for more details, UNODC Executive Director Jose Maria Costa, CND, 'Making Drug Control "Fit for Purpose"'. Building on the UNGAS's Decade Report by the Executive Director of the UN Office on Drugs and Crime as a Contribution to the Review of the Twentieth Special Session of the General Assembly of 7 March 2008, UN Doc. E/CN.7/2008/CRP.17, p. 10.

135 Daniel Wolfe, and Kasia Malinowska-Sempruch, 'Illicit Drug Policies and the Global HIV Epidemic: Effects of UN and National Governments Approaches', 2004, pp. 24 et seq.

136 Barrett et al., *supra* note 81, pp. 31 et seq. Cf. also in this regard Bewley-Taylor, *supra* note 4, 171: 'the United Nations Convention still stand as a major obstacle to the introduction of pragmatic approaches to drug use on a national level'.

137 Damon Barrett and Manfred Nowak, 'United Nations and Drug Policy: Towards a Human Rights-based Approach', in: Aristotle Constantinides and Nikos Zaikos (eds), *Essays in Honour of Kalliopi Koufa*, 2009, 449, p. 2. (available at https://papers.ssrn.com/sol3/papers.cfm?abstract_id=1461445).

138 William B. McAllister, 'Reflections of a Century of International Drug Control', in: John Collins (ed.), *Governing the Global Drug Wars*, Special Report, 2012, 10 (13). As to the reliance on supply reduction see already, Simon Davies, 'International Law, The Final Solution, in: P.A O'Hare et al. (eds), *The Reduction of Drugs-Related Harm*, Routledge, New York and London 1992, 62.

risks today are not exclusively related to the perils of non-medical drug use, albeit that these risks should not be neglected.[139] Risky behaviours associated with non-medical drug use, most notably the risk of HIV/Aids infection of intravenous drug users, are of great concern. Many States have neglected these perils and treated the complex socio-psychological phenomenon of widespread, harmful, non-medical drug use as a criminal issue rather than a health-care issue.[140] Additionally, drug detention centres – where suspected drug users are held against their will without due process and are subjected to forced labour – are a serious human rights concern in many States.[141] Consensus seems to be growing that such zero tolerance policies are not proving the desired results of terminating non-medical drug use, while they are overburdening criminal justice systems.[142]

Such policies can result in human rights violations. Drug users' liberty and life are protected by international human rights law just as with any other individual.[143] This also applies to the right to the highest attainable standard of health that also protects drug users (Art. 12 (1) ICESCR).

It is against the background of the rights of individual drug users that the provisions of the UN Drug Conventions on demand have to be assessed. These obligations can be distinguished as three categories:

- First, an obligation to penalize illicit drug use (Art. 3 (2) 1988 Convention).
- Second, an obligation to adopt non-penal measures of demand reduction by treatment and prevention of drug abuse (Art. 38 (1) Single Convention; Art. 20 (1) 1971 Convention; Art. 14 (4) 1988 Convention).
- Third, an obligation to replace criminal punishment with treatment (Art. 36 (1) (b) Single Convention; Art. 22 (1) (b) 1971 Convention; Art. 3 (4) (b)–(d) 1988 Convention).

139 Cf. e.g. as to the risks of overdose with opiates; UNODC and WHO, 'Opioid Overdose: Preventing and Reducing Opioid Overdose Mortality', 2013, pp. 1 et seq.

140 UNODC Executive Director Jose Maria Costa, CND 'Making Drug Control "Fit for Purpose"'. Building on the UNGAS's Decade Report by the Executive Director of the UN Office on Drugs and Crime as a Contribution to the Review of the Twentieth Special Session of the General Assembly of 7 March 2008, UN Doc. E/CN.7/2008/CRP.17, p. 12.

141 Human Rights Watch, 'Torture in the Name of Treatment: Human Rights Abuses in Vietnam, China, Cambodia, and Lao PDR', 2012. In March 2012, 12 UN entities issued a joint statement calling on States to 'close' such institutions (ILO, UNHR, UNDP, UNESCO, UNFPA, UNHCR, UNICEF, UNODC, UNW, WFP, WHO, UNAIDS) Joint Statement, Compulsory Drug Detention and Rehabilitation Centres, March 2012 (available online at: www.unaids.org/sites/default/files/en/media/unaids/contentassets/documents/document/2012/JC2310_Joint%20Statement6March12FINAL_en.pdf).

142 Cf. in this regard the statement by William R. Brownfield, Assistant Secretary, Bureau of International Narcotics and Law Enforcement Affairs, 9 October 2014 (available online at: https://2009-2017.state.gov/j/inl/rls/rm/2014/232824.htm).

143 This does not mean that a right to drug use can be approved, see *infra* 4.5.

As will be shown, these obligations do not inhibit States from adopting health-oriented approaches towards drug use, but at the same time fail to establish a system that effectively protects the health of drug users and establishes a comprehensive legal framework on how to cope with illicit drug use and addiction.

6.3.1 No obligation to penalize drug use

Article 3 (2) 1988 Convention contains a provision to penalize illicit drug use:

> Subject to its constitutional principles and the basic concepts of its legal system, each Party shall adopt such measures as may be necessary to establish as a criminal offence under its domestic law, when committed intentionally, the possession, purchase or cultivation of narcotic drugs or psychotropic substances for personal consumption contrary to the provisions of the 1961 Convention, the 1961 Convention as amended or the 1971 Convention.

The action of drug use or consumption itself is not penalized. States parties are merely required to establish as an offence the possession, purchase or cultivation with the additional intent to consume these substances.[144] This, however, amounts to an indirect penalization of drug consumption, since it is impossible to consume these substances without possessing them.[145]

By referring to the 1971 Convention and the Single Convention – in its initial and amended form – the drafters sought to integrate the distinction between licit and illicit use made by those treaties into the 1988 Convention. Thus, it is the possession, purchase and cultivation of drugs for other than medical and scientific purposes which States are required to penalize.

The provision is of little relevance for States parties. Constitutional courts have relied heavily on the constitutional safeguard clause of Art. 3 (2) and stricken down domestic implementation laws penalizing illicit drug use.[146] Additionally, the States parties are by no means required to actually carry out the offences established by Art. 3 (2) 1988 Convention. As Art. 3 (4) (a) 1988 Convention clarifies, States parties are allowed to replace punishment with treatment.

Therefore, nothing in the international drug control system prevents States from replacing criminalization of drug users by treatment.[147] This, however, does not mean that States parties could simply legalize narcotic drugs or psychotropic substances by establishing a regulated market. States remain bound by the fundamental imperative to limit all drug-related activities, including drug use, to medical and scientific purposes, and they have to generally prevent

144 Commentary 1988 Convention, Art. 3, MN 3.95.

145 *Ibid.*

146 Cf. in this regard Neil Boister, *Penal Aspects of the UN Drug Conventions*, p. 125 with further references; cf. also Supreme Court of Argentina Arriola, *Sebastiàn y otros s/ causa* n°9080, Judgment of 25 August 2009, MN 25; cf. also the German Federal Constitutional Court Judgement of 9 March 1994, BVerfGE 90, 145 Abweichende Meinung Richter Sommer para. 251.

147 Krzysztof Krajewski, 'How Flexible are the UN Drug Conventions?', *IJDP* Vol. 19 1999, 329 (333; 335).

non-medical and non-scientific drug use.[148] Moreover, Art. 3 (2) 1988 Convention clearly incites penalization of drug use by States parties. Albeit a growing number of States parties seem to shift drug policies from incarceration of drug users towards health-related measures, this shift is not unequivocally reflected in UNGA resolutions or INCB practice due to a lack of consensus on the issue.[149]

The key to resolving whether States can adopt heath-oriented treatment for the benefit of individual drug users is not related to the crime versus treatment dichotomy, but requires carving out what the treatment of illicit drug users means under the UN Drug Conventions.

6.3.2 The indeterminacy of treatment under the UN Drug Conventions and the right to the highest attainable standard of health

States parties are obliged under all three UN Drug Conventions to take measures for the treatment and prevention of drug use. However, the vague wording of Art. 38 (1) Single Convention and Art. 20 (1) 1971 Convention[150] does not spell out what States are supposed to do in this regard.

Article 14 (4) 1988 Convention is not more precise, but allows States parties to adopt treatment measures as spelled out in recommendations by the UN, the WHO, other specialized agencies and 'other competent international organizations'.

Therefore, the UN Drug Conventions as a whole do not resolve the question of treatment. It is clear that States have to do something in order to cope with illicit drug use, but these treaties leave unresolved what that something is. Article 14 (4) does give some hints, by directing the attention of States parties to the expertise of competent institutions, but fails to impose mandatory obligations of what measures of treatment ought to look like. Such guidance is be direly needed. This rather vague conception of treatment under the Drug Conventions in itself is not incompatible with health-oriented approaches towards illicit drug use.

However, there is nothing within the UN Drug Conventions that expressively obligates States parties to adopt human rights-conforming treatment of drug users. Article 38 (1) Single Convention, Art. 20 (1) 1971 Convention and Art. 14 (4) 1988 Convention merely obligate States to adopt 'appropriate measures'. It is not laid out what measures could be considered as appropriate or – perhaps more importantly – what measures would have to be considered as inappropriate.[151]

148 This means States have to prevent non-medical and non-scientific drug use by adopting administrative measures; cf. *supra* 4.2.3.

149 Cf. UNGA, Outcome Document UNGASS 2016, 2016, UN Doc. A/Res-S/30/1, para. 1; INCB Annual Report 2016, para. 35.

150 Both provisions almost have an identical wording with the sole difference that Art. 38 (1) Single Convention applies to drugs, whereas Art. 20 (1)1971 Convention applies to psychotropic substances. Art. 38 (1) was included into the Single Convention by the 1972 Protocol and is framed after Art. 20 (1).

151 Such a concretization is also not provided for by Art. 38 (2) Single Convention and Art. 20 (2), which demand States to 'promote the training of personnel in the treatment, after-care, rehabilitation and social reintegration of abusers of drugs'. These provisions are not mandatory obligations but only obligate States parties to promote this training as far as possible. For a different view, however, cf. UNODC, Drug Policy Provisions from the International Drug Control Conventions, 2014, pp. 8 et seq.

This is problematic from the perspective of the right to health (Art. 12 (1) ICESCR). The right to the highest attainable standard of health requires that States adopt treatment measures that are compatible with scientific evidence,[152] and it involves a right to quality and evidence-based health care measures.[153] As was rightly remarked by the UN Special Rapporteur on the Right of Everyone to the Enjoyment of the Highest Attainable Standard of Physical and Mental Health '*[t]reatment that is not evidence-based should never be used*'.[154] Additionally, the right to the highest attainable standard rules out, at least in general, coerced forms of treatment of drug users which remain a common practice in many States where drug users are held in so-called detention centres.[155] The reference to appropriate measures of the UN Drug Conventions has to be read in this light. States are thus not obligated by the UN Drug Conventions to resort to forms of treatment of drug users that contradict scientific evidence. Another question is whether the UN Drug Conventions inhibit States parties from adopting health-oriented approaches towards drug use.

6.3.3 Do the UN Drug Conventions involve inhuman treatment of drug users?

It has been argued that the wording of Art. 36 (1) (b) Single Convention, allowing States parties to replace detention with treatment, would suggest an approval for coercive forms of drug treatment.[156] The wording of Art. 36 (1) (b) may be somewhat unclear in this regard by obliging States 'to [...] provide that such

152 CESCR, General Comment No. 14, The Right to the Highest Attainable Standard of Health, 2000, UN Doc E/C.12/2000/4, para. 12 (d).

153 Report of the Special Rapporteur on the Right of Everyone to the Enjoyment of the Highest Attainable Standard of Physical and Mental Health (Anand Grover), 2009, UN Doc. A/64/272, para. 32.

154 Report of the Special Rapporteur on the Right of Everyone to the Enjoyment of the Highest Attainable Standard of Physical and Mental Health (Anand Grover), 2010, UN Doc. A/65/255, para. 91 (italics added).

155 This issue remains debated among scholars; Saul Takahashi, 'Drug Control, Human Rights, and the Right to the Highest Attainable Standard of Health: By No Means Straightforward Issues', *HRQ* Vol. 31 2009, 748 (775) argues against a blanket prohibition; for a different opinion cf. Simon Flacks, 'Drug Control, Human Rights, and the Right to the Highest Attainable Standard of Health: A Reply to Saul Takahashi', *HRQ* Vol. 33 2011, 856 (862 et seq.); Richard Lines, *Drug Control and Human Rights in International Law*, pp. 93 et seq. with further references. It is also not clarified by the practice of treaty bodies and international court; see CESCR, General Comment No. 14, The Right to the Highest Attainable Standard of Health, 2000, UN Doc. E/C.12/2000/4, para. 8, where the Committee did not rule out 'coercive medical treatment'; the UNODC and WHO considered that such forms may be compatible with human rights law in exceptional cases but has not renewed this assessment in recent years; cf. UNODC and WHO, Principles of Drug Dependence Treatment, March 2008, p. 10.

156 Barrett et al., *supra* note 81, p. 29. The wording of Art. 22 (1) (b) 1971 Convention is slightly different in this regard. Albeit it is phrased in an imperative form, the word 'shall' is omitted here.

abusers *shall* undergo measures of treatment, education, after-care, rehabilitation and social reintegration in conformity with paragraph 1 of article 38'.[157]

The *telos* of Art. 36 (1) (b) argues, however, against such a line of interpretation. Article 36 (1) (b) merely allows States to replace punishment with treatment and, therefore, cannot be invoked as obliging States parties to provide for involuntary treatment of drug offenders. This reading is furthermore suggested by the reference of Art. 36 (1) Single Convention to Art. 38 (1) Single Convention. The latter does not mention any forms of coerced treatment. Thus, although the Single Convention does not rule out such forms of treatment, it cannot be argued that such compulsory treatment would be suggested by this treaty.

Likewise it was held that the fourth and fifth preambular paragraphs of the Single Convention would lead to a stigmatization of drug users. They read as follows: 'Recognizing that addiction to narcotic drugs constitutes a serious evil for the individual and is fraught with social and economic danger to mankind, Conscious of their duty to prevent and combat this evil'.[158]

This demonization of drug addiction would be without parallel in international law, as even the genocide convention, the apartheid convention and the torture convention would not contain such a rigid condemnation of the acts that they prohibit.[159] This stigmatizing language would result in describing a threat which States would subsequently exploit in order to resort to such drastic measures incompatible with their human rights obligations.[160]

Linking inhuman treatment of drug addicts with the Single Convection's preamble seems hardly convincing. The language used in the above-mentioned provision does not forcibly involve a stigmatization of individual drug users. Indeed, such a language would seem problematic as soon as it contained a rhetoric describing individuals – drug users or drug traffickers alike – as threats or scourges. This is not the case, as the UN Drug Conventions merely express the contempt for addiction of the States parties. It is also clear that today such a language would not be used today in a multilateral treaty and that some States tend to exploit threats described by international law for various reasons. However, establishing a direct link between such language and human rights abuses seems unconvincing.

157 Art. 22 (1) (b) Single Convention almost has the same wording but the term 'shall' is omitted.
158 By the same token, the second preambular para. of the 1971 Convention notes with concern the social problem resulting from drug abuse and preambular para. 1 of the 1988 Convention voices concerns over the illicit production, traffic and demand for narcotic drugs and psychotropic substances as posing a threat to the health and welfare of human beings; cf. for this argument already, Barrett et al., *supra* note 81, p. 11; cf. for a more elaborated line of argumentation, Rick Lines, '"Deliver Us from Evil" – The Single Convention on Narcotic Drugs, 50 Years On', *International Journal on Human Rights and Drug Policy* Vol. 1 2010, 2; cf. also in this regard Damon Barrett, 'Reflections on Human Rights and International Drug Control' in: John Collins (ed.), *Governing the Global Drug Wars*, Special Report, LSE Ideas 2012, 55.
159 Lines, *supra* note 159, 2 (8) with further references.
160 See as to this argumentation Richard Lines, *Drug Control and Human Rights in International Law*, pp. 62 et seq.

6.3.4 The limits of treatment under the UN Drug Conventions: Wither the harm-reduction approach

Despite all vagueness of treatment measures under the UN Drug Conventions, one simple truth should not be lost from sight. The long-term goal of treatment is the termination of non-medical and non-scientific drug use. This idea is prevalent within the Art. 38 (1) Single Convention and Art. 20 (1) 1971 Convention; both provisions are entitled 'measures against the abuse' of narcotic drugs and psychotropic substances respectively.

The axiom of equating treatment of illicit drug use with its very termination is challenged by the harm-reduction approach. Albeit there is no recognized definition of harm reduction, a useful starting point is provided for by the NGO 'Harm Reduction International', whereby '[h]arm Reduction refers to policies, programmes and practices that aim primarily to reduce the adverse health, social and economic consequences of the use of legal and illegal psychoactive drugs without necessarily reducing drug consumption.'[161]

For many human rights advocates a support for harm-reduction measures constitutes an indispensable cornerstone of health-oriented and evidence-based drug policies.[162] The harm-reduction approach developed in European inner city districts in the 1980s in order to protect intravenous drug users from HIV/Aids.[163] Today, the term 'harm reduction' has a wider connotation and covers all sorts of measures and interventions aimed at protecting drug users from health-related risks caused by drug use.[164] The most well-known harm-reduction measures are:

- Opioid maintenance therapy: where an addicted drug user uses opioids under medical surveillance – e.g. methadone or heroin – in order to mitigate withdrawal symptoms;
- Needle exchange programmes: where individuals are provided with sterile syringes in order to prevent injecting drug users from being inflicted with HIV/Aids;

161 Cf. in this regard, Harm Reduction International, What is Harm Reduction (available online at: https://www.hri.global/files/2010/08/10/Briefing_What_is_HR_English.pdf). Similar consideration pre-dates the label harm reduction; the ECDD already argued in 1974:

> The broad purpose of preventive measure should be to prevent or reduce the severity of problems associated with the non-medical use of dependence-producing drugs. This goal is at once broader, more specific, and with respect to certain drugs in many countries, more realistic than the prevention of-non-medical use per se [WHO Expert Committee on Drug Dependence, 20th Report, WHO Technical Report Series No 551, 1974, p. 32].

162 Andrew Ball, 'HIV, Injecting Drug Use and Harm Reduction: A Public Health Response', *Addiction* Vol. 102 2007, 684 (685).

163 David Bewley-Taylor, *International Drug Control: Consensus Fractured*, pp. 41 et seq.

164 This, for example, is the case for naloxone, a narcotic antagonist reversing overdose; see as to this issue WHO, Community Management of Opioid Overdose, 2014, *passim*.

- Drug consumption rooms: where drug users can consume illicitly acquired drugs without being prosecuted under the supervision of street workers and/or medical personnel.[165]

Harm-reduction measures have been frequently associated with the right to the highest attainable standard of health as guaranteed by Art. 12 ICESCR.[166] Many have written about the legality of harm-reduction measures under the current legal framework and approved their compatibility with the present legal framework.[167] The more fundamental problems of all of these harm-reduction measures, however, all too often remained unclear.

The harm-reduction approach as a whole focuses on the reduction of drug-related harms, but is not concerned with a limitation of drug use. This causes potential frictions with a system whose aim is to *limit* drug use to medical and scientific purposes.[168] These frictions have not been sufficiently clarified and laid out by the States parties and in particular the INCB. This explains their incoherent treatment of harm-reduction measures.

6.3.4.1 States parties and drug control institutions' incoherent practice on harm-reduction measures

States parties have struggled over supportive statements with regard to 'harm reduction'. The controversies led to a crack in the so-called Vienna Consensus during the 2008 CND session.[169] States were unable to agree whether the final declaration should contain a supportive reference to harm-reduction measures. A coalition of 26 States adopted an interpretative statement, whereas they would interpret the reference to 'related support services' as comprising

165 Cf. David Bewley-Taylor, *International Drug Control: Consensus Fractured*, pp. 41 et seq. with further details.

166 Cf. e.g. Takahashi, supra note 156, 749 (763 et seq.); cf. e.g. Report of the Special Rapporteur on the Right of Everyone to the Enjoyment of the Highest Attainable Standard of Physical and Mental Health (Anand Grover), UN Doc. A/65/255, 2010, paras 50 et seq.

167 Cf. e.g. David Spivack, *A Fourth International Convention for Drug Policy*, pp. 17 et seq.; Legal Affairs section United Nations Drug Control Programme, Flexibility of Treaty Provisions as regards Harm Reduction Approaches, 30 September 2002, UN Doc. E/INCB/2002/W.13/SS.5 (available online at: www.undrugcontrol.info/images/stories/un300902.pdf); Takahashi, *supra* note 156, 749 (765 et seq.); David Bewley-Taylor and Martin Jelsma, 'Fifty Years of the 1961 Single Convention on Narcotic Drugs: A Reinterpretation', TNI Series on Legislative Reform of Drug Policies No. 12 (2011), pp. 9 et seq.; Ian Malkin, Richard Eliott and Rowan McRae, 'Supervised Injection Facilities and International Law', *JDI* Vol. 33 2003, 539; UNODC, Drug Policy Provisions from the International Drug Control Conventions, 2014, pp. 11 et seq.

168 See *supra* Chapter 4.

169 As to this notion cf. *supra* note 88.

'harm-reduction measures'.[170] This interpretative statement was rejected by a number of States *inter alia* because these measures were incompatible with the UN Drug Conventions. [171] Despite calls to the contrary by the European Union[172] and civil society, the term 'harm reduction' is, likewise, not contained within the UNGASS 2016 outcome document.[173]

These controversies are misleading, however. Despite all the turmoil caused by a supportive statement for the umbrella term of 'harm-reduction measures', States parties have continuously – directly and indirectly – supported individual harm-reduction measures without using this term. This is, for example, true with regard to needle exchange programmes, which has been supported for some time by CND resolutions[174] and more lately by the UNGASS 2016 outcome document. Thereby, UNGA supports 'injecting equipment programmes', which is a synonym for needle exchange programmes.[175] This shows that the debate amongst States parties on harm-reduction measures has become somewhat Kafkaesque. States are unable to agree on the general label 'harm reduction', while supporting specific harm-reduction measures because of their efficacy of combating Aids.

The assessment of harm-reduction measures by the INCB is hardly more consistent. The INCB has voiced concerns over HIV/Aids for intravenous drug users since its 1986 Annual Report.[176] In its 1993 Annual Report, the INCB underlined 'the importance of certain aspects of "harm reduction" as a tertiary prevention strategy for demand reduction purposes', while simultaneously underlining 'that "harm reduction" programmes are not substitutes for demand reduction programmes'.[177] Thus, the INCB cautiously approved a harm-reduction strategy subject to certain limits, without laying out in the abstract where those 'limits of latitude' lie.[178]

170 CND, Report of the Fifty-second Session, ECOSOC Official Records No. 8 No. 8, 14 March 2008 and 11–20 March 2009, UN Doc. E/2009/28 para. 155.

171 CND, Report of the Fifty-second Session, ECOSOC Official Records No. 8 No. 8, 14 March 2008 and 11–20 March 2009, UN Doc. E/2009/28 paras 156 et seq.

172 European Union Common Position on UNGASS 2016, paras 11 and 14 (available online at: www.unodc.org/documents/ungass2016/Contributions/IO/EU_COMMON_POSITION_ON_UNGASS.pdf).

173 Cf. UNGA, Outcome Document UNGASS 2016, 2016, UN Doc. A/Res-S/30/1, para. 1.

174 Cf. CND Resolution 45/1, 2002 UN Doc. E/2002/28, para. 6; *id.* Resolution 46/2, 2003, UN Doc. E/2003/28/Rev.1, para. 4.

175 David Bewley-Taylor and Martin Jelsma, 'UNGASS 2016: A Broken or B-r-o-a-d Consensus?', Drug Policy Briefing No. 45, June 2016, 5; UNGA, Outcome Document UNGASS 2016, 2016, UN Doc. A/Res-S/30/1, para. 1 (o).

176 INCB Annual Report 1986, para. 11; *id.* Annual Report 1987, para. 2; *id.* Annual Report, 1988, para. 1; *id.* Annual Report 1989, para. 10.

177 INCB Annual Report 1993, para. 29. Cf. for further approval of harm reduction by the INCB, INCB Annual Report 2000, para. 445 but cf. for a highly sceptical assessment of harm reduction by then INCB president, Hamid Ghodse, 'Harm Reduction: The Idea and the Ideology', *The Journal of Drug Policy and Practice* Vol. 1 2007 Issue 4.

178 Cf. for this formulation, David Bewley-Taylor and Martin Jelsma, 'The UN Drug Control Conventions: The Limits of Latitude', TNI Series on Legislative Reform of Drug Policies No. 18 March 2012.

Those limits can only be assessed when taking a look at the evaluation of individual harm-reduction measures by the INCB. Despite some initial scepticism, the INCB today accepts the legality of opioid substitution therapy.[179] It also – although not expressed in an unequivocal manner[180] – seems to consider sterile syringe programmes to be in line with the UN Drug Conventions under the condition that they do not '*facilitate or promote drug abuse*'.[181] According to the Board, facilitation and promotion of drug abuse is to be approved when States parties allow the operation of drug consumption rooms. The operations of 'such sites [is] contrary to the fundamental provisions of the international drug control treaties, which oblige state parties to ensure that drugs are used only for medical and scientific purposes'.[182]

The Board has repeatedly reiterated this point of view,[183] although the differentiation between drug injection rooms and needle exchange programmes is factually difficult to sustain[184] and was not shared by the legal affairs section of the UNODC's predecessor, the United Nations Drug Control Programme, when it advised the INCB on the matter.[185]

The different treatment of drug consumption rooms, on the one hand, and needle exchange programmes, on the other hand, reveals fundamental inconsistencies. A closer look at those two measures shows that both interventions facilitate, to a certain extent, non-medical and non-scientific drug use. A State allowing for the provision of an individual drug user with needles, tolerates that

179 Cf. for its initial position, INCB Annual Report 1994, para. 327; *id.* Annual Report 1995, para. 385; *id.* Annual Report 2003, para. 222. Cf. e.g. *id.* Annual Report 2003, para. 222. The INCB initially was very critical with regard to heroin maintenance; cf. Diane Steber Buechli and Ruth Dreifuss, 'Swiss Drug Policy in International Context: Fought, Ignored, Admired', in: Collins John (ed.), *Governing the Global Drug Wars*, Special Report, LSE Ideas, 2012, 43 (45 et seq.). It, however, does not seem to have retained this position, Germany was not criticized after implementing such a programme, although the programme was remarked on; cf. INCB Annual Report 2009, para. 698.

180 For such an interpretation cf. e.g. Human Rights Watch, 'International Harm Reduction Association: Building Consensus', A Reference guide to Human Rights and Drug Policy, 2009, p. 1; Takahashi, *supra* note 156, 749 (766), but this is not unequivocally shared as the President of the INCB in 2002 publicly spoke out against needle exchange programmes; quoted in: Julia Buxton, *The Political Economy of Narcotics: Production, Consumption and Global Markets*, p. 162

181 INCB Annual Report 1987, para. 2; *id.* Annual Report 1988, para. 7; *id.* Annual Report, 2003, para. 221.

182 INCB Annual Report 2003, para. 326.

183 INCB Annual Report 2011, para. 289. The issue came up again, when the Supreme Court of Canada ruled in *(Attorney General) v. PHS Community Services Society*, 2011 SCC 44, [2011] 3 S.C.R. 134 that a denial to exempt a drug consumption room from operating would violate the right to life, liberty and security of person as guaranteed by the Canadian Charter of human rights; the INCB criticized this judgment vividly; INCB Annual Report 2011, para. 289.

184 Takahashi, *supra* note 156, 749 (765).

185 Legal affairs section UNDCP, Flexibility of Treaty Provisions as regards Harm Reduction Approaches, 2002, UN –Doc. E/INCB/2002/W.13/SS.5, paras 21 et seq.; this paper is widely quoted but never was officially commented by the INCB (available online at: www.undrugcontrol.info/images/stories/un300902.pdf).

these needles will be used for illicit drug use. The same is *mutatis mutandis* true for drug consumption rooms. A State which allows the operation of drug consumption rooms, tolerates the fact that drugs will be used within a safe setting. This is not to say that such practices are not permissible within the present legal framework, but to clarify the more underlying problem of harm-reduction measures under the present status quo: there are harm-reduction measures that do effectively deviate from the limitation of drugs to medical and scientific purposes which are considered as compatible with the UN Drug Conventions.

6.3.4.2 Towards a more coherent approach for determining the legality of harm-reduction measures

A more accurate assessment of the legality of harm-reduction measures under the current *lex lata* involves a three-step assessment of harm-reduction measures.

The first question that a State has to ask under the present legal framework is whether the harm-reduction measure involved complies with the obligation to limit drug use to medical and scientific purposes. If this is the case, the legality of harm-reduction measures under the present legal framework has to be approved.

Arguably, however, a harm-reduction measure not limiting drugs to medical and scientific purposes may likewise be compatible with the UN Drug Conventions' provisions on treatment. The second sentence of Art. 14 (4) 1988 Convention allows States to base demand-reduction strategies on recommendations by international organizations. It seems viable to read Art. 14 (4) as allowing for any harm-reduction measure contained within such a recommendation. Despite the more general concern of Art. 14 (4) to lower illicit demand, the second sentence of Art. 14 (4) can be read as allowing States parties to the UN Drug Conventions to base their demand-reduction strategies on the recommendations of international organizations, even when these measures deviate from medical and scientific purposes. Moreover, the reference to 'international organizations' has to be read as comprising institutions that do not fulfil the criteria of international organizations under international law. This is true because of the *telos* of this provision is to ensure that the States parties to the UN Drug Conventions are enabled to take into account external scientific expertise when they treat drug users. This means that the expertise of international institutions such as the INCB, the EMCDDA, the UNODC or the ECDDA may also be considered, when States adopt demand-reduction measures.[186]

Additionally, an important consideration follows from Art. 38 (1) Single Convention and Art. 20 (1) 1971 Convention.[187] These provisions reveal that

186 It cannot be reconstructed why States decided to open up the 1988 Convention to the expertise of such institutions. The initial proposal for what should later become Art. 14 (4) merely contained a binding reference to the multidisciplinary outline and did not mention recommendations of the UNGA or other institutions; OR I 1988 Convention, p. 150. The *travaux préparatoires* to the 1988 Convention do not clarify why the recommendations of these institutions were integrated into the final text; OR II 1988 Convention, pp. 303 et seq., 306.

187 Art. 38 Single Convention; Art. 20 1971 Convention.

treatment does not necessarily have to be identical to the *prevention* of abuse. Prevention of drug abuse refers to the imperative to counter non-medical drug use, whereas treatment comprises the measures for the sake of the well-being of the individual drug user. The provisions stipulate that the 'the parties shall [...] take all practicable measures for the prevention of abuse of drugs *and* for [...] treatment of the persons involved'.[188] The difference between prevention of non-medical drug use, on the one hand, and treatment of non-medical drug use, on the other hand, is an idea that was also reiterated by the States parties to the UN Drug Conventions on the Guiding Principles on demand reduction adopted by the UNGASS in 1998.[189] If prevention of drug abuse and treatment of drug users are not similar one may well imagine situations in which treatment might entail the need to accept the social reality of illicit drug use in order to prevent the user from suffering perilous harm, despite the fact that such a form of treatment was not recommended by an institution mentioned in Art. 14 (4) 1988 Convention.

This leads to the adoption of a three-layered test with regard to harm-reduction measures:

- First, it has to be determined whether the form of treatment can be considered to involve medical drug use.[190] If this is the case, the legality of the treatment measure cannot be called into doubt.
- Second, in case the measure facilitates non-medical drug use, it has to be assessed whether the measure at hand is recommended specifically by Art. 14 (4) 1988 Convention. If this is the case, the legality of the measure can be approved.
- Third, if the measure (a) involves non-medical and drug use, and (b) is not recommended by a specialized agency nor mentioned by Art. 14 (4), one can nevertheless consider whether there are circumstances requiring the toleration of non-medical drug use in order to prevent perilous harms for the drug user. Especially in cases where scientific evidence seems to indicate that a measure could be viable to reduce incurable diseases, most notably HIV/Aids, a State may resort to such a measure. This will have to be assessed on a case-by-case basis.

One could argue that such an approach would contradict and misconceive the central objective of the international drug control system of limiting all drug-related activities to medical and scientific purposes. Indeed, the present book has shown that the limitation of drugs to medical and scientific purposes is only

188 Art. 38 (1) Single Convention (italics added). This interpretation is not accepted by the Commentaries of the Single Convention and the 1971 Convention; cf. Commentary 1972 Protocol, Art. 15, MN 10; Commentary 1971 Convention, Art. 20, MN 10.

189 UNGA, Declaration on the Guiding Principles of Demand Reduction, 1998, UN Doc. A/Res/S-20/3, para. 8 (b) (i).

190 Cf. as to the meaning of medical drug use, *supra* 4.2.4.

subjected to very narrow exceptions.[191] Nevertheless, a line of argumentation opening the UN Drug Conventions for harm-reduction measures seems plausible, albeit somewhat at odds with the fundamental objective of limiting drugs to medical and scientific purposes.

It has to be remembered that perilous threats for drug users, like Aids, were not existent when the Single and 1971 Conventions were adopted. It would seem a strange result to require State parties to renounce modern approaches to the treatment of drug use that were unforeseeable when the foundations for the international drug control system were laid. Additionally, while at odds with the limitation of drugs to medical and scientific purposes, harm-reduction measures do not mean that a State explicitly allows for non-medical and non-scientific purposes. They can, therefore, not be equated with the creation of a regulatory market for drugs.[192] Harm-reduction measure merely involve that a State refrains from preventing non-medical and non-scientific purposes in certain circumstances. Thus, although harm-reduction measures – at least in some cases – may be at odds with limiting drugs to medical and scientific purposes, they do not fully contravene this goal. Even more so because the reliance on harm-reduction measures does not mean that States would have to renounce the long-term goal of terminating the non-medical drug use. On the contrary, harm-reduction measures may serve this goal because they often provide for the first-time contact of drug users with treatment institutions.

6.3.4.3 Assessment of individual harm-reduction measures

The above-mentioned three-layered test also leads to viable results for individual harm-reduction measures. This can be shown with regard to opioid substation therapy, needle exchange programmes and drug consumption rooms.

Opioid substitution therapy or heroin maintenance complies with the limitation of drugs to medical and scientific purposes. As has been outlined above, medical drug use can be approved when an individual uses drugs in accordance with sound medical practice and the use is controlled by an individual exercising medical functions.[193] This is the case for this form of treatment. The drug user will only use the drug under medical authority. The substance that is prescribed, heroin, methadone or any other narcotic drug would seem irrelevant in this regard.

Needle exchange programmes deviate from the limitation of drugs to medical and scientific purposes. Albeit that they do not involve the provision of drugs for individuals for other than medical or scientific purposes, they facilitate non-medical and non-scientific drug use. An individual will use these sterile syringes for intravenous drug use occurring outside the control of an individual

191 Cf. *supra* 4.3.

192 Cf. as to the incompatibility of a regulatory drug market with the international drug control system *supra* 4.3.3.

193 Cf. *supra* 4.2.7.

exercising medical functions; this cannot be considered as medical drug use.[194] It is the purpose of these programmes to protect the individual using drugs for such purposes from being inflicted with blood-transmittable diseases. Such practices, nevertheless, are legal under the UN Drug Conventions because they are contained within the recommendations of WHO's Technical Guide and thereby are a viable form of treatment as outlined by Art. 14 (4) 1988 Convention.[195]

Drug consumption rooms remain the most hotly debated harm-reduction measure. Although these rooms are supervised, the drug use that occurs there cannot be considered as medical drug use. The user decides autonomously on his or her drug use. Additionally, and in contrast to needle exchange programmes, drug consumption rooms cannot be subsumed under Art. 14 (4) 1988 Convention. They are neither contained within the Technical Guide nor within any other recommendation of an institution falling under Art. 14 (4). Nevertheless, States are not barred from taking this form of treatment. Drug consumption rooms are considered effective to prevent HIV and to protect the drug user in the case of an overdose.[196] Thus, the need to prevent non-medical drug use may be subjected to the protection of the health of the drug users in this case. This does not mean that treatment of an individual always outweighs prevention of non-medical drug use. The case may be different for harm-reduction measures which do not lead to a protection of the health of the drug user.

6.3.5 Conclusion

The UN Drug Conventions do not satisfactorily resolve the issue of demand reduction and illicit drug use. Albeit States are not required to penalize non-medical and non-scientific drug use, it remains unclear how they are supposed to treat non-medical drug use.[197] The vagueness of treatment is problematic in light of the underlying objective of the international drug control system to limit drugs to medical and scientific purposes. The obligations on treatment may seem *prima facie* too narrow in order to allow for forms of treatment that deviate from this approach.

It has been shown that this problem can be dealt with by adopting an interpretation of the UN Drug Conventions that balances treatment of drug users with the imperative to limit drugs to medical and scientific purposes. Thus, more health-oriented approaches to drug users are feasible under the present legal framework. However, it is also true that the UN Drug Conventions do

194 Cf. *supra* 4.2.7.

195 Technical Guide, p. 12; cf. also for an earlier support by the ECDD, ECDD, 30th[h] Report, WHO Technical Report series No. 873, 1998, p. 4.

196 Technical Guide p. 22; cf. also in this regard Georgina MacArthur et al., 'Interventions to Prevent HIV and Hepatitis C in People who Inject Drugs: A Review of Reviews to Assess Evidence of Effectiveness', *IJDP* Vol. 25 2014, 34 (46).

197 Cf. for reform proposals with regard to demand reduction, Spivack David, *A Fourth International Convention for Dug Policy.*

not oblige States parties to provide for such policies. There is no individual obligation that would entitle a drug user to up-to-date health-oriented treatment. Such an obligation only derives from the right to the highest attainable standard of health, which has to be considered when interpreting the UN Drug Conventions. Thus, the same need of contextualizing the UN Drug Conventions within international human rights law that has been described in the previous section with regard to drug supply,[198] also applies to the demand side. When implementing the obligations of the UN Drug Conventions, States parties simultaneously have to protect the health and other human rights of drug users. Nevertheless, a more robust protection of drug users by the UN Drug Conventions is desirable.

The promise of the first preambular paragraph of the Single Convention to serve the health and welfare of mankind is not yet fulfilled by the operative provisions of the treaties. States parties and drug control institutions have to bring it to life. The possibility to adopt more health-oriented approaches towards drug use puts pressure on the actors inside the international drug control system to move States in this direction.

6.4 Fairness and the premise of the international drug control system to limit drugs to medical and scientific purposes by relying on a control of drug supply

This book has so far exclusively analysed the international drug control system from a positivistic view. It has sought to provide for an understanding of international drug control's norms and institutions in accordance with the current *lex lata*. It has left more underlying questions of the system's legitimacy untouched. The following section will widen this angle somewhat. In spite of dismantling some of the contemporary challenges to the international drug control system, it will ask whether the current approach of the system to limit drugs to medical and scientific purposes can be considered as 'fair'. This is deemed necessary because of the claim that the manner by which the burdens are allocated within the international drug control system today is unfair. This concerns the relationship between drug-producing, drug transit and drug-consuming States.

6.4.1 The opposition between drug-producing, drug transit and drug-consuming States as a problem of fairness

The international drug control system has, for the last century, been marked by opposition between States along the drug supply chain.[199] The division between drug-producing, drug transit and drug-consuming States in its classical form suggests that drugs – the coca leaf/cocaine, opium/opiates and cannabis – are

198 See *supra* 6.2.3.

199 Cf., e.g. already as to this opposition, Quincy Wright, 'The Opium Conferences', *AJIL* Vol. 19 1925, 559 (568).

produced and trafficked in States of the global South. Their illicit use, however, occurs in industrialized States of the global North. International drug trafficking cartels gain a lot of financial resources from bringing these substances from their origins to drug-consuming States, where the retail market for drugs lies.

One may question the viability of this differentiation for today's drug markets, as these markets have become incredibly complex.[200] Psychotropic substances and new psychoactive substances can be produced in laboratories everywhere in the world.[201] Similarly, cannabis is also grown and produced everywhere, including the classical drug-consuming States of Europe and North America.[202] Furthermore, consumption of drugs has become a pressing problem in many States where drugs are produced and trafficked.[203]

Nevertheless, the classical distinction of States along the drug supply chain still works with two substances. According to UNODC figures, the quasi-totality of cocaine produced still emanates from three States from South America – Bolivia, Peru and Colombia.[204] Likewise, OAS reports that 80 per cent of the cocaine consumed in the United States flows through Mexico.[205] The same is true for the opiate market. Despite all efforts, Afghanistan, according to the information of the UNODC, remains by far the biggest opium producer, making up for about 80 per cent of the opium produced for other than medical and scientific purposes worldwide.[206]

More importantly for this book, there are specific aspects of the world drug problem which exclusively concern so-called 'drug-producing' and 'drug transit' States. Indeed, the toll posed by international drug trafficking cartels is enormous. Mexico has been torn by the immense violence surrounding international drug trafficking cartels for over a decade.[207] The same is true for the decades-long internal violence within Colombia that was partly caused and fuelled by international trade in cocaine. The problem is not limited to Central and South America; Western Africa has emerged as an important hub for cocaine

200 INCB Annual Report 2012, para. 16.

201 With regard to psychoactive substances, see UNODC, 2014 Global Synthetic Drugs Assessment, 2014, UN Publication, Sales No.E14.XI.6 2014, *passim*.

202 UNODC, World Drug Report 2014, UN Publication, Sales No. E.14.XI.7, p. 39.

203 E.g. according to UNODC data, cocaine use is expanding in South and Central America, UNODC, World Drug Report 2014, UN Publication, Sales No. E.14.XI.7, p. xi.

204 UNODC, World Drug Report 2017, Part III Market Analysis of Plant-based Drugs Opiates, Cocaine, Cannabis, 2017, UN Publication, Sales No. E.17.XI.6). 34.

205 OAS, Report on the Drug Problem in the Americas in 2013, 2013, p. 47.

206 UNODC, World Drug Report 2017, Part III Market Analysis of Plant-based Drugs Opiates, Cocaine, Cannabis, 2017, UN Publication, Sales No. E.17.XI.6, p. 14.

207 Cf. e.g. as to this conflict and with a differing view regarding the conflict's classification, Carina Bergal, 'The Mexican Drug War: The Case for a Non-International Armed Conflict Classification', *Fordham Int'l L. J.* Vol. 34 2011, 1042; Patrick Gallahue, 'Mexico's "War on Drugs": Real or Rhetorical Armed Conflict', *Humanitäres Völkerrecht Informationsschriften* Vol. 24 2011, 34.

smuggling.[208] In 2012, the United Nations Security Council (UNSC) adopted a resolution under Chapter VII of the UN Charter in response to a *coup d'état* in Guinea Bissau of generals connected to international drug trafficking cartels.[209] The UNSC – after having expressed its concerns over the impact of drug trafficking in the region numerous times – decided that drug trafficking posed a threat to international peace and security.[210] To this day, the dynamics between violence and the international drug trade are not fully understood.[211] It is all the more difficult – if impossible – to normatively examine whether this violence is rooted within the norms of provisions of the international drug control system.[212] The point made here – more narrowly – is that drug-producing and drug transit States are considerably affected by the world drug problem.

Conversely, in drug-consuming States the drug problem – albeit causing considerable costs, notably in the health care and justice systems – has not reached similar existential dimensions. Hence, drug-producing and drug transit States seem to be troubled the most by the world drug problem in its present form. Drug-producing and drug transit States have repeatedly reminded the international community of the need to viably reduce the demand for drugs, which in their narrative is fuelling the insecurity and corruption within their borders. They ensured a key role in the run-up to the all three UNGA special sessions on drugs.[213] Thus, before calling for the first UNGA 1990 Special Session on drugs, then President of Colombia Virgilio Barco Vargas appealed:

> [to] effectively stop the demand for these illicit drugs. It is the insatiable demand for drugs that fuels narco-terrorism and is one of the greatest threats to democracy in Latin America. Those who consume cocaine are contributing to the assassination of my people by the criminal drug cartels.[214]

208 UNODC, Transnational Organized Crime in West Africa: A Threat Assessment, 2013, p. 3.

209 *Ibid.*, p. 16.

210 UNSC Resolution 2039 (2012), Peace and Consolidation in West Africa, 2012, UN Doc. S/Res/2039 (2012) preambular para. 18.

211 Cf. for a useful starting point, OAS, Report on the Drug Problem in the Americas in 2013, 2013, pp. 75 et seq.; cf. also as to this Damon Barrett, 'Security, Development and Human Rights: Normative, Legal and Policy Challenges for the International Drug Control System', *IJDP* Vol. 21 2010, 140 (141).

212 The creation of a drug market that provides for the economic foundation of these cartels has been labelled as an unintended consequence of the international drug control system by then UNODC Deputy Director Antonio Maria Costa, UNODC Deputy Director Antonio Maria Costa, CND, 'Making Drug Control "Fit for Purpose"'. Building on the UNGASS Decade. Report by the Executive Director of the UN Office on Drugs and Crime as a Contribution to the Review of the Twentieth Special Session of the General Assembly, 2008, UN Doc. E/CN.7/2008/CRP.17, p. 10. It is already difficult to determine precisely the notion of 'unintended consequences'; cf. as to this problem, Pierre-Arnaud Chouvy, 'A Typology of Unintended Consequences of Drug Crop Reduction', *JDI* Vol. 43 2012, 216. The indeterminacy of this term makes it rather ill-suited for a legal analysis of these treaties.

213 See as to this, David Bewley-Taylor and Martin Jelsma, 'UNGASS 2016: A Broken or B-r-o-a-d Consensus?', Drug Policy Briefing No. 45, June 2016, pp. 2 et seq.

214 Address by Virgilio Barco Vargas, President of the Republic of Colombia, 1989, UN Doc. A/44/PV.13, p. 12; for the call for the first special session, cf. *ibid.*, pp. 17 et seq.

By the same token, ahead of the second UNGA special session on drugs, in a widely remarked letter to the UN Secretary General, Mexico declared in 1993: 'Since drug consumption is the driving force that generates drug production and trafficking, the reduction in demand becomes the radical – albeit long-term solution of the problem.'[215]

Almost 20 years later, in 2012, while the preparation for the 2016 UNGASS was underway, Colombia, Guatemala and Mexico concluded:

> 1. That the consumption of illegal drugs is a powerful stimulus for the activities of criminal organizations in all regions of the world [...];
> 3. That, with their enormous financial resources, transnational criminal organizations are capable of penetrating and corrupting State institutions [...];
> 5. That, until the flow of resources from drug and weapon consumers to criminal organizations is stemmed, these organizations will continue to threaten our societies and governments;
> 6. That, consequently, the approach maintained to date by the international community with regard to drugs should be reviewed as a matter of urgency, with a view to stemming the flow of capital from the illegal drug market.[216]

Thus, some drug-producing and drug transit States have raised the same issue for the last 25 years by calling on drug-consuming States to lower the demand for drugs. At first sight the critique that they are advancing seems to be one of effectiveness: we have to be become more effective with reducing drug demand in order to keep away the financial flows from drug trafficking cartels, which are destabilizing our States and societies.

There is, however, another issue that is driving these States. A lack of effectiveness alone cannot explain why a certain number of States are constantly urging the international community to increase their effectiveness in reducing demand. Why for other States does this action not seem to be of similar vital interest? Arguably, the debate on the problems caused by 'our insatiable demand for drugs'[217] is in reality – at least in part – a discussion over a lack of fairness.[218]

Civil society representatives, consisting of elder statesmen from drug-producing and drug transit States have explicitly outlined the need for a fair burden sharing with regard to the abundant costs created by illicit drug trafficking and illicit drug production. Thus, the West African Commission on Drugs appealed:

215 Letter from Mexico to the Secretary General, 1993, UN Doc. A/C.3/48.2, para. 25.

216 Joint Declaration of Colombia, Guatemala and Mexico to the UN, 2012, UN Doc. A/67/493.

217 Cf. in this regard also the statement by then Secretary of State Hillary Rodham Clinton: 'Our insatiable demand for illegal drugs fuels the drug trade', *New York Times*, 25 March 2009 (available online at: www.nytimes.com/2009/03/26/world/americas/26mexico.html?_r=0).

218 Cf. already in this regard M. Cherif Bassiouni, 'Critical Reflections on International and National Control of Drugs', *DJILP* Vol. 18 1990, 311 (313).

> We urge the international community to share the burdens created by the rise in trafficking through West Africa, which neither produces nor consumes most of the drugs that transit their regions. Nations whose citizens consume large amounts of illicit drugs must play their part and seek humane ways to reduce the demand for drugs.[219]

By the same token, its predecessor, the Latin American Commission on Drugs and Democracy, five years earlier had appealed to European and North American States to take action in order to viably reduce the demand for drugs:

> The long-term solution for the drug problem is to reduce drastically the demand for drugs in the main consumer countries. The question is not to find guilty countries and allocate blame for this or that action or inaction, but to reiterate that the United States and the European Union share responsibility for the problems faced by our countries, insofar as their domestic markets are the main consumers of the drugs produced in Latin America. It is, thus, pertinent for us, Latin Americans, to ask them as partners to design and implement policies leading to an effective reduction in their levels of drug consumption and, as a consequence, in the overall scope of the narcotics criminal activities.[220]

These claims are similar in that they lament a lack of fairness within the contemporary drug control system. The term 'fairness' is of course difficult to grasp. According to the late Thomas M. Franck, 'fairness' is *inter alia* based on the 'core principle' that 'inequalities in access to, or the distribution of, goods must be justified by demonstrating that the inequality benefits not only to its beneficiaries, but also, in absolute terms everyone else'.[221]

We will rely on this concept of fairness because it is well suited to the present analysis. When applying this understanding of fairness to the international drug control system, the critique advanced by drug-producing and drug transit States is that they are taking measures of incredible high costs in order to prevent the flow of drugs to users in drug-consuming States, without receiving any benefits.

The next question that comes up is whether this perceived lack of fairness is attributable to the norms and provisions of the international drug control system. Finding a normative imbalance within the international drug control system that

219 West African Commission on Drugs, 'Not Just in Transit: Drugs, the State and Society in West Africa', 2014 p. 5.

220 Latin American Commission on Drugs and Democracy, 'Drugs and Democracy: Toward a Paradigm Shift', 2009, p. 7.

221 Thomas M. Franck, 'Fairness in the International Legal and Institutional System', *RdC* Vol. 240 1993 III, 9 (36). The other fundamental core of fairness, according to Franck, is that a global community cannot include any group that believes to be entitled to an "automatic trumping element" that supersedes the interests of all the other stakeholders; cf. as to this *ibid.* (34 et seq.).

would systematically disadvantage such States is far from self-evident. Much of the criticism caused by the supply orientation and perceived imbalances of drug control is in reality caused by realpolitik. So-called drug-consuming States' – most notably the United States – used the label of 'narco States' in order to further their own political agenda and relied on controversial steps, such as the irregular rendition of drug traffickers or self-defence, under Art. 51 of the Charter in order to counter drug trafficking.[222] Such steps – problematic as they are – are not rooted within the UN Drug Conventions nor international law in general.[223]

The fact that supply orientation may be partly an outcome caused by political and economic inequality of the actors involved does not preclude that it may also be traced within the legal framework. It has to be examined whether a lack of fairness remains prevalent in the premise of the international drug control system to resolve the world drug problem primarily by controlling drug supply.

6.4.2 Imbalance of supply orientation within the international drug control system

6.4.2.1 Supply orientation as a historical premise to resolve the world drug problem

Supply orientation is certainly historically rooted within the legal framework.[224] The lesson that was drawn from the Chinese opium epidemic at the turn of the century was that the key to resolving the world drug problem was to control drugs at their source.[225] China became the biggest opium consumer in the course of the nineteenth century because it had been unable to control the opium supply within India. Several statements from the United States during the early period of the drug control system show that its objective was to resolve its

222 A very drastic example in that regard is the United States' invasion of Panama in 1990, in the aftermath of which the former President Noriega was charged with drug trafficking in Florida; cf. Ved Nanda, 'Agora U.S. Forces in Panama: Defenders, Aggressors or Human Rights Activists?', *AJIL* Vol. 84 1990, 494. During this time the US official position was that drug trafficking could trigger the right to self-defence under the Charter; Statement of the Legal Advisor of the US Department of State of 1989 in that regard, statement by then legal Adviser of the Department of State, Abraham D. Sofaer, quoted in: *AJIL* Vol. 84 1990, 724 (727). Cf. also with regard to so-called 'irregular renditions' against drug traffickers, Charles Kallenbach, '*Plomo o Plata*: Irregular Rendition as a Means of Gaining Jurisdiction over Colombian Drug Kingpins', *NYU JILP* Vol. 23 1990, 169.

223 Cf. also in this regard resolutions by the UNGA, where the UNGA underlined that the principles of the Charter – most notably the prohibition of the use of force – have to be respected in the fight against drug abuse and drug trafficking, UNGA Resolution 45/147, 1990, UN Doc. A/Res/45/147; *id.* Resolution A/RES/46/101, 1991, UN Doc. A/Res/46/101; *id.* Resolution 47/98, 1992, UN Doc. A/Res/47/98.

224 Cf. also in this regard, e.g. Catherine Carstairs, 'The Stages of the International Drug Control System', *Drug and Alcohol Review* Vol. 24 2005, 57 (59).

225 Cf. *supra* 3.1.2.1.1.

own drug problem by gaining control over drug supply.[226] It was aware that to this end international cooperation was indispensable because the supply for cocaine and opiates emanated from the territory of other States. This also explains why there were no obligations in the drug control treaties before the Single Convention to lower the illicit demand for drugs or provide for treatment of drug addicts.[227] There was no perceived need for such obligations. Once the supply for drugs would be controlled, there would be no more drug addiction and non-medical drug use because drugs for other than medical and scientific purposes would simply be not available.

This means that initially drug-producing States were held accountable for resolving the health-related by problem of drug-consuming States by preventing the flow of drugs into the latter's territories.

6.4.2.2 Supply orientation today

6.4.2.2.1 REVEALING SUPPLY ORIENTATION: COMPARING DEMAND- AND SUPPLY-ORIENTED OBLIGATIONS

The earlier concept of resolving the world drug problem by exclusively reducing drug supply is mitigated by the contemporary legal framework. As has been shown, all three Drug Conventions contain obligations on demand reduction and treatment (Art. 38 Single Convention; Art. 20 1971 Convention; Art. 14 (4) 1988 Convention).

This means that supply orientation of the contemporary legal framework is forcibly relative. It can only be correctly assessed when comparing the demand-related obligations with supply-related obligations. As has been shown above, States are obligated to control the licit production and trade for drugs. Their compliance with those obligations can be objectively verified by the INCB (Art. 19 Single Convention; Art. 16 1971 Convention).[228] Additionally, States are obligated to counter the illicit supply by adopting penal sanctions and ensuring their effective cooperation.[229] These obligations are clear and enforceable.

In contrast, the legal framework leaves the question on how to handle illicit drug demand unresolved. The vague content of demand-reduction obligations has already been discussed. States can basically rely on the obligations of demand reduction and treatment to justify any kind of policy with regard to drug users – ranging from zero tolerance policies to health-oriented approaches.[230] Their

226 Cf. with regard to the US viewpoint, Hamilton Wright, 'The International Opium Conference', *AJIL* Vol. 6 1912, 865 (868); cf. also H.J.Res., 453 451 Stat. 1431: the effective control of [habit-forming] drugs can only be obtained by limiting their production to the quantity required for strictly medicinal and scientific purposes'.

227 Cf. for a reference of those treaties *supra* Chapter 3.

228 Cf. *supra* 6.1.

229 Cf. *supra* 6.2.

230 Cf. *supra* 6.3.

adherence to demand-reduction obligations cannot be objectively monitored. Thus, it is unclear what States have to do in order to cope with a widespread demand for drugs for other than medical and scientific purposes. Additionally, as has been shown, the obligation to penalize illicit drug use is subjected to notable loopholes (Art. 3 (2) 1988 Convention) and the whole system of cooperation to combat illicit drug supply by extradition, law enforcement and other means as outlined by the 1988 Convention is not extended to the penalization of illicit drug use.[231]

Seen from this perspective – despite some progresses – the obligations on demand reduction are an alien element within the UN Drug Conventions. These treaties remain based on the un-outspoken premises that drug use will be prevented by ensuring that the production of drugs will be limited to medical and scientific purposes and combatting drug supply for all other ends. The potential drug user, seeking drugs for other than medical and scientific purposes, would not – if these obligations would be fulfilled in practice – have the substances available in order to do so. This was shared by the parties to the Single Convention. The following statement of the Soviet delegate reveals the direction of the UN Drug Conventions in order to resolve the world drug problem: 'the work of drug control should be directed towards preventing the development of drug addiction by regulating the licit supply of dangerous drugs and by stamping out the illicit'.[232]

This puts pressure on States where drugs are produced and trafficked for other than medical and scientific purposes at high scales. This pressure is critical from a fairness perspective. Drug-producing and drug transit States have to adopt costly measures for reducing drug supply for the potential benefit of drug-consuming States, while no verifiable indicators for a reduction of demand exist. This pressure is even exacerbated by the way prominent actors address the inability of States to viably reduce illicit drug supply.

6.4.2.2.2 THE PRACTICE OF SANCTIONS: EXACERBATING SUPPLY ORIENTATION

The INCB has invoked Art. 14 Single Convention with regard to Afghanistan for the last 16 years.[233] It has made its consultations with this State public. This

231 Cf. *supra* 6.3.1.

232 OR I Single Convention, pp. 107 et seq.

233 INCB Annual Report 2001, paras 231 et seq.; *id.* Annual Report 2002, paras 231 et seq.; *id.* Annual Report 2002, paras 185 et seq.; *id.* Annual Report 2003, paras 198 et seq.; *id.* Annual Report 2003, paras 198 et seq.; *id.* Annual Report 2004, paras 205 et seq.; *id.* Annual Report 2005, paras 201 et seq.; *id.* Annual Report 2006, paras 160 et seq.; *id.* Annual Report 2007, paras 195 et seq.; *id.*, Annual Report 2008, paras 224 et seq.; *id.* Annual Report 2009, paras 213 et seq.; *id.* Annual Report 2010, paras 159 et seq.; *id.* Annual Report 2011, paras 123 et seq.; *id.* Annual Report 2012, paras 143 et seq.; *id.* Annual Report 2013, paras 129 et seq.; *id.* Annual Report 2014, paras 204 et seq.; *id.* Annual Report 2015, paras 231 et seq.; *id.* Annual Report 2016, paras 287 et seq., *id.* Annual Report 2017, paras 229 et seq.

is the second most severe measure at its disposal to address non-compliance of a State party with the provisions of the Single Convention (Art. 14 (1) (d) Single Convention). In the meantime, drug-consuming States were simultaneously unsuccessful in reducing their own demand for opiates.[234] The INCB never publicly invoked Art. 14 against a State because it would fail to address widespread demand for drugs.

This is far from suggesting that invoking Art. 14 vis-à-vis a State where drug demand remains unabated would seem a viable step. Conversely, requesting one of the poorest States in the world to control its illicit opium cultivation and production as long as illicit demand for opiates remains unabated seems deprived of any economic logic. Such steps to single out drug-producing States perpetuate the impression that the blame for the world drug problem is allocated to States unable to control the supply for drugs, whilst in reality, and despite all efforts, classical drug-consuming States in the meantime have not achieved any results in reducing their illicit drug demand.

The US decertification procedure is even more problematic in this regard. The procedure freezes any US assistance for 'major drug producing [...] or drug transit States' failing to comply with their obligations under the international counternarcotics agreements.[235] To current knowledge, there are no comparable measures in which drug-producing States would freeze assistance to drug-consuming States because of their inability to curb illicit drug demand.

This shows that the approach to resolving the world drug problem by reducing supply and reallocating the blame on those States where drug supply comes from, remains rooted within the implementation of the international drug control system. Such steps cannot claim to be fair. Undermining the fairness of the international drug control system imperils compliance with this system and, equally, in the long term puts its very existence into question.[236] It is therefore no coincidence that two concepts have seen the light of the day which challenge the imbalance inherent to the contemporary drug control system.

6.4.3 Challenging supply orientation

Two, albeit interrelated, approaches can be distinguished which were designed in order to correct the overall reliance of the international drug control system on a reduction of drug supply.

234 UNODC, Contribution of the Executive Director of the United Nations Office on Drugs and Crime to the High-Level Review of the Implementation of the Political Declaration and Plan of Action on International Cooperation Towards an Integrated and Balanced Strategy to Counter the World Drug Problem, to be conducted by the Commission on Narcotic Drugs in 2014, 2013, UN Doc. UNODC/ED/2014/1, paras 19 et seq. This statement concerns the period from 2009 to 2013.

235 Italics added; Section 706 (1) Foreign Relations Authorization Act, FY 2003 (Public Law 107–228).

236 Cf. in general, Franck, *supra* note 222, 9 (42).

6.4.3.1 Balanced approach

First is the balanced approach. The call for a balanced approach was made in the final declaration to the 1987 Conference on drug abuse and illicit drug trafficking.[237] Preambular para. 1 of the Declaration of the International Conference on Drug Abuse and Illicit Trafficking provided a clear commitment to combat drug abuse, by adopting '*urgent measures to strengthen international co-operation through a balanced, comprehensive and multidisciplinary approach*'.[238] Calls for a balanced approach have since been made numerous times by the UNGA.[239] The idea behind the approach is that the limitation of drugs to medical and scientific purposes can only be achieved once illicit drug supply and drug demand are simultaneously lowered.

The obligation contained in Art. 14 (4) was negotiated into this treaty by drug-producing and drug transit States in order to ensure more accountability of drug-consuming States to finally fulfil their promise of reducing illicit demand.[240] The same is true for the targets set by UNGASS in 1998 and the CND in 2009.[241] It was hoped that by setting precise targets to viably reduce the demand for, and the supply of, drugs a better equilibrium could be established between the obligation's various actors on the drug supply chain.[242]

After roughly 20 years, the growing tensions within the international drug control system stand proof that this idea has failed. This is far from suggesting

237 138 States assembled in accordance with UNGA, 1985, UN Doc. A/Res/40/122. The Conference adopted a non-binding 'Comprehensive Multidisciplinary Outline of Future Activities in Drug Abuse Control'.

238 The International Conference on Drug Abuse and Illicit Trafficking, Vienna, 17–26 June 1987, UN Doc. A/CONF.133/12, p. 88, para. 1 (italics added); cf. also UNODC, UNODC, World Drug Report 2008, UN Publication, Sales No. E.08.XI.1, pp. 203 et seq.

239 UNGA, Political Declaration, 1998, UN Doc. A/Res/S-20/2, para. 2; *id.* Resolution 54/132, 1999, UN Doc. A/Res/54/132, para. 1; *id.* Resolution 55/65, 2000, UN Doc. A/Res/55/65, para. 1; *id.* Resolution 56/124, 2001, UN Doc. A/Res/56/124, para. 1; *id.* Resolution 57/174, 2002,UN Doc. A/Res/57/174, para. 1; *id.* Resolution 58/141, 2003 UN Doc. A/Res/58/141, para.1; *id.* Resolution 59/163, 2004, UN Doc. A/Res/59/163, para.1; *id.* Resolution 60/178, 2005, UN Doc. A/Res/60/178, para. 1; *id.* Resolution 61/183, 2006, UN Doc. A/Res/61/183, para.1; *id.* Resolution 62/176, 2007, UN Doc. A/Res/62/173, para. 1; *id.* Resolution 63/197, 2008, UN Doc. A/Res/63/197, para.1; *id.* Resolution 64/182, 2009, A/Res/64/182, para.2; *id.* Resolution 65/233, UN Doc. A/Res/65/233, para. 2; *id.* Resolution 66/183, 2011, UN Doc. A/Res/66/183; *id.* Resolution 67/193, UN Doc. A/Res/67/193, 2012, para. 2; *id.* Resolution 68/197, 2013, UN Doc. A/Res/68/2013, para. 2; *id.* UNGA Resolution 69/201, 2014, UN Doc. A/Res/69/201, para. 2. The UNGA had already invoked this concept before 1998 UNGASS, cf. *id.* Resolution 49/168, 1994, A/RES/49/168, para. III.3; *id.* Resolution 50/148, 1995, UN Doc. A/RES/50/148, para. IV.5; *id.* Resolution A/RES/51/64, 1996, para. III.3; *id.* Resolution 52/92, 1997, A/RES/52/92, para. III.3.

240 OR II 1988 Convention, p. 304.

241 Cf. as to these targets *supra* 1.1.

242 Cf. as to these goals set by UNGASS, Martin Jelsma, 'Drugs in the UN System: The Unwritten History of the 1998 United Nations General Assembly Special Session on Drugs', *IJDP* Vol. 14 2003, 181 (191 et seq.).

that an equality between reducing demand and supply would not be necessary. The approach, however, to ultimately correct the imbalance between supply and demand by aiming for the eradication of non-medical drug use and non-medical drug production of drugs was *in fine* unsuccessful. The idea behind the balanced approach is to maximize the effectiveness of the international drug control system without addressing its lack of fairness; this cannot work out.

Because of the existing imbalances within the hard law – demanding precise and verifiable steps of States parties to eradicate illicit supply and control licit supply, while at the same time leaving the demand issue to the entire discretion of the States parties – requiring a verifiable reduction of drug demand and supply *in fine* solely perpetuates these imbalances. Another concept that was developed by the UNGA simultaneously with the balanced approach could be more successful in order to overcome drug control's current challenges.

6.4.3.2 Shared responsibility

The idea of shared responsibility means that the world drug problem cannot be resolved by controlling drug supply alone. To the contrary, States on both ends of the drug supply chain ought to seek for a solution of the world drug problem by cooperating in a spirit of solidarity.[243]

The roots of this idea date back to the 1980s. In 1984, the UNGA – by adopting its resolution on the Declaration on the Control of Drug Trafficking and Drug Abuse – declared that the '*eradication of the trafficking in narcotic drugs is the collective responsibility of all States, especially those affected by problems relating to illicit production, trafficking and abuse*'.[244] The idea to tackle the illicit traffic in drugs as a collective responsibility is also outlined by preambular para. 10 of the 1988 Convention. The Commentary to the 1988 Convention rightly states that this recognition 'places the Convention in the category of multilateral treaties responding to general concerns or interests affecting all States within the international community in a similar manner'.[245]

In subsequent years, the UNGA slightly modified the principle and invoked the idea of shared responsibility in countering illicit drug supply, traffic and demand.[246] From UNGASS 1998 onwards, the UNGA spoke of a common and shared responsibility in taking action against the world drug problem.[247]

243 Cf. INCB Annual Report 2012, para. 1.

244 UNGA Resolution 39/142, 1984, UN Doc. A/Res/39/142 (italics added); cf. also in this regard UNGA Resolution, A/RES/43/122, 1988, UN Doc. A/Res/43/122, para. 2; *id.* Resolution A/RES/44/142, 1989, UN Doc. A/Res/33/142, para. 3.

245 Commentary 1988 Convention, Preamble, 10th para., MN 0.21.

246 UNGA Resolution 46/103, 1991, A/Res/46/013, preambular para. 2; *id.* Resolution 47/99, 1992, A/Res/47/99, preambular para. 8; *id.* Resolution 48/12, 1993, UN Doc. A/Res/48/12, para. 1; *id.* Resolution 49/168, 1994, A/Res/49/168, para. 1; *id.* Resolution 50/148, 1995, A/Res/50/148, para. II.1; *id.* Resolution 51/64,1996, A/Res/51/64, para. II.1.

247 UNGA, Political Declaration, 1998, UN Doc. A/Res/S-20/2, para. 2; *id.* Resolution 54/132, 1999, UN Doc. A/Res/54/132, para. 1; *id.* Resolution 55/65, 2000, UN Doc. A/Res/55/65, para. 1; *id.* Resolution 56/124, 2001, UN Doc. A/Res/56/124, para. 1; *id.* Resolution 57/174, 2002,UN Doc. A/Res/57/174, para. 1; *id.* Resolution 58/141, 2003, UN Doc. A/

The international drug control system does not only presuppose universal participation of the international community striving towards the goal of exclusive reduction of drugs to medical and scientific purposes. It is also intended that the effort that this achievement requires be distributed equally between the States and actors involved. Stemming from this perspective, this book construes the international drug control system as a field of shared responsibility, moving away from conceptions where international obligations have actually been breached.[248]

The central actors of the international drug control system have to bring this concept to life. During UNGASS 2016, the UNGA stressed the importance of 'common and shared responsibility'.[249] Pledges were made to strengthen technical assistance including, where appropriate, financial assistance, and to establish best practices as well as international cooperation in this regard.[250] It remains to be seen whether such pledges will be transferred into policies which effectively address the problems caused by international drug trafficking cartels and enhance the situation of those individuals that are exposed to the violence and insecurity caused by international drug trafficking.

6.4.3.3 Paving the way forward for the international drug control system

Diverging interests of different States parties in a legal regime of global scale is of course an inevitable result of the diverse world we live in. Indeed, the economic inequalities as well as cultural differences, to name only a few factors, require balancing diverging interests when States cooperate on a global scale. This is a problem of which all fields of the law of cooperation are confronted with.[251]

Res/58/141, para.1; *id.* Resolution 59/163, 2004, UN Doc. A/Res/59/163, para.1; *id.* Resolution 60/178, 2005, UN Doc. A/Res/60/178, para. 1; *id.* Resolution 61/183, 2006, UN Doc. A/Res/61/183, para.1; *id.* Resolution 62/176, 2007, UN Doc.A/Res/62/173, para. 1; *id.* Resolution 63/197, 2008, UN Doc. A/Res/63/197, para.1; *id.* Resolution 64/182, 2009, A/Res/64/182, para.2; *id.* Resolution 65/233, UN Doc. A/Res/65/233, para. 2; *id.* Resolution 66/183, 2011, UN Doc. A/Res/66/183, para. 2; *id.* Resolution 67/193, UN Doc. A/Res/67/193, 2012, para. 2; *id.* Resolution 68/197, 2013, UN Doc. A/Res/68/2013, para. 2; *id.* UNGA Resolution 69/201, 2014, UN Doc. A/Res/69/201, para. 2.

248 UNGA, Outcome Document UNGASS 2016, 2016, UN Doc. A/Res-S/30/1, para. 6.

249 UNGA, Outcome Document UNGASS 2016, 2016, UN Doc. A/Res-S/30/1, para. 6 (a)-(e).

250 A distinction needs to be drawn between shared responsibility for breaches of international obligations and shared responsibility in a wider sense; see for this distinction, André Nollkaemper and Dov Jacobs, 'Shared Responsibility in International Law: A Conceptual Framework', *Mich. J.Int'l L.* Vol. 34 2013, 359 (366). They distinguish the term 'shared responsibility' from the term 'shared accountability' which is not linked to the breach of an international obligation; *ibid.*, 369. With regard to shared responsibility in the former sense, see in particular, Patrick Gallahue, 'International Drug Control', in: André Nollkaemper and Ilias Plakokefalos (eds), *The Practice of Shared Responsibility in International Law*, 162. It is the latter concept that is considered here; see already in this regard Geiß and Wisehart, *supra* note 1, 368 (400 et seq.)

251 See with regard to the imbalance between powerful States shaping transnational criminalization and other States in general, Neil Boister, 'The Concept and Nature of Transnational Criminal Law', in: Neil Boister and Robert J. Currie (eds), *Routledge Companion of Transnational Criminal Law*, 11 (13).

Solidarity and fair burden sharing on a global level is still in an embryonic state. However, three ideas can be advanced in order to show a way forward for the international drug control system.

The first idea is to provide flexibility for the various actors in the different supply chains. A more flexible framework is provided by international environmental law, where it is recognized that although all States have their part to play in preserving the environment as a common responsibility, this responsibility may differ from one State to another ('common but differentiated responsibility').[252] By the same token, WTO law allows for separate but differential treatment for State parties in order to allow for developing States to adopt domestic trade policies deviating from the most favoured nation clause in order to permit viable economic growth.[253]

The second idea is to facilitate accountability between the various actors on the drug supply chain. Accountability is not a one way street. This means that drug-consuming States have to be at the very least aware that their drug demand causes problems in drug-producing States and vice versa. It also involves setting up mechanisms between States parties where solidarity is organized and institutionalized. States have to be enabled to learn from each other as how to cope with illicit drug supply and demand in accordance with human rights and scientific evidence.

Most importantly, however, States parties have to implement the idea of common and shared responsibility into their real practice. This means primarily to refrain from adopting measures that openly contradict the conception of common and shared responsibility. Drug-producing and drug transit States remain being blamed for the inability of the international drug control system to reach the goal of limiting drugs to medical and scientific purposes. This has to stop. States individually and through international institutions have to unequivocally express that the 'world drug problem' is not caused by a limited number of States, but that it is a common task which affects all of us and which needs to be dealt with in a spirit of solidarity.

Such suggestions would of course have to be spelled out in greater detail in the future. They may also seem little realistic given the current polarization of the international drug control system. They are, however, direly needed in order to prevent the erosion of the international drug control system. As the current tensions within this system show, institutional forms of international cooperation cannot simply be imposed on a universal level by defending a pre-existing status quo.

This concerns the goals of international cooperation, as well as the means by which these goals are reached. Overall objectives need to be accepted universally and have to be attained coherently and in a spirit of mutual solidarity. When this is not the case, the foundation for international cooperation is likely to be undermined in the long term. International cooperation is most likely to thrive in fields which either factually require international cooperation because of their transnational scope or demand international cooperation because of their normative importance for the international community. When both of these prerequisites are missing, the chances for continued and viable institutionalized international cooperation are slim.

252 Lavanya Rajamani, *Differential Treatment in International Environmental Law*, pp. 24 et seq.
253 Ellen Hey, 'Common but Differentiated Responsibilities', *MPEPIL*, 2012.

States have to acknowledge their diverging interests while not losing sight of their common goals. If these diverging interests are addressed in a spirit of solidarity meaningful results can be achieved. The achievement of such solutions for the international drug control system could stand proof that the international law of cooperation has a role to play in the future. International cooperation is indeed direly needed more than ever to resolve mankind's numerous problems on a global scale. The international drug control system could stand proof that international cooperation indeed can be recalibrated and reformed. This would set a positive precedent for the law of cooperation in general. Such a positive precedent is desperately needed today as global cooperation continuous to be the only way in which mankind can deal with the numerous problems of global scale.

6.4.4 Conclusion

It has been shown that States where cocaine and opiates are illicitly produced and trafficked predominantly challenge the international drug control system because of a perceived lack of burden sharing of the dire consequences posed by illicit drug supply. Indeed, this imbalance between drug-producing and drug transit States, on the one hand, and drug-consuming States, on the other hand, is engrained to a certain extent within the legal framework. It stems from the premise on which the international drug control system was erected. This premise remains present within today's legal framework. Albeit supply orientation today is relativized, the international drug control system predominantly tries to achieve the goal of limiting drugs to medical and scientific purposes by controlling drug supply for those ends and supressing all other drug supply. Demand reduction and treatment of non-medical drug use is still deprived of a mandatory content. This problem has been detected and challenged but not overcome. This is a fundamental problem of fairness within the entire international drug control. It has the potential to further undermine the legitimacy of this system if States are not ready to find remedies for this problem soon.

The balanced approach to limit drugs to medical and scientific purposes by agreeing to a universal eradication of illicit demand and supply, as currently carried out by the UNGA, seems rather to reinforce the imbalances of the hard law between a reduction of demand and supply. The idea to achieve more solidarity between all actors of the drug supply chain, by construing the world drug problem as a common and shared responsibility, seems more viable in order to overcome this imbalance between supply and demand. It has, however, not led to concrete results and is openly contradicted by the practice of blaming and singling out individual drug-producing and drug transit States as bearing the sole responsibility for the inability of the system to universally limit drug demand and supply to medical and scientific purposes.

6.5 Conclusion

This chapter has shown the means by which the international drug control system embraces to reach its overall objective of limiting drugs to medical and scientific purposes. It was concluded that the system predominantly aims to limit drugs to medical and scientific purposes by controlling the licit supply chain and supressing all other supply. The control of the licit supply chain means primarily a reduction of the supply available to the amount required for medical and scientific purposes. The goal of ensuring the availability of drugs to medical and scientific purposes as spelled out in the preamble of the 1971 Convention and the Single Convention is hardly operationalized. It is only an effective obligation for narcotic drugs (Art. 9 (4) Single Convention) and it is rather the subsequent practice of drug control's institutions that has put this goal to the fore in the last years.

The suppression of illicit drug supply occurs by obliging States parties to adopt and carry out penal sanctions. These obligations potentially restrict the human rights of individuals targeted by such sanctions. Their rights are not ensured by the UN Drug Conventions but by international human rights law. Providing for human rights-conforming measures against illicit drug trafficking requires implementation of the obligations arising from the UN Drug Conventions in light of the simultaneously applicable human rights obligations. This seems sufficient in order to ensure human rights-conforming treatment of drug traffickers, albeit it does not resolve all problems for international cooperation with States with differing human rights obligations.

The demand-related obligations of the UN Drug Conventions leave enough leeway in order to provide for up-to-date demand reduction that conforms with human rights and scientific evidence. An obligation to implement and carry out penal sanctions for drug users cannot be approved. The obligations on treatment and the prevention of drug use are vague and deprived of a mandatory normative core. When assessing the obligations of treatment in light of the right to the highest attainable standard of health it becomes clear that despite this vagueness, States are not allowed to provide treatment measures for drug users that contradict scientific evidence. Additionally, compulsory treatment of drug users has to be confined to exceptional situations. Harm-reduction measures are possible under the current legal framework. The normative difficulty of these measures relate to the fact that such measures may possibly deviate from the requirement to limit drugs to medical and scientific purposes. Nevertheless, harm-reduction measures comply with the international drug control system when they are recommended by a competent international institution such as the WHO, or when the harm-reduction measure (possibly) prevents perilous drug-related harm for the drug user. Not all measures of drug treatment have to simultaneously embrace the prevention of further non-medical drug use.

Lastly, the system remains based on the premise that a limitation of drug demand and supply alike to medical and scientific purposes will be predominantly ensured by limiting the supply available to medical and scientific purposes and suppressing the supply for all other ends. This orientation towards a reduction of drug supply has so far not been corrected despite several attempts. Demand reduction remains too vague and under-devolved on a universal level, and States do not have comprehensive obligations in this regard. Additionally, the blame for a persisting world drug problem is all too often placed on States where the supply for narcotic drugs for other than medical and scientific purposes comes from. This seems incompatible with the reiterated call of the international community to construe the world drug problem as a common and shared responsibility.

7 Concluding remarks and outlook

This concluding chapter summarizes the book's essential findings. Based on these results, short-term proposals will be made, as well as recommendations for where the international drug control system should go in the long term.

The results of this study can be summarized in ten conclusions: conclusions 1–5 relate to the objective of the international drug control system;

Conclusion 1: The international drug control system is centred on the objective of limiting drugs to medical and scientific purposes.[1] This limitation of drugs forms the fundamental point of reference for all drug-related activities. Drug-related activities complying with this norm are allowed and licit, whereas drug-related activities deviating from this norm have to be considered illicit and are prohibited. The distinction between licit and illicit drug-related activities is drawn by assessing the intended or actual drug use. Medical drug use denotes drug use that is carried out under *de lege artis* medical assistance. Scientific drug use refers to drug use that is carried out under the authority of a person exercising scientific functions. The limitation of drugs to medical and scientific purposes is the common object and purpose of all three UN Drug Conventions and has been reinforced by countless subsequent instruments of the various institutions within the international drug control system.

Conclusion 2: There is only very limited leeway for States to deviate from the central objective of limiting all drug-related activities to medical and scientific purposes. The exceptions in this regard, contained exclusively within the Single Convention, are narrow and concern the use of drugs within industrial settings for the production of meat or of soft drinks. A regulatory market for cannabis cannot rely on any of these exceptions and is therefore violating the limitation of this substance to medical and scientific purposes, as spelled out by the Single Convention. Reservations under the Single Convention and the 1971 Convention are no viable means to deviate from the limitation of drugs to medical and scientific purposes. The vast majority of the international community ratified these treaties and accordingly could only insert reservations to those treaties by denouncing them in the first place and subsequently reacceding to them with

1 In the following lines, the term 'drugs' is used to designate psychotropic substances as well as narcotic drugs, unless otherwise spelled out.

reservations. Such a procedure is only legal provided that no other State party object to such a step; this is highly improbable. Thus, deviating from the limitation of drugs to medical and scientific purposes requires treaty amendment.

Conclusion 3: The Single Convention and the 1971 Convention are inconsistent as far as the termination of traditional drug use for other than medical or scientific purposes is concerned. Whereas under the Single Convention traditional drug use of cannabis, opium and the coca leaf had to be terminated within a transitional period ending in 1989, the 1971 Convention allows for the traditional drug use of plant-based hallucinogens by indigenous peoples for an indeterminate period.

Conclusion 4: Albeit the material scope of the international drug control system can be modified and hence is theoretically flexible, this flexibility in effect is very limited. This has a twofold implication. First, the Single Convention remains applicable for substances of which the WHO determines produce cannabis-, cocaine/coca. or opiate-like effects. This means that cannabis and cocaine/coca, as well as opiates, will never be exempted from the Single Convention's scope of control without treaty amendment, even if scientific evidence would suggest that they have high therapeutic use and low risk for drug abuse. Second, the WHO does not regularly review whether all psychotropic substances and narcotic drugs should remain covered by the limitation to medical and scientific purposes.

Conclusion 5: International human rights law is not incompatible with the fundamental leitmotif of the international drug control system to limit drugs to medical and scientific purposes. Currently, a human right to recreational drug use cannot be approved. The relationship between international human rights law and the limitation of drug-related activities to medical and scientific purposes is not without tensions. The rights of indigenous peoples to traditional coca use and the limitation of coca leaf to medical and scientific purposes as spelled out by the Single Convention clash. Within the particular normative environment of South America, an indigenous right to traditional coca use can be approved. The lack of the flexibility of the Single Convention with regard to traditional coca use is particularly troublesome. In consequence, States will either breach their obligations to allow for traditional coca use for indigenous peoples or have to fail to abide by the limitation of the coca leaf to medical and scientific purposes. Conclusions 6–10 relate to the premises which the international drug control system embraces to reach the goal of limiting drugs to medical and scientific purposes:

Conclusion 6: The controlled economy regulating the production, manufacture and traffic of drugs, as erected by the Single Convention and the 1971 Convention hardly operationalizes the goal of ensuring the drugs for medical and scientific purposes. Rather it limits the amount of drugs available to medical and scientific needs. Article 9 (4) Single Convention is the sole operative provision to provide for narcotic drugs for medical and scientific purposes. No similar obligation exists for psychotropic substances. Besides this rather isolated provision, the goal of providing for the availability of drugs is merely contained within the preamble of the 1971 Convention and the Single Convention. The ECOSOC, the CND, preambles to the INCB and finally the UNGA have prioritized this goal in the last few years. This prioritization has so far failed to outline concretely when domestic drug control systems do impede the availability of drugs beyond what is required to ensure their limitation to medical and scientific purposes.

Conclusion 7: Albeit the illicit supply of drugs destined for other than medical or scientific purposes is combatted by punitive and sanction-oriented obligations, this suppressive set of obligations does not contradict contemporary international human rights law. Suppressive obligations of the UN Drug Conventions – most notably the 1988 Convention – have to be interpreted against the background of applicable human rights norms in order to ensure drug control measures conforming to human rights.

Conclusion 8: In contrast to the control of supply, demand reduction still is hardly elaborated within the international drug control system. It is unclear how States have to handle illicit drug use. The obligation to penalize non-medical or non-scientific drug use under Art. 3 (2) 1988 Convention is deprived of practical effect. Treatment is not spelled out by clear-cut obligations with a mandatory content. In order to provide for health-oriented responses to drug use and addiction, the obligations of the UN Drug Conventions on treatment have to be interpreted against the background of the right to the highest attainable standard of health.

Conclusion 9: Key harm-reduction measures are legal under the UN Drug Conventions. Albeit harm reduction measures partly deviate from the requirement to limit drugs to medical and scientific purposes, such measures are legal when necessary in order to prevent perilous harm for the drug user involved. The UN Drug Conventions allow for balancing the treatment of the individual drug user with the imperative to effectively ensure that all drug-related activities are limited to medical and scientific purposes.

Conclusion 10: The narrow focus of the international drug control system on reducing drug supply is problematic for States where narcotic drugs are produced and trafficked at high scales. Because of a perceived lack of burden sharing and fairness, these drug-producing and drug transit States challenge the current approach of the international community of limiting drugs to medical and scientific purposes by predominantly controlling and reducing drug supply. A lack of fairness can be recognized because of vague demand-reduction obligations that do not impose on States to adopt clear-cut measures to viably reduce illicit drug demand, while in the meantime States have enforceable and verifiable obligations to control and reduce drug supply. This puts drug-producing and drug transit States under pressure. They have to reduce the illicit drug supply for the sake of drug-consuming States without receiving any benefits. This lack of burden sharing is not corrected by the balanced approach of equally eradicating the illicit demand and supply for drugs at the same time, which has been repeatedly invoked by the UNGA since UNGASS 1998. This is true because the balanced approach aims to enhance the effectiveness of the international drug control system, without addressing its lack of fairness. A more viable approach for correcting these imbalances is to construe the world drug problem as a common and shared responsibility. It addresses the lack of fairness within the international drug control system by demanding solidarity between all actors along the drug supply chain.

It is against the background of conclusions 6–10 that the following short-term recommendations should be adopted by the UNGA:

Recommendation 1: The UNGA should clearly lay out the need for drug-control measures to respect international human rights law. This concerns both supply- and demand-reduction measures. Instead of general statements on drug control's respect of human rights, the UNGA should clarify which substantial human rights need to be respected, including, but not limited to, the right to health of drug users, the right to life of suspected drug traffickers and habeas corpus rights of individuals suspected of drug-related offences. The UNGA should underline that drug control measures may never become a pretext for States to deviate from international human rights law.

Recommendation 2: The obligation to ensure the availability of narcotic drugs and psychotropic substances as outlined by Art. 9 (4) Single Convention and the preambles of the Single Convention and the 1971 Convention needs to be strengthened. The UNGA should further concretize the steps that States need to take in order to ameliorate the availability of narcotic drugs and psychotropic substances for medical and scientific purposes. It needs to clarify when domestic drug-control systems handle narcotic drugs and psychotropic substances over-restrictively and curtail their availability beyond what is needed to limit them to medical and scientific purposes.

Recommendation 3: Treatment needs to be further strengthened by the UNGA. Three aspects have to be emphasised in this regard:

- *First, member States have to rule out what measures of treatment States should not resort to.* It should be made clear that the term 'appropriate measures' of treatment in accordance with Art. 38 (1) Single Convention, Art. 22 (1) 1971 Convention and Art. 14 (4) 1988 Convention is limited to measures in accordance with the right to the highest attainable standard of health as contained within Art. 12 ICESCR. The UNGA, thereby, should lay down that the right to health requires States parties to adopt measures that are evidence based.
- *Second, member States have to point out which measures of treatment States may adopt under the UN Drug Conventions.* It should be made clear that States may resort to core harm-reduction measures under the present legal framework, including opiate substitution therapy and drug consumption rooms. The need to balance health-oriented treatment of the individual drug user with the long-term goal of terminating non-medical drug use has to be formulated.
- *Third, member States have to clarify what States have to do at the very least with regard to treatment of drug users.* All member States should pledge that they will adopt measures of treatment as outlined in the WHO's Technical Guide in the near future.

Recommendation 4: The UNGA should demand more fairness between the various actors along the drug supply chain. It should ensure that drug-producing and drug transit States are not left alone with their problems caused by the demand for drugs in drug-consuming States. The concept of shared responsibility needs to be strengthened and backed up by concrete action. Efforts to contain drug supply need to be acknowledged and compensated for to a certain extent. Compensation could take many forms, including, but not limited to, alternative development programmes for farmers involved in illicit crop cultivation. Financial contributions should also ensure structures of good governance to counter the violence and corruption caused by the international drug trade. The UNGA should speak out against the blaming and shaming of drug-producing and drug transit States for the prevalence of the world drug problem.

These recommendations could be adopted by the UNGA in the near future as they do not require any treaty amendment. The UNGA is the sole institution where all the States parties to the UN Drug Conventions assemble on a regular basis. When adopting unanimous decisions, the UNGA can be the true key player for further development of the international drug control system and develop the interpretation of the UN Drug Conventions. Its recommendations can constitute subsequent practice that authoritatively influences the understanding of the provisions of the UN Drug Conventions. It is important in this regard that the UNGA should link as far as possible the above-mentioned recommendations with norms and provisions of the UN Drug Conventions.

The above-mentioned recommendations' commonality is that they exclusively relate to the premises by which the international drug control system aims to reach the goal of limiting drugs to medical and scientific purposes. However, the current situation requires consideration as to whether the exclusive reduction of drugs to medical and scientific purposes should remain the first guiding principle for drug control in the future. As was remarked almost 40 years ago, a truly viable long-term goal for the universal drug control system is the minimization of harm caused by drug use.[2]

It is this aspect that forms the concern of the health and welfare of mankind. This concern, as announced within preambular para. 1 of the UN Drug Conventions, has to be widened. The health and welfare of mankind should not be a mere justification for limiting drugs to medical and scientific purposes. Rather, it is out of this concern that all drug-related harms should be prevented if possible and at least mitigated.

2 Kettil Brunn, Lynn Pan and Ingemar Rexed, *The Gentlemen's Club: International Control of Drugs and Alcohol*, p. 290: 'the goal of the international drug control system should be reformulated as to the minimization of harmful effects of drug use'. Robin Geiß and Daniel Wisehart, '"Concerned with the Health and Welfare of Mankind..." The UN Drug Conventions – A Suitable Legal Framework for the 21st Century?', *MPYbUNL* Vol. 19 2014, 368 (404); Damon Barrett and Manfred Nowak, 'United Nations and Drug Policy: Towards a Human Rights Based Approach', in: Aristotle Constantinides and Niko Zaikos (ed.), *Essays in Honour of Kalliopi Koufa*, 449.

Against this background, the concept of common and shared responsibility has to be updated. It is not the world drug problem but the health and welfare of mankind that should be considered as a common and shared responsibility. This common and shared responsibility should form the overarching backbone of all drug control efforts. This should be the guiding principle for post UNGASS 2016 and the drug control system as a whole in the future. Hence, the UNGA should not simply reiterate the goals set by UNGASS 1998 and the CND review of 2009 to eradicate or substantially lower illicit drug demand, supply and traffic within a ten-year period. Rather, it should invoke the guiding principle that the harm caused by illicit drug demand, supply and traffic has to be considerably reduced within the years to come.[3]

The powers of the UNGA are not unlimited. The UNGA cannot simply modify the fundamental premise of the UN Drug Conventions to limit drugs to medical and scientific purposes. It should, however, point out the simple fact that the limitation of drugs to medical and scientific purposes should only apply in the first place to those substances where scientific evidence indicates that this is really necessary. Drugs that do not pose a threat to human health should not be subjected to the international drug control system. The UNGA should ask the WHO to regularly carry out scientific review of all substances targeted to medical and scientific purposes.[4] It should request the CND to abide by this scientific evidence and take scheduling decisions which conform with the recommendations of the WHO in this regard.

The UNGA is not a conference of the States parties that can amend the UN Drug Conventions. It cannot simply abrogate the fundamental prerogative of the UN Drug Conventions to limit drugs to medical and scientific purposes. The fate of this objective is in the hands of the States parties. Whether the universal limitation of drugs to medical and scientific purposes will stand the test of time seems to be more questionable today than ever. A growing number of States want to deviate from this norm. Instead of adopting questionable interpretations of the UN Drug Conventions and thereby falsely suggesting that those treaties would allow for a regulatory market for drugs, a frank dialogue is required. This dialogue should start as soon as possible, should the limitation of drugs to medical and scientific purposes – a global norm to which the vast majority of the entire international community has subscribed to – not become a pure mockery. Otherwise, the international drug control system would become an ‘emperor without clothes’, a veritable farce, where the actors suggest complying with norms from which they, in reality, deviate. This would indeed be problematic for the architecture of international law as a whole. It would question the law’s general ability to resolve problems of global magnitude, and set a poor example for other treaties and treaty systems.

3 Cf. for similar conclusions to modify the goals of drug policies, IDPC, The Road to UNGASS 2016: Process and Policy Asks from the IDPC, November 2014, p. 3.

4 Cf. E. Danenberg et al., ‘Modernizing Methodology for the WHO Assessment of Substances for the International Drug Control Conventions’, *Drug and Alcohol Dependence* Vol. 131 2013, 175 (181).

Frank dialogue on the future of the international drug control system should commence by addressing the question of whether a universal limitation of drug use to medical and scientific purposes is necessary. In spite of the clash between the limitation of drugs to medical and scientific purposes and the cultural rights of indigenous peoples as far as the coca leaf is concerned, more flexibility to deviate from the limitation of drugs to medical and scientific purposes is certainly needed. The Single Convention should contain a similar option to the 1971 Convention allowing for traditional drug use by indigenous peoples for an indeterminate period. States might need in general to recalibrate what aspects of the world drug problem need to be handled on a universal level and what questions can, and should, be left to the discretion of individual States parties.

Relying on the guiding principle of minimizing drug-related harm also seems viable in this regard. States could be left with a margin of discretion on how to minimize the harms associated with drug use. Minimizing the harms caused by drug use does not necessarily involve that drug use is to be treated identically on a global sphere. Seen from this perspective, States may adopt different approaches with regard to drug use, dependent on their cultural and economic context. This margin of appreciation has its limits, where a failure of restricting drug use in a State's own territory leads to a lack of control within another State. This idea would involve a fair balance between the need for universality in drug control and the respect for differing cultural traditions with regard to drugs.

Bibliography

Abi Saab, Georges, 'Whither the International Community?', *EJIL* Vol. 9 1998, pp. 248–265

Aguinacoa, Andrés and Barra, Aram, 'Cannabis for Personal Use in the Supreme Court of Mexico: Legal Case and Potential for Policy Change', *IJDP* Vol. 50 2017, pp. 9–10

Aislinger, Harry J., 'The Implementation of Treaty Obligations Regulating the Traffic in Narcotic Drugs', *AmULR* Vol. 8 1959, pp. 108–116

Alvarez, Jose and Kingsury, Jose, 'AJIL at 111', *AJIL* Vol. 111 2017, pp. 1–6

Anaya, S. James, *Indigenous Peoples in International Law*, Oxford University Press, Oxford and New York 2000

Anaya, S. James, 'International Human Rights and Indigenous Peoples: The Move toward the Multicultural State', *AJICL* Vol. 21 2004, pp. 13–61

Anderson, D. R., 'Reservations to Multilateral Conventions: A Re-examination', *ICLQ* Vol. 13 1964, pp. 450–481

Arp, Björn, 'Denunciation Followed by Re-Accession with Reservations to a Treaty: A Critical Appraisal of Contemporary State Practice', *NILR* Vol. 61 2014, pp. 141–165

Asra, Husain, Brown, Marty Skemp and Maurer, Martha A., 'Do National Drug Control Laws Ensure the Availability of Opioids for Medical and Scientific Purposes?', *Bulletin of the World Health Organization* Vol. 92 2014, pp. 108–113

Aust, Anthony, *Modern Treaty Law and Practice*, 2nd edn, Cambridge University Press, Cambridge and New York 2007

Ayoagi, Melissa T., 'Beyond Punitive Prohibition: Liberalizing the Dialogue on International Drug Policy', *NYU JILP* Vol. 37 2005, pp. 555–610

Ball, Andrew, 'HIV, Injecting Drug Use and Harm Reduction: A Public Health Response', *Addiction* Vol. 102 2007, pp. 684–690

Barrett, Damon, 'Reflections on Human Rights and International Drug Control' in: Collins, John (ed.), *Governing the Global Drug Wars* Special Report, LSE Ideas 2012, pp. 55–62 (available online at: www.lse.ac.uk/IDEAS/publications/reports/pdf/SR014/SR-014-FULL-Lo-Res.pdf)

Barrett, Damon, 'Security, Development and Human Rights: Normative, Legal and Policy Challenges for the International Drug Control System', *IJDP* Vol. 21 2010, pp. 140–144

Barrett, Damon, 'Unique in International Relations? A Comparison of the International Narcotic Control Board and the Human Rights Treaty Bodies', International Harm Reduction Association 2008 (available online at: www.ihra.net/files/2010/06/16/Barrett-UniqueinInternationalRelations.pdf)

Barrett, Damon, Jelsma, Martin and Bewley-Taylor, David, 'Fatal Attraction: Brownfield's Flexibility Doctrine and Global Drug Policy Reform', *Huffington Post*, 18 November 2014 (available online at: www.huffingtonpost.co.uk/damon-barett/drug-policy-reform_b_6158144.html?utm_hp_ref=tw)

Barrett, Damon, Lines, Rick, Schleifer, Rebecca, Elliott, Richard and Bewley-Taylor, David, 'Recalibrating the Regime: The Need for a Human Rights-based Approach to International Drug Policy', The Beckley Foundation Drug Policy Programme, 2008 (available online at: www.ihra.net/files/2010/06/16/BarrettRecalibratingTheRegime.pdf)

Barrett, Damon and Nowak, Manfred, 'United Nations and Drug Policy: Towards a Human Rights-based Approach' in: Constantinides, Aristotle and Zaikos, Nikos (eds), *Essays in Honour of Kalliopi Koufa*, Martinus Nijhoff Publishers, Leiden and Boston 2009, pp. 449–477 (available online at: http://papers.ssrn.com/sol3/papers.cfm?abstract_id=1461445)

Barrett, Damon and Vermann, Philip, *Article 33: Protection from Narcotic Drugs and Psychotropic Substances*, Martinus Nijhoff Publishers, Leiden and Boston 2012

Bassiouni, M. Cherif, 'An Appraisal of the Growth and Developing Trends of International Criminal Law', *RIDP* Vol. 45 1974, pp. 405–433

Bassiouni, M. Cherif, 'Critical Reflections on International and National Control of Drugs', *DJILP* Vol. 18 1990, pp. 311–337

Bassiouni, M. Cherif and Wise, Edward M., Aut Dedere Aut Judicare*: The Obligation to Extradite or Prosecute in International Law*, Martinus Nijhoff Publishers, Leiden and Boston 1995

Bassiouni, M. Cherif (ed.), *International Criminal Law: Vol. I, Sources, Subjects, and Contents*, 3rd edn, Martinus Nijhoff Publishers, Leiden and Boston 2008

Bayer, I. and Ghodse, H., 'Evolution of International Drug Control, 1945–1995', *Bulletin on Narcotics* Vol. 51 1999 no. 1, pp. 1–19

Beigbeder, Yves, 'World Health Organization (WHO)' in: Wolfrum, Rüdiger (ed.), *MPEPIL*, Oxford University Press, Oxford and New York 2012

Bennett, Wells and Walsh, John, 'Marijuana Legalization is an Opportunity to Modernize International Drug Treaties', Center for Effective Public Management at Brookings, 2014 (available online at: www.brookings.edu/wp-content/uploads/2016/06/CEPMMJLegalizationv4.pdf)

Bergal, Carina, 'The Mexican Drug War: The Case for a Non-International Armed Conflict Classification', *FILJ* Vol. 34 2011, pp. 1042–1088

Bernhardt, Rudolf, Geck, Wilhelm Karl, Jaenicke, Günther and Steinberger, Helmut (eds), *Völkerrecht als Rechtordnung Internationale Gerichtsbarkeit Menschenrechte: Festschrift für Hermann Mosler*, Springer, Heidelberg and New York 1983

Bettati, Mario, 'Le contrôle international des stupéfiants', *RGDIP* Vol. 78 1974, pp. 170–225

Bewley-Taylor, David, 'Challenging the UN Drug Conventions: Problems and Possibilities', *IJDP* Vol. 14 2003, pp. 171–179

Bewley-Taylor, David, *International Drug Control: Consensus Fractured*, Cambridge University Press, Cambridge and New York 2012

Bewley-Taylor, David, *The United States and International Drug Control 1909–1997*, Pinter, New York 1997

Bewley-Taylor, David and Jelsma, Martin, 'Fifty Years of the 1961 Single Convention on Narcotic Drugs: A Reinterpretation', TNI Series on Legislative Reform of Drug Policies No. 12, 2011

Bewley-Taylor, David, Blickman, Tom, and Jelsma, Martin, 'The Rise and Decline of Cannabis Prohibition: The History of Cannabis in the UN Drug Control System and Options for Reform', TNI, 2014 (available online at: www.swansea.ac.uk/media/TNI-GDPO_Rise-and-Decline_web.pdf)

Bewley-Taylor, David and Jelsma, Martin, 'Regime Change: Re-visiting the 1961 Single Convention on Narcotic Drugs', *IJDP* Vol. 23 2012, pp. 72–81

Bewley-Taylor, David and Jelsma, Martin, 'The UN Drug Control Conventions: The Limits of Latitude', TNI Series on Legislative Reform of Drug Policies No. 18, March 2012 (available online at: http://papers.ssrn.com/sol3/papers.cfm?abstract_id=2184316&download=yes)

David Bewley-Taylor and Jelsma, Martin, 'UNGASS 2016: A Broken or B-r-o-a-d Consensus?', Drug Policy Briefing No. 45, June 2016 (available online at: www.tni.org/files/publication-downloads/dpb_45_04072016_web.pdf)

Bewley-Taylor, David and Trace, Mike, 'The International Narcotics Control Board: Watchdog or Guardian of the UN Drug Control Conventions', The Beckley Foundation Drug Policy Programme Report No. 7, 2006 (available online at: http://archive.beckleyfoundation.org/pdf/Report_07.pdf)

Bogaard, W., 'International Control of the Legitimate Trade in Narcotic Drugs', *NYIL* Vol. 3 1972, pp. 97–133

Boisson de Chazournes, Laurence, 'Subsequent Practices, and "Family-Resemblance": Towards Embedding Subsequent Practice in its Operative Milieu', in: Nolte, Georg (ed.), *Treaties and Subsequent Practice*, Oxford University Press, Oxford and New York 2013, pp. 53–69

Boister, Neil, book review: 'Commentary on the United Nations Convention Against Illicit Traffic in Narcotic Drugs and Psychotropic Substances UN Doc E/CN.7/590', *ICLQ* Vol. 55 2001, pp. 466–467

Boister Neil, 'Human Rights Protections in the Suppression Conventions', *HRLR* Vol. 2 2002, pp. 199–227

Boister, Neil, *An Introduction to Transnational Criminal Law*, Oxford University Press, Oxford and New York 2012

Boister, Neil, *Penal Aspects of the UN Drug Conventions*, Kluwer Law International, The Hague 2001

Boister, Neil, '"Transnational Criminal Law"?', *EJIL* Vol. 14 2003, pp. 953–976

Boister Neil, 'The Concept and Nature of Transnational Criminal Law', in: Boister, Neil and Currie, Robert J. (eds), *Routledge Companion of Transnational Criminal Law*, Routledge, Abingdon 2015, pp. 11–27

Boister Neil and Currie, Robert J. (eds), *Routledge Companion of Transnational Criminal Law*, Routledge, Abingdon 2015

Boiteux, Luciana, Chernicharo, Luciana Peluzio and Alves, Camila Souza, 'Human Rights and Drug Conventions: Searching for Humanitarian Reason in Drug Laws', in: Labate, Beatriz Caiuby and Cavnar, Clancy (eds), *Prohibition, Religious Freedom, and Human Rights: Regulating Traditional Drug Use*, Springer, Heidelberg and New York 2014, pp. 1–25

Bone, Melissa, 'From the Sacrilegious to the Sacramental: A Global Review of Rastafari Cannabis Case Law', in: Labate, Beatriz Caiuby and Cavnar, Clancy (eds), *Prohibition, Religious Freedom, and Human Rights: Regulating Traditional Drug Use*, Springer, Heidelberg and New York 2014, pp. 89–109

Borgen, Christopher, 'Treaty Conflicts and Normative Fragmentation', in: Hollis, Duncan (ed.), *The Oxford Guide to Treaties*, Oxford University Press, Oxford and New York 2012, pp. 448–471

Bossuyt, Marc, *Guide to the Travaux Préparatoires of the International Covenant on Civil and Political Rights*, Martinus Nijhoff Publishers, Dordrecht 1987

Brandeis, Jason, 'The Continuing Vitality of *Ravin v. State*: Alaskans Still Have a Constitutional Right to Possess Marijuana in the Privacy of their Homes', *ALR* Vol. 29 2012, pp. 175–236

Bridge, James, 'The Commission on Narcotic Drugs on the Final Road to UNGASS 2016: Progress Made, But a Long Way Still to Go', 2016 (available online at: https://idpc.net/blog/2016/03/the-commission-on-narcotic-drugs-on-the-final-road-to-ungass-2016-progress-made-but-a-long-way-still-to-go)

Brunn, Kettil, Pan, Lynn and Rexed, Ingemar, *The Gentlemen's Club: International Control of Drugs and Alcohol*, The University of Chicago Press, Chicago and London 1975

Brunnée, Jutta, 'Compliance Control', in: Ulfstein, Geir, Zimmermann, Andreas and Marauhn, Thilo (eds), *Making Treaties Work: Human Rights. Environment and Arms Control*, Cambridge University Press, Cambridge and New York 2007, pp. 373–389

Burgorgue-Larsen, Laurence and de Torres, Amaya Úbeda, *The Inter-American Court of Human Rights: Case Law and Commentary*, Oxford University Press, Oxford and New York 2011

Buxton, Julia, 'The Historical Foundations of the Narcotic Drug Control Regime', The World Bank Development Research Group Macroeconomics and Growth Team, March 2008 (available online at: http://elibrary.worldbank.org/doi/pdf/10.1596/1813-9450-4553)

Buxton, Julia, *The Political Economy of Narcotics: Production, Consumption and Global Markets*, Zed Books, London and New York 2006

Cabranes, Jose, 'International Law and Control of the Drug Traffic', *Int'l L.* Vol. 7 1973, pp. 761–769

Carstairs, Catherine, 'The Stages of the International Drug Control System', *Drug and Alcohol Review* Vol. 24 2005, pp. 57–65

Chatterjee, S. K., *Legal Aspects of International Drug Control*, Martinus Nijhoff Publishers, The Hague and Boston 1981

Chatterjee, S. K., 'The WHO Expert Committee on Drug Dependence', *ICLQ* Vol. 28 1979, pp. 27–51

Chouvy, Pierre-Arnaud, 'A Typology of Unintended Consequences of Drug Crop Reduction', *JDI* Vol. 43 2012, pp. 216–230

Churchill, Robin and Ulfstein, Geir, 'Autonomous Institutional Arrangements in Multilateral Environmental Agreements: A Little Noticed Phenomenon in International Law', *AJIL* Vol. 94 2003, pp. 623–659

Clapham, Andrew and Robinson, Mary (eds), *Realizing the Right to Health*, Swiss Human Rights Book Series, Rüffer & Rub, Zürich 2009

Cohrssen, John and Hoover, Lawrence, 'The International Control of Dangerous Drugs', *J. Int'l L. & Econ.* Vol. 9 1974, pp. 81–112

Collins, John (ed.), 'Governing the Global Drug Wars Special Report', LSE Ideas 2012 (available online at: http://eprints.lse.ac.uk/47122/1/Governing%20the%20global%20drug%20wars(published).pdf)

Comment, 'The Convention on Psychotropic Substances: Domestic Consequences of Ratification', *Iowa L. Rev.* Vol. 63 1978, pp. 950–974

Corten, Olivier and Klein, Pierre (eds), *The Vienna Convention on the Law of Treaties: A Commentary*, Oxford University Press, Oxford and New York 2011

Coulson, Carolyn and Caulkins, Jonathan P., 'Scheduling of Newly Emerging Drugs: A Critical Review of Decisions over 40 Years', *Addiction* Vol. 107 2011, pp. 766–773

Courtwright, David, 'Foreword: Drug Use and Prohibition: Three Reform Traditions', in: Labate, Beatriz Caiuby and Cavnar, Clancy (eds), *Prohibition, Religious Freedom, and Human Rights: Regulating Traditional Drug Use*, Springer, Heidelberg and New York 2014, pp. v–viii

Crawford, Emily, 'Proportionality', in: Wolfrum, Rüdiger (ed.), *MPEPIL*, Oxford University Press, Oxford and New York 2012

Crawford, James, *State Responsibility: The General Part*, Cambridge University Press, Cambridge and New York 2013

Crawford, James (ed.), *The Rights of Peoples*, Oxford University Press, Oxford and New York 1988

Crema, Luigi, 'Disappearance and New Sightings of Restrictive Treaty Interpretation', *EJIL* Vol. 21 2010, pp. 681–700

Cressey, Daniel, 'The Cannabis Experiment', *Nature* Vol. 524 2015, pp. 280–283

Currie, Robert J., book review: 'Neil Boister, *An Introduction to Transnational Criminal Law*', *JICJ* Vol. 13 2015, 1166–1169

Currie, Robert. J., 'The Protection of Human Rights in the Suppression of Transnational Crime', in: Boister, Neil and Currie, Robert J. (eds), *Routledge Companion of Transnational Criminal Law*, Routledge, Abingdon 2015, pp. 27–41

Dahlgren, Stephan and Stere, Roxana, 'The Protection of Children from Illicit Drugs – A Minimum Human Rights Standard: A Child-Centered vs. a User-Centered Drug Policy', Fri Förlag in cooperation with World Federation Against Drugs, the Swedish Society for Sobriety and Social Upbringing and the Swedish Carnegie Institute, 2012

Daillier, Patrick, Forteau, Matthias and Pellet, Alain (Nguyen Quoc Din †), *Droit International Public*, 8th edn, LGDJ Paris 2009

Danenberg, E., Sorge, L.A., Wieniawski, W., Eliott, S., Amato, L. and Scholten, W., 'Modernizing Methodology for the WHO Assessment of Substances for the International Drug Control Conventions', *Drug and Alcohol Dependence* Vol. 131 2013, pp. 175–181

Davidson, Colin, 'New Psychoactive Substances', *Progress in Neuro-Psychopharmacology & Biological Psychiatry* Vol. 39 2012, pp. 219–220

Davies, Simon, 'International Law, The Final Solution', in: O'Hare, P.A., Newcome, R., Matthews, A., Buning, E.C. and Drucker, E. (eds), *The Reduction of Drug-Related Harm*, Routledge, New York and London 1992

Dinstein, Yoram, 'Cultural Rights', *Isr.Y.B.Hum.Rts* Vol. 9 1979, pp. 58–81

Don, Allison E., 'Lighten Up: Amending the Single Convention on Narcotic Drugs', *Minn. J. Int'l L.* Vol. 23 2014, pp. 213–243

Dopagne, Frédéric, 'Art. 4', in: Corten, Olivier and Klein, Pierre (eds), *The Vienna Convention on the Law of Treaties: A Commentary*, Oxford University Press, Oxford and New York 2011

Dörr, Oliver, 'Art. 31', in: Dörr, Oliver and Schmalenbach, Kirsten (eds), *Vienna Convention on the Law of Treaties: A Commentary*, Springer, Heidelberg and New York 2012

Dörr, Oliver and Schmalenbach, Kirsten (eds), *Vienna Convention on the Law of Treaties: A Commentary*, Springer, Heidelberg and New York 2012

Dreier, Horst, 'Art. 2 I', in: Drier, Horst (ed.), *Grundgesetz Kommentar*, 3rd edn, Mohr Siebeck, Tübingen 2013

Dreier Horst (ed.), *Grundgesetz Kommentar*, 3rd edn, Mohr Siebeck, Tübingen 2013

Dupuy, Réné-Jean, 'Communauté international et disparités de développement: Cours générale de Droit International Public', *RdC* Vol. 165 1979 IV, pp. 9–232

Eick, Chirstophe, 'Art. 20', in: Simma, Bruno, Khan, Daniel-Erasmus, Nolte, Georg and Paulus, Andreas (eds), *The Charter of the United Nations*, 3rd edn, Oxford University Press, Oxford and New York 2012

EMCDDA, *Perspectives on Drugs: Controlling New Psychoactive Substances*, 2013

Engel, Salo, 'Integration of International Legislation', *AJIL* Vol. 45 1951, pp. 770–780

Engle, Karen, 'On Fragile Architecture: The UN Declaration on the Rights of Indigenous Peoples in the Context of Human Rights', *EJIL* Vol. 22 2011, pp. 141–163

Fazey, Cindy S.J., 'The Commission on Narcotic Drugs and the United Nations International Drug Control Programme: Politics, Policies and Prospects for Change', *IJDP* Vol. 14 2003, pp. 155–169

Fitzmaurice, Gerald, 'The Law and Procedure of the International Court of Justice: Treaty Interpretation and other Treaty Points', *BYBIL* Vol. 28 1951, pp. 1–28

Gerald Fitzmaurice, 'The Law and Procedure of the International Court of Justice 1951–4: Treaty Interpretation and Other Treaty Points', *BYBIL* Vol. 33 1957, pp. 203–293

Fitzmaurice, Gerald, 'Reservations to Multilateral Conventions', *ICLQ* Vol. 2 1953, pp. 1–26

Flacks, Simon, 'Drug Control, Human Rights, and the Right to the Highest Attainable Standard of Health: A Reply to Saul Takahashi', *HRQ* Vol. 33 2011, pp. 856–877

Franck, Thomas M., 'Fairness in the International Legal and Institutional System', *RdC* Vol. 240 1993 III, pp. 9–498

Franoini, Francesco and Scheinin, Martin (eds), *Cultural Human Rights*, Brill, Leiden 2008

Friedmann, W., 'General Course in Public International Law', *RdC* Vol. 127 1969 II, pp. 39–246

Gallahue, Patrick, 'The Death Penalty for Drug Offences – Global Overview 2011: Shared Responsibility and Shared Consequences', Harm Reduction International, 2011 (available online at: www.hri.global/files/2014/08/06/IHRA_DeathPenaltyReport_Sept2011_Web.pdf)

Gallahue, Patrick, 'International Drug Control', in: Nollkaemper, André and Plakokefalos, Ilias (eds), *The Practice of Shared Responsibility in International Law*, Cambridge University Press, Cambridge and New York 2017

Gallahue, Patrick, 'Mexico's "War on Drugs": Real or Rhetorical Armed Conflict', *Humanitäres Völkerrecht Informationsschriften* Vol. 24 2011, pp. 39–46

Gallahue, Patrick and Lines, Rick, 'The Death Penalty for Drug Offences: Global Overview 2015 – The Extreme Fringe of Global Drug Policy', Harm Reduction International, 2015 (available online at: www.hri.global/files/2015/10/07/DeathPenaltyDrugs_Report_2015.pdf)

Gallahue, Patrick and Lines, Rick, 'The Death Penalty for Drug Offences: Global Overview', Harm Reduction International, 2010

Gallahue, Patrick, Saucier, Roxanne and Barrett, Damon, 'Partners in Crime: International Funding for Drug Control and Gross Violations of Human Rights', Harm Reduction International, 2012 (available online at: www.hri.global/files/2012/06/20/Partners_in_Crime_webl.pdf)

Gardiner, Richard, *Treaty Interpretation*, Oxford University Press, Oxford and New York 2008

Geiß, Robin and Wisehart, Daniel, '"Concerned with the Health and Welfare of Mankind..." The UN Drug Conventions – A Suitable Legal Framework for the 21st Century?', *MPYbUNL* Vol. 19 2014, pp. 368–404

Ghodse, Hamid, 'Harm Reduction: The Idea and the Ideology', *The Journal of Global Drug Policy and Practice* Vol. 1 2007 Issue 4, pp. 1–4 (available online at: www.globaldrugpolicy.org/Issues/Vol%201%20Issue%204/Harm%20Reduction.pdf)

Giacca, Gilles and Riedel, Eibe, 'Art. 68', in: Simma, Bruno, Khan, Daniel-Erasmus, Nolte, Georg and Paulus, Andreas (eds), *The Charter of the United Nations*, 3rd edn, Oxford University Press, Oxford and New York 2012

Gilmore, Norbert, 'Drug Use and Human Rights: Privacy, Vulnerability, Disability and Human Rights Infringements', *JCHLP* Vol. 12 1996, pp. 355–447

Global Commission on Drug Policy, 'War on Drugs: Report of the Global Commission on Drug Policy', 2011 (available online at: www.globalcommissionondrugs.org/wp-content/themes/gcdp_v1/pdf/Global_Commission_Report_English.pdf)

Goodrich, Leland M., 'New Trends in Narcotics Control', International Conciliation No. 530 1960, pp. 180–242

Gootenberg, Paul, 'Secret Ingredients: The Politics of Coca in US–Peruvian Relations, 1915–65', *JLAS* Vol. 36 2004, pp. 233–265

Grabenwarter, Christoph, *European Convention on Human Rights: Commentary*, C.H. Beck/Hart Publishing, Oxford 2014

Gregg, Robert W., 'The Single Convention for Narcotic Drugs', *Food, Drug, Cosmetic Law Journal* Vol. 16 1961, pp. 187–208

Gregg, Robert W., 'The United Nations and the Opium Problem', *ICLQ* Vol. 14 1964, pp. 96–115

Griffiths, Paul, Evans-Brown, Michael and Sedefov, Roumen, 'Getting Up to Speed with the Public Health and Regulatory Challenges Posed by New Psychoactive Substances in the Information Age', *Addiction* Vol. 108 2013, pp. 1700–1703

Hafner, Gerhard, 'Subsequent Agreements and Practice: Between Interpretation, Informal Modification and Formal Agreement', in: Nolte, Georg (ed.), *Treaties and Subsequent Practice*, Oxford University Press, Oxford and New York 2013

Hallam, Christopher, 'The International Drug Control Regime and Access to Controlled Medicines', TNI Series on Legislative Reform of Drug Policies, December 2014 (available online at: www.tni.org/en/report/international-drug-control-regime-and-access-controlled-medicines)

Hallam, Christopher, Bewley-Taylor, David and Jelsma, Martin, 'Scheduling in the International Drug Control System', TNI Series on Legislative Reform of Drug Policies, June 2014 (available online at: www.tni.org/files/download/dlr25_0.pdf)

Heilmann, Daniel, 'The International Control of Illegal Drugs and the UN Treaty Regime: Preventing or Causing Human Rights Violations?', *Cardozo J. Int'l & Comp. L.* Vol. 19 2011, pp. 237–286

Heilmann, Daniel, 'Narcotic Drugs and Psychotropic Substances', in: Wolfrum, Rüdiger (ed.), *MPEPIL*, Oxford University Press, Oxford and New York 2012

Helfer, Laurence, 'Not Fully Committed? Reservations, Risk and Treaty Design', *YJIL* Vol. 31 2006, pp. 367–382

Henkin; Louis (ed.), *The International Bill of Rights: The Covenant on Civil and Political Rights*, Columbia University Press, New York 1981

Hermanns-Clausen, Maren, Kneisel, Stefan, Szabo, Bela and Auwärter, Volker, 'Acute Toxicity Due to the Confirmed Consumption of Synthetic Cannabinoids: Clinical and Laboratory Findings', *Addiction* Vol. 108 2013, pp. 534–544

Hoijer, Olof, *Le trafic de l'opium et d'autres stupéfiants. Étude de droit international et histoires diplomatique*, Editions Spes, Paris 1925

Hollis, Duncan (ed.), *The Oxford Guide to Treaties*, Oxford University Press, Oxford and New York 2012

Hood, Roger and Hoyle, Caroline, *The Death Penalty: A Worldwide Perspective*, 4th edn, Oxford University Press, Oxford and New York 2008

Hudak, John, 'Colorado's Rollout of Legal Marijuana is Succeeding: A Report on the State's Implementation of Legalization', Center for Effective Public Management at Brookings, July 2014 (available online at: www.brookings.edu/wp-content/uploads/2016/06/CEPMMJCOonepager.pdf)

Human Rights Watch, 'Global State of Pain Treatment: Access to Medicines and Palliative Care', 2011 (available online at: www.hrw.org/report/2011/06/02/global-state-pain-treatment/access-medicines-and-palliative-care)

Human Rights Watch, 'Torture in the Name of Treatment: Human Rights Abuses in Vietnam, China, Cambodia, and Lao PDR', 2012 (available online at: www.hrw.org/sites/default/files/reports/HHR%20Drug%20Detention%20Brochure_LOWRES.pdf)

Hunt, Neil, 'Public Health or Human Rights: What Comes First?', *IJDP* Vol. 15 2004, pp. 231–237

Husak, Douglas, *Drugs and Rights*, Cambridge University Press, Cambridge and New York 1992

Jaenicke, Karl Günther and Steinberger, Helmut (eds), *Völkerrecht als Rechtordnung Internationale Gerichtsbarkeit Menschenrechte Festschrift für Hermann Mosler*, Springer, Heidelberg and New York 1983

Jelsma, Martin, 'Drugs in the UN System: The Unwritten History of the 1998 United Nations General Assembly Special Session on Drugs', *IJDP* Vol. 14 2003, pp. 181–195

Jelsma, Martin, 'Lifting the Ban on Coca Chewing: Bolivia's Proposal to Amend the 1961 Single Convention', TNI Series on Legislative Reform of Drug Policies No. 11, March 2011 (available online at: www.tni.org/files/download/dlr11.pdf)

Jelsma, Martin, 'UNGASS 2016: Watershed Event or Wasted Opportunity?', 2016 (available online at: www.tni.org/en/article/ungass-2016-watershed-event-or-wasted-opportunity)

Jelsma, Martin, 'UNGASS 2016: Prospects for Treaty Reform and UN System-Wide Coherence on Drug Policy', 2016 (available online at: www.unodc.org/documents/ungass2016//Contributions/Civil/Transnational_Institute/Jelsma_United_Nations_final.pdf)

Jojarth, Christine, *Crime, War and Global Trafficking: Designing International Cooperation*, Cambridge University Press, Cambridge and New York 2009

Joseph, Sarah and Castan, Melissa, *The International Covenant on Civil and Political Rights: Cases Materials and Commentary*, 3rd edn, Oxford University Press, Oxford and New York 2013

Kälin, Walter and Künzli, Jörg, *The Law of International Human Rights Protection*, Oxford University Press, Oxford and New York 2009

Kallenbach, Charles, '*Plomo o Plata:* Irregular Rendition as a Means of Gaining Jurisdiction over Colombian Drug Kingpins', *NYU JILP* 1990 Vol. 23, pp. 169–216

Keller, Helen and Grover, Leena, 'General Comments of the Human Rights Committee and Their Legitimacy', in: Ulfstein, Geir and Keller, Helen (eds), *UN Human Rights Treaty Bodies: Law and Legitimacy*, Cambridge University Press, Cambridge and New York 2012, pp. 116–199

Khan, Daniel-Erasmus, 'Art. 20', in: Simma, Bruno, Khan, Daniel-Erasmus, Nolte, Georg and Paulus, Andreas (eds), *The Charter of the United Nations*, 3rd edn, Oxford University Press, Oxford and New York 2012

King, L.A. and Kickman, A.T., 'A Brief History of "New Psychoactive Substances"', *Drug Testing and Analysis* Vol. 3 2011, pp. 401–403

Kingsbury, Benedict, 'Indigenous Rights', in: Wolfrum, Rüdiger (ed.), *MPEPIL*, Oxford University Press, Oxford and New York 2012

Kirk, James, 'Coca, Cocaine and the Rights of Indigenous Peoples', *TCLR* Vol. 10 2007, pp. 77–97

Klein, Eckart, 'Specialized Agencies', in: Wolfrum, Rüdiger (ed.), *MPEPIL*, Oxford University Press, Oxford and New York 2012

Klein, Axel, Metaal, Pien and Jelsma, Martin, 'Chewing over Khat Prohibition: The Globalization of Control and Regulation of an Ancient Stimulant', TNI Series on Legislative Reform of Drug Policies, January 2012 (available online at: www.tni.org/files/download/dlr17.pdf)

Klein, Eckart and Schmahl, Stefanie, 'Art. 11', in: Simma, Bruno, Khan, Daniel-Erasmus, Nolte, Georg and Paulus, Andreas (eds), *The Charter of the United Nations*, 3rd edn, Oxford University Press, Oxford and New York 2012

Klinger, Stefanie, *Die Implementierungsmechanismen der UN Drogenkonventionen von 1961, 1971 und 1988*, Duncker & Humblot, Berlin 1999

Kohona, Palitha, 'Some Notable Developments in the Practice of the UN Secretary General as Depositary of Multilateral Treaties: Reservations and Declarations', *AJIL* Vol. 99 2005, pp. 433–450

Krajewski, Krzysztof, 'How Flexible are the United Nations Drug Conventions?', *IJDP* Vol. 10 1999, pp. 328–339

Küfner, Stefanie, Rabe, Drew and Sonczyk, Barbara, 'The Santo Daime Church: The Protection of Freedom of Religion Under International Law', Amsterdam International Law Clinic, 2007 (available online at: www.bialabate.net/wp-content/uploads/2008/08/Santo-Daime1.AILC.FINAL-REPORT.14.03.07.pdf)

Labate, Beatriz Caiuby and Cavnar, Clancy (eds), *Prohibition, Religious Freedom, and Human Rights: Regulating Traditional Drug Use*, Springer, Heidelberg and New York 2014

Labate, Beatriz and Feeny, Kevin, 'Ayahuasca and the Process of Regulation in Brazil and Internationally: Implications and Challenges', *IJDP* Vol. 23 2012, pp. 154–161

Lande, Adolf, 'The Adjustment of the International Opium Administration to an Eventual Dissolution of the League of Nations', *CLR* Vol. 45 1945, pp. 392–411

Lande, Adolf, 'La Codification du droit international des stupéfiants', *AFDI* Vol. 2 1956, pp. 557–571

Lande, Adolf, 'The Single Convention on Narcotic Drugs, 1961', *International Organization* Vol. 16 1962, pp. 776–797

Lande, Adolf, 'Geleitwort' in: Wartburg, Walter von (ed.), *Drogenmissbrauch und Gesetzgeber, Methodik und Möglichkeit einer optimalen Kontrolle des Missbruachs von Drogen und Arzneimitteln*, Experentia Supplementum Vol. 21 1974, pp. V–VII

Latin American Commission on Drugs and Democracy, Drugs and Democracy: Toward a Paradigm Shift', 2009 (available online at: www.opensocietyfoundations.org/sites/default/files/democracy_20090218.pdf)

Lauterpacht Hersch, 'Restrictive Interpretation and the Rule of Effectiveness in the Interpretation of Treaties', *BYBIL* Vol. 29 1949, pp. 48–85

Le Petit Robert, *Dictionnaire alphabétique et analogique de la langue française*, Le Robert, Paris 2013

Leinwand, Mark A., 'The International Law of Treaties and United States Legalization of Marijuana', *Colum. J. Transnat'l L.* Vol. 10 1971, pp. 413–441

Levine, Harry, 'Global Drug Prohibition: Its Uses and Crises', *IJDP* Vol. 14 2003, pp. 145–153

Levroy, Bernard, 'Drug Trafficking', in: Boister, Neil and Currie, Robert J. (eds), *Routledge Companion of Transnational Criminal Law*, Routledge, Abingdon 2015, pp. 229–247

Levroy, Bernard, Bassiouini, M. Cherif and Thony, Jean-François, 'The International Drug Control System', in: Bassiouni, M. Cherif (ed.), *International Criminal Law: Vol. I, Sources, Subjects, and Contents*, 3rd edn, Martinus Nijhoff Publishers, Leiden 2008, pp. 855–905

Lines, Rick, '"Deliver Us from Evil?" – The Single Convention on Narcotic Drugs, 50 Years On', *International Journal on Human Rights and Drug Policy* Vol. 1 2010, pp. 3–13

Lines, Richard, *Drug Control and Human Rights in International Law*, Cambridge University Press, Cambridge and New York 2017

Lines, Richard, Barrett, Damon and Gallahue, Patrick, 'Guest Post: Has the US Just Called for Unilateral Interpretation of Multilateral Obligations?', 18 December 2014 (available online at: http://opiniojuris.org/2014/12/18/guest-post-us-just-called-unilateral-interpretation-multilateral-obligations/)

Lowes, Peter, *The Genesis of International Narcotics Control*, Librarie Droz, Geneva 1966

MacArthur, Georgina, Velzen, Eva van, Palmateer, Norah, Kimber, Jo, Pharris, Anastasia, Hope, Vivian, Taylor, Avril, Roy, Kirsty, Aspinall, Esther, Goldberg, David, Rhodes, Tim, Hedrich, Dagmar, Salminen, Mika, Hickman, Matthew and Hutchinson, Sharon, 'Interventions to Prevent HIV and Hepatitis C in People who Inject Drugs: A Review of Reviews to Assess Evidence of Effectiveness', *IJDP* Vol. 25 2014, pp. 34–52

McAllister, William B., *Drug Diplomacy in the Twentieth Century: An International History*, Routledge, London 2000

McAllister, William B., 'Reflections of a Century of International Drug Control', in: Collins, John (ed.), *Governing the Global Drug Wars*, Special Report, LSE Ideas, 2012, pp. 10–16

McClean, David, *Transnational Organized Crime: A Commentary on the UN Convention and its Protocols*, Oxford University Press, Oxford and New York 2007

McGrory Glenn, 'Reservations of Virtue? Lessons from Trinidad and Tobago's Reservation to the First Optional Protocol', *HRQ* Vol. 23 2001, pp. 769–826

McNair, Lord, *The Law of Treaties*, Clarendon Press, Oxford 1961

Malkin, Ian, Eliott, Richard and McRae, Rowan, 'Supervised Injection Facilities and International Law', *JDI* Vol. 33 2003, pp. 539–578

Marks, Stephen, 'Access to Essential Medicines as a Component of the Right to Health', in: Clapham, Andrew and Robinson, Mary (eds), *Realizing the Right to Health*, Swiss Human Rights Book Series, Rüffer & Rub, Zürich 2009, pp. 82–101

Mason, Cody T., 'Coca Leaves and Colorado: International Law and the Shifting Landscape of Drug Reform', *Md. J. Int'l L.* Vol. 29 2014, pp. 238–268

Maurer, Martha, Gilson, Aaron, Husain, S. Asra and Cleary, James, 'Examining Influences on the Availability of and Access to Opioids for Pain Management and Palliative Care', *JPPCP* Vol. 27 2013, pp. 255–260

May, Herbert, 'The Single Convention on Narcotic Drugs: Comments and Possibilities', *Bulletin on Narcotics* Vol. 7 1955 No. 1, pp. 1–14

Mbenge, Makane Moïse, 'Preamble', in: Wolfrum, Rüdiger, *MPEPIL*, Oxford University Press, Oxford and New York 2012

Mechlem, Kerstin, 'Treaty Bodies and the Interpretation of Human Rights', *Vand. J. Trant'l L.* Vol. 42 2009, pp. 902–947

Meng, Werner, 'Art 57', in: Simma, Bruno, Khan, Daniel-Erasmus, Nolte, Georg and Paulus, Andreas (eds), *The Charter of the United Nations*, 3rd edn, Oxford University Press, Oxford and New York 2012

Meng, Werner, 'Art 60', in: Simma, Bruno, Khan, Daniel-Erasmus, Nolte, Georg and Paulus, Andreas (eds), *The Charter of the United Nations*, 3rd edn, Oxford University Press, Oxford and New York 2012

Metaal Pien, 'Coca in Debate: The Contradiction and Conflict between the UN Drug Conventions and the Real World', in: Labate, Beatriz Caiuby and Cavnar, Clancy (eds), *Prohibition, Religious Freedom, and Human Rights: Regulating Traditional Drug Use*, Springer, Heidelberg and New York 2014, pp. 25–45

Milanovic, Marko, *Extraterritorial Application of Human Rights Treaties: Law, Principles and Policy*, Oxford University Press, Oxford and New York 2011

Müller, Daniel, 'Art. 20', in: Corten, Olivier and Klein, Pierre (eds), *The Vienna Convention on the Law of Treaties: A Commentary*, Oxford University Press, Oxford and New York 2011

Müller, Daniel, 'Reservations and Time: Is There Only One Right Moment to Formulate and to React to Reservations?', *EJIL* Vol. 24 2013, pp. 1113–1134

Musto, David, *The American Disease: Origins of Narcotic Control*, Expanded Edition, Oxford University Press, Oxford and New York 1987

Nadelmann, Ethan, 'Global Prohibition Regimes: The Evolution of Norms in International Society', *International Organization* Vol. 44 1990, pp. 479–526

Nanda, Ved, 'Agora: U.S. Forces in Panama: Defenders, Aggressors or Human Rights Activists?', *AJIL* Vol. 84 1990, pp. 494–503

New York City Bar, 'The International Drug Control Treaties: How Important are They to US Drug Reform', Committee on Drugs and the Law, August 2012 (available online at: www2.nycbar.org/pdf/report/uploads/3_20072283-InternationalDrugControlTreaties.pdf)

Nollkaemper, André and Jacobs, Dov, 'Shared Responsibility in International Law: A Conceptual Framework', *Mich. J. Int'l L.* Vol. 34 2013, pp. 359–438

Nolte, Georg (ed.), *Treaties and Subsequent Practice*, Oxford University Press, Oxford and New York 2013

Nowak, Manfred, *U.N. Covenant on Civil and Political Rights: CCPR Commentary*, 2nd edn, N. P. Engel, Kehl 2005

O'Keefe, Roger, 'Cultural Life, Right to Participate in, International Protection', in: Wolfrum, Rüdiger (ed.), *MPEPIL*, Oxford University Press, Oxford and New York 2012

O'Keefe, Roger, 'The "Right to Take Part in Cultural Life" under Article 15 of the ICESCR', *ICLQ* Vol. 47 1998, pp. 904–923

Obokata, Tom, 'Illicit Cycle of Narcotics from a Human Rights Perspective', *NQHR* Vol. 25 2007, pp. 159–187

Orakhelashvili, Alexander, 'Art. 30', in: Corten, Olivier and Klein, Pierre (eds), *The Vienna Convention on the Law of Treaties: A Commentary*, Oxford University Press, Oxford and New York 2011

Pellet, Alain, 'Art. 19', in: Corten, Olivier and Klein, Pierre (eds), *The Vienna Convention on the Law of Treaties: A Commentary*, Oxford University Press, Oxford and New York 2011

Pellet, Alain, 'Art. 55 alinéas a et b', in: Pellet, Alain, Cot, Jean Pierre and Forteau, Mathias (eds), *La Charte des Nations Unies*, Economica, Paris 2005

Pellet, Alain, Cot, Jean Pierre and Forteau, Mathias (eds), *La Charte des Nations Unies*, Economica, Paris 2005

Peters, Anne, 'Treaties, Unequal', in: Wolfrum, Rüdiger (ed.), *MPEPIL*, Oxford University Press, Oxford and New York 2012

Petersen, Nils, 'Life, Right to, International Protection', in: Wolfrum, Rüdiger (ed.), *MPEPIL*, Oxford University Press, Oxford and New York 2012

Pfeiffer, Sven, 'Rights of Indigenous Peoples and the International Drug Control Regime: The Case for Traditional Coca Leaf Chewing', *GoJIL* Vol. 5 2013, pp. 287–324

Prott, Lyndel, 'Cultural Rights as Peoples' Rights in International Law', in: Crawford, James (ed.), *The Rights of Peoples*, Oxford University Press, Oxford and New York 1988, pp. 93–107

Raemy, Charest Gabrielle, 'The Visionary Vine: When Domestic Religious Freedom and International Law Conflict', *TJICL* Vol. 12 2004, pp. 435–460

Rajamani Lavanya, *Differential Treatment in International Environmental Law*, Oxford University Press, Oxford and New York 2006

Ree, Erik van, 'Drugs as a Human Right', *IJDP* Vol 10 1999, pp. 89–98

Reins, Thomas, 'Reform, Nationalism and Internationalism: The Opium Suppression Movement in China and the Anglo-American Influence, 1900–1908', *Modern Asian Studies* Vol. 24 1991 pp. 101–142

Renborg, Bertil A., 'The Grand Old Men of the League of Nations: What They Achieved and Who They Were', *Bulletin on Narcotics* Vol. 15 1964 Issue 4, pp. 1–11

Renborg, Bertil A., 'International Drug Control', Carnegie Endowment for International Peace, Washington 1947

Renborg, Bertil A., 'International Control of Narcotics, Law and Contemporary Problems', *Law and Contemporary Problems* Vol. 22 1957, pp. 86–112

Renborg Bertil A., 'Principles of International Control of Narcotic Drugs', *AJIL* Vol. 37 1943, pp. 436–459

Reuter, Peter, 'The Dangerous Charm of the Unknown', *Addiction* Vol. 107 2012, pp. 1902–1903

Reuter, Paul, 'The Obligations of the States under the Single Convention on Narcotic Drugs, 1961', *Bulletin on Narcotics* Vol. 20 No. 4 1968, pp. 3–7

Richards, David A. J., 'Drug Use and the Rights of the Person: A Moral Argument for Decriminalization of Certain Forms of Drug Use', *Rutgers L. Rev.* Vol. 33 1981, pp. 607–687

Riedel, Eibe, 'Health, Right to, International Protection', in: Wolfrum, Rüdiger (ed.), *MPEPIL*, Oxford University Press, Oxford and New York 2012

Riedel, Eibe and Arend, Jean-Michel, 'Art. 55 (c)' in: Simma, Bruno, Khan, Daniel-Erasmus, Nolte, Georg and Paulus, Andreas (eds), *The Charter of the United Nations*, 3rd edn, Oxford University Press, Oxford and New York 2012

Röben, Volker, 'Art. 60' in: Simma, Bruno, Khan, Daniel-Erasmus, Nolte, Georg and Paulus, Andreas (eds), *The Charter of the United Nations*, 3rd edn, Oxford University Press, Oxford and New York 2012

Röben Volker, 'Conference (Meeting) of States Parties', in: Wolfrum, Rüdiger (ed.), *MPEPIL*, Oxford University Press, Oxford and New York 2012

Room, Robin, 'Legalizing a Market for Cannabis for Pleasure: Colorado, Washington, Uruguay and Beyond', *Addiction* Vol. 109 2014, pp. 345–351

Room, Robin and Mackay, Sarah, 'Roadmaps to Reforming the UN Drug Conventions', A Beckley Foundation Report, 2012

Room, Robin and Pagila, Angela, 'The International Drug Control System in the Post-Cold War Era: Managing Markets or Fighting a War', *Drug and Alcohol Review* Vol. 18 1999, pp. 305–315

Room, Robin and Reuter, Peter, 'How Well Do International Drug Conventions Protect Public Health', *The Lancet* Vol. 379 2012, pp. 84–91

Samuels, J.W., 'International Control of Narcotic Drugs and International Economic Law', *Can. Y. B. Int'l* Vol. 7 1969, pp. 192–223

Sands, Philippe, 'Art. 40', in: Corten, Olvier and Klein, Pierre (eds), *The Vienna Convention on the Law of Treaties: A Commentary*, Oxford University Press, Oxford and New York 2011

Santos, Juan Manuel, 'Re-examining the Drug Problem through a Fresh Lens', in: Collins. John (ed.), *Governing the Global Drug Wars*, Special Report, LSE Ideas 2012, pp. 2–4

Saul, Ben, Kinley, David and Mowbray, Jaqueline, *The International Covenant on Economic, Social and Cultural Rights*, Oxford University Press, Oxford and New York 2014

Schabas, William A., *The Abolition of the Death Penalty in International Law*, 3rd edn, Cambridge University Press, Cambridge and New York 2002

Schaus, Annemie, 'Art. 27', in: Corten, Olivier and Klein, Pierre (eds), *The Vienna Convention on the Law of Treaties: A Commentary*, Oxford University Press, Oxford and New York 2011

Schwarzenberger, Georg, *Economic World Order: A Basic Problem of International Economic Cooperation*, Manchester University Press, Manchester 1970

Schwarzenberger, Georg, *Power Politics: A Study of International Society*, 2nd edn, Stevens, London 1951

Seely, Kathryn, Lapoint, Jeff, Moran, Jeffery and Fattore, Liana, 'Spice Drugs are More than Harmless Herbal Blends: A Review of the Pharmacology and Toxicology of Synthetic Cannabinoids', *Progress in Neuro-Psychopharmacology & Biological Psychiatry* Vol. 39 2012, pp. 234–243

Seya, Marie-Josephine, Gelders, Susanne, Uzoma, Obianuju, Milani, Barbara and Scholten, Willem, 'A First Comparison Between the Consumption of and the Need for Opioid Analgesics at Country, Regional, and Global Levels', *JPPCP* Vol. 25 2011, pp. 6–18

Simma, Bruno, 'From Bilateralism to Community Interest in International Law', *RdC* Vol. 250 1994 VI, pp. 217–384

Simma, Bruno, Khan, Daniel-Erasmus, Nolte, Georg and Paulus, Andreas (eds), *The Charter of the United Nations*, 3rd edn, Oxford University Press, Oxford and New York 2012

Sinha, Jay, 'The History and Development of the Leading International Drug Control Conventions', Prepared for the Senate Special Committee on Illegal Drugs, Law and Government Division, 21 February 2001, Library of Parliament of Canada Research Branch (available online at: www.parl.gc.ca/content/sen/committee/371/ille/library/history-e.htm#ABSTRACT)

Sloan, Blaine, 'General Assembly Resolutions Revisited (Forty Years Later)' *BYBIL* Vol. 58 1987, pp. 39–151

Soanes, Chaterine and Stevenson, Angus, *Concise Oxford English Dictionary*, 11th edn, Oxford University Press, Oxford and New York 2006

Sohn, Louis B., 'The Rights of Minorities', in: Henkin, Louis (ed.), *The International Bill of Rights: The Covenant on Civil and Political Rights*, Columbia University Press, New York 1981

Sorel, Jean-Marc and Boré-Eveno, Valérie, 'Art. 31' in: Corten, Olivier and Klein, Pierre (eds), *The Vienna Convention on the Law of Treaties: A Commentary*, Oxford University Press, Oxford and New York 2011

Spivack, David, *A Fourth International Convention for Dug Policy*, The Senlis Council, Brussels 2004

Sproule, D.W. and St-Denis, Paul, 'The UN Drug Trafficking Convention: An Ambitious Step', *Can. Y. B. Int'l* Vol. 27 1989, pp. 263–294

Starke, J.G., 'The Convention of 1936 for the Suppression of the Illicit Traffic in Dangerous Drugs', *AJIL* Vol. 31 1937, pp. 31–43

Steber Buechli, Diane and Dreifuss, Ruth, 'Swiss Drug Policy in International Context: Fought, Ignored, Admired', in: Collins, John (ed.), *Governing the Global Drug Wars*, Special Report, LSE Ideas, 2012

Stoll, Peter-Tobias, 'Art. 55 (a)-(b)', in: Simma, Bruno, Khan, Daniel-Erasmus, Nolte, Georg and Paulus, Andreas (eds), *The Charter of the United Nations*, 3rd edn, Oxford University Press, Oxford and New York 2012

Sumnall, H.R., Evans-Brown, M. and McVeigh, J., 'Social, Policy and Public Health Perspectives on New Psychoactive Substances', *Drug Testing and Analysis* Vol. 3 2011, pp. 515–523

Takahashi, Saul, 'Drug Control, Human Rights, and the Right to the Highest Attainable Standard of Health: By No Means Straightforward Issues', *HRQ* Vol. 31 2009, pp. 748–776

Takahashi, Saul, *Human Rights and Drug Control: The False Dichotomy*, Hart Publishing, Portland 2016

Taylor, Ally, 'Addressing the Global Tragedy of Needless Pain: Rethinking the United Nations Single Convention on Narcotic Drugs', *J. L. Med. & Ethics* Vol. 35 2007, pp. 556–570

Thoumi, Francisco E., 'A Modest Proposal to Clarify the Status of Coca in the United Nations Conventions', *Crime, Law & Social Change* Vol. 42 2004, pp. 297–307

Thoumi, Francisco, 'The International Drug Control Regime's Straight Jacket: Are There Any Policy Options?', *Trends Organ. Crim.* Vol. 13 2010, pp. 75–86

Tieya, Wang, 'International Law in China: Historical and Contemporary Perspectives', *RdC* Vol. 221 1990 II, pp. 195–369

Tobin, John, *The Right to Health in International Law*, Oxford University Press, Oxford and New York 2012

Tomuschat, Christian, 'Protection of Minorities under Article 27 of the International Covenant on Civil and Political Rights', in: Bernhardt, Rudolf, Geck, Wilhelm Karl, Jaenicke, Günther and Steinberger, Helmut (eds), *Völkerrecht als Rechtordnung Internationale Gerichtsbarkeit Menschenrechte Festschrift für Hermann Mosler*, Springer, Heidelberg and New York 1983, pp. 949–981

Tomuschat, Christian, 'United Nations General Assembly', in: Wolfrum, Rüdiger (ed.), *MPEPIL*, Oxford University Press, Oxford and New York 2012

Trocki, Carl, *Opium, Empire and the Global Political Economy: A Study of the Asian Opium Trade 1750–1950*, Routledge, London, 1999

Tupper, Kenneth and Labate, Beatriz, 'Plants, Psychoactive Substances and the International Narcotics Control Board: The Control of Nature and the Nature of Control', *Human Rights and Drugs* Vol. 2 2012, pp. 17–28

Tyagi, Yogesh, 'The Denunciation of Human Rights Treaties', *BYBIL* Vol. 67 2008, pp. 87–193

Ulfstein, Geir, 'Treaty Bodies and Regimes', in: Hollis, Duncan (ed.), *The Oxford Guide to Treaties*, Oxford University Press, Oxford and New York 2012, pp. 428–447

Ulfstein, Geir and Keller, Helen (eds), *UN Human Rights Treaty Bodies: Law and Legitimacy*, Cambridge University Press, Cambridge and New York 2012

Ulfstein, Geir, Zimmermann, Andreas and Marauhn, Thilo (eds), *Making Treaties Work: Human Rights, Environment and Arms Control*, Cambridge University Press, Cambridge and New York 2007

UNODC, 'The Challenge of New Psychoactive Substances, A Report from the Global SMART Programme', 2013 (available online at: www.unodc.org/documents/scientific/NPS_2013_SMART.pdf)

UNODC, 'Drug Policy Provisions from the International Drug Control Conventions', 2014 (available online at: www.unodc.org/documents/hlr/Drug_policy_provisions_from_the_international_drug_control_Conventions.pdf)

UNODC, 'Ensuring Availability of Controlled Medications for the Relief of Pain and Preventing Diversion and Abuse: Striking the Right Balance to Achieve the Optimal Public Health Outcome', Discussion Paper based on a Scientific Workshop, 2011 (available online at: www.unodc.org/docs/treatment/Pain/Ensuring_availability_of_controlled_medications_FINAL_15_March_CND_version.pdf)

UNODC, 'UNODC and the Promotion and Protection of Human Rights', 2012 (available online at: www.unodc.org/documents/justice-and-prison-reform/UNODC_Human_rights_position_paper_2012.pdf)

UNODC, 'World Drug Report 2008', UN Publication, Sales No. E.08.XI.1

UNODC, 'World Drug Report 2013', UN Publication, Sales No. E.13.XI.6

UNODC, 'World Drug Report 2014,' UN Publication, Sales No. E.14.XI.7

UNODC and WHO, 'Opioid Overdose: Preventing and Reducing Opioid Overdose Mortality', 2013 (available online at: www.unodc.org/docs/treatment/overdose.pdf)

Vignes, Claude-Henri, 'La Convention sur les Substances Psychotropes', *AFDI* Vol. 17 1971, pp. 641–656

Vignes, Claude-Henri, 'Les modifications apportées à l'Organe internationale de contrôle par les amendements à la Convention unique sur les stupéfiants', *AFDI* Vol. 18 1972, pp. 629–648

Villiger, Mark E., *Commentary to the 1969 Vienna Convention on the Law of Treaties*, Martinus Nijhoff Publishers, Leiden and Boston 2009

Vrdolijak, Ana Filipa, 'Self-determination in Cultural Rights', in: Franoini, Francesco and Scheinin, Martin (eds), *Cultural Human Rights*, Brill, Leiden 2008, pp. 41–78

Waddell, Ian G., 'International Narcotics Control', *AJIL* Vol. 64 1970, pp. 310–324

Wallach, Phillip, 'Washington's Marijuana Legalization Grows Knowledge, Not Just Pot: A Report on the State's Strategy to Assess Reform', August 2014 (available online at: www.brookings.edu/wp-content/uploads/2016/06/CEPMMJWallach.pdf)

Walsh, Charlotte, 'Drug and Human Rights: Private Palliatives, Sacramental Freedoms and Cognitive Liberty', *IJHR* Vol. 14 2010, pp. 425–441

Wang, Drong, *China's Unequal Treaties Narrating National History*, Lexington Books, Oxford 2005

Ward, Tara, 'The Right to Free, Prior, and Informed Consent: Indigenous Peoples' Participation Rights within International Law', *NUJIHR* Vol. 10 2011, pp. 54–84

Wartburg, Walter P. von, 'Drogenmissbrauch und Gesetzgeber, Methodik und Möglichkeit einer optimalen Kontrolle des Missbrauchs von Drogen und Arzneimitteln', Experentia Supplementum Vol. 21, Birkhäuser Verlag, Basel and Stuttgart 1974

Weil, Prosper, 'Towards Relative Normativity in International Law?', *AJIL* Vol. 77 1983, pp. 413–442

West African Commission on Drugs, 'Not Just in Transit: Drugs, the State and Society in West Africa', 2014 (available online at: www.wacommissionondrugs.org/wp-content/uploads/2014/11/WACD-Full-Report-Eng.pdf)

WHO, 'Access to Controlled Medications Programme: Improving Access to Medications Controlled under International Drug Conventions', April 2012 (available online at: www.who.int/medicines/areas/quality_safety/ACMP_BrNote_Genrl_EN_Apr2012.pdf?ua=1)

WHO, 'Access to Controlled Medicines Programme: Ensuring Balance in National Policies on Controlled Substances – Guidance for Availability and Accessibility of Controlled Medicines, 2011 (available online at: www.unodc.org/docs/treatment/Pain/WHO_encuring_balance_controlled_substances.pdf)

WHO, 'Community Management of Opioid Overdose', 2014 (available online at: http://apps.who.int/iris/bitstream/10665/137462/1/9789241548816_eng.pdf?ua=1&ua=1)

WHO, 'Narcotic & Psychotropic Substances: Achieving Balance in National Opioids Control Policy – Guidelines for Assessment, WHO Doc. WHO/ED/QSM/2000.4, 2000

WHO, 'WHO's Role, Mandate and Activities to Counter the World Drug Problem: A Public Health Perspective', 2014 (available online at: http://www.unodc.org/documents/ungass2016/Contributions/UN/WHO/WHO_Role_and_Mandate_to_counter_the_worlds_drug_problems_2014.pdf)

Wolfe, Daniel and Malinowska-Sempruch, Kasia, 'Illicit Drug Policies and the Global HIV Epidemic: Effects of UN and National Governments Approaches', Open Society Institute, New York 2004 (available online at: www.hivpolicy.org/Library/HPP000536.pdf)

Wolfrum, Rüdiger (ed.), *MPEPIL*, Oxford University Press, Oxford and New York 2012

Wong, John, *Deadly Dreams: Opium and the Arrow War (1858–1860) in China*, Cambridge University Press, Cambridge and New York 1998

Wright, Hamilton, 'The International Opium Commission', *AJIL* Vol. 3 1909 pp. 648–673 (Part I); pp. 828–868 (Part II)

Wright, Hamilton, 'The International Opium Conference', *AJIL* Vol. 6 1912, pp. 865–889 (Part I); pp. 108–139 (Part II)

Wright, Hamilton, 'The International Opium Conference, *AJIL* Vol. 7 1913, pp. 108–139

Wright, Quincy, 'The American Withdrawal from the Opium Conference', *AJIL* Vol. 18 1925, pp. 348–355

Wright, Quincy, 'The Narcotics Convention of 1931', *AJIL* Vol. 28 1934, pp. 475–486

Wright Quincy, The Opium Conferences, *AJIL* Vol. 19 1925, pp. 559–568

Wright, Quincy, 'The Opium Question', *AJIL* Vol. 18 1924, pp. 281–295

Xanthaki, Alexandra, 'Indigenous Cultural Rights in International Law', *Eur. J.L. Reform* Vol. 2 2000, pp. 343–367

Yupsanis, Anthanasios, 'The International Labour Organization and Its Contribution to the Protection of the Rights of Indigenous Peoples', *Can. Y. B. Int'l L.* Vol. 49 2011, pp. 117–176

Ziemele, Ineta, 'Privacy, Right to, International Protection', in: Wolfrum, Rüdiger (ed.), *MPEPIL*, Oxford University Press, Oxford and New York 2012

Index

For Product Safety Concerns and Information please contact our EU representative GPSR@taylorandfrancis.com
Taylor & Francis Verlag GmbH, Kaufingerstraße 24, 80331 München, Germany

www.ingramcontent.com/pod-product-compliance
Ingram Content Group UK Ltd.
Pitfield, Milton Keynes, MK11 3LW, UK
UKHW011004180926
475701UK00004B/546
* 9 7 8 0 3 6 7 5 8 4 9 9 3 *